THE LONG FIFTEENTH CENTURY

Douglas Gray
J. R. R. Tolkien Professor of English Literature and Language at the University of Oxford

THE LONG FIFTEENTH CENTURY

ESSAYS FOR DOUGLAS GRAY

EDITED BY
HELEN COOPER
AND
SALLY MAPSTONE

CLARENDON PRESS · OXFORD
1997

Oxford University Press, Great Clarendon Street, Oxford OX2 6DP
Oxford New York
Athens Auckland Bangkok Bogota Bombay
Buenos Aires Calcutta Cape Town Dar es Salaam
Delhi Florence Hong Kong Istanbul Karachi
Kuala Lumpur Madras Madrid Melbourne
Mexico City Nairobi Paris Singapore
Taipei Tokyo Toronto
and associated companies in
Berlin Ibadan

Oxford is a trade mark of Oxford University Press

Published in the United States by
Oxford University Press Inc., New York

© The several contributors 1997

All rights reserved. No part of this publication may be reproduced,
stored in a retrieval system, or transmitted, in any form or by any means,
without the prior permission in writing of Oxford University Press.
Within the UK, exceptions are allowed in respect of any fair dealing for the
purpose of research or private study, or criticism or review, as permitted
under the Copyright, Designs and Patents Act, 1988, or in the case of
reprographic reproduction in accordance with the terms of the licences
issued by the Copyright Licensing Agency. Enquiries concerning
reproduction outside these terms and in other countries should be
sent to the Rights Department, Oxford University Press,
at the address above

British Library Cataloguing in Publication Data
Data available

Library of Congress Cataloging in Publication Data
Data available

ISBN 0-19-818365-8

1 3 5 7 9 10 8 6 4 2

Typeset by Graphicraft Typesetters Ltd., Hong Kong
Printed in Great Britain
on acid-free paper by
Biddles Ltd.,
Guildford and King's Lynn

Preface

DOUGLAS GRAY retires as J. R. R. Tolkien Professor of English Literature and Language in 1997. This volume marks that retirement by providing a collection of essays to accompany one of his most significant contributions to medieval studies, *The Oxford Book of Late Medieval Verse and Prose* (1985). In choosing to connect this tribute to Douglas with that anthology we hope to convey an appreciation of the range and depth of his scholarship, and the particular importance of late medieval literature within it. The bibliography of published writings which concludes this volume reflects the range, in date, genres, and themes, of Douglas's work. It also charts his recurrent interest in the later Middle Ages, a period that for him, as his own preface to the *Oxford Book* states, extends well into the sixteenth century, a view that provides some justification for our own designation of it as 'the long fifteenth century'. Douglas's book on the religious lyric pays serious attention to the character of fifteenth-century poetry, and his study of Henryson was and remains a turning-point in the understanding of the Scottish, English, and Continental heritage of one of the fifteenth century's most remarkable poets. In the *Oxford Book* Douglas opened up a memorably rich and varied array of both late medieval verse and late medieval prose. He was concerned, in a manner characteristically humane and searching, to convey the character of literature produced during a period that he describes as one of 'profound change, of apparently contradictory impulses, and sometimes of an acute tension beneath a harmonious surface'. These essays are designed to follow that pattern of seeing the period whole but appreciating its diversities. They pursue the revaluation of the nature of late medieval literature and culture in which Douglas has done so much pioneering work, and which is surely where much future study and research should lie. The long fifteenth century has been too long neglected.

We are very grateful to all the contributors to this volume for responding so gamely and generously to a series of demanding deadlines; and to Douglas himself for his benign interest in the project (it was impossible to keep it from him!). We are conscious, however, that in focusing the subject of this book so specifically we have deprived some of Douglas's friends and admirers of the opportunity of contributing to a collection in his honour. We know none the less that they and his many other friends and devotees around the world will join us in dedicating this volume to him with every good wish for a long and productive retirement.

HELEN COOPER
SALLY MAPSTONE

Contents

Contributors — ix

Abbreviations — x

Introduction — 1
    Helen Cooper

1. 'Dysemol daies and fatal houres': Lydgate's *Destruction of Thebes* and Chaucer's *Knight's Tale* — 15
    James Simpson

2. Hoccleve and the Middle French Poets — 35
    John Burrow

3. Kingship and the *Kingis Quair* — 51
    Sally Mapstone

4. Frames and Narrators in Chaucerian Poetry — 71
    Helen Phillips

5. The Verse Forms of Jon the Blynde Awdelay — 99
    Eric Stanley

6. Poetic Originality in *The Wars of Alexander* — 123
    Peter Dronke

7. Counter-Romance: Civil Strife and Father-Killing in the Prose Romances — 141
    Helen Cooper

viii *Contents*

8. The Ballad and the Middle Ages 163
   Richard Firth Green

9. 'Send thine heart into purgatory': Visionaries
   of the Other World 185
   Robert Easting

10. Fleshly Monks and Dancing Girls: Immorality
    in the Morality Drama 205
    Malcolm Godden

11. 'Abject odious': Feminine and Masculine in
    Henryson's *Testament of Cresseid* 229
    Felicity Riddy

12. 'Spekyng for one's sustenance': The Rhetoric of
    Counsel in *Mum and the Sothsegger*,
    Skelton's *Bowge of Court*, and Elyot's
    Pasquil the Playne 249
    Helen Barr and Kate Ward-Perkins

13. Justification by Faith: Skelton's *Replycacion* 273
    Vincent Gillespie

14. *Visio Baleii*: An Early Literary Historian 313
    Anne Hudson

A Bibliography of the Published Writings of
Douglas Gray 331
   Joerg O. Fichte

Select Bibliography 337

Index 353

Contributors

HELEN BARR is Fellow and Tutor in English, Lady Margaret Hall, Oxford.

JOHN BURROW is Winterstoke Professor of English, University of Bristol.

HELEN COOPER is Professor of English Language and Literature, University College, Oxford.

PETER DRONKE is Professor of Medieval Latin Literature, University of Cambridge.

ROBERT EASTING is Reader in English Language and Literature, Victoria University of Wellington.

JOERG O. FICHTE is Professor of Medieval English, University of Tübingen.

VINCENT GILLESPIE is Fellow and Tutor in English, St Anne's College, Oxford.

MALCOLM GODDEN is Rawlinson and Bosworth Professor of Anglo-Saxon, University of Oxford.

RICHARD FIRTH GREEN is Associate Professor of English, University of Western Ontario.

ANNE HUDSON is Professor of Medieval English, University of Oxford.

SALLY MAPSTONE is Joanna Morse Memorial Fellow and Tutor in English, St Hilda's College, Oxford.

HELEN PHILLIPS is Senior Lecturer in English, University of Nottingham.

FELICITY RIDDY is Professor of English, Centre for Medieval Studies, University of York.

JAMES SIMPSON is Fellow of Girton College and University Lecturer in English, University of Cambridge.

ERIC STANLEY is Rawlinson and Bosworth Professor Emeritus of Anglo-Saxon, University of Oxford.

KATE WARD-PERKINS is Fellow and Tutor in English, St Edmund Hall, Oxford.

Abbreviations

Archiv	*Archiv für das Studium der neueren Sprachen*
EETS	Early English Text Society
ELH	*English Literary History*
ELN	*English Language Notes*
ES	*English Studies*
IMEV	*The Index of Middle English Verse*, ed. Carleton Brown and Rossell Hope Robbins (New York, 1943); *Supplement*, ed. Rossell Hope Robbins and John L. Cutler (Lexington, Ky, 1965)
IMEP	*Index of Middle English Prose* (vol. iv, Cambridge, 1976; Supplement, 1965)
IPMEP	*Index of Printed Middle English Prose*, ed. R. E. Lewis, N. F. Blake, and A. S. G. Edwards (New York and London, 1989)
Manual	*A Manual of the Writings in Middle English 1050–1500*, ed. J. Burke-Severs and Albert E. Hartung (New Haven, Conn.), vol. i (1967), vol. ii (1970) vol. iii (1972), vol. iv (1973), vol. v (1975) vol. vi (1980), vol. vii (1986), vol. ix (1993)
MÆ	*Medium Ævum*
MED	*Middle English Dictionary*, ed. J. Kurath *et al.* (Ann Arbor, Mich., 1956–)
MLQ	*Modern Language Quarterly*
N&Q	*Notes and Queries*
OBLMVP	*The Oxford Book of Late Medieval Verse and Prose*, ed. D. Gray (Oxford, 1985)
OED	*Oxford English Dictionary*, ed. J. A. H. Murray, H. Bradley, W. A. Craigie, and C. T. Onions (Oxford, 1933)
PMLA	*Publications of the Modern Language Association of America*
PQ	*Philological Quarterly*
RES	*Review of English Studies*
SATF	Société des anciens textes français
SP	*Studies in Philology*

SSL	*Studies in Scottish Literature*
STC	*A Short-Title Catalogue of Books printed in England, Scotland and Ireland and of English Books printed Abroad 1475–1640*, ed. A. W. Pollard and G. R. Redgrave, rev. W. A. Jackson, F. S. Ferguson, and K. F. Pantzer, 3 vols. (1976–91)
STS	Scottish Text Society
TEAMS	Consortium for Teaching in the Middle Ages, University of Western Michigan
YES	*Year's Work in English Studies*

EDITORIAL NOTE

Punctuation of texts, and some spellings (þ, ȝ, u/v/w, i/j, and Scots ß) have been modernized to match the practice of *OBLMVP*.

Introduction

Douglas Gray's *Oxford Book of Late Medieval Verse and Prose*,[1] to which the present collection of essays is intended as a companion volume, was a landmark work in the study of the literature of the end of the Middle Ages. The brilliance of other forms of the arts in the England of the period is unmistakable. It was in this period that the architecture of stone learned to fly, in the vaulting of Norwich Cathedral, the chapel of King's College, Cambridge, or Henry VII's chapel in Westminster Abbey. English music acquired through the work of John Dunstable and his contemporaries a pre-eminence in continental Europe unparalleled before or since.[2] By contrast, the 'long fifteenth century', from the death of Chaucer to the Reformation, was for long regarded as a literary wilderness,[3] its only writers of acknowledged status being Sir Thomas Malory (who could himself be presented as a rather inadequate translator of material too good for him) and John Skelton (whose eccentricity in terms of a 'great tradition' of English poetry marked him as an outsider who need not be taken too seriously). Scottish poetry did markedly better, with the unignorable names of Henryson, Dunbar, and Douglas; but they were too often

---

[1] *The Oxford Book of Late Medieval Verse and Prose*, edited by Douglas Gray with a note on grammar and spelling in the fifteenth century by Norman Davis (hereafter *OBLMVP*), was first published by the Clarendon Press, Oxford, in 1985.

[2] See Reinhard Strohm, *The Rise of European Music 1380–1500* (Cambridge, 1993), 197–266, 377–411; he describes the period after 1400 as characterized 'by a massive adoption of England's music by continental musicians, and an admiration for her composers the like of which neither William Byrd nor Henry Purcell were to enjoy' (p. 197). At the end of the period, Scotland too produced an outstanding composer in Robert Carver: see D. James Ross, *Musick Fyne: Robert Carver and the Art of Music in Sixteenth-Century Scotland* (Edinburgh, 1993).

[3] C. S. Lewis bears a heavy responsibility both for confirming this attitude and making it appear respectable: see his characterization of the period as 'a history of decay' (*English Literature in the Sixteenth Century, excluding Drama* (Oxford, 1954), 120). Such dismissiveness was finely challenged by David Lawton in his 'Dullness and the Fifteenth Century', *ELH* 54 (1987), 761–99.

presented as rare candles in a large darkness. The *Oxford Book* changed all that. Here were represented writer after writer, text after text, that were striking, vibrant—that, in contrast to the customary picture of the period as the great producer of unreadable texts, seized the imagination, challenged set ways of thinking, and raised issues of a sophistication that twentieth-century critics had too often assumed had died with the great poets of the age of Richard II.

Douglas Gray's anthology was at once a sign of a new interest in the period,[4] and set new standards and enlarged the boundaries for its study. The essays given here build on the foundations laid by the *Oxford Book*. We have tried to convey something of the same idea of the richness of literary production of the period by giving attention to less well known works as well as the more famous authors, even though we could not reflect the whole range of the 'diversities of many wonderful things', the 'nifles, trifles and merry jests', the letters, phrase-books, and textbooks that make the anthology so full of arresting surprises.[5] We therefore give comparatively little space to many of the major figures who have received their proper share of attention elsewhere: to Dunbar, Douglas, or More, for instance, or to some of those writers who have only recently been made the subject of significant study but who have caught up fast on their previous neglect, such as Margery Kempe and Caxton. We hope that this emphasis on the breadth of literary activity over the long fifteenth century—from the first generation of post-Chaucerian poets at the start of the collection to Bale's retrospective survey from the mid-sixteenth century at the end—will, like the *Oxford Book*, help to change the way the period is perceived.

---

[4] Besides the increasing numbers of studies of individual authors, one might mention two collections of essays specifically designed to open up the century in new ways: the survey of criticism edited by R. F. Yeager, *Fifteenth-Century Studies: Recent Essays* (Hamden, Conn., 1984); and the special edition of *Modern Language Quarterly*, 53/1 (1992), 'Tradition and Innovation in Fifteenth-Century Poetry', ed. A. S. G. Edwards. Lois A. Ebin, in her Introduction to her *Illuminator, Makar, Vates: Visions of Poetry in the Fifteenth Century* (Lincoln, Nebr. and London, 1988), discusses both the neglect of the period and its importance 'for the profound changes in the literary process' that characterize it. A collection that includes generous coverage of Scottish literature of the period is the special issue of *SSL*, 26 (1991), on 'The Language and Literature of Early Scotland'.

[5] See especially *OBLMVP* 1, 2, 9, 17, 23.

Perception has indeed been at the root of the period's neglect. Scholars of the late fourteenth century have looked at the poets who claimed to be writing in the Chaucerian tradition, and decided that they are not Chaucer;[6] scholars of the Scottish 'Chaucerians' have too often defined them as nothing else. Studies of the alliterative revival treat it as a fourteenth-century phenomenon, and give little or no attention to its vibrant continuation through to the sixteenth century. The origins of the ballad have been set in the eighteenth century, and so there has been little exploration further back. The prose romances, with the exception of Malory—who has frequently been treated as if he had no English context—have lain largely ignored, outside the scope of scholars of metrical romance or of the early modern novel. Many of the essays in this collection addres these issues of misrepresentation, misattribution, and incomprehension. The opening three, by James Simpson, John Burrow, and Sally Mapstone, show how innovative were the poets writing in the generation after Chaucer, Lydgate, Hoccleve, and James I; in the fourth, Helen Phillips analyses the richness of the play of variations in Chaucerian framed poems across the whole century, their narratological experimentation, and their ability to open up new areas of experience; for later in the period, Felicity Riddy demonstrates the arresting disparities between Chaucer and Henryson. Peter Dronke's essay on the *Wars of Alexander*—of uncertain date, but limited only by its copying c.1450—is a reminder of the vitality of alliterative poetry into the fifteenth century and beyond: the vitality that produced in England *Scotish Feilde* on the battle of Flodden of 1513, and in Scotland Dunbar's magnificent *Tua Mariit Wemen and the Wedo*.[7]

---

[6] The *OBLMVP* was an honourable exception to this and the succeeding examples: cf. *OBLMVP* 6 for the Chaucerian poems. Contrast A. C. Spearing's summary in *Medieval to Renaissance in English Poetry* (Cambridge, 1985), 120: 'The persistent distortion of Chaucer's achievement that is represented by the poetry of most of his disciples meant that the work of the literary Renaissance, which Chaucer had begun single-handed, had to be done all over again in the sixteenth century'; or Seth Lerer's argument, in his otherwise finely detailed *Chaucer and his Readers* (Princeton, NJ, 1993), 116, that 'Chaucer's authority infantilized, diminished, or dulled the self-presentations of those writers who would follow him'. The influence of Chaucer is treated with more nuancing by Ebin, *Illuminator, Makar, Vates*, and in Julia Boffey and Janet Cowen (eds.), *Chaucer and Fifteenth-Century Poetry*, King's College London Medieval Studies, 5 (London, 1991).

[7] See *OBLMVP* 1E, 19C.

Richard Firth Green offers a fine demonstration of the persistence of oral tradition that puts beyond doubt the origins of many ballads in the fifteenth century.[8] Malory's centrality to the larger context of contemporary English prose romances is explored by Helen Cooper,[9] in an essay that emphasizes their radical differences from the better-studied metrical romances. Such rereadings comprise an essential revision of those surveys of literary history that overlook the contributions of the fifteenth century and conflate its texts with those of periods regarded as more interesting.

The long fifteenth century is also overdue for revaluation since the criteria for what makes literature 'interesting' have changed so radically in the past few decades, in response to a recognition of the narrowness and insufficiency of traditional canons of taste. Romantic and post-Romantic criteria of aesthetic value, with their emphasis on the revelation of the individual poet's soul in delightful and apparently spontaneous verse, are the worst possible criteria to bring to the century's writing: not because its literature is 'bad' (as the *Oxford Book* showed, much of it is excellent by any standards), but because it operates by different principles. The recent emphasis on the historical dimension of literature, its active and often fully conscious participation in the moment of its own production, opens up text after text in this period of exceptional political and cultural disturbance.

At the simplest, this consciousness is a reflection of the troubled politics of the century. The Lancastrian usurpation of the throne by Henry IV in 1399 left a legacy of recurring rebellion by the rival dynastic Yorkist line, culminating in the civil wars of the Roses. Even the strong reign of Henry V (1409–22) was marked by conspiracy by dynastic rivals and rebellion by supporters of Lollardy, England's first home-grown heresy, which had emerged in the late fourteenth century and which the

---

[8] Gray's section on 'Ballads and Verse Romances' (*OBLMVP* 12) concentrates interestingly on popular narratives that occupy the overlapping generic ground between the medieval metrical romance and the traditional ballad.

[9] Cf. *OBLMVP* 14. Malory's place within the broader context of English culture is explored by Felicity Riddy, *Sir Thomas Malory* (Leiden, 1987).

Lancastrian kings set out to suppress unmercifully. Henry V's triumphs in France culminated in the Treaty of Troyes of 1420 and his marriage to Katherine de Valois, which was intended to lead to Lancastrian inheritance of the French crown; all that his son, a mere nine months old at the time of his father's death, did inherit was an unsure claim to the English throne, an unwinnable war in France, and his maternal grandfather's insanity, which itself made the Yorkist move to fill the vacuum at the centre of power all but inevitable. The passing on of the crown was typically a matter of violence: the murder of Richard II in 1399 set the pattern for the murders of Henry VI in 1471 and Edward V in 1483, and the genealogical turbulence it created lasted beyond the death of Richard III at Bosworth to the carnage of the battle of Stoke of 1487. Scotland experienced an analogous series of power vacuums, beginning with the imprisonment of James I in England from 1406 to 1424; but that country had had its civil wars (and wars of independence) a century earlier, and its political community knew the stabilizing value of an otherwise uninterrupted dynasty. Despite a series of assassinations and violent deaths (James I was murdered in 1437, James III died in a rebellion against him in 1488; James II was killed at the siege of Roxburghe in 1460, and James IV at the battle of Flodden, 1513), and the ensuing minorities, no serious alternative to the Stewart line was ever posited. As Sally Mapstone suggests, this may account for the distinct character of the political literature produced in Scotland. Religious disturbance was similarly a distinctively English phenomenon: Lollardy never took hold north of the Border, and the suppression of Roman Catholicism, which marks the end of the 'long fifteenth century' in England, was there delayed until the 1550s.

The political disruptions in England were occasionally seen at the time, and have been regarded since, as related to a falling away in literary composition;[10] but in fact many works of the period engage deeply with the moment of their production.

---

[10] See p. 143 below for the connection made by John Metham in the 1440s between civil unrest and the scarcity of new chivalric works.

There was no belief in the Middle Ages that poetry was a private matter, for either poet or audience. It is not just that writers reflect, consciously or unconsciously, the moment and circumstances of their writing; rather, that they saw one of the writer's roles as being that of social or political commentator. Lydgate is now being revealed as just such a commentator on the tangled politics of power and dissent in the early decades of the century, with their dread of heresy, their brief triumph of jingoistic nationalism succeeded by the anxieties attendant on the power struggles around an infant sovereign.[11] James Simpson's revaluation of his *Siege of Thebes*—or, as he shows it should more properly be called, *The Destruction of Thebes*—gives it its full weighting as a work with an agenda independent of its role as a further Canterbury tale, as an intervention in politics at a more ominous moment than has been assumed; not a clumsy imitation of the *Knight's Tale*, but a critique of it. The prose romances too appear in Helen Cooper's essay not as fantasy exercises in poetic justice as expressed in happy endings, but as presenting worlds all too recognizable to readers living through the civil disturbances of the century. More overtly political or satiric writing opens up problematic issues of authorial complicity and integrity, to which authors of the period were fully and explicity alert. Helen Barr and Kate Ward-Perkins look at the problems raised in political writing after Langland and Gower,[12] of the impossibility of giving advice that will be heard when one is speaking from the margin, and the impossibility of speaking disinterestedly when one is speaking from the centre. Their three principal texts span the whole

---

[11] Gray's selections from Lydgate (*OBLMVP* 4, especially 4B) make the same point, as does his opening the whole anthology with a section entitled 'The Mutability of Worldly Changes'. The roles of Lydgate and Hoccleve within the Lancastrian polity are explored by Larry Scanlon, *Narrative, Authority, and Power: The Medieval Exemplum and the Chaucerian Tradition* (Cambridge, 1994), 298–350, and by Paul Strohm, 'Hoccleve, Lydgate, and the Lancastrian Court', in *The Cambridge History of Medieval English Literature: Writing in Britain, 1066–1547*, ed. David Wallace (Cambridge, forthcoming).

[12] Cf. *OBLMVP* 8, 24, 26. On the whole issue of the relationship between poet and prince, see Richard Firth Green, *Poets and Princepleasers: Literature in the English Court in the Late Middle Ages* (Toronto, 1980). For an overview of the relationship between politics and literature in the period, see V. J. Scattergood, *Politics and Poetry in the Fifteenth Century* (London, 1971).

chronological range of this volume, from Henry IV to Henry VIII, and the range of alliterative and stanzaic verse and prose: *Mum and the Sothsegger*, Skelton's *Bowge of Court*, and Thomas Elyot's *Pasquil the Playne*.

The role of the poet is an explicit issue in many of these works, though it is expressed in ways very different from later periods and therefore again has been easy to underestimate. Chaucer first introduced the Muses into English poetry, but the kind of spontaneous inspiration they are now taken to represent would have seemed bizarre and inappropriate to fifteenth-century poets. Verse was still an open alternative to prose in many areas of discourse; fifteenth-century poetry was public in its concerns and implied no restriction of audience—indeed, the existence of oral poetry, such as the ballads that Richard Firth Green describes, made some forms of verse accessible to the non-literate where prose could not run. Earlier literatures typically epitomize their cultures in verbal form: the Old Testament for the Jews, Virgil for the self-representation of Augustan Rome, *The Battle of Maldon* and *La Chanson de Roland* for earlier medieval cultures that measured virtue by renown. That the major functions of poetry were praise and blame was, as Vincent Gillespie shows in his essay, an idea still active among early humanist apologists for poetry.[13] The modern distrust of public poetry, of literature written from the centre rather than from the margins, is largely a post-Romantic phenomenon, and one endorsed by the rise of modern totalitarian states. The fifteenth century is perhaps too close to the imminent Renaissance privileging of the individual for it to be seen sufficiently clearly how much it belongs with this earlier belief in poetry as culturally central. The inscription in late medieval literature of an endorsement of orthodox piety, morality, and political stability is not a sign of complicity or bland conformity, but

---

[13] See p. 305 below. The idea reached the early humanists through Averroes' commentary on Aristotle's *Poetics* as translated by Hermann the German (the *Poetics* being unknown in their original form in the Middle Ages); see A. J. Minnis and A. B. Scott (eds.), *Medieval Literary Theory and Criticism c.1100–c.1375: The Commentary Tradition* (Oxford, 1988), 277–307. The continuing role of 'shame culture' in the fifteenth century is discussed with reference to Malory by D. S. Brewer in his introduction to *The Morte Darthur Parts Seven and Eight by Sir Thomas Malory* (London, 1968), 23–35.

evidence of the value accorded to the written word and the status of the author in upholding social and religious ideals that were all too obviously ignored or absent in the world of action. The poet typically writes on behalf of the common weal, and his poetry, even when it appears most inward (in religious writings, especially when it appears most inward), can speak for the whole community. And so for Hoccleve, as John Burrow shows, personal piety can be embodied in the re-expression of another's words, in the translation into his own mother tongue of the devotional beliefs common to the whole of Catholic Europe. The visionaries, whose subject-matter comes to them not from any metaphorical Muses but direct from God, receive as individual revelation information about the general condition of humanity after death, as they send their hearts into purgatory—the title Robert Easting takes for his study (and it is worth noting that the primacy of purgatory in these visions accords with this enforcement of orthodoxy, since the Lollards questioned its existence). John Skelton, in Vincent Gillespie's exposition, finds at the heart of his humanist-inspired defence of poetry and of his own role as poet that orthodox faith and true poetic inspiration are two sides of the same coin: his Muse is the Holy Ghost.

Texts are rooted in social practices as much as in political or religious beliefs, and two essays in particular in this collection address those connections. Sally Mapstone's discussion of *The Kingis Quair* shows how its replication of the model of the 'king of love' gives a glimpse into the courtly ethic of play and pastime and its intersection with the more serious ethics of government. Performance of a more formal kind is addressed by Malcolm Godden, whose revelations about the use of women as actors in plays and pageants allow a sight of a world in which women are much more visible, in every sense, than has commonly been thought: the image of the monks of the great monastery of Bury creating their own literal representations of wicked women, and the contrasting image of the secular monarch turning his back in shame from a dance 'of young ladies with bared bosoms', sum up beautifully the tensions and contradictions to be found even within the public culture of the later Middle Ages—and it is in keeping with many of the findings of feminist-oriented scholarship that women should be at the focus of such tensions.

There is abundant evidence of an increasing, though generally more orthodox, participation of women in written culture in this period, whether in the many records of their ownership of books, their readiness to communicate by letter (as the many women of the Paston family abundantly demonstrate), the illiterate Margery Kempe's desire that her dictated record of her life should be preserved in written form, or in activities such as Dame Eleanor Hull's devotional translations.[14] The post-Chaucerian framed poems also bore a considerable potential for giving expression to the subjectivity of women, an area too often silent in medieval literature; as Helen Phillips demonstrates, their speakers are on a number of occasions female, whether those voices are dramatically conceived or are those of actual authors—and although the gender of the authors of anonymous works must be speculative, it would be irrational to assume that they must always be male.[15] Fifteenth-century England may not have produced a woman writer of the status of Christine de Pizan, but her works were read and on occasion translated; she therefore provided a model of secular female authorship to set alongside the Continental women visionaries whose works were also being translated at this period—Catherine of Siena, Bridget of Sweden, Marguerite Porete—and indeed England's own women mystics, from Julian of Norwich at the start of the century through Kempe herself and the Benedictine nun whose vision of purgatory is described by Robert Easting.

Not every account of women's experience, however, may be

---

[14] The literature on this issue has been expanding rapidly in recent years, and a full bibliography would be impracticable; but see in particular Carol M. Meale, '... alle the bokes that I haue of latyn, englisch and frensch: Laywomen and their Books in Late Medieval England', in Meale (ed.), *Women and Literature in Britain 1150–1500*, Cambridge Studies in Medieval Literature, 17 (Cambridge, 1993), 128–58; Julia Boffey, 'Women Authors and Women's Literacy in Fourteenth- and Fifteenth-Century England', ibid. 159–82.

[15] For an especially shrewd discussion of the possibility of female authorship of poems customarily ascribed to men, see Sarah McNamer, 'Female Authors, Provincial Setting: The Re-Versing of Courtly Love in the Findern Manuscript', *Viator*, 22 (1991), 279–310.

quite what it seems. Chaucer had used above all the comparatively naturalistic medium of story, rather than his own framed poems, to offer an exploration of women's subjectivity. Robert Henryson appears to do something comparable in *The Testament of Cresseid*, as Douglas Gray shows with particular sensitivity in his own study of the poet:[16] Cresseid enlarges beyond the types she would seem to exemplify, of the fickle woman, the lady lamenting her abandonment, the penitent magdalene, or moral exemplum. In this collection, Felicity Riddy offers a radical challenge to all such readings, to argue instead that the significance of the leprous Cresseid to Henryson is as the abject that must be expelled in order for Troilus's own *trouthe* to be constructed; and the incipient humanist reading of her character is dissolved into 'different genres that provide discontinuous subject positions', testamentary, moralizing, subject to time, forsaken, outcast.

Such a conclusion demands a rethinking of basic questions about the presentation of subjectivity in late medieval literature. Troilus himself functions less as an individual, by this reading, than as an exemplary 'stable masculine identity' reassuring to male readers who look to poets to establish moral certainties in a less comforting world. This refocusing of interpretation would offer a new kind of alignment for the *Testament* with the strong tendency in the literature of the period to place its primary emphasis on what is common to the experience of being human rather than on what is unique: on the individual as everyman. But there is an awareness in the fifteenth century too that 'every*man*' need not in every instance be male. The eponymous protagonist of the morality play of that name is gendered male as a dramatic character and by virtue of the masculine pronouns applied to him, but the life-experiences, and death-experiences, ascribed to him are kept remarkably gender-inclusive: he is abandoned as death approaches, for instance, by both Beauty and Strength, the archetypal female and male attributes.[17]

---

[16] Douglas Gray, *Robert Henryson* (Leiden, 1979).
[17] A full text of *Everyman* is given in OBLMVP 21. The eponymous protagonist of *Mankind* (OBLMVP 16), by contrast, is presented specifically as male, even though the name itself equally allows the possibility of representing humanity in general.

This emphasis on what is held in common does not however mean that a sense of subjectivity, of the uniqueness of individual experience as it is registered inwardly, is necessarily absent in the later Middle Ages. Again, it is too easy to imagine the literary representation of subjectivity to be predominantly a post-Romantic phenomenon, with its roots certainly in the Renaissance, perhaps arguably in the work of Chaucer—but here too the fifteenth century demands more attention. The problem here is not any late medieval lack of interest in the matter, but the unfamiliarity of the means of representation. Dream vision; framed poetry, in which the subjective experience of a first-person narrator encloses some other event or episode; discontinuous or serial poetry—these are the typical forms of the period through which subjective experience is explored, and which provide the space and structure for the juxtaposition of counter-experiences against which to define such subjectivity. These forms are ideally suited for the debating and analysis of problematic psychological matters: rival constructions of identity, self-representation, the nature of love, the relationship of lover and beloved. It is these methods that are chosen by many authors in the Chaucerian tradition, whose concern with such issues has been occluded by their choice of the less 'naturalistic' of Chaucer's own forms. Literary imitation itself can enable poets to find the voice for such expression (Petrarchism offers a particularly famous example); Hoccleve, as John Burrow demonstrates in this volume, finds the models for his own remarkable self-representation in the French *dits* that had also inspired Chaucer.

It was not self-expression that made a medieval poet, however, but the act of making poetry; and that required a mastery of the arts of language, rhetoric, and metre. As Helen Phillips notes, writers of the period might well find inexplicable our relative lack of interest in matters such as the choice and mastery of a variety of stanza-forms and the refinement of the language. Douglas Gray himself is perhaps the master-expositor of medieval lyrics to the late twentieth century,[18] and it is appropriate

---

[18] Douglas Gray, *Themes and Images in the Medieval English Religious Lyric* (London and Boston, 1972).

that one of the essays in this collection should concentrate on the issue of lyric craftsmanship. A poet in the fifteenth century was a 'maker', Scots *makar*: yet the associations of the term with fine workmanship have again paradoxically lowered the evaluation of the writers of this period, to being mere artisans of words, as if inspiration alone might have produced better poetry. Just as the low literary reputation of the whole century for long resulted in a broad refusal to credit it with alliterative poetry and ballads, so the one English lyric poet of the first part of the period for whom we have both a name and a substantial corpus of work, John Audelay, has been denied authorship of the outstanding poem of the manuscript that preserves his works. *The Three Dead Kings*, a remarkable and gruesome poem on the appearance of three dead to three living, has been attributed to Anon instead of Audelay largely on the grounds that Anon wrote better poetry. Eric Stanley's essay establishes Audelay's alertness to genre, his interest in the craft of poetry, his virtuosity in combining alliteration, complex stanza forms, and intricate rhyme schemes: the result is like seeing a darkly varnished picture after cleaning. Audelay emerges as a much finer and more innovative artist than one could see before, and the concomitant reattribution to him of *The Three Dead Kings* gives him back a poem of grim imaginative intensity.

If the Chaucerians and Audelay demonstrate in different ways the richness of vernacular English traditions of poetry, that does not mean that late medieval literature was merely insular or parochial, in retreat from Chaucer's own cosmopolitanism. Fifteenth-century poets, like Chaucer, look to France for literary models and inspiration; as John Burrow points out, it is sometimes hard to distinguish direct French poetic influence from such influence as mediated by Chaucer. Such debt to literary models, even direct translation, need not imply the loss of originality. The innovatory elements in Lydgate, Hoccleve, and the framed poems are all demonstrated in the course of this volume. Medieval Latin too was a tradition to be used, not just replicated in the vernacular. The late flowering of the Alexander legend in both English and Scots in this period provides some particularly fine treatments of material with a long

European history.[19] Peter Dronke's close study of *The Wars of Alexander* illustrates both the author's respect for his Latin original and the brilliance and detail of his own contribution. Mainstream Classical literature and contemporary humanist writings were also increasingly penetrating England in translation,[20] as well as being read by those literate in Latin. The essays by Vincent Gillespie and by Helen Barr and Kate Ward-Perkins show the penetration of these new humanist ideas into English traditions of religious and political writing, in ways that bring together social and private considerations, the individual anxieties of the poetic voice and the obligations laid on the poet by his duty to God and to the common weal.

It may have been a combination of such factors—Chaucer's own awareness, inherited by his followers, of his place in a tradition of poetry; the French poets' self-consciousness about transmitting a coherent canon of work; the humanist stress on individual responsibility and achievement—that governed the form taken by John Bale's survey of English writing. Bale himself was a product of the long fifteenth century, born in 1495, and living on into the reign of Elizabeth. His life covers the period in which the primary form for the circulation of writing shifted from manuscript to print; his survey included both forms, and itself exists in both printed and manuscript versions.[21] In the final essay in this collection, Anne Hudson explores how this early scholar of cultural studies looked back on the achievements of English writing in the century preceding his own, and how his premisses have helped to shape our own conception of literary history. The triumvirate of great English poets, Chaucer, Gower, and Lydgate, had been frequently invoked in the later part of the century; Bale constructs an entire canon of English

---

[19] Gray includes a section from the Prose *Alexander*, *OBLMVP* 14A; on that text see also p. 141 below, and pp. 52, 63–4 on the *Buik of King Alexander the Conquerour*. For a general survey, see Gerrit H. V. Bunt, *Alexander the Great in the Literature of Medieval Britain*, Medievalia Groningana, 14 (Groningen, 1994).

[20] Cf. *OBLMVP* 17A–E, representing Boethius, Petrarch as Latin author, Claudian (the first hexameter translation to be attempted in English), and Buonaccorso da Montemagno.

[21] On the conditions and processes of publication in the century before the advent of printing in Britain, see Jeremy Griffiths and Derek Pearsall (eds.), *Book Production and Publishing in Britain 1375–1475* (Cambridge, 1989).

writing based not on texts, but on authors. Like modern literary and historical scholars with their concerns for issues of gender, power, and dissent, Bale has his own agenda of issues of crucial concern to his particular cultural moment, for him consisting of the record of past English resistance to Roman Catholicism. But he is most like the modern scholars who have written, or who will read, this present book, and the one to whom it is dedicated, in that he is interested in vernacular texts as such: the first man to study English literature as a discipline in its own right and with its own history.

1 'Dysemol daies and fatal houres': Lydgate's Destruction of Thebes and Chaucer's Knight's Tale

JAMES SIMPSON

Lydgate's poem known as the *Siege of Thebes* is in every respect a much darker, more saturnine work than has been commonly allowed. The strongest manuscript tradition, endorsed by Lydgate from within the work, calls it the *Destruction of Thebes*, and destruction is indeed its subject.[1] In this it may well answer to the period of its composition, which in my view is after the death of Henry V. So far from being any simple celebration of Henry and the Treaty of Troyes (May 1420), its themes of fraternal strife and civic destruction answer more convincingly to events that followed Henry's death. Henry's brothers Humphrey, Duke of Gloucester, and John, Duke of Bedford, both threatened to fill the vacuum created by Henry's

---

I dedicate this article with pleasure to Douglas Gray, who astonished me in 1980 by suggesting that I apply for a job. Without this suggestion I would have waited a good many years before attempting such a thing. Aside from his rich published work, I also learnt a great deal about Chaucer and about teaching from Douglas's affable yet probing conduct of a seminar on *Troilus and Criseyde* in 1979.

[1] The editors of the most authoritative edition state that 'as a matter of fact, the question of the title has been settled by Lydgate himself, who in his *Fall of Princes* calls our poem "The Sege of Thebes"' (Axel Erdmann and Eilert Ekwall (eds.), *Lydgate's 'Siege of Thebes'*, 2 vols., EETS ES 108, 125 (1911, 1930), ii. 2). The reference is to *Fall of Princes* I. 3724: 'For in the siege of Thebes ye may it reede' (*Lydgate's Fall of Princes*, ed. Henry Bergen, 4 vols., EETS ES 121–4 (1924–7), i. 103). The title *The Destruction of Thebes* is however required both by the poem's action and by its naming within the work—the 'siege and destruccioun / Of worthy Thebes' (ll. 184–5), and 'the destruccioun / Of myghty Thebes' (ll. 4606–7). This is what the oldest and best manuscript (British Library, Arundel MS 119, followed by nine other manuscripts and two printed texts) calls the poem in its colophon: 'Here endeth the destruccioun of Thebes' (fo. 79ʳ). (See Erdmann and Ekwall, pp. 1, 38.)

death on 31 August 1422; in December of that year Parliament determined that Bedford should be Protector in England whenever he was in the country, and that Gloucester (Protector while Bedford was in France) must give way to his older brother.[2] Questions of dating and title, however, are not the principal concern of this article: both those questions are in part dependent on how we understand the nature of Lydgate's project,[3] and it is to that larger question that this article is devoted. I argue that Lydgate enlists the energies of Chaucer's Theban narrative, the *Knight's Tale*, to shape a powerful, prudential admonition concerning the treacherousness of history.

I

Twentieth-century scholars of Lydgate's Theban poem have, on the whole, understood it to exemplify the value of 'truthe' in politics; Adrastus, Tydeus, and Polymyte exemplify faith-keeping, while Eteocles offers the anti-type.[4] This account of

---

[2] For the historical situation, see, for example, M. H. Keen, *England in the Later Middle Ages: A Political History* (London and New York, 1973), 409–12. For the consensus position on dating, see Erdmann and Ekwall, ii. 8–10. The strongest argument for a *terminus a quo* is the clear citation of the Treaty of Troyes (May 1420) at ll. 4690–3 and 4702–3. Lydgate probably did write a work, *The Serpent of Division* (ed. Henry Noble MacCracken (London and New Haven, 1911)), in the first year of the reign of Henry VI (beginning in September 1422), which drew on classical example (the Roman Civil War) to warn against the disastrous consequences of civil strife. MacCracken argues that ll. 4660–88 of the *Destruction* are a recollection of the themes and vocabulary of the *Serpent of Division* (p. 5). That argument with regard to vocabulary is unfortunately not watertight, but the passage from the *Destruction* is unquestionably identical in theme to the *Serpent*. The strongest argument in favour of 1421 is by Johnstone Parr, who uses astronomical evidence to date the poem to April 1421 ('Astronomical Dating for Some of Lydgate's Poems', *PMLA* 67 (1952), 251–8).

[3] Erdmann and Ekwall, for example, argue for a date prior to the death of Henry V on what are clearly interpretative grounds: 'it is evident that Lydgate could not possibly have composed the fourteen above mentioned lines (4690–703), so full of joy at the happy ending of the war and of hopefulness for the future, if the bright political outlook had been already darkened by the sudden death of England's youthful king' (ii. 9). But if Tydeus 'is clearly conceived in the image of Henry V' (Walter F. Schirmer, *John Lydgate: A Study in the Culture of the Fifteenth Century*, trans. Ann E. Kemp (London, 1952), 64; see also Derek Pearsall, 'Lydgate as Innovator', *MLQ* 53 (1992), 5–22 (p. 14)), then it is surely significant that this brilliant figure dies disastrously in the poem (ll. 4199–239).

[4] The major article arguing this position is Robert W. Ayers, 'Medieval History, Moral Purpose, and the Structure of Lydgate's *Siege of Thebes*', *PMLA* 73 (1958), 463–74. Accounts of the poem as exemplary in mode, and as a mirror of princes along the general lines established by Ayers, are consistently repeated in *Siege* criticism: see, for

the poem has a certain force, for there are indeed inset passages praising the virtue of 'truthe'. One could, for example, cite the long addition Lydgate makes to his source in his narration of Eteocles' first council session (ll. 1725–91). There some counsel Eteocles to be faithful to the pact whereby each brother should rule in alternate years, while others encourage him to remember that he is 'a knyght, / And to holde of force, more than of right, / Duryng his lyf lordship of the toun' (ll. 1785–7).[5] In his own voice, Lydgate interjects to cite the example of Nehemiah, who through fidelity 'Gat hym licence to reedifie / The wallys newe of Jerusalem' (ll. 1740–1); he contrasts that with the example of Ethiocles, through whose duplicity 'Thebes with his walles olde / Distroied was' (ll. 1776–8).

These references to cities either destroyed through double, faithless speech or edified through faith-keeping suggest further that 'truthe' is not merely the explicit theme of the poem. The direct address to rulers in such passages implies that the work is itself an example of truth-telling, an example which conforms with the constructive political role assigned to poetry in the work's opening. There Lydgate records the myth of Amphion building the walls of Thebes through the 'armonye of his swete song' (l. 203), a *fabula* which Lydgate, following Boccaccio, rationalizes as meaning that a king can build literal cities, and political harmony, through eloquence (ll. 213–92). As has been argued, Lydgate's poem about the rise and fall of a city implies a Ciceronian, almost architectural role for truth-telling poetry in political construction.[6]

---

example, John M. Ganim, *Style and Consciousness in Middle English Narrative* (Princeton, 1983), 110, 114; A. C. Spearing, *Medieval to Renaissance in English Poetry* (Cambridge, 1985), 83; and Lee Patterson, 'Making Identities in Fifteenth-Century England: Henry V and John Lydgate', in Jeffrey N. Cox and Larry J. Reynolds (eds.), *New Historical Literary Study: Essays in Reading Texts, Representing History* (Princeton, 1993), 69–107 (p. 77). Patterson also recognizes the deeper complexity of the poem in his final section, where he tentatively suggests that Lydgate wrote a poem 'that incorporated its own opposite' (p. 97).

[5] All citations of the *Destruction/Siege of Thebes* are from the edition of Erdmann and Ekwall. I have modernized letter-forms for thorn and yogh; omitted editorial diacritics; and omitted caesural virgulae.

[6] For the Ciceronian myth about the constructive powers of rhetoric, see *De inventione*, I. 2. 2–3. Lois A. Ebin, 'Lydgate's Views on Poetry', *Annuale Mediaevale*, 18 (1977), 76–105 (esp. pp. 97–105) makes a convincing case that Lydgate contributes substantially

This account of the poem's theme and rhetorical posture is not by any means eccentric to what the poem says about itself. And if we left the matter there, we would have a poem that conforms to the kind of (rather tedious, neat) thing we expect of Lydgate: a poetry of moral exemplarism. But the poem's ethical interest extends well beyond 'truthe'. For Middle English writers concerned to define a secular ethics appropriate to political action, 'truthe' is one aspect of that ethical nexus, the Cardinal Virtues. 'Truthe', translating *fides*, is an aspect of Justice,[7] but the poem is equally concerned to exemplify other virtues in this system, and especially the virtue of Prudence. Focus on this virtue takes us closer to the historical quality of Lydgate's imagination in this poem.

One of the great sources for ethical thinking of this kind in the medieval period, Cicero's *De officiis*,[8] defines the essential difference between humans and animals as the capacity to think with discrimination across time:

> Man, however, is a sharer in reason; this enables him to perceive consequences, to comprehend the causes of things, their precursors and their antecedents, so to speak; to compare similarities and to link and combine future with present events; and by seeing with ease the whole course of life to prepare whatever is necessary for living it.[9]

---

to a political poetics; this material has subsequently been incorporated into and developed by the same author's *Illuminator, Maker, Vates: Visions of Poetry in the Fifteenth Century* (Lincoln, Nebr. and London, 1988), 39–48.

[7] For the reception of the Cardinal Virtues into English poetry, see J. D. Burnley, *Chaucer's Language and the Philosophers' Tradition*, Chaucer Studies, 2 (Cambridge, 1979).

[8] The contents of the *De officiis* were easily available to medieval writers in the summary possibly by William of Conches, the *Moralium dogma philosophorum* (ed. John Holmberg, *Gulielmus de Conchis: Das Moralium dogma philosophorum* (Paris, Uppsala, and Leipzig, 1929)). This work survives in over ninety manuscripts; there are over forty more of the Old French translation; see Philippe Delhaye, 'Une adaption du *De officiis* au xiie siècle: le *Moralium dogma philosophorum*', *Recherches de théologie ancienne et médiévale*, 16 (1949), 227–58.

[9] 'Homo autem, quod rationis est particeps, per quam consequentia cernit, causas rerum videt earumque praegressus et quasi antecessiones non ignorat, similitudines comparat rebusque praesentibus adiungit atque annectit futuras, facile totius vitae cursum videt ad eamque degendam praeparat res necessarias' (*De officiis*, ed. Walter Miller (Cambridge, Mass. and London, 1913), 1. 4. 11; p. 12). The translation is taken from Cicero, *On Duties*, ed. M. T. Griffin and E. M. Atkins (Cambridge, 1991), 6.

The person, according to Cicero, who relies on prudence and wisdom (*prudentia consilioque fidens*) will anticipate the future by reflection on the past, and will never be reduced to saying '*Non putaram*'—'I hadn't thought of that'.[10] In Lydgate's poem this virtue of prudential foresight is consistently practised by the aged. Among the Argives Adrastus (who advises Polymyte that he should 'prudently tak hede' in not going to Thebes, l. 1835), and especially Amphiorax (who is consulted about the war as 'on that was ful prudent and right wyce / And circumspecte in his werkes alle', ll. 2796–7), both represent the virtue of practical prudence. On the Theban side it is Jocasta who promotes prudential wisdom, as she foresees the military disaster that will befall Eteocles if he insists on fighting (ll. 3648–708). All the aged figures, in fact, embody prudence, by foreseeing events, and by giving advice not to undertake enterprises that cannot be completed; when the young Theban soldiers abuse Amphiorax, for example, Lydgate pauses to digress on the impetuosity of youth, whereas

> age experte no thyng undertaketh
> But he to-forn be good discrecioun,
> Make a due examynacioun
> How it wil tourne outher to badde or good.
> . . . .
> The olde, prudent in al his governaunce,
> Ful longe a-forn maketh purveaunce;
> But youth allas be counsail wil not wyrke,
> For which ful ofte he stumbleth in the dyrke.   (ll. 2952–62)

And just as the poem presents itself as an example of truth-telling, so too is it an example of prudential thought, produced by a relatively aged figure (Lydgate represents himself as almost 'fifty yere of age' in the Prologue (l. 93)). The whole poem is

---

[10] *De officiis*, I. 23. 81; p. 82. The *locus classicus* in Middle English literature is, of course, Criseyde's lament for her lack of prudence (*Troilus and Criseyde*, V. 743–9). The *Moralium dogma* summarizes Cicero's discussion of prudence thus: 'Prudentiam diximus esse discretionem rerum bonarum et malarum et utrarumque. Hec namque uirtus discernit bona a malis et bona ab inuicem, mala ab inuicem... Huius partes sunt prouidentia, circumspectio, cautio, docilitas' (ed. Holmberg, I. A; p. 8).

an act of purveyance, reflecting prudentially as it does over exempla from the past, and equally applying an implicit pressure on the present and future of the readers for whom the poem was designed. The positive model of the poem is not merely the truthful ruler; it is a much broader, Ciceronian model of the ruler who is at once wise and eloquent. The marriage of Oedipus and his mother Jocasta, which provokes the 'utter ruyne' of Thebes (l. 850), is contrasted with the marriage of Mercury and Philology, recalled from Martianus Capella's *De nuptiis* (ll. 823–74); Lydgate, in line with a long tradition, interprets this fable as signifying the Ciceronian marriage of 'sapience' and 'eloquence' (ll. 839–44), a marriage that would, by implication, edify the polis.[11]

But the poem's own praise of prudence is not simply a matter of static moral exempla, however frequent Lydgate's references to that virtue.[12] On the contrary, Lydgate promotes the virtue of prudence only to underline the unpropitious historical circumstances that must constrain its confidence. Once we accept Lydgate's invitation to set static moral exempla (either of 'truthe' or of prudence) into the dynamic structure of both the *Destruction of Thebes* and the *Knight's Tale*, we arrive at an understanding of the genuinely Statian quality of Lydgate's poem. The actual source for the *Destruction* is, most probably, the *Roman de Edipus*, a prose redaction of the *Roman de Thebes*;[13]

---

[11] For the interpretation of Martianus's text as an allegory whose significance encapsulates Cicero's coupling of wisdom and eloquence, see Gabriel Nuchelmans, 'Philologie et son mariage avec Mercure jusqu'à la fin du xii siècle', *Latomus*, 16 (1957), 84–107. The key text is Cicero, *De inventione*, 1. 1. 1, where he says that 'sapientiam sine eloquentia parum prodesse civitatibus, eloquentiam vero sine sapientia nimium obesse plerumque, prodesse numquam'; see Cicero, *De inventione*, ed. and trans. H. M. Hubbell (London and Cambridge, Mass., 1949), 2.

[12] Citations relevant to prudence (much more common, incidentally, than those relevant to 'truthe') are as follows: ll. 221, 681–2, 763–72, 818, 1104–11, 1730, 1835–43, 1940, 2219, 2601, 2682, 2794–818, 2941–84, 3121, 3411, 3443, 3639, 3653–708, 3938, 4168. It should also be mentioned that the two other Cardinal Virtues (or aspects thereof) are also exemplified by Tydeus (courage) and Adrastus (liberality, an aspect of justice): see ll. 2174–235 for courage, and ll. 2689–736 for liberality.

[13] For convincing arguments that the source of the *Destruction* is 'almost certainly a complete text of the *Roman de Edipus*', see Alain Renoir, 'The Immediate Source of Lydgate's *Siege of Thebes*', *Studia Neophilologica*, 33 (1961), 86–95. For the French text, see *Le Roman de Edipus, Filz du Roy Layus* (Paris: Pierre Sergent, s. xvi (undated); repr. Paris, 1858)). Elsewhere, Renoir rightly characterizes the *Roman de Edipus* thus: 'It resembles the magnificent *Roman de Thebes* in about the same degree as the comic-book

here I want to argue that Lydgate is entering into conversation not with the French text, but rather with the *Knight's Tale*. Like Chaucer's poem, Lydgate's cannot be read in terms of static moral exemplarism; when read as dynamic wholes, *and as themselves part of a whole*, both the *Destruction of Thebes* and the *Knight's Tale* illuminate in each other a deep pessimism about the value of human enterprise and construction, whether that construction be political, architectural, or poetic.

In the larger field of Lydgate scholarship, the sum of my argument here implies disagreement with the following accounts of Lydgate (examples, in my view, of posterity's condescension): that he is 'medieval' and his humanism only skin deep;[14] and that he is overawed by Chaucer's presence.[15] For the moment, however, let me turn to Lydgate's dark and powerful sense of historical forces, forces that negate the enterprise of prudential, truthful eloquence.

2

It is the Knight who interrupts the tragedies of the Monk in the *Canterbury Tales*; by the Knight's reckoning, the Monk may as well tell stories which trace the opposite trajectory, of moving

---

version of *Macbeth* resembles Shakespeare's tragedy, and it is written in the same spirit for a naive audience' (*The Poetry of John Lydgate* (London, 1967), 134). For thirteenth- and fourteenth-century prose redactions of twelfth-century *romans antiques*, see the references given by Barbara Nolan, *Chaucer and the Tradition of the 'Roman Antique'*, Cambridge Studies in Medieval Literature, 15 (Cambridge, 1992), 328 n. 11.

[14] This is the view of Derek Pearsall, consistently held across publications spanning twenty-two years; see his *John Lydgate* (London, 1970), 14–16, and 'Lydgate as Innovator': 'My argument has always been that Lydgate's importance and his claim on our attention is his representative and noninnovatory medievalness' (p. 5). See also Spearing, *Medieval to Renaissance*, 83–8, for the same view. The tradition of humanism in which Lydgate's work stands is admirably elucidated by Nolan, *Chaucer and the Tradition of the 'Roman Antique'*.

[15] See especially Spearing, *Medieval to Renaissance*, 88–110, which has it that there exists an Oedipal relationship between Chaucer and his fifteenth-century followers, springing from the 'widespread anxiety among his poetic descendants about the impossibility of the task they were undertaking' (p. 107). See also Seth Lerer, *Chaucer and his Readers: Imagining the Author in Late Medieval England* (Princeton, 1993) for an elaboration of the same position. My argument here is rather that Lydgate's address to the *Canterbury Tales* is anything but anxious, infantile, and unsophisticated; Lydgate confidently lays claim to the *Tales*, by harnessing their energy to his own project (and vice versa).

from misery to happiness (*Canterbury Tales*, VII. 2767–79[16]). Of course there are many *examples* of tragic fall, the Knight implies, but if there is nothing *inherent* in the universe that provokes such fall, then why not provide comedy?—'Swich thyng is gladsom, as it thynketh me, / And of swich thyng were goodly for to telle' (VII. 2778–9). Lydgate, himself a Benedictine 'Monk of Bury' (and represented as such in the Prologue to the *Destruction*), takes up the challenge of tragedy where Chaucer's Monk had been chased from the field: on the return trip to London, Lydgate imagines a scene in which he joins the pilgrimage to tell a tale. But the first tale on the imagined return to London is no mere replacement of the Monk's tragedies; it is instead much more ambitious, directed to the first tale of the outward journey from London, that of the Knight: Lydgate's poem, that is, relates the events of Theban history beginning with the construction of the city by Amphion, and leading right up to exactly the point that the *Knight's Tale* begins, the destruction of the same city by Theseus. This answering to the Knight by the cleric Lydgate is characteristic of the consistent debate between knights and clerics within Lydgate's poem.[17]

The first tale on the way back answers, then, to the first tale out: this initial patterning pulls a reader into it, creating a complex set of relationships, in which events that are recounted *later* in the fictional time of the newly enlarged *Canterbury Tales* happen *earlier* in history. As this Lydgatian version of the *Canterbury Tales* progresses, that is, so are we increasingly pulled *backwards* to its beginning. If we put the two poems together, as Lydgate unquestionably invites us to do, then we have a poem constructed 'preposterously', or back-to-front—a narrative ordering with a long history, and recommended by the *artes poetriae* as by far the most sophisticated ordering.[18]

[16] All citations from the works of Chaucer are from *The Riverside Chaucer*, ed. Larry D. Benson, 3rd edn. (Oxford, 1988).

[17] See Ebin, 'Lydgate's Views on Poetry', 98–100 for examples in the *Destruction* of the opposition (traditional in humanist writing) between *miles* and *clericus*.

[18] For the notion of praeposterous, or back-to-front order, see my *Sciences and the Self in Medieval Poetry: Alan of Lille's 'Anticlaudianus' and John Gower's 'Confessio Amantis'*, Cambridge Studies in Medieval Literature, 25 (Cambridge, 1995), 75–81.

Many earlier readers of the *Canterbury Tales*, in both manuscript and printed editions, did in fact read the poem in this way, since they found Lydgate's poem presented as a Canterbury tale, placed as it was at the end of the *Canterbury Tales*.[19]

What thematic gains does Lydgate derive from this formal patterning? Most obviously, we realize that the events of the *Knight's Tale* are but a reflex of the larger, predominant patterns of Theban history: as we head back towards the *Knight's Tale*, we see that the fraternal dispute of Palamon and Arcite is but a replay, on a smaller scale, of the sibling hatred between the sons of Oedipus, the hatred which is responsible for the destruction of Thebes. In the larger scheme offered us by Lydgate, the Argive Adrastus plays the part of Athenian Theseus in Chaucer's poem: Adrastus's first act in the poem is to contain and resolve the violent rivalry between Polymyte and Tydeus, just as he consoles Lycurgus for the death of his infant son in terms strikingly similar to Theseus's consolation for the death of Arcite. But there is a consistent pattern to these echoes: the *Destruction of Thebes* plays out in fully political, military, and historical terms what was presented in a more restricted frame by Chaucer's Knight: Adrastus's liberal welcome to the soldiers to war (ll. 2671–736) recalls Theseus's liberality in preparations for a tournament (I. 2190–206); the viciousness of the tournament in Chaucer (I. 2601–22) expands into the really bloody description of the war in Lydgate (e.g. ll. 4317–48). Lydgate 'unsprings' Chaucer's poem: whereas the personal history of the lovers Palamon and Arcite might consistently tend towards (and imply) political and even cosmological questions, the political and cosmological forces of the narrative are turned back towards the resolution of personal conflict; Lydgate, by contrast, sets his narrative squarely within the realm of politics.

---

[19] See John M. Bowers, 'The *Tale of Beryn* and the *Siege of Thebes*: Alternative Ideas of the *Canterbury Tales*', *Studies in the Age of Chaucer*, 7 (1985), 23–50 (pp. 39–40), for evidence that five of the fifteenth-century witnesses to the poem were attached to the *Canterbury Tales*, and that the early editors of Chaucer (Stow, Speght) both printed Lydgate's poem 'along with the rest of the Chaucer canon' (p. 40). For a full list of the thirty manuscripts, see 'John Lydgate', by Alain Renoir and C. David Benson, in *A Manual of the Writings in Middle English 1050–1500*, gen. ed. Albert E. Hartung, vol. vi (New Haven, 1980), 1809–920, and 2071–175 (p. 2155).

Of course it involves personal histories, but those are not allowed to obscure the fate of cities in this story: the *occupatio* for Arcite's funeral (I. 2913–66) is echoed in Lydgate's poem by an *occupatio* for the funeral of *all* the Greek warriors (ll. 4565–87). This passage has been largely extended from its contracted, one-dimensional source in the *Roman de Edipus*, clearly in order to activate memories of the *Knight's Tale*:

> But what shuld I any lenger dwelle
> The olde ryytes by and by to telle,
> Nor th'obsequies in order to devise;
> Nor to declare the manere and the guyse
> How the bodyes wer to asshes brent,
> Nor of the gommes in the flaumbe spent,
> To make the ayre swetter of relees,
> As fraunc encence mirre and aloes;
> Nor how the wommen round aboute stood,
> Some with mylk and some also with blood,
> And some of hem with urnes made of gold,
> Whan the asshes fully weren made cold,
> T'enclosyn hem of gret affeccioun
> And bern hem hom into her regioun.   (ll. 4565–78)[20]

But if this sonorous passage does activate powerful memories of the *Knight's Tale*, it does so precisely in order to mark differences: whereas Chaucer's *occupatio* refers to the funeral rites of a single warrior, this speech registers the loss of an entire army—the governing class of an entire city, indeed. The destructive patterns of Theban history that are largely repressed in the *Knight's Tale* (and which are also, it should be remarked in passing, palpable behind the narrative of *Troilus and Criseyde*[21]) here reassert themselves in panoramic gravity. The *Knight's Tale* begins and ends with a marriage; Lydgate's poem begins

---

[20] Compare *Knight's Tale*, ll. 2882–912. Compare also the *Roman de Edipus* at this juncture: 'Quant ce fut faict grant douleur reprenoyent aux corps des Grecz mettre en cendre et en sepulture faire, nul ne pourroit dire la grant douleur que les dames demenoient et faisoient. Ie ne vueil mye de chascun compter la sepulture, car ie ne pourroye ne ne scauroye' (*Le Roman de Edipus*, fo. K. ii^{r-v}).

[21] For which see Winthrop Wetherbee, *Chaucer and the Poets: An Essay on 'Troilus and Criseyde'* (Ithaca, NY and London, 1984), 111–44, and Lee Patterson, *Chaucer and the Subject of History* (London, 1991), 126–36.

with the construction of a city, while its narrative ends with the collapse of that same city—'the destruccioun / Of myghty Thebes shortly, and no more' (ll. 4606–7).

Lydgate reveals a central feature of Chaucerian narrative in widening the focus in this way: we see how Chaucer, in both the *Knight's Tale* and *Troilus and Criseyde*, takes up classical stories through personal histories, and implies the larger patterns of Theban or Trojan history within a more enclosed space. So Lydgate's Canterbury tale, in at least this respect, relates to its companion not through rivalry (as most other 'pairs' within the *Canterbury Tales* do), but rather by means of intelligent commentary, by giving historical depth and resonance to the 'heroical pageants' of Chaucer's poem.[22] Lydgate expands Chaucer's story both historically and discursively—historically from the story of Palamon and Arcite to the history of Thebes behind it, and discursively from a story focused on individuals to a consistently political narrative.

3

Lydgate, then, enlarges the discursive boundaries of his Chaucerian model. What are we to say, though, of the dispositional *hysteron-proteron* we observe when we put the *Destruction* beside the *Knight's Tale*? For in this newly constructed version of the *Tales*, we have, as I have said, a back-to-front ordering of the Theban story, whereby events that are historically *prior* to those narrated in the *Knight's Tale* are narrated *after* it. The events of the *Destruction* are fictionally posterior but historically prior to the narrative of the *Knight's Tale*. What insights on both poems does this offer?

Here I want first to suggest that the events of Lydgate's poem foreshadow and foreclose possibilities within the *Knight's Tale*. Whereas Chaucer's narrative might appear to declare the constructive possibilities of prudential political management, the space for such prudential political action is drastically

---

[22] The phrase 'heroical pageants' is a note by Gabriel Harvey made c.1598 in the margins of his copy of the *Knight's Tale*. It is cited in Derek Brewer (ed.), *Chaucer: The Critical Heritage*, 2 vols. (London, 1978), i. 122.

narrowed in the *Destruction of Thebes*. And this narrowing happens, of course, as we move back into the *Knight's Tale*, where Theseus extols the virtues of heroic action, and seems to practise the virtue of constructive, political prudence. As we face the prospect of Theseus again, the values he promotes seem hopelessly foreclosed in the larger, malevolent, Saturnine context of Theban history, a history into which Theseus (like Adrastus before him) has now been drawn. Whereas Theseus's 'Jovial' account of the cosmic order (I. 2987–3069) would have it that destructive cosmic forces are contained, the *Destruction* reinstates Saturn as the force whose 'cours... hath so wyde for to turne', and 'Hath moore power than woot any man' (I. 2454–5).

I argued in Section 1 that any exemplary reading of the *Siege* should attend to prudence as a virtue practised both by models within the poem and by the poem itself: the aged figures in the *Destruction* all reflect prudentially across time by way of judging the practical possibilities of the present, just as the poem itself can be described as a prudential act. But what is the real achievement of prudential reflection in this poem?

The first act of philosophical reflection ends in the defeat of reason: once Laius knows that his child has been conceived, he summons 'dyvynoures and philosophres', who are to calculate the child's 'fate and disposicioun' (ll. 358–68). They do so in a process described with elaborate exactitude (ll. 369–99), only to discover Saturn in Scorpio, 'Hevy-chered malencolik and loth', with Mars and Venus equally unpropitious; their (correct) conclusion is that 'with his swerd his fader shal be slawe; / Ther may no man helpe it nor excuse' (ll. 398–9).

This defeat of reason sets the pattern for each prudential act in the poem. As I mentioned earlier, the figure who most fully embodies the prudence of age in the *Destruction of Thebes* is Amphiorax, 'ful prudent and right wyce / And circumspecte in his werkes alle' (ll. 2796–7), who can 'aforn ful opynly dyvyne / Thyngges begonne how they shulde fyne' (ll. 2811–12). Consulted by the parliament of Adrastus on the question as to whether or not the Argives should go to war against Thebes, Amphiorax at first tries to hide, recognizing that such a war will destroy him and the 'moste parte of the blood royal' (l. 2824). Discovered, he addresses the parliament with eloquence, truthfulness, and prudence, expressing

> His cleer conceyte in verray sikernesse,
> Nat entryked with no doublenesse,
> Her dysemol daies and her fatal houres,
> Her aventurys and her sharpe shoures,
> The froward soort and the unhappy stoundys,
> The compleyntes of her dedly woundys,
> The wooful wrath and the contrariouste
> Of felle Mars in his cruelte. (ll. 2891–8)

This speech, however, which attempts to avert the historical malevolence destroying both Thebes and Argos, is met with abuse and derision, especially by the 'sowdeours, / And of lordes regnyng in her flours' (ll. 2935–6); the poem consistently contrasts philosophical, historically informed counsel with knightly bluster. And if this prudential figure is initially ignored and abused by the chivalric young, in the final negotiations to prevent war he is again ignored—'for al his elloquence / He had in soth but lytyl audience' (ll. 3811–12). But figures who now stand against Amphiorax are not the wild and impetuous young: here Amphiorax speaks in opposition to the eminently just speech of Tydeus (ll. 3764–805), and is himself silenced by the aged Adrastus, who 'bad hym to be stille' (l. 3813). The *De nuptiis* coupling of wisdom and eloquence (inverted in the wedding feast of Oedipus and Jocasta, ll. 823–52) is again ignored.

The space for rational, politically prudent action is, then, radically limited in Lydgate's poem. Jocasta's efforts at negotiation are equally destroyed, by the chance killing of the Theban tigers. It is appropriate, then, that Amphiorax should be the first Argive hero to die, entirely swallowed up by the earth, just as the discursive space for prudential counsel has been narrowed to vanishing point. The Lydgate-persona (who until this point has been full of praise for Amphiorax) does a sudden volte-face as Amphiorax disappears; he imitates the *Troilus and Criseyde* epilogue in his dismissal of Amphiorax's useless pagan skills:

> Lo here the mede of ydolatrie,
> Of rytys old and of fals mawmetrye.
> Lo what avayllen incantaciouns
> Of exorsismes and conjurisouns... (ll. 4047–50)

If Chaucer had written these lines, I have no doubt that we would distrust them as much as many of us distrust the antihumanist *Troilus* epilogue, with its dismissal of 'payens corsed olde rites' and 'wrecched worldes appetites' (*Troilus and Criseyde*, V. 1849–51): after all, it is precisely the skills of prudent foresight that could have averted the destruction of two armies. The role of Amphiorax the 'dyvynour' (e.g. l. 4096) in Lydgate's poem has altogether disappeared in the *Knight's Tale*, leaving only the rueful voice of the Knight as he points to the gap: 'I nam no divinistre; / Of soules fynde I nat in this registre' (I. 2811–12). Lydgate's poem, after the event (as it were), prepares the way for that silence.

Amphiorax disappears, Tydeus is shot dead, Parthenope is killed, Ypomedon 'casuelly was drownyd' (l. 4248), Eteocles murders Polymyte as Polymyte attempts to save his brother's life; Adrastus dies in solitary misery; the entire Argive force, which has acted with courage and justice, is destroyed:

> For when Amphiorax and Tydeus,
> Ipomedon, Parthonope also
> Were ded, and slayn proude Campaneus,
> And when the wrecched Thebans, bretheren two,
> Were slayn, and kyng Adrastus hom ago,
> So desolat stod Thebes and so bare
> That no wight coude remedie of his fare.

This stanza from Chaucer's *Anelida and Arcite* (ll. 57–63) allows a vision of the whole scene of carnage and desolation, even if the brief poem of which it is a part then recoils back into Anelida's extraordinarily intense and personal 'poynt of remembraunce' (ll. 211, 350). The same is true of Cassandra's survey of Theban history in *Troilus and Criseyde* (V. 1456–519), where the force of the bare historical narrative of Theban disaster bears in upon Troilus's own intense and personal pain. In the conclusion of Lydgate's poem, by contrast, the focus remains on the desolation of the political figure Adrastus, as he receives the powerfully grave company of Grecian women, come to bury their husbands. Lydgate focuses briefly on Adrastus's impotence to help the women, 'wisshing his herte parted wer on tweyne' (l. 4490), before the women turn instead to Theseus, and Lydgate turns instead to Chaucer, 'as my mayster Chaucer list endite' (l. 4501) for the source of his narrative. Whereas Chaucer consistently fragments and personalizes his Theban narratives,[23] Lydgate's seamless join with the beginning of the *Knight's Tale* reinserts Chaucer's text into an unequivocally historical, political narrative; it equally places the most severe constraints on whatever glimpses of prudential wisdom the *Knight's Tale* might have seemed to offer.

In the *Knight's Tale* the death of Arcite elicits the philosophical consolation of Theseus's 'First Mover' speech. The *Destruction*, as we have seen, has a long *occupatio* for the funeral of the Greek warriors that structurally and rhetorically matches the *occupatio* for Arcite's funeral; but at this point the *Destruction* offers no speech of consolation equivalent to the philosophic consolation offered by Theseus. Adrastus, the figure from whom we might expect such a speech, is now broken and impotent. But there *is* an equivalent speech in the *Destruction*, made by Adrastus. It is placed much earlier in the poem (ll. 3409-49), in an apparent digression, as a consolation for Lycurgus on the accidental death of his baby son (fatally bitten by a snake while his nurse Ipsiphyle saved the parched Greeks by leading them to water). In the larger structure of both the *Destruction* and *Knight's Tale* this speech serves as a comment both on the fate of the just Argives, and on Theseus's philosophical optimism. All life, says Adrastus, is 'but an exile'; no one is safe from death. At the equivalent point in the *Knight's Tale* speech, Theseus focuses on Arcite's fame as the saving grace of his life. Adrastus, however, is confronting the death of a baby; he can only say that whoever dies in youth 'is eskaped

---

[23] He fragments, for example, the story of Arcite, apparently the same figure in both the *Knight's Tale* and *Anelida and Arcite* (a bad surprise for the reader who puts the narratives together); the same is true of Theseus in both the *Knight's Tale* and the 'Legend of Ariadne' in the *Legend of Good Women* (another bad surprise).

al the woode rage, / Al sorowe and trouble of this present lyff'. This is a very limited and unconvincing form of consolation—it is as if the optimistic Theseus had been transformed into the grim Egeus—and indeed there are clear echoes of Egeus's desolating speech of 'consolation' here. Just as Egeus has it that 'we been pilgrymes, passynge to and fro. / Deeth is an ende of every worldly soore' (I. 2848–9), so too does Adrastus (in a speech added by Lydgate) console Lycurgus with images of futile movement:

> And our lif her, who taketh hed ther-to,
> Is but an exile and a pilgrymage,
> Ful of torment and of bitter rage,
> Lich a see rennyng to and fro,
> Swyng an ebbe whan the flood is do,
> Lytil space abidyng at the fulle. (ll. 3418–23)

Adrastus concludes, apparently like Theseus, by counselling prudent patience before the decree of the gods:

> Wher-for best is, as semeth unto me,
> No man gruche but, of hegh prudence,
> The sonde of goddis tak in pacience. (ll. 3442–4)

But this amounts to the extinction of prudence, given the nature of the gods whose influence governs Theban history, and from whose influence the baby, according to Adrastus, is well clear. The fundamental pessimism of this speech not only underwrites the fate of the Argives in Lydgate's poem, but it also points forward to the fragility of Theseus's philosophical optimism.

4

The exercise of prudence requires, among other things, understanding of beginnings: from an appraisal of beginnings, one judges the possibilities of final outcomes—'age provydeth every thing / Or he begynne to casten the endyng' (ll. 2945–6). The *Destruction of Thebes*, however, cautions against prudential confidence by underlining the difficulty of grasping clearly demarcated origins.

The Lydgate-persona, explicitly at least, tries to contain the disasters of Theban politics within an ethical frame: Eteocles is described as 'Rote of unreste and causer of unpes' (l. 4260), 'Of al this sorowe verraye sours and welle' (l. 4290). This perspective on the story is not unlike one of the main currents of *Knight's Tale* criticism in this century, which has focused on ethical differences between Palamon and Arcite, as if these differences (such as they are) were the point of Chaucer's narrative.[24] But can the unrest of either narrative be convincingly traced back to, and held within, origins of this kind? The very movement of the *Destruction of Thebes* takes us back into Theban history, revealing that the possible ethical differences between Palamon and Arcite have deeper roots than can be accounted for by reference to individual character. Statius himself poses the question of beginnings in the *Thebaid*—'Where should I begin?' he asks in the first lines of the poem—since '*longa retro series*', far back runs the sequence of events (I. 1–17).[25] And Lydgate is by no means insensitive to this aspect of the history: he consistently stresses the Saturnian, melancholic strain in the Theban royal family, coupled with a furious, Martian spirit (e.g. ll. 387–99, 467–74, 2037). Even the opening, mythic account of the origins of Thebes, stressing as it does the founding, constructive powers of Amphion's eloquence and prudential wisdom, cannot help but evoke another, anterior founding myth—that of Cadmus, whose is an altogether darker story of fratricidal violence and exile (by Amphion).[26]

---

[24] Such readings might be said to originate with Dryden, according to whom Arcite is 'violent in his Love, and unjust in the Pursuit of it' (*The Poems and Fables of John Dryden*, ed. James Kinsley (London, 1970), 527), and reach their apogee in A. H. Markwardt, *Characterization in Chaucer's 'Knight's Tale'*, University of Michigan Contributions to Modern Philology, 5 (1947).

[25] A line possibly evoked by the Knight's conclusion of his tale: 'What may I conclude of this longe serye?' (I. 3067).

[26] See Patterson, *Chaucer and the Subject of History*, 75, for a similar point about the Cadmian beginnings of Theban history. Lydgate had access to the Ovidian account of Cadmus through Boccaccio, *Genealogia deorum gentilium libri* (ed. Vincenzo Romano, 2 vols. (Bari, 1951), ii. 43 and v. 30 respectively). Lydgate offers a fuller account of the myth of Cadmus founding Thebes in his *Fall of Princes*, I. 1842–2170. This account has Cadmus's story beginning and ending in exile; all his efforts at familial and civic construction come to nothing—'Loo heer the fyn of Cadmus everideel, / His childre slayn and his allies all, / And he hymsilffe fro Fortunys wheel, / Whan he lest wend, ful sodenli is fall' (*Lydgate's Fall of Princes*, I. 2108–11; i. 58).

So behind the constructive founding myth of Amphion lies a story of usurpation and exile, a story which will be replicated as Thebes moves towards its destruction. Any attempt to 'ground' the city in texts is susceptible to shifting foundations:

> But sothly yit some expositours,
> Groundyng hem upon olde auctours,
> Seyn that Cadmus the famous olde man,
> Ful longe afor this cite first began
> And the ground of the bieldyng sette. (ll. 293–7)

And this same uncertainty about grounding origins characterizes the Lydgate narrator's account of the feud between Eteocles and Polymyte. The epilogue to Part II of the *Destruction*, for example, offers an ethical account of Theban collapse— Lydgate points to lack of 'truthe' as 'The firste grounde and roote of this ruyne' (l. 2549). The Prologue to Part III, immediately following, cancels that ethical account by insisting on an inevitable recursion to chaos in Theban history, where the political construction of the city is precariously poised between choleric astrological and physiological forces:

> O cruel Mars ful of malencolye,
> And of thy kynde hoot combust, and drye,
> (As the sperkles shewen fro so ferre,
> By the stremes of thi rede sterre,
> In thy spere as it aboute goth)
> What was cause that thow were so wroth
> With hem of Thebes? Thorgh whoos fervent ire
> The cite brent and was sette a-fyre,
> As bookes olde wel reherce konne,
> Of cruel hate rooted and begunne,
> And engendred, the story maketh mynde,
> Oonly of blood corrupt and unkynde,
> Bynfeccioun called orygynal,
> Causyng a strif dredful and mortal,
> Of which the meschief thorgh al Grece ran. (ll. 2553–68)

Along with Mars, indeed, 'Satourn old with his frosty face... Malencolik and slowgh of mocioun' (ll. 3–5) is the presiding spirit of the poem's own fictional narration: the Prologue opens with a *chronographia* evoking the first sentence of the *Canterbury Tales*, but equally marking the way time has moved on: the Sun has now passed out of the Ram, and Saturn stands in (malevolent) opposition to the Moon (ll. 1–8). Pale, drained Lydgate's promise to follow the 'law' of the Host by telling 'some tale of myrth or of gladnesse' (l. 168) is made in a context of unpropitious, more powerful natural forces whose sources are infected at root.

As we move to the end of the *Destruction*, we move back to the beginning of the *Knight's Tale*; but as we do, we see that Lydgate's presentation of Theban history offers not merely the historical 'pretext' of the Knight's poem, by widening its historical and discursive boundaries; we can also see how the irresistible backward pull of history forecloses what limited possibilities for constructive human activity the *Knight's Tale* might have offered. Lydgate's reading of the *Knight's Tale* squares with the pessimistic readings of that tale by scholars in the later twentieth century.[27] History, from the point of view of the *Destruction of Thebes*, looks bleak in both directions: backwards into the Theban past, and forwards into the *Knight's Tale*. And, after all, to move forward into the *Knight's Tale* is, ultimately, to move backwards: back into the *Canterbury Tales*, backwards into the same patterns of Theban history, and back to Troynovant.

---

[27] See especially K. A. Blake, 'Order and the Noble Life in Chaucer's *Knight's Tale*', *MLQ* 34 (1973), 3–19, and Patterson, *Chaucer and the Subject of History*, ch. 3.

2 Hoccleve and the Middle French Poets

JOHN BURROW

Consideration of Thomas Hoccleve's relationships with the vernacular poetry of his time has concerned itself largely with Geoffrey Chaucer—understandably so, given his allusions to his 'maister deere and fadir reverent'.[1] There has accordingly been little study of Hoccleve's relationship to the French poetry current when he wrote, especially the writings of such Middle French poets as Guillaume de Machaut, Jean Froissart, Oton de Granson, Eustache Deschamps, Christine de Pizan, and Alain Chartier. Although the circulation of manuscripts of these poets in England remains to be studied, several English writers in the time of Chaucer and beyond show knowledge of them, Hoccleve included. I hope at least to suggest some lines of enquiry which may profitably be pursued further in his case.[2]

Hoccleve's intimate familiarity with the French language itself requires no demonstration. French was, with Latin, the language of Privy Seal documents at the time. In the enormous Formulary which the poet compiled for the benefit of juniors and successors towards the end of his life, after some thirty-eight years' work in the Privy Seal office, 704 of the 885 specimen documents are in French, with the rest all in Latin (none in English).[3] The drafting and copying of such texts must have

---

[1] *Regiment of Princes*, l. 1961, ed. F. J. Furnivall, EETS ES 72 (1897). On Hoccleve's relation to John Gower, see Charles R. Blyth, 'Thomas Hoccleve's Other Master', *Mediaevalia*, 16 (1993), 349–59.

[2] The most recent study of Chaucer's relation to Middle French poetry is by James I. Wimsatt, *Chaucer and his French Contemporaries: Natural Music in the Fourteenth Century* (Toronto, 1991).

[3] The two-volume edition by E.-J. Y. Bentley, 'The Formulary of Thomas Hoccleve', Ph.D. thesis (Emory, 1965), counts 1,110 items; but her numbering skips two, and I exclude 223 short 'Exordies et Extraitz des Lettres'. Hoccleve's petitions to the King's Council are in French: nos. 9 and 63 in the Appendix to J. A. Burrow, *Thomas Hoccleve*, Authors of the Middle Ages, 4 (Aldershot, 1994).

occupied much of his working time at the Westminster office. It is also quite possible that his duties took him across the Channel to Calais. During some years in the reign of Henry V the Privy Seal was divided into two sections, one in England and the other in France; and in May 1418 Hoccleve's underclerk, John Welde, was rewarded for his labours in that office 'during the last three years both at Calais and in the kingdom of England'.[4] So, when the old beadsman in the *Regiment of Princes* observes that Hoccleve must be 'wele leerid' in French as well as in Latin and his own English, having worked so long at the Privy Seal, one can believe him—even though the poet in reply claims only a smattering of all three ('ful smal is my taast').[5]

Three of Hoccleve's surviving poems are known to be versions of French pieces.[6] *The Letter of Cupid*, dated 1402, is a free rendering of *L'Epistre au dieu d'amours*, composed some three years earlier by the French poetess then fashionable in English court circles, Christine de Pizan.[7] *The Complaint of the Virgin*, 'translatee au commandement de ma dame de Hereford' according to the poet's French endnote, has its source in a passage in Guillaume de Deguileville's *Pelerinage de l'ame*

---

[4] For the Welde document, see *Hoccleve's Works: The Minor Poems*, ed. F. J. Furnivall and I. Gollancz, EETS ES 61 and 73 (1892, 1925), in one volume revised by Jerome Mitchell and A. I. Doyle (1970), p. lxii n. 5. On the Privy Seal in France, see A. L. Brown, 'The Privy Seal Clerks in the Early Fifteenth Century', in D. A. Bullough and R. L. Storey (eds.), *The Study of Medieval Records: Essays in Honour of Kathleen Major* (Oxford, 1971), 262.

[5] *Regiment of Princes*, ll. 1854–62. The beadsman suggests that Hoccleve might address a complaint to Prince Henry in French or Latin. It is to this that the poet's reply refers. There is no evidence that he composed anything but prose in either language.

[6] M. C. Seymour, *Selections from Hoccleve* (Oxford, 1981), p. xvi, counts the story of the Virgin's sleeves (Gollancz, *Minor Poems*, nos. VI–VII) among poems translated from the French, but I know of no evidence for this. Beverly Boyd says that 'the story has not been found in Latin or in French' (*The Middle English Miracles of the Virgin* (San Marino, Calif., 1964), 119).

[7] The English and French poems are edited and translated by Thelma S. Fenster and Mary Carpenter Erler, *Poems of Cupid, God of Love* (Leiden, 1990). See also J. C. Laidlaw, 'Christine de Pizan, the Earl of Salisbury and Henry IV', *French Studies*, 36 (1982), 129–43. Douglas Gray, introducing his selection from Hoccleve, characterizes the *Letter* as a 'spirited version': *OBLMVP*, p. 48. Hoccleve no doubt knew of the debate or 'quarrel' over the *Roman de la Rose* in which Christine had become involved by 1402. He makes his own contributions to the long-running exchanges on the woman question in the *Letter of Cupid* (recalling at ll. 316–22 Chaucer's representations of male infidelity in his *Legend of Good Women*) and also in his *Dialogue*, ll. 661–826, where he defends the *Letter* against charges of anti-feminism.

Hoccleve and the Middle French Poets 37

(c.1358), and so looks back to an earlier generation of French poets. Deguileville's writings had continued to interest English readers—witness the complete English translation of the *Ame*, dated 1413, into which Hoccleve's *Complaint of the Virgin* came to be included.[8] Another of Hoccleve's religious poems also has a French source, his *Balade to the Virgin and Christ*, headed by him 'Ceste balade ensuyante feust translatee au commandement de mon Meistre Robert Chichele'. Its source is a fourteenth-century Anglo-French poem beginning 'En mon deduit a moys de May', which has been identified in three manuscripts.[9]

All three translated pieces take liberties with their French originals. In rendering the couplets of Deguileville and Pizan, Hoccleve chose to write rhyme-royal stanzas, and these commonly drift away from the French in the course of their seven lines, having started close. The stanzas of eight octosyllabic lines in the Anglo-French poem are rendered into 'Monk's Tale' stanzas, and these also tend to drift away from the French. But Hoccleve was capable of representing the original with great fidelity. One may compare, for instance, the first stanza of his *Balade to the Virgin and Christ* (Furnivall no. XVIII) with the French:

> En mon deduit a moys de may
> Pensant aloy iuxt une boscage
> Les floures divers divisay
> Oseux chauncheantz a lour usage
> De cele disport me confortay
> Mes une pense point mon corage
> Que morir mestoit mes quant ne say
> Ne ou devenir a quele ostage.

---

[8] An edition of the English *Ame* is in progress: Rosemarie Potz McGerr (ed.), *The Pilgrimage of the Soul: A Critical Edition of the Middle English Dream Vision*, vol. i (New York, 1990). None of the other English verse translations scattered through the *Pilgrimage* is by Hoccleve, as has sometimes been claimed.

[9] The first 120 lines of this poem were identified in St John's College Cambridge MS G. 5 by H. E. Sandison in C. F. Fiske (ed.), *Vassar Mediaeval Studies* (New Haven, 1923), 235–45, from which I quote below. Two further copies have recently been identified by C. S. Stokes, who prints the remaining forty lines in *MÆ* 64 (1995), 74–84.

This is Hoccleve's version:

> As that I walkid in the monthe of May
> Besyde a grove in an hevy musynge,
> Floures dyverse I sy, right fressh and gay,
> And briddes herde I eek lustyly synge,
> That to myn herte yaf a confortynge.
> But evere o thoght me stang unto the herte,
> That dye I sholde / and hadde no knowynge
> Whanne, ne whidir, I sholde hennes sterte.

There may remain to be discovered other places where Hoccleve draws directly on French poetic sources; but I am concerned here rather to indicate certain more general features of his writings which bear comparison with Middle French verse. Some of these features he shares with Chaucer, but by no means all. Indeed, in some respects Hoccleve may be better understood as, say, an English Deschamps than as a latter-day Chaucer.

Not that the French and Chaucerian connections can always be distinguished. English readers commonly regard the rhyme-royal stanza as peculiarly Chaucerian; but Hoccleve would also have met it as a regular stanza form in French balades, where it is known as the 'balade de vii bastons'. The same is true of what English scholars call the 'Monk's Tale stanza', an eight-line stanza rhyming ababbcbc known as the 'double croisée' in French.[10] Nor would a reader accustomed to the rules of French poetry have found anything unfamiliar in the syllabic structure of the lines which make up these stanzas in Hoccleve. The survival of three holograph copies of his work, containing some 7,000 lines of verse, has enabled Judith Jefferson to demon-

---

[10] See Ernest Langlois, *Recueil d'arts de seconde rhétorique* (Paris, 1902; repr. Geneva, 1974). One treatise printed by Langlois says that all balade stanzas must begin with a 'croisée de rime', abab (p. 206). Where this is repeated, the result is a 'double croisée', ababbcbc (p. 59). In what the English call rhyme royal, a 'croisée' is followed by an 'adjunct' b-rhyme and a pair of new rhyme sounds, cc, hence: ababbcc (p. 207). All the nine poems headed 'balade' in the Hoccleve holographs have stanzas conforming to one of these two types: 'double croisée' for Furnivall, *Minor Poems*, nos IV, V, VI, VIII, XIII, XIV, XVIII; 'balade de vii bastons' for Furnivall no. XVII and Gollancz no. IX.

strate that the English poet adheres just as strictly as his French contemporaries to a fixed syllable-count. A Hoccleve line must have ten, or eleven, syllables.[11] A detailed comparison between his metrical usage, so consistently realized in the holographs, and that of the French poets shows up more specific similarities. Thus, the holographs have Hoccleve deploying variant forms of words and endings systematically in order to maintain the required number of syllables, variants such as *han* and *have*, *fownden* and *fownde*, *as* and *as that*; and the editor of his younger French contemporary, Alain Chartier (d. 1430), observes the same device in Chartier's verse: 'Chartier makes use of morphological doublets, such as *Elle/El* or *telle/tel*, for purely metrical reasons'.[12] Again, Hoccleve normally elides final unstressed *-e* where the mid-line caesura intervenes before a following initial vowel or *h*; but he occasionally lets it stand in hiatus there, a licence which Middle French poets also allow themselves.[13] How much of this, one may speculate, did Hoccleve learn from his master Chaucer, and how much from his reading of French poetry? Chaucer's apology for lines which may 'fayle in a sillable' (*House of Fame*, l. 1098) shows that he was concerned about the syllable-count. Yet this is a feature most easily disrupted by the scribes, as one can see by comparing the scribal and holograph texts of Hoccleve's *Series*; so the fact that we have no holograph copies of Chaucer's verse makes it very difficult to determine exactly what, in this matter, his disciple could have learned from him. My own impression, for what it is worth, is that Hoccleve shows himself much more ready than Chaucer to subordinate rhythmical considerations to the prepotent demands of the syllable-count. In this respect he may be regarded as more Gallic than his master—perhaps too Gallic, indeed, for native readers have commonly failed

---

[11] Judith A. Jefferson, 'The Hoccleve Holographs and Hoccleve's Metrical Practice', in D. Pearsall (ed.), *Manuscripts and Texts: Editorial Problems in Later Middle English Literature* (Cambridge, 1987), 95–109.

[12] *The Poetical Works of Alain Chartier*, ed. J. C. Laidlaw (Cambridge, 1974), 55. Jefferson gives many examples from Hoccleve.

[13] For example, *Dialogue with a Friend*, l. 496: 'To muse longe / in an hard mateere'. For the French practice, see G. Lote, *Histoire du vers français*, première partie, *Le Moyen Âge*, 3 vols. (Paris, 1949–55), iii. 81–2. Lote's whole section 'Le compte des syllables', pp. 73–133, is relevant.

either to notice or, if it is noticed, to appreciate his expertise in syllabic verse.[14]

However, French readers would also have found things to surprise and shock them in the English poets' verse-technique. They would have been surprised to see the 'balade de vii bastons' employed in long poems such as Chaucer's *Troilus* or Hoccleve's *Regiment of Princes,* for that was a short-poem stanza in French; and they would have been shocked by Hoccleve's so-called 'balades'. Unlike Chaucer's, these consistently fail to conform to the French type. This required three stanzas, with the same rhyme-sounds in the same order throughout and a refrain, with or without an envoy. Of the nine poems distinguished by Hoccleve himself as 'balades' in the holographs, only two (Furnivall nos. V and VI) have common rhymes in the same order—but in four, not three, stanzas. The rest vary either the rhyme-sounds or the order in which they appear. None of the nine has a refrain; and they also vary in length, having three, four, five, six, and even in one case twenty stanzas. It seems, in fact, that Hoccleve understood the term 'balade' quite loosely, as indicating simply a shortish poem in the kinds of stanza that figure in French balades, or on occasion just the stanza itself:

> On swich mateere / by god that me made,
> Wolde I bestowe many a balade.[15]

Hoccleve's 'balades' show him at a further remove than Chaucer from French formal models; but there are other features of his *œuvre* which suggest a closer affinity with current French developments than can be attributed to his English master. Among these features is the survival of three holograph

---

[14] One might contrast Furnivall's dismissive comment, 'so long as he can count ten syllables by his fingers, he is content' (*Minor Poems*, p. xli), with the fine appreciation shown by the Dutch scholar J. H. Kern in several remarkable but neglected early studies, e.g. 'Zum Texte einiger Dichtungen Thomas Hoccleve's', *Anglia*, 39 (1916), 389–494. The question of the rhythmic structure of Hoccleve's verse is currently being addressed again by Judith Jefferson. I remain to be convinced that 'a high proportion of his lines move naturally in a five-stress pattern with alternating stresses', as Norman Davis says in *OBLMVP*, p. 494.

[15] *Dialogue with a Friend*, ll. 550–1. For an account of the French balade, see Lote, *Le Moyen Âge*, ii. 270–85. An example from Deschamps, in 'double croisée' stanzas, is printed below. Professor Laidlaw points out to me that Christine de Pizan and, especially, Deschamps occasionally extend their balades beyond three stanzas.

manuscripts devoted entirely to Hoccleve's own 'minor poems': Durham University Library MS Cosin V. iii. 9, and Huntington Library MSS HM 111 and 744. The two Huntington manuscripts, whether or not they originally formed a single codex, together contain twenty-nine shorter pieces, with no duplication between them; and they have plausibly been described as 'the earliest extant "collected poems" made by a known English author'.[16] Such single-author codexes were not unheard of in the later Middle English period; but Middle French poetry offers many more examples, as Sylvia Huot has shown.[17] Machaut, Froissart, Granson, Deschamps, Christine de Pizan, and Charles d'Orléans are chief among those whose works are found in manuscripts of this kind. The huge collected Deschamps, Bibl. Nat. MS fr. 840, containing no less than fifteen hundred items by that poet, was evidently produced after his death;[18] but in other cases these 'clerc-écrivains' themselves organized, supervised, and sometimes even copied the collections. Thus, a note at the beginning of Bibl. Nat. MS fr. 1584 reads: 'Vezci l'ordenance que G. de Machaut vuet qu'il ait en son livre'.[19] The best example of such an anthology not only organized but also copied by the author comes from Italy, where single-author codexes had developed at about the same time as in France: Petrarch's holograph copy of his *Rerum Vulgarium Fragmenta*, MS Vaticano Latino 3195.[20] Hoccleve's French

[16] John M. Bowers, 'Hoccleve's Huntington Holographs: The First "Collected Poems" in English', *Fifteenth-Century Studies*, 15 (1989), 27–51, at p. 27.
[17] Sylvia Huot, *From Song to Book: The Poetics of Writing in Old French Lyric and Lyrical Narrative Poetry* (Ithaca, NY, 1987), esp. ch. 7: 'The Vernacular Poet as Compiler: The Rise of the Single-Author Codex in the Fourteenth Century', and the following chapters on Machaut and Froissart.
[18] See *Œuvres complètes*, ed. Le Marquis de Queux de Saint-Hilaire and Gaston Raynaud, SATF, 11 vols. (Paris, 1878–1903), xi. 101–6, for an account of this MS. Also M.-H. Tesnière, 'Les Manuscrits copiés par Raoul Tainguy', *Romania*, 107 (1986), 282–368; pp. 313–16 and 340–2.
[19] Cited by Huot, *From Song to Book*, 274 in her chapter on this MS. Cf. ibid. 211: 'Guillaume de Machaut and Jean Froissart, and after them such writers as Christine de Pizan and Charles d'Orléans, evidence an involvement with the process of compilation and book production that was not apparent in the poets of the thirteenth century. The codices of Machaut and Froissart were almost certainly organized by the authors themselves.' In England, John Gower presents the nearest parallel.
[20] H. Wayne Storey traces the development of the single-author 'poetry book' in thirteenth- and fourteenth-century Italy: see his *Transcription and Visual Poetics in the Early Italian Lyric* (New York, 1993).

contemporary Christine de Pizan is also held to have played a part in copying those many manuscripts of her own works over which she certainly also exercised personal supervision.[21] A later and rather different example is the scribal copy of his poems which Charles d'Orléans kept as his private 'libellus' and added to in his own hand. One may compare this to Guillaume de Machaut's 'livre ou je met toutes mes choses', though this last has not survived.[22]

Sylvia Huot observes that 'the compilation of anthologies devoted solely to the career of a single vernacular poet entails a new kind of poetic authority';[23] but it should be remarked that such single-author codexes were not necessarily recognizable as such by their medieval readers. How would an early user of the Huntington manuscripts have recognized them as holographs?[24] Nor would the fact that Hoccleve's name makes four scattered appearances in them have been enough to establish the common authorship of all their contents. Indeed, one may wonder on what grounds the excellent eighteenth-century editor George Mason came to the conclusion that the poems in HM 111 'were all written by Thomas Hoccleve'.[25] However, the case of the third holograph, the Durham MS, is quite different; for here the presence, if not the 'authority', of a single

---

[21] See J. C. Laidlaw, 'Christine de Pizan: From Scriptorium to Database and Back Again', *Journal of the Institute of Romance Studies*, 1 (1992), 59–67. Sandra Hindman maintains that British Library MS Harley 4431, a large book containing twenty-nine of Christine's works, was 'entirely written' by the poet herself: 'The Composition of the Manuscript of Christine de Pizan's Collected Works in the British Library: A Reassessment', *British Library Journal*, 9 (1983), 93–123. See also Fenster and Erler, *Poems of Cupid*, 22–3.

[22] On Bibl. Nat MS fr. 25458 of the poems of Charles, see P. Champion, *Le Manuscrit autographe des poésies de Charles d'Orléans* (Paris, 1907). For Guillaume's 'livre', see S. J. Williams, 'An Author's Role in Fourteenth-Century Book Production: Guillaume de Machaut's "Livre ou je met toutes mes choses"', *Romania*, 90 (1969), 433–54.

[23] Huot, *From Song to Book*, 6.

[24] Furnivall came to doubt his original belief that Hoccleve himself copied the texts: *Minor Poems*, p. xlix; but the demonstration by H. C. Schulz has been accepted by all recent scholars: 'Thomas Hoccleve, Scribe', *Speculum*, 12 (1937), 71–6.

[25] *Poems by Thomas Hoccleve, Never Before Printed: Selected from a MS in the Possession of George Mason* (London, 1796), 1. Mason's selection includes both the poems in which HM 111 inscribes the poet's name: the *Male Regle* (heading and l. 351) and the *Balade and Chanson to Henry Somer* (l. 25). In HM 744 the name occurs in Lady Money's roundel (l. 1 etc.). HM 111 is defective at the beginning and HM 744 at the end, so it is possible that one or both originally contained some further indication of authorship.

writer, named as 'Hoccleve' and as 'Thomas' by the friend, cannot be missed.

Although as a compilation of miscellaneous pieces linked together it might be compared with Chaucer's *Canterbury Tales*, the sequence in the Durham MS known as the *Series* has no real precedent in English. Its true affinities lie, I believe, with the French *dit*, as that developed in the fourteenth century. Huot, observing that 'the dit and the single-author codex are related phenomena', cites a brilliant essay on the former by Jacqueline Cerquiglini, many of whose observations are directly applicable to Hoccleve's *Series*.[26] Referring chiefly to the *dits* of Machaut (especially his *Voir Dit*) and Froissart, Cerquiglini identifies two salient characteristics of the genre, both of which, she argues, depend upon its essentially bookish nature. These are: discontinuity, and the representation of an authorial *je*.[27] Thus, in the *Voir Dit* the varied and 'discontinuous' ingredients in the text—prose letters and lyric poems—are represented as having been written by Machaut himself and his mistress in the course of their developing relationship which the poem as a whole describes. By thus eliding the distinction between author and narrator—'la représentation de l'énonciateur dans l'énoncé', as Cerquiglini puts it—Machaut achieves a 'montage' effect: 'Le montage, comme l'indique Machaut, consiste précisément à faire tenir ensemble, selon une technique de l'étagement, des choses qui existent ou qui peuvent exister par ailleurs, antérieurement'.[28] Hence Cerquiglini can describe *Voir Dit* as a work 'se retournant, sans cesse, sur sa propre écriture', a self-referential 'méta-écriture'.[29] As in other French *dits*, accordingly, the *je* characteristically represents him- or herself as a writer, a *clerc*: 'le *je* du *dit* donne à découvrir le clerc'.[30]

At first sight, a comparison between Hoccleve's *Series* and the *dits* of such French poets as Machaut or Froissart may

---

[26] Huot, *From Song to Book*, 213; Jacqueline Cerquiglini, 'Le Clerc et l'écriture: Le *Voir Dit* de Guillaume de Machaut et la définition du dit', in Hans Ulrich Gumbrecht (ed.), *Literatur in der Gesellschaft des Spätmittelalters* (Heidelberg, 1980), 151–68.

[27] 'Le dit est un genre qui travaille sur le discontinu' (p. 158); 'le dit est un discours qui met en scène un "je"' (p. 160).

[28] Cerquiglini, 'Le Clerc et l'écriture', 161, 159.

[29] Ibid. 160, 155.   [30] Ibid. 165.

seem distinctly unpromising. Neither in the *Series* nor anywhere else in his writings does Hoccleve show any interest in such lyrics and narratives of *fin amour* as occupy Machaut's *Voir Dit*, Froissart's *Espinette Amoureuse*, or Granson's *Livre Messire Ode*. The *Series* is certainly no *dit amoureux*. Hoccleve and the friend with whom he discusses his troubles and his writings may be clerks, but they are not clerks in love; and the inset writings themselves—two *Gesta Romanorum* stories with their moralizations, and *Learn to Die*—belong to a world of moral and spiritual discourse far removed from that of the courtly lover. However, as Cerquiglini herself observes, 'ce n'est donc pas la *nature* des "ingrédients" qui fait le *dit*, selon nous, mais bien leur *mode* de mise en présence, leur montage'.[31] Leaving aside the actual 'ingredients', then, one can see in the *Series* exactly those characteristics which Cerquiglini singles out in the French *dits*. Hoccleve's work 'met en scène un "je"', who is identified by name with its author and who is represented as projecting and writing those discontinuous compositions which go to make up the whole. This is precisely the technique of 'montage' or layering ('étagement') which Cerquiglini describes as making an ensemble out of 'choses qui existent ou qui peuvent exister par ailleurs, antérieurement'. *Learn to Die*, after all, does appear as a free-standing independent item in HM 744; and it may have been composed before ever Hoccleve conceived the *Series*, as indeed may the *Gesta* stories. Similar considerations do apply to some of the Canterbury stories; but Chaucer's poem, so far from 'se retournant, sans cesse, sur sa propre écriture', goes out of its way to discourage any consideration of the tales as writings—either by the pilgrim narrator or even, one might say, by Chaucer himself. As an example of 'meta-écriture', in fact, the *Series* has no full English precedent. Its origins lie rather, I believe, in Hoccleve's French reading.[32]

---

[31] Cerquiglini, 'Le Clerc et l'écriture', 158.
[32] Specific parallels are to be found between the *Series* and French *dits*. Thus, the setting of Hoccleve's opening complaint, with its solitary poet suffering at the end of November from a 'thowgtfull maladye', may be compared with the opening of Machaut's *Jugement dou Roy de Navarre*, also set in November, with the poet alone in his chamber suffering from melancholy: 'Si que la merencoloie / Tous seuls en ma chambre et pensoie'

Hoccleve and the Middle French Poets

In the course of her discussion, Cerquiglini notes 'le rapport du *dit* à l'actualité': 'Dans la mesure où c'est un *je* qui parle dans le *dit*, *je* individué, *je* typé, il a à se situer par rapport à l'ici et au maintenant, il a à dire le rapport au temps présent, à l'actualité'.[33] Certainly the *Series* involves just such a sense of the here and now: the current discontents of the poet himself in the aftermath of his mental illness, problems with the coinage, the regency of Duke Humphrey, and the like. However, it is not only in *dits* that late medieval French poets engage with 'actualities'; and for my last Anglo-French comparison I turn to the balades and rondeaux of Eustache Deschamps, to be considered in relation to some of Hoccleve's shorter poems in the Huntington MSS.

Like Hoccleve, Deschamps (b. *c*.1340) belonged to that growing body of 'fonctionnaires', officials serving some royal or noble master, which produced so many of the vernacular writings in late medieval France and England. Whether or not Hoccleve had read Deschamps, as Gervase Mathew once very plausibly suggested, their works have many points in common, most strikingly in those poems of complaint and petition which reflect their common circumstances as minor functionaries dependent upon the favour of great ones and their financial officers.[34] Thus, in HM 111 Hoccleve addresses petitionary complaints to the King's Treasurer Lord Furnival (the *Male Regle*), to the Lord Chancellor Thomas Langley (Furnivall no. XII), and to the Under-Treasurer Henry Somer (Furnivall no. XIII). In each case he looks to the officer for his help in ensuring the payment of 'arrerages' due to him and, in the Somer poem, to

---

(ll. 37–8). In Machaut's poem, too, the visit of a friend later (l. 468) brings relief. On autumnal melancholy as characteristic of the Middle French poets, see Jacqueline Cerquiglini-Toulet, *La Couleur de la mélancolie* (Paris, 1993).

[33] Cerquiglini, 'Le Clerc et l'écriture', 165. For a general account of 'le rapport à l'actualité' in the poetry of late medieval France, see Claude Thiry, 'La Poésie de circonstance', ch. ix in D. Poirion (ed.), *La Littérature française aux xive et xve siècles*, vol. i, *Grundriss der romanischen Literaturen des Mittelalters*, vol. viii/1 (Heidelberg, 1988), 111–38.

[34] Gervase Mathew, *The Court of Richard II* (London, 1968), 58. Paul Zumthor, stressing the impersonality of most French medieval poetry, notes that his generalization does not apply to the new class of 'fonctionnaires écrivains', among whom he counts Deschamps: *Essai de poétique médiévale* (Paris, 1972), 68.

three Privy Seal colleagues. Chaucer himself also wrote three poems of this petitionary sort, addressed respectively to three dukes of the King's Council (*Fortune*), a friend at court (*Scogan*), and King Henry IV (*Complaint to his Purse*); but Hoccleve displays his personal circumstances, by way of complaint, with a richness of detail which recalls Deschamps rather than Chaucer.[35] The French poet, in such various official capacities as *bailli*, *huissier d'armes*, and royal messenger, addressed many poems of 'supplication' to a variety of possible benefactors—the King himself, dukes, and officials from the Chancellor down—asking for due payment of his 'gaiges' and complaining of his straitened circumstances.[36] Since it is difficult to focus on any single Deschamps poem in the monstrous profusion of his collected works, it may be permissible to print one of his petitionary balades in full here, for comparison with Hoccleve's *Male Regle*. Deschamps has been suffering, he says, for five years from a sickness, that is, lack of money; but he has now been promised a cure, to be administered after All Saints' Day. Yet he still cannot sleep for worry ('penser'), because he knows that there are many other poor souls clamouring for payment. So he appeals in the envoy to three officials: Jean le Flament and Pierre de Metz, both royal treasurers, and Guy Crestien, Master of Requests (the officer who dealt with petitions) in the King's household. He asks them to act on his behalf to ensure that he will get his 'medicine' in full, when the time comes, from Jaques Hemon, the Receiver-General of taxes:

> J'ay par cinq ans esté en maladie,
> Dont mire nul ne m'a voulu guerir,
> De pou d'argent, ou maint homme mendie;
> Or ay trouvé qui m'a fait l'uis ouvrir
> De surgien pour mes plaies garir,
> Li quelz m'a dit que je seray tous sains;

---

[35] See V. J. Scattergood, 'Begging Poems', in A. J. Minnis, with V. J. Scattergood and J. J. Smith, *The Shorter Poems*, Oxford Guides to Chaucer (Oxford, 1995), 503–12. See also 'The Poet as Petitioner', in J. A. Burrow, *Essays on Medieval Literature* (Oxford, 1984), 161–76.

[36] Examples in the *Œuvres complètes* are: nos. 90, 247, 250, 618, 679, 788, 864, 866, 902, 903, 919, 1168, 1190, 1206, 1375, 1378, 1408, 1425, 1439, 1497.

> Mais il me fault endurer et soufrir
> Le mal que j'ay jusqu'après la Toussains.
>
> Si n'ay espoir en chose qu'on me die,
> Pour le penser qui ne me laist dormir
> Et la paour que j'ay qu'om ne m'oublie
> Pour autres gens que je voy poursuir;
> Tant de povres a un huis requerir
> Fait leurs clamours escondire et leurs plains.
> Pour l'amour Dieu, vueilliez faire fenir
> Le mal que j'ay jusqu'après la Toussains.
>
> Après ce jour, je, Eustace, supplie
> Que vous vueillez a mon mal secourir
> Et ordonner en l'apothicairie
> Jaque Hemon chose qui puist tenir
> Sanz recoupper, qui me face adoucir
> De povreté les maulx dont je suis plains;
> Si non, bien sçay que me fera mourir
> Le mal que j'ay jusqu'après la Toussains.
>
> Flament, Pierre, Crestien, je vous prie,
> Garissiez moy, vous estes souverains,
> Ou autrement perdre fera ma vie
> Le mal que j'ay jusqu'après la Toussains.[37]

In the much longer and more elaborate *Male Regle*, Hoccleve relates his own 'maladie de pou d'argent' to real physical illness: 'My body and purs been at ones seeke'.[38] Both sicknesses,

---

[37] 'For five years I have been suffering from a disease which no doctor has wished to cure—lack of money, from which many a man suffers; but now I have found someone who has opened for me the door to a surgeon who can cure my wounds; and he has said that I will be completely cured, but I must wait and endure the illness that I have until after All Saints' Day. All the same, I have no faith in what I am told, because of the worry which deprives me of sleep and my fear that I may be forgotten amongst all the other petitioners I see. Having so many poor people pressing their claims at a door results in their cries and complaints being rejected. For God's sake, please put an end to the illness that I have until after All Saints' Day. After that day I, Eustace, beg that you will consent to relieve my suffering and arrange with the apothecary's shop of Jaques Hemon for something that can come without deductions and so ease the evils of poverty, of which I have quite enough. If not, I know I shall die from the illness that I have until after All Saints' Day. Flament, Pierre, Crestien, I beg you to arrange my cure, for you have the power, or else it will cause me to die of the illness that I have until after All Saints' Day' (no. 902 in *Œuvres complètes*). The editor identified the persons named in the index in vol. x.

[38] *Male Regle*, l. 409; see also ll. 130, 337–8, 349–50, 387, 395. Elsewhere Deschamps shows himself ready, like Hoccleve, to admit details of his actual bodily distresses into

he says, have their origin in the same youthful misrule, the extravagance and dissipation of which he now regrets. The long moralizing account of the poet's earlier misdemeanours makes the *Male Regle* a much riskier 'begging poem' than the Deschamps, for the petitioner has evidently only himself to blame for his current illness and poverty; yet it turns out to be 'pursuing' the same end:[39]

> By coyn, I gete may swich medecyne
> As may myn hurtes alle, that me greeve,
> Exyle cleene / and voide me of pyne.   (446–8)

Both Deschamps and Hoccleve specify quite exactly what they want—payment due last Michaelmas, in Hoccleve's case—and both name the financial official from whom they hope to receive it. Also, each poem is addressed, not directly to that official, but to others who may act as friendly intermediaries in the case. Hoccleve's version of this indirect approach (so characteristic of the court life of the time) is much more fanciful than the French poet's appeal to three royal functionaries. He asks the god Health to have a word on his behalf with the Treasurer, thus incidentally managing to convey his best wishes for the health of the great man; and the final appeal, from which I quoted above, is addressed not to the lord himself but to the god. Such witty indirection is characteristic of the sophisticated begging poetry of functionaries such as Hoccleve and Deschamps.[40] As the *Male Regle* puts it:

> Who-so him shapith mercy for to crave
> His lesson moot recorde in sundry wyse.   (397–8)

---

his verse: e.g. nos. 797 (diarrhoea), 834 (toothache), and 1449 (various). He also couples bodily with financial distress in another poem comparable with the *Male Regle*: no. 178, beginning 'J'ay le cuer bon, mais le corps ne puet rien; / Argent me fault, mais trover ne le puis', with the refrain 'Il ne me fault que finance et bon corps'.

[39] 'Pursue' forms part of the language of petition in both English and French. Compare l. 12 of the Deschamps balade quoted above with *Male Regle*, l. 426, and *Regiment of Princes*, ll. 1534 and 1848.

[40] Daniel Poirion makes an observation on Deschamps which could equally well apply to Hoccleve: 'Comme Colin Muset et Rutebeuf qui amusaient les autres en racontant leurs soucis d'argent ou de ménage, Deschamps joue pour la cour la comédie du *Moi*. Il propose au public la mise en scène parfois douloureuse, mais souvent comique de sa propre existence. Et c'est parfois pour obtenir sans importuner les avantages qu'il convoite' (*Le Poète et le prince* (Paris, 1965), 232).

English readers of Deschamps will find much else there to remind them of Hoccleve; and comparisons with other Middle French poets could also, I believe, be pursued with profit. It is not the purpose of this essay to minimize Hoccleve's debt to Chaucer. He could, after all, have learned the art of indirection in petitionary poetry from the *Envoy to Scogan*; and it was Chaucer, not Machaut or Deschamps, whom he celebrated as the founder and master of the poetic tradition in which he worked, and whose death he deplored in the *Regiment of Princes*. Yet even here one may note that such celebration of a dead vernacular poet, unprecedented in England before the death of Chaucer, has its earlier parallel in the poems that Deschamps wrote in honour of his dead master Guillaume de Machaut, 'le noble rethorique'.[41]

---

[41] *Œuvres complètes*, nos. 123 and 124, also 447. James Wimsatt considers these in his chapter on Chaucer and Deschamps, *Chaucer and his French Contemporaries*, 246–8. See also Cerquiglini-Toulet, *La Couleur de la mélancolie*, 41–2.

3 Kingship and the Kingis Quair

SALLY MAPSTONE

The murder of James I in Perth on 20 February 1437 was preceded by a number of omens. An Irish woman stopped the king on a crossing of the water of Leith to tell him that if he continued the journey he would not return alive, a warning that tallied with a prophecy that the king himself had recently read. James also dreamt that he was attacked in his chamber by 'a cruell serpente and an horrible toode'. And one of his squires dreamt that the king was to be murdered by Robert Graham, indeed one of his assailants. So at least testifies a contemporary account of James's death surviving in an English translation, by John Shirley, of an untraced Latin original.[1] This account goes on to describe another episode which took place a short time before the murder:

Where uppon a day the king plaide at the chesse with oone of his knyghttis, whomme in pleying wyesse he clepyd 'King of Love', for he was a lusti man, ful amorowse and moche medled hym in loves arte. And as it cam the kyng to mynde of the prophesye spokenn of to-for, the king saide to this knyght, 'Sir, Kynge of Love,' quod hee, 'It is not long agoone sithe I redde a prophessie in a olde booke, that I saw howe that this yere schulde a kinge be slayne in this lande. And yee wotte wille, Sir Allisaundre, there be no moo kynges in this reaum but

---

[1] M. Connolly, 'The Dethe of the Kynge of Scotis: A New Edition', Scottish Historical Review, 71 (1992), 46–69. The credibility of this account was distrusted by earlier historians, e.g. E. W. M. Melville, James I, King of Scots, 1406–1437 (London, 1936), 243, but recent studies have argued for its importance: e.g. M. H. Brown, ' "That Old Serpent and Ancient of Evil Days": Walter, Earl of Atholl and the Death of James I', Scottish Historical Review, 71 (1992), 23–45, and M. Brown, James I (Edinburgh, 1994), 172–93. See also M. H. Brown, ' "I have thus slain a tyrant": The Dethe of the Kynge of Scotis and the Right to Resist in Early Fifteenth-Century Scotland', Innes Review, 47 (1996), 24–44.

yee and I, and therfore I counseile you that yee be welle ware, for I lette you [wit] that I schal ordeyne for my seure keping sufficeauntly, I trust to Godde, for I am undur your knyhthode as in the seruice of love.' And thus the king in his solas plaide with the knyght.[2]

The reliability of these *obiter dicta* cannot be confirmed, but there are convincing elements in them. The playful idea of a King of Love appointed within a courtly setting and capable of disrupting the normal hierarchy features at length in parts of the two fifteenth-century Scots Alexander romances derived from the popular *Voeux du Paon*, the earliest of which, *The Buik of Alexander*, was completed by 1438.[3] (The naming of the Scots knight as Alexander is an interesting detail in this connection.) But the separation of the roles of King of Scots and King of Love also sheds a revealing retrospective light on the particular nature of the project of the protagonist of the *Kingis Quair*, the poem long, if contentiously, associated with James I.[4] The *Kingis Quair* posits a fusion of personal and public roles, of King of Love and King of Scots, highly appropriate for the opening of James's reign but less easily sustained by the end of it. The poem's relation to the reign of James I provides a valuable interpretative paradigm for the practice of Scottish kingship in the fifteenth century. And its distribution of emphases also shows an early concern with issues that were to assume great significance in one of the most popular genres of late medieval Scottish writing, the literature of 'advice to princes'.

The *Kingis Quair* is more commonly seen, however, as a

---

[2] *Dethe of the Kynge of Scotis*, 55; another MS reads 'kynghood' for 'knyhthode' at the end of James's remarks.

[3] *The Buik of Alexander*, ed. R. L. Graeme Ritchie, 4 vols., STS NS 12, 13, 21, 25 (Edinburgh and London, 1921–9; the episode is in vol. ii); *The Buik of King Alexander the Conquerour*, ed. J. Cartwright, 2 vols., STS, 4th ser. 16, 18 (Edinburgh, 1986; Aberdeen 1990).

[4] The poem survives in one MS, Bodleian Library, Oxford, Arch. Selden. B. 24, dated c.1488–1500. See J. Boffey and A. S. G. Edwards (introd.), *A Facsimile of Bodleian Library, Oxford, MS Arch. Selden. B.* 24 (Woodbridge, 1997). The second scribe of the MS attributes the poem to 'Iacobus primus scotorum rex Illustrissimus' (fo. 211ʳ). At the poem's opening is written in a sixteenth-century hand, 'Heirefter followis the quair Maid be King James of Scotland the first callit the kingis quair and Maid quhen his Maiestie wes in England' (fo. 191ᵛ). For summaries of discussion of the authorship of the *Kingis Quair* see the introductions to the editions by J. R. Simon (*Le Livre du roi*, Bibliothèque de Philologie Germanique, 21 (Paris, 1967)), M. P. McDiarmid (1973), and J. Norton-Smith (Leiden, 1981). Quotation is taken from the last of these editions.

poem 'dealing with personal rather than public issues' and foregrounding the healing power of love.[5] Such readings emphasize the poem's debt to Chaucerian tradition, while at the same time pointing up the inventiveness of its response to that legacy. It will be argued here, in contrast, that an important element in the creation of that individual Scottish response lies in the poet's concern to deal with both love *and* Scottish kingship, giving meaning to the treatment of love within a consciously public context. For the *Kingis Quair* is a poem both about love and about self-government. It is also conspicuously optimistic about the relation and practice of those two forces in a manner that places it in striking contrast to poems on which it self-consciously draws, Chaucer's *Knight's Tale* and *Troilus and Criseyde*. Its optimistic treatment of love has more in common with Lydgate's *Temple of Glass*, but the context in which the *Kingis Quair* considers it is much broader, encompassing encounters not only with Venus but with Minerva and Fortune. It is indeed the element of determined confidence in the *Kingis Quair*'s conclusion that has occasionally led to its critical denigration.[6] The poem insists on the compatibility of human love and Christian virtue—in Minerva's words, ' "Desire", quod sche, "I nyl it noght deny / So thou it ground and set in Cristin wise"' (988-9). This is an outlook that distinguishes it pointedly from the separation of Christian and human love at the end of *Troilus*, and focuses this difference more sharply than Lydgate does in the *Temple of Glass*. Similarly, the poem reworks Boethian warnings against trusting in Fortune into the idea of the strategic employment of prudent foresight —again in Minerva's terms, ' "oft gude fortune flourith with gude wit"' (929). Such tenets take a combative approach to the fatalism of *Troilus*, and with their attendant Christian colouring deny the problematical juxtaposition of Boethian stoicism and a malign pagan universe afforded by the *Knight's Tale*.

[5] R. J. Lyall, 'The Literature of Lowland Scotland, 1350-1700', in P. H. Scott (ed.), *Scotland: A Concise Cultural History* (Edinburgh, 1993), 77-98 (p. 80).
[6] For example, Simon, *Le Livre du roi*, 250: '*Le Quair* offre certes un contenu didactique, mais l'heureuse issue de la narration se prêtait mal à des conclusions morales très profondes.' For summary accounts of critical views up to 1978 see W. Scheps and J. A. Looney, *Middle Scots Poets: A Reference Guide to James I of Scotland, Robert Henryson, William Dunbar, and Gavin Douglas* (Boston, 1986), 16-51.

Moreover, whereas in much fifteenth-century English writing an underlying Boethianism is often related to a dark or troubled world-view,[7] the revisionist reading of the *Consolation* in the Scots *Kingis Quair* prompts a series of reflections that lead ultimately to the optimistic way of seeing already remarked upon. But for all the *Kingis Quair*'s liberties with the lessons of the *Consolation*, the presence of that text as the trigger for the protagonist's reflections itself points to the important role of the narrator in the poem not only as lover but as moral exemplar. The *Kingis Quair* invites further comparison with ethical and political English fifteenth-century texts in which Boethianism was a key element, even while it offers a different response to those Boethian concerns.

Although the dream episode of the *Kingis Quair* contains crucial moral lessons, the poem itself is not primarily a dream-vision narrative. In this too it is different from some of its Chaucerian antecedents which juxtapose a reading experience with a dream narrative, or from the *Temple of Glass*, where the narrator does not read before he sleeps but falls asleep within fifteen lines of the poem's opening. The *Kingis Quair*'s narrator's reflections on past events in his life are inspired by a reading of Boethius, but their presentation as a deliberate act of poetic composition affords the narrator both a greater interpretative control of his material and a greater distance from his source text than if his role had been dominantly that of a dreamer. The narrator of *The Book of the Duchess* falls asleep 'ryght upon my book' (274) containing the story of Ceyx and Alcyone and wakens with it in his hand. His literal closeness to his text seems connected not only to its shaping influence upon his dream but to his inability to offer any distilled interpretation of that dream on his awakening. The narrator of the *Kingis Quair*, in contrast, shuts his book 'and at my hede it laide' (52) early in the poem as he lies wakefully thinking. Preoccupied as he is by his thoughts and the task of writing a poetic account of what happened to him, the narrator uses that act of composition to consolidate a learning process which the body of the

---

[7] D. Lawton, 'Dullness and the Fifteenth Century', *ELH* 54 (1987), 761–99.

poem itself describes.[8] Unlike the abrupt conclusion to *The Book of the Duchess*, the *Kingis Quair*'s ending is extended and in its own way analytical as sense is made of the narrator's experience and, within that, his dream. Behind that interpretative posture lies the poem's consistent concern with self-rule.

On a biographical or autobiographical level the poem interacts with key events in the life of James I: his capture at sea as a 12-year-old boy by the English *en route* to France in March 1406; his captivity as an English prisoner for eighteen years thereafter; his marriage to Joan Beaufort in February 1424 and his subsequent release. These episodes are synthesized into an interpretation which consistently relates them to the narrator's emotional and intellectual state. The image of the steerless and endangered ship translated from the reality of the abortive journey to France becomes a metaphor for the protagonist's own youthful mental and emotional insecurity seen from a distanced perspective:

> I mene this by myself, as in partye.
> Though nature gave me suffisance in youth,
> The rypenesse of resoun lak[it] I
> To governe with my will... (106–9)

The metaphor is of course a Boethian one, but it was also common to the literature of kingship. As the late fourteenth-century Scottish chronicler John of Fordun put it, 'a country without a king [is], beyond a doubt, like a ship amid the waves of the sea, without rower or steersman'.[9] The context of this allusion in the *Kingis Quair* gains added retrospective weight when it is remembered that the news of James's abduction in 1406 prompted the demise of his father Robert III and the beginning of James's minority within an indeed kingless country. The necessity that the king who returned in 1424 be ready to assume firm government of a country that had lacked a

---

[8] Cf. W. Quinn, 'Memory and the Matrix of Unity in the *Kingis Quair*', *Chaucer Review*, 15 (1981), 332–55.
[9] John of Fordun, *Chronica Gentis Scotorum*, ed. W. F. Skene, 2 vols. (Edinburgh, 1871–2), ii. 289. For the Latin original, see i. 293.

monarch for eighteen years was thus a heightened one, and one of which the *Kingis Quair* shows its own awareness.

A greater sleight of hand is at work in the celebrated moment when the *Kingis Quair's* narrator falls in love:

> forquhy my wittis all
> Were so overcom with plesance and delyte
> Onely throu latting of my eyen fall,
> That sudaynly my hert became hir thrall
> For ever, of free wyll... (282–6)

This subjection of wit to will is permitted by the poem's ultimate vantage-point, as presented by a well-meaning Venus (vastly revised from her Chaucerian precedents and more positively depicted still than her Lydgatian precursor in the *Temple of Glass*),[10] and emphatically spelt out by Minerva, in which an earthly love founded in Christian virtue is both beneficial and rational. Love here, unlike its traditionally disabling and unreasonable image, is linked to what is reasoned ('"Lat wisedom ay to thy will be iunyt"' (931)) and what is successful:

> sen that it is so,
> That in vertew thy lufe is set with treuth
> . . . .
> I will pray full fair
> That Fortune be no more therto contrair. (1003–8)

Emerging from the dream in which his instruction has taken place, the narrator presents himself as one prepared to appeal to Venus on behalf of those who deserve to attain love, 'So that it hir and resoun noght displese' (1288), and as one established in 'blisse with hir that is my sovirane' (1267). In human terms, a very King of Love indeed.

But he does not call himself so. That pun (for that it surely is) on Joan's role as his 'sovirane' in love and his queen is the closest the poem's narrator comes to describing himself *as* king. The attributions surrounding the poem in its manuscript are far more explicit on the identification of the author as king

---

[10] See L. Ebin, 'Boethius, Chaucer and *The Kingis Quair*,' *PQ* 53 (1974), 321–41 (p. 332), and G. Kratzmann, *Anglo-Scottish Literary Relations 1430–1550* (Cambridge, 1980), 58–9.

than the poem ever is about its main protagonist. If, as the opening note states, the *Kingis Quair* was 'Maid quhen his Majestie wes in Ingland' and the poem was composed before James had returned to Scotland officially as king, that might offer one, slightly technical, explanation for this reticence.[11] The absence of specific description of James as king may have a deliberate reference to his own kingly absence from his realm, particularly if the poem was written during the four-month period that encompassed his marriage, release, and return to Scotland. But also relevant here is the intended role of the poem's narrator. In depicting him as a figure for whom love and courtship are part of the process of acquiring a mature balance between wisdom and desire, the poem also offers him as one who can act as both an exemplar and an instructor to other earthly mortals. Venus and Minerva criticize the 'negligent' (802), 'double and inconstant' (954) world and support the narrator only when it is clear that he is opposed at heart to this kind of corruption. Venus urges him to encourage mankind to reform; Minerva promises him success if he adheres to her doctrine.

Wise and mature self-government as a prerequisite for good practical kingship was a staple element of the advice to princes tradition, in which examples of immature and unreasonable monarchs illustrated common forms of kingly failure. But an added aspect of advisory writing was the exemplary model that monarchs should offer to all men, self-governors of their own mental and emotional realms. The *Kingis Quair* draws on both aspects of this tradition. On one level it makes sense of James's exile in England in terms of his acquisition of the reasoned virtue necessary for good kingly rule; on another it turns him into an exemplary figure who is a man like other men: ' "tell

---

[11] Arch. Selden. B. 24, fo. 191ᵛ. James was married in February 1424 and travelled slowly north thereafter before entering Scotland in early April. He was crowned in Scone on 21 May. Some commentators reject the rubric's claim (and that of John Major, see n. 32, below) that the poem was written in England, on the grounds that its perspective 'suggests that several years had passed and had given the king the opportunity to develop the philosophic detachment exhibited' (J. MacQueen, 'Poetry—James I to Henryson', in R. D. S. Jack (ed.), *The History of Scottish Literature*, vol. i: *Origins to 1660* (Aberdeen, 1989), 55–72, 56). But the poem can equally be read as suggesting both a closeness to a completed episode of the king's life and a new distance on it that fits well with the start of James's reign.

on, man, quhat thee befell"' (77). The articulation of this idea through the setting of a love relationship is a further aspect of this, since the *Kingis Quair* makes much of the susceptibility of all men to love.

The poem thus elegantly connects these kingly roles—referring unmistakably to James I's experience in a way that makes something positive of it for him and for his subjects. What he is said to be and what he represents are successful and exemplary images. The first major surviving Scots poem before the *Kingis Quair*, John Barbour's *Bruce* (c.1375), had marked the inauguration of Stewart rule by depicting Robert II's illustrious ancestor as an exemplary monarch.[12] Now in the *Kingis Quair* a king figure himself takes on the role of both dispenser and recipient of advice. It is not usual to term these poems advice to princes literature, and they are both generically broader than that (though this itself is a recurrent element of much subsequent Scottish advice to princes writing), but their concerns set the agenda for what was to become one of the most dominant modes of late medieval Scottish literature.

The semi-concealed references to kingship are perhaps at their most provoking in the narrator's encounter with Fortune, the third female goddess he meets in the inset educational dream-vision. His vulnerability, emphasized in Fortune's scornful description of him as 'feble' (1178) and 'wrechit' (1184) and her irreverent grasping of him by the ear, is still apparent. The protagonist wakes from his dream at the very moment that Fortune, stressing her innate capriciousness ('"Thus, quhen me likith, up or doun to fall"' 1202), sets him upon the wheel, and the poem might seem here, almost despite itself, to acknowledge the basic instability of worldly fortunes against which its confident finale seems so determined to set itself. But the representation of the workings of fortune within the *Kingis Quair* again makes good sense within the literature and iconographic traditions of kingship.[13]

---

[12] L. A. Ebin, 'John Barbour's *Bruce*: Poetry, History and Propaganda', *SSL* 9 (1972), 218–47.

[13] For further analysis of Fortune's role, J. MacQueen, 'Tradition and the Interpretation of the *Kingis Quair*', *RES* NS 12 (1961), 117–31.

The vividness of the scene with Fortune is probably indebted to the ubiquitous illustrations of Fortune and her wheel in manuscripts of the *Consolation of Philosophy*. As regular an element in the picture as Fortune turning her wheel was the presence of a king or a number of king figures. One strand of iconographical tradition, current to the end of the fifteenth century, showed four kings in various positions of rising and falling on the wheel, often accompanied by the legend *Regnabo, regno, regnavi, sum sine regno*. But current too in the later Middle Ages was a variation featuring the king atop the wheel but figures from other estates, such as soldiers or burgesses, or simply other men, in the position of ascending or descending.[14] These two versions encapsulate one of the paradoxes of late medieval kingship: kings were presented as undeposable, subject only to divine sanction, and yet, in practice, they not infrequently were removed. As we shall see, Scotland and Scottish advisory writers had their own particular variation on this phenomenon.[15] In drawing on these traditions to inform its protagonist's encounter with Fortune the *Kingis Quair* is making yet another allusion to kingship, and working its own commentary on it.

For Fortune herself acknowledges that she must implement an alteration for the better in the narrator's life, and her recognition of that looks back to Minerva's statement that a change for the good in his life (and success in love) will be the results of the acquisition of a prudent virtue. An understanding of the workings of fortune is a part of this. When Fortune spells out her inherent instability to the narrator the poem returns to a more orthodox acknowledgement of Boethian counsel than it is sometimes claimed to have.[16] It is what it does with this knowledge that makes the difference. The *Kingis Quair* takes an understanding of the nature of fortune into an active engagement

---

[14] P. Courcelle, *La Consolation de Philosophie dans la tradition littéraire, antécédents et posterité de Boece* (Paris, 1967), 142–52 and plates 65–86.
[15] On both late medieval and Scottish context see R. Mason, 'Kingship, Tyranny and the Right to Resist in Fifteenth Century Scotland', *Scottish Historical Review*, 66 (1987), 125–51.
[16] e.g. by S. Kohl, 'The Kingis Quair and Lydgate's *Siege of Thebes* as Imitations of Chaucer's *Knight's Tale*', *Fifteenth-Century Studies*, 2 (1979), 119–34; the best appraisal of the poem's response to the *Consolation* is Ebin, 'Boethius, Chaucer, and The Kingis Quair'.

with the pursuit of worldly happiness. It is also important that this encounter with Fortune takes place within the narrator's own mind, within the dream upon which he is now reflecting at a greater distance. A common device of advice to princes literature was to depict or allegorize advice-giving in such a way as to suggest that at best the prime advisory context was the king's own mental realm, and that in this sense the regulatory principles of self-government came essentially from within himself. Dream does this perhaps a little more obliquely, exploiting the ambiguity of the extent to which visionary encounters of this sort come from within the protagonist, or come to him from outside. But the suggestion that love, wisdom, and fortune are all aspects of the narrator's mental world which need to be brought into correct alignment heightens the sense that the state of the protagonist's guiding consciousness is not only the poem's organizing principle but one of its prime concerns.

The net effect of the dream and the narrator's reception of it within the *Kingis Quair* is thus that the capriciousness of Fortune is not denied (indeed, ll. 57–64 early on in the poem show, retrospectively, a received appreciation of it), but the argument that its workings can be withstood or even avoided by prudent self-regulation is more strongly endorsed, to the extent that Fortune's wheel can eventually be thanked by the narrator (1321). Beyond this, the once apparently malign workings of fortune are seen in the penultimate stanza to be part of a divine plan, 'Causit from hevyn quhare powar is commytt' (1367). This is another way of presenting the kingly exile as a beneficial learning process, and establishing a divinely sanctioned pattern to what had earlier seemed an unjust sequence of events. Kingly stability on the wheel of Fortune is to be understood as dependent on something beyond the control of Fortune herself.

An emphasis upon the king as 'bot a man', a marked concern with the dangers of young and ill-advised rulers, a strong sense of the final sanction on monarchical power being a divine one, and an abiding optimism about the potential of misguided monarchs for reform are all distinctive features of the fifteenth-century Scottish advice to princes tradition, particularly when contrasted with the outlook of much late medieval English political writing.[17] All of these things characterize *Lancelot of the Laik* (probably composed in the late 1460s or 1470s), another Scottish poem which yokes a courtly love-story with an exploration of good kingship, and whose connections with the *Kingis Quair* are enhanced by its employment of the 'anglicizing' literary dialect first found in that poem.[18] Within the lengthy advice to princes section of *Lancelot*, far exceeding that in its French source, the ill-fortune of the nation is explained as due to Arthur's falling away from the practice of kingly virtue. The king's poor example has had a deleterious influence upon his subjects. The prominent attention given to wisdom and virtue in the *Kingis Quair* now finds fuller expression in the paradigmatic relationship between king and people:

> Thus if o king stud lyk his awn degree,
> Vertuis and wys than shuld his puple bee,
> Only set by vertew hyme to ples,
> And sore adred his wisdom to disples.
> And if that he towart the vicis draw,
> His folk shal go on to that ilk law.   (1977–82)

Stressed too are the perils of and to young rulers who will not act well when they come to the 'yheris of Resone' (1652) and, in clear association with this, a definition of the role of the monarch that places its emphasis less on his innate royalty and more on the value of his governing function and the praise from his people which that inspires: 'What is o prince? quhat is o governoure / Withouten fame of worschip and honour?' (1523–4). Linked to this are the repeated sentiments that a king who fails to govern properly or to reform will be summarily judged by the vengeful will of God, 'as has ben hard or this / Of every king that wirketh sich o mys' (1887–8). The Scottish

---

[17] S. Mapstone, 'The Advice to Princes Tradition in Scottish Literature, c.1450–1500' (D.Phil. thesis, University of Oxford, 1986); for a comparison with English writing, S. Mapstone, 'The Scots, the French, and the English: An Arthurian Episode', in G. Caie, R. Lyall, and K. Simpson (eds.), *A European Sun* (forthcoming). For the king as 'bot a man' see the advice from Aristotle to Alexander from *The Buik of King Alexander the Conquerour* on pp. 63–4 below; but this point is one that Alexander also makes himself: ' "Suppois your king ye ordant me, / Yit am I nothing bot a man as ye" ' (2479–80).
[18] Ed. W. W. Skeat, EETS OS 6 (1895; repr. 1965). Quotation is from this edition.

poet, however, has selected a section from the Arthurian story which enables him to present the king in a finally positive light; although the poem does not survive complete, enough remains to show that Arthur acts upon the advice delivered to him and the fortunes of the nation commensurately improve. This is the point also being made in the *Kingis Quair*. Bad fortune is linked with bad or youthful self-government; good fortune with a prudent God-fearing kingship. That such texts articulate the notion of kingly deposition through the idea of divine retribution is often a way of avoiding confronting the real circumstances in which a king might be removed. But Scottish works more commonly explore these issues in order to produce a positive outcome and outlook.

Though there is marked love-interest in *Lancelot of the Laik*, the roles of king and lover are essentially separated in this poem. The love-plot focuses on Lancelot, whose distinction as both lover and knightly exemplar inevitably invites some comparison with Arthur, but the disturbing potential in this juxtaposition is made much less prominent in this Scottish work than it is in its English near contemporary, Malory's *Arthuriad*. This subjection in emphasis of the amatory to the political or ethical in texts involving both is a continuing aspect of late medieval Scottish writing through poems such as *The Buik of King Alexander the Conquerour* to Dunbar's *Golden Targe* and belatedly in David Lindsay's mid-sixteenth-century *Satyre of the Thrie Estaitis*. The degree of attention paid to a love relationship within a kingly context in the *Kingis Quair* is to this extent unusual within Scottish literary tradition but the concern to link it to a state of ethical and moral harmony was influential upon the course of much following advisory writing.[19]

Indeed, the *Kingis Quair* marks an early manifestation of distinctive currents in Scottish advice to princes literature that

---

[19] For stimulating discussion of the poem (which does not, however, consider it within the advice to princes tradition) as 'very much the king's book . . . celebrat[ing] an ultimately certain choice, the authority of sovereign love, and of the sovereign word', see L. Fradenburg, *City, Marriage, Tournament: Arts of Rule in Late Medieval Scotland* (Madison, Wis. 1991), 130–4. MacQueen has argued that the *Kingis Quair* inaugurated a tradition of Scottish courtly lyrics, but cites few examples before the end of the fifteenth century (*Ballatis of Luve*, ed. J. MacQueen (Edinburgh, 1970)).

respond to the political climate of late medieval Scotland. The installation of the Stewart dynasty in the last quarter of the fourteenth century brought with it a greater if gradually established stability to Scottish political life after the English and civil wars of the previous hundred years. It was a dynasty, however, repeatedly interrupted throughout the fifteenth century by periods of minority rule, as Robert III, James I, and James II all died before their heirs were old enough to take on the throne. This was not, moreover, a new problem. The thirteenth and fourteenth centuries had also seen troublesome minorities, and it was the absence of an heir to Alexander the III that had precipitated the wars of independence with England. But although all the fifteenth-century kings had to assert themselves with some force on taking up their thrones, and despite the deaths of James I and III during rebellions of sorts against them, the stability of Stewart rule was never seriously threatened by a viable long-term alternative. But it could be opposed, as it was under both James I and James III, when a significant section of the political community objected to royal policy. That such objections were often related to a royal desire to encroach more deeply into local power-bases than members of the nobility would have wished is itself a telling comment on power relations in late medieval Scotland.[20] Though this was a situation they regularly tried to alter, Scottish kings were closer in terms of money and territory to the most powerful members of their aristocracy than were their French or English neighbours; and the less centralized, more localized nature of Scottish justice was another aspect of this. Scottish writing on kingship throughout this period reveals a related set of tenets: a deeply held belief in the unifying power of kings, accompanied by a stress upon the reciprocal bond between king and people, and a resistance to elevating the image of the Stewart dynasty or the idea of kingship itself. As the 'Regiment of Princis' in *The Buik of King Alexander the Conquerour* puts it:

---

[20] J. M. Brown, 'The Exercise of Power', in J. M. Brown (ed.), *Scottish Society in the Fifteenth Century* (London, 1977), 33–65, and J. Wormald, *Court, Kirk, and Community: Scotland 1470–1625* (London, 1981), 3–26.

> Ane king is bot a man be him allane.
> Quhat is he wourth, bot as a stok or stane,
> Bot gif he for his wourschip mak defence,
> And gar his folk mak him obedience?
> Quhat is ane king worth bot discretioun
> Off hie prudence to governe his regioun
> Bot as ane ass war crounit in scornyning?
> . . . .
> For giff thow will that God and man lufe the,
> Schaw forth gud will ay to thi commintie. (9971–86)

As far as literary patronage went, Scottish kings themselves seem to have to some extent acquiesced in this. Whereas nearly all fifteenth-century English rulers, claimants, or heirs to the throne received or commissioned advice to princes literature, the reverse is true of Scotland, where until the very end of the century such texts were generally produced in aristocratic or clerical milieux often ultimately with an eye to the king but not immediately for him.[21] The exception here is indeed the *Kingis Quair*, whose close association with James I as king is in this context another aspect of its 'Englishness'. But its Scottishness manifests itself through the poem's nexus of concerns. The clustering of Scottish texts on kingship during minorities and at the beginnings of reigns proper and the repeated reference to problems of minority rule within them gives a particularly Scottish slant to the familiar theme of young and uncounselled monarchs: strong kingly rule is encouraged, but only if the monarch has the maturity to instigate it with discrimination. As the mid-fifteenth-century chronicler of the *Liber Pluscardensis*, reflecting on the aftermath of the murder of James I, put it: 'But alas that our kings should so often be young men in whose time justice is often halting; and the reason for this is that they are not wise nor skilful to recognise the way of equity and justice'.[22]

The *Kingis Quair* engages with these issues by showing a process whereby unstable youthfulness is replaced by virtuous

---

[21] S. Mapstone, 'Was there a Court Literature in Fifteenth-Century Scotland?', *SSL* 26 (1991), 410–22. On English ownership see also N. Orme, *From Childhood to Chivalry: The Education of the English Kings and Aristocracy 1066–1530* (London, 1984), 94–7.

[22] *Liber Pluscardensis*, ed. F. J. H. Skene, 2 vols. (Edinburgh, 1877–80), ii. 291. For the Latin original, see i. 391.

and wise maturity, and where the king figure is presented in a way that encourages connections with other men. The poem also makes that figure a locus for the strongly positive worldview at its conclusion as he makes sense of the pattern of the past and speaks of his present bliss. There is a correspondence here with the way in which James I approached the government of his kingdom after his return to Scotland. As his most recent biographer writes, 'James presented himself as a restorer of order and peace in the kingdom.'[23] But his kingly practice in the years that followed illustrated both the pros and cons of Stewart monarchy. The early years saw an attention to legislation and a concern to confirm his authority in Scotland, particularly in the rebellious Highlands; after 1430, however, the reign was characterized by a greater concentration on his own accumulation of wealth and an interest in ostentation, as evinced by the rebuilding of Linlithgow Castle as a palace rather than a fortified residence, and less attention to the administration of justice.

The 'striking paradox' whereby the political community were probably relieved at the death of a Stewart monarch but remained loyal to the Stewart line in his successor was repeated again in the reigns of James II and James III.[24] The gulf between the image of James I offered in the *Kingis Quair* and the reputation of the king at his death illustrates a tension between ideal and reality that was a feature of Stewart kingship. But as important here is the ideological weight of that exemplary image. While the murder of the king in 1437 by members of his own household and at the instigation of members of his family was an indication of the degree to which James I had lost popularity, there was little doubt that his young son would eventually inherit the throne. And the power of the stabilizing image of Stewart kingship is well witnessed a few years later in the response to his death of the chronicler Walter Bower. Concluding his *Scotichronicon* in the 1440s during the disruptive years of James II's minority when a number of political factions were

---

[23] Brown, *James I*, 117.
[24] Mason, 'Kingship, Tyranny and the Right to Resist', 142.

disputing control of government, Bower images James I as the classic exemplary ruler. Establisher of justice and peace, prudent and virtuous, James is also presented as skilled in many arts and subjects, including philosophy and literature. The image Bower purveys straddles the public and personal sides of kingly life to construct an ideal model, and one which it is especially hoped that his son will be able to imitate. Reference to this brings with it both the association of good rule with good fortune and the familiar concerns about royal immaturity:

> Thus even if our king the law-giver and leader is dead, we should nevertheless not give way to grief over his death, for he has left someone like him as his heir, with indeed the same name. If only he can be no less fortunate until his dying day! So far this young man furnishes a lively reputation for himself, at least in the eyes of his unoffending subjects. God be praised that signs of virtue are being consolidated as he enters the early years of full age! But as the proverb has it: 'While the grass grows, the calf is weak.'[25]

The ideological value of this idealized image is clear: only a replica can supply the kind of order the country needs. Bower's lengthy encomium to James I brings out to the full the potential of the exemplary ideas that lie behind the construction of the narratorial figure in the *Kingis Quair*.

Was James I then that poem's author? No other named author has ever been convincingly put forward, but the lateness of the poem's end-of-century manuscript and its attributions to James have given cause for dispute, despite the fact that the *Kingis Quair*'s linguistic mixture makes sense as the production of a native Scot who had spent considerable time in England and absorbed much English literature.[26] The evidence that the poem itself offers shows clearly that it is 'about' James; it does not demonstrate conclusively that it is by him. The poem certainly presumes an aristocratic audience who would pick up its allusions to James I and its play on ideas of kingship. It is possible to envisage the *Kingis Quair* as produced in an aristocratic

---

[25] W. Bower, *Scotichronicon*, vol. viii, ed. D. E. R. Watt (Aberdeen, 1987), 216–17.
[26] Simon (ed.), *Le Livre du roi*, 35–112; C. D. Jeffrey, 'Anglo-Scots Poetry and *The Kingis Quair*', in J.-J. Blanchot and C. Graf (eds.), *Actes du 2ᵉ Colloque de Langue et de Littérature Écossaises (Moyen Âge et Renaissance)* (Strasbourg, 1978), 207–21.

household, perhaps for William Sinclair, whose father Henry had been a close friend of James's and in captivity with him. William was himself a significant presence on James's council from 1424, and, like several subsequent members of his family, he was a noted literary patron. It was indeed in his family that the *Kingis Quair* was preserved and copied.[27] On balance, however, there is more good evidence for James's authorship of the poem than there is against it. While it may be said that until James VI no other Scottish monarch showed an interest in literary composition, no other Scottish monarch had quite James I's background.

Also neglected perhaps is the other evidence concerning James's literary compositions. In addition to describing James as eagerly applying himself to 'the art of literary composition' Bower gives an earlier instance of James's spontaneous composition of a Latin couplet at the time of his arrest of the rebellious Lord of the Isles and other members of his family in 1428:

> He craftily invited each of them to come individually to the tower [where the council was meeting] and had each put separately into close confinement. In the meantime while all this was taking place, the king composed a verse, saying to those standing around: 'Ad turrim fortem ducamus caute cohortem. / per Christi sortem meruerunt hii quia mortem' (Let us conduct this company to a strong tower with care, for, by Christ's death, these men deserve death).[28]

In the light of his own experience and in the context of the *Kingis Quair* it is quite credible that the contemplation of imprisonment should inspire James I to compose this business-like epigram. Now in the crucial early years of his reign when he was at his most brutal as well as his most energetic, this is very much the work of the King of Scots rather than the King of Love.

---

[27] William Sinclair commissioned the three translations (one of an advisory text, the *Secretum Secretorum*), completed by Sir Gilbert Hay in 1456. Arch. Selden. B. 24 seems to have been copied for his grandson Henry Sinclair, 3rd Lord Sinclair, who was also the patron of Gavin Douglas's translation of Virgil's *Aeneid* in 1512.

[28] Bower, Scotichronicon, viii. 258–9, but emending *forte* to *fortem*, and with altered translation. This is the correct reading, and is also cited in this form by John Major, *A History of Greater Britain*, ed. and trans. A. Constable, Scottish History Society, 10 (Edinburgh, 1892), 358.

The sixteenth-century chronicler, John Major, who also quotes these verses, remarks with slight disapproval: 'He treated the last syllable of the adverb *cautè* as short, whereas it is long; but some allowance may well be made for kings when they take to extempore verse-making'.[29] It is Major too who, unlike Bower, refers to the quality of James's compositions in Scots: 'When he wrote the language of his own country he showed the utmost ability.'[30] Major refers to three specific pieces, one of which, 'an ingenious little book about the queen', looks like a reference to the *Kingis Quair*, another of which, *At Beltayn*, is probably related to but not identical with *Peblis to the Play*, and the third, *Yas sen*, has not been securely identified.[31] Despite these vagaries, this degree of detail lends weight to the credibility of James's activity as a poet and as the likely author of the *Kingis Quair*. But notable too is Major's emphasis on James's composition of these works before his return to Scotland, 'while he was yet in captivity and before his marriage . . . because he was at that time kept a prisoner in the castle where the lady [Joan Beaufort] dwelt with her mother, or even in his own chamber'.[32] While at the very opening of his reign the *Kingis Quair* blends the images of the King of Love and the King of Scots to suggest that James is ripe to rule and right to be a model to his subjects, it seems likely that after his return to Scotland it was the assertive role of King of Scots that dominated James's thoughts. By the end of his reign the coalescence of public and personal roles had become more problematic still for him. Ironically, perhaps, in the greater luxury of the latter years of his reign James had more cause to claim the recreational role of King of Love, but in the edgy days before his murder it was his identity as King of Scots that concerned him. And if in the

[29] Major, *History*, 358.   [30] Ibid. 366.
[31] For discussion see *The Kingis Quair*, ed. W. W. Skeat, STS NS 1 (Edinburgh and London, 1911), pp. xvi–xxi, and *The Kingis Quair*, ed. McDiarmid, 46–7. Another intriguing statement on the transmission of the *Kingis Quair* is that by the nineteenth-century bibliographer George Paton that 'There are people alive who remember to have seen the Kings Quair in a printed pamphlet long before Mr. Tytler's copy [1783, the first known printed edition] but now no where to be found.' See W. Beattie, 'Some Early Scottish Books', in G. W. S. Barrow (ed.), *The Scottish Tradition* (Edinburgh, 1974), 107–20 (p. 108).
[32] Major, *History*, 366.

Kingis Quair James had been trying to set out both a poetic manifesto and an ethical or political one, it was the ethical content of his work that particularly interested later fifteenth-century writers, who found less to pursue in the 'courtly' side of the *Kingis Quair*—possibly because of the absence of much stimulus for a literary culture at the Scottish court after James I and until James IV.[33] Both the poetic definition of James's image in the *Kingis Quair* and its uneasy relation to his own practice as king gave important early definition to ideas of kingship in late medieval Scotland.

[33] Mapstone, 'Court Literature', *passim*; but see also the discussion of the *Kingis Quair* as primarily a 'courtly' work for an aristocratic audience, in R. J. Goldstein, 'Writing in Scotland, 1058–1560', in D. Wallace (ed.), *The Cambridge History of Medieval English Literature: Writing in Britain, 1066–1547* (Cambridge, forthcoming).

4 Frames and Narrators in Chaucerian Poetry

HELEN PHILLIPS

1. Chaucerian poetry

'Chaucerian' poetry is not a precise term. To define it simply as poetry that imitates Chaucer would be both too wide and too narrow. Critically it makes most sense to see it as the English and Scottish subgroup within a larger tradition: the tradition of *dits amoureux* and associated lyric genres, which developed in French literature from the thirteenth century and continued to flourish on both sides of the Channel for two centuries after Chaucer. 'Chaucerian' is obviously not the right term for all of this (indeed, there is no good term for the whole tradition: 'courtly' or *dits amoureux* are in their own ways just as far from being adequate), but when considering writing in English within that wider tradition, 'Chaucerian' has the advantage both of familiarity (established especially by Skeat's seminal 1897 anthology, *Chaucerian and other Pieces*) and of marking the centrality of Chaucer for composition in these genres in England and Scotland.

Historically, views both on the value of Chaucerian verse and on what constitutes Chaucer-like writing have fluctuated. In practice today 'Chaucerian' usually denotes lyrics in the forms Chaucer brought into English from French, especially complaints, ballades, and envoys, and also lyrico-narratives: those framed narratives whose titles typically work variations on *Court*, *Dream*, *Palace*, *Temple*, *Parliament*, *Cupid*, *Love*, *Ladies*, and *Venus*, and make up a large part of the late medieval and Tudor anthologies containing poetry by Chaucer and other writers.[1] In structure they consist of a core of lyric, debate, or narrative, frequently including allegory, enclosed in one or more framing sections. Though narrative in overall form, they tend to be lyric in their essential subject-matter, and often contain interpolated lyrics. Scribes, compilers, and printers of verse anthologies (such as Bodleian Library, Fairfax MS 16, or the early printed editions of Chaucer), keen to increase the number of texts with the qualities contemporary readers admired in Chaucer, included in their own concept of Chaucer-like writing a much wider range of genres: sixteenth-century editions of Chaucer include among their additions misogynist poems, proverbs, prophecy, and anti-Catholic satire.

It is easy to forget, because for a long time the modern arbiters of literary history allowed only certain writers of the late medieval and Tudor period, such as Skelton or Malory, to be deserving of extensive critical and editorial attention, that the poetry we call Chaucerian formed for about two centuries an important part in readers' and writers' sense of what English literature was. Chaucerian poetry creates originality from conventionality, working variations on familiar motifs, often with unostentatious sophistication. Unity of design (easily missed by modern readers with alien expectations) is typically wrought through consistency of tone and mood or through sequences of episodes with repeated patterning.

Chaucerian poetry coincides happily with several recent critical interests: for example, studies in literary reception, translation, and narratology, and the revolution during the last twenty years in codicology and printing history, which has brought together bibliographical, textual, critical, art-historical, and sociohistorical interpretation into an interdisciplinary study of the history of the book. Love being the main subject of Chaucerian literature, feminist approaches have revealed complexity and seriousness disregarded by earlier criticism. The Chaucerian framed narrative, employing structures which engender surface fragmentation and discontinuities, shifts in point of view and

---

[1] 'Lyrico-narrative' is a term popularized by S. Huot, *From Song to Book: The Poetics of Writing in Old French Lyric and Lyrical Narrative Poetry* (Ithaca, NY, 1987), 1–2, 83–90, 219–41, 302–37.

narrative level, and with its predilection for literary imitations and resonances, is a form that encouraged narratological and metafictional self-consciousness; and the recent revaluation of this poetry owes much to the late twentieth-century critical preoccupation with self-reflexive literature and the concept of postmodernism.[2] Lydgate, of course, might find inexplicable our relative lack of interest in other things clearly of importance to fifteenth-century Chaucerian poets and readers, such as the choice and mastery of a variety of stanza-forms, aureate experimentation, the refinement of the national language, or concern for literature as a vehicle for moral counsel.

Chaucer's importance for late medieval writing is incalculable, not only for the inspiration of his art and the obvious gifts of subjects, styles, genres, and metres, for which he virtually created the English forms, but also in the confidence he gave English poets—which included confidence to use the literary past, and within it the very traditions inherited from him, freshly and audaciously. He also inspired the establishment of a lucid and flexible English courtly style, which mingles the colloquial and the grand, the light-hearted with the profound. Yet in important respects, Chaucerian literature in England and Scotland owes as much to French writing as to Chaucer: in the beginning to the great tradition of lyric *formes fixes* and *dits amoureux*, and the achievement of Chaucer's French predecessors and contemporaries such as Machaut, Froissart, and Deschamps, which inspired Chaucer; but also, after Chaucer, to French fifteenth-century developments.[3] The Chaucerian items in Douglas Gray's

---

[2] See, for example, J. S. Norman, 'A Postmodern Look at a Medieval Poet: The Case of William Dunbar', *SSL* 26 (1991), 343–55. This is not just a modern approach. William Baldwin's *Beware the Cat*, ed. W. A. Ringler, Jr. and M. Flachmann (San Marino, Calif., 1988), cat-classic, religious satire, and Shandyesque spoof, shows Renaissance awareness of the metafictional potential of the *House of Fame* (see pp. 31–3).

[3] See J. Boffey, 'English Dream Poems of the Fifteenth Century and their French Connections', in D. Maddox and S. Sturm-Maddox (eds.), *Literary Aspects of Courtly Culture*, International Courtly Literature Society (Cambridge, 1994), 113–21; J. M. Smith, *The French Background to Middle Scots Literature* (Edinburgh, 1934), 60–4, 164–5; J. S. Norman, 'William Dunbar: Grand rhétoriqueur', in J. D. McClure and M. R. G. Spiller (eds.), *Bryght Lanternis: Essays on the Language and Literature of Medieval and Renaissance Scotland* (Aberdeen, 1989), 179–93. Critics of French *dits amoureux*, such as Poirion, Zumthor, Brownlee, Wimsatt, Zink, Huot, and Cerquiglini, paved the way for critical revaluation of English Chaucerian writing.

Oxford Book of Late Medieval Verse and Prose typify this continuing double heritage. The *Lover's Mass*, with allusions to the *Legend of Good Women* and *Troilus* in its 'Epistle', belongs to the peculiarly medieval genre of liturgical parody, the prime example of which is de Condé's *Messe des oiseaux* (c.1330).[4] The *Floure and the Leafe*, decorated, like many courtly works, with French song phrases, belongs to a fashion for poems using the motif of the Flower and the Leaf which, like the marguerite/daisy poems, apparently began in France, became popular in the culturally bilingual Ricardian English court, and inspired later English writers, particularly as a result of Chaucer's use of both motifs in the *Legend of Good Women*.[5] The *Letter of Dydo* (before 1526) and the English *Belle Dame sans Mercy* (c.1450) are both translations from French, both with significant English modifications. The *Letter* adapts part of Octavien de Saint-Gelais' *Epistres d'Ovide* (1496) to create a framed complaint, whose heroine, as Boffey shows, reflects the Dido of Chaucer's *Legend* and *House of Fame*.[6] Sir Richard Roos's translation of the *Belle Dame*, attributed to Chaucer in Pynson's 1526 edition, gained new framing sections, first from the translator, and then in 1526 from the printer. This English *Belle Dame* with its additional framing sections can be seen as an English contribution to the extraordinary cycle of literary responses and imitations generated by Alain Chartier's original

---

[4] The extant text, Bodleian Library, Fairfax MS 16, is not macaronic, nor comprehensive liturgical imitation like the *Messe*, *Court of Love*, *Book of Cupid*, *Death of the Duke of Suffolk*, or *Harmony of Birds*. Its Oryson and Epistle—no liturgical epistle but a *letter* to the fraternity of lovers, requesting prayers—lack liturgical imitations. The *Messe* is ambiguously irreverent (see Huot, *From Song to Book*, 221-2), with its eucharist-rose and love-obsessed nuns: de Condé included a volte-face conclusion condemning impiety. Liturgical formulas were used for satire, from *Renart* to the *Dyrge made by the Commons of Kent* during Cade's Rebellion. The English *Lover's Mass* is less a parodic Mass than a set of skilful love-lyrics using echoes of religious phrases, very like Charles d'Orléans' 'My gostly fadir'. English bird-masses, e.g. Lydgate's *Birds' Devotions* or the *Harmony of Birds* (and Chaucerian birds generally), are usually reverent or moralistic. See W. A. Davenport, 'Bird Poems from *The Parliament of Fowls* to *Phillip Sparrow*', in J. Boffey and J. Cowen (eds.), *Chaucer and Fifteenth-Century Poetry*, King's College, London, Medieval Studies, 5 (London, 1991), 66-83.

[5] *The Floure and the Leafe and the Assembly of Ladies*, ed. D. A. Pearsall (Manchester, 1980), 22-9.

[6] J. Boffey, 'Richard Pynson's *Book of Fame* and the *Letter of Dydo*', *Viator*, 19 (1988), 339-53. See G. Schmitz, *The Fall of Women in Early English Narrative Verse* (Cambridge, 1990), 39-43. *Dydo* is STC 5068.

Belle Dame sans Merci (1424) for over a century.⁷ Chartier's central image, of cruel beauty, was already long familiar in both French and English literature: for instance, in Richard de Fournival's *Bestiaire d'Amours* (c.1250) or the English *Merciless Beauty*, uncertainly attributed to Chaucer himself.

For the topic considered here, narrators and frames, French examples have a particular value, since the authors of French *dits* tend (as does Dunbar) towards an overt virtuosity which brings to the surface narratological games and devices typical of late medieval writing in these genres, which are less immediately visible, though just as much present, in the generally more understated English style.

The styles and genres we call Chaucerian, and especially the framed narrative, flourished in both France and Britain to the late sixteenth century, with national differences, and not static but subject to cultural, political, and technological change (including the transitions from manuscript to print, and from patron to printer), fashion, and commercial stimulus.⁸ Fashions developed, among them encyclopaedic didacticism; pro- and anti-feminist controversy; poems about honour; and writings influenced by the movement encouraged by the *Cour amoureuse*, Christine de Pizan, and Chaucer's *Legend of Good Women*, for poetry promoting virtuous love and respect for women. In English the envoy took on a literary life of its own. Legal allegories became popular, especially in France. The framed complaint was fruitfully combined with the Falls of Princes tradition and the genre of admonitory revelations from the next world, to produce overheard laments by contemporary political figures fallen from power.⁹ Seasonal, *chanson d'aventure*, and dream prologues were prefaced to all sorts of subjects: political satire, parody, bawdy, propaganda—a development illustrating how

---

[7] See A. Piaget, 'La *Belle Dame sans merci* et ses imitations', *Romania*, 30 (1901), 22–48, 317–51; 31 (1902), 315–49; 33 (1904), 179–208; 34 (1905), 375–428, 559–97; W. Söderhjelm, 'La Dama senza Mercede', *Revue des langues modernes*, 35 (1891), 95–127.

[8] C. J. Brown, *Poets, Patrons, and Printers: Crisis of Authority in Late Medieval France* (Ithaca, NY, 1995), discusses the changing figure of the narrator with the advent of printing.

[9] e.g. *Lament for the Duchess of Gloucester* (1428, IMEV 3720), *Metrical Visions*, the *Mirror for Magistrates*, *Leicester's Ghost* (1602).

much Chaucerian structures, far from being exclusively 'courtly' or consciously retrospective literary modes (though they were both those things), came also be treated by writers as a standard contemporary literary language.[10] For devotional texts such as Brampton's *Penitential Psalms* (*c*.1420) and Bradshaw's *Lyfe of Saint Werburge* (*c*.1513), the addition of translators' prologues using the Chaucerian motif of the early-waking narrator suggest appropriately monastic associations.[11] 'Go little book' envoys (sometimes moved to the prologue section of the frame), with their conciliatory humility, proved attractive to political poets, as in Cavendish's *Metrical Visions* (*c*.1550: a particularly obsequious example, 'Crepe forthe my boke . . .', 2384).[12] Machaut, Froissart, and de Granson had often used framed narratives as showcases for inset lyrics, and English Chaucerian frames sometimes enclose lyric collections, as in Skelton's *Garland of Laurel*, Charles d'Orléans' English ballades, and the Renaissance miscellany the *Court of Venus* (printed *c*.1537).[13]

Why were Chaucerian forms so popular so long? There is, obviously, the attraction of their characteristic subject-matter—love, melancholy, and morality; and the perceived elegance of their style, as well as admiration for Chaucer and a sense of the importance (actually overestimated) of these genres in the *œuvre* of the great English national poet. Above all, however, it must surely have been their formal potentialities which excited writers. First, and often in the most simple sense, they encourage

---

[10] Though typically attached to the ensuing narrative with an air of abruptness, these prefaces are often aptly chosen: e.g. the London *aventure* prologue to *Twelve Letters Save England* (*c*.1461, IMEV 700), and the countryside *aventure* prologue to the *Duty of Prelates*, with its virtuous shepherds. J. M. Davidoff, *Beginning Well: Framing Fictions in Late Middle English Poetry* (London and Toronto, 1988), provides a conspectus of the use of frames; on differences between French and English, see pp. 36–46.

[11] Henry Bradshaw, *Life of Saint Werburge*, ed. C. Horstmann, EETS OS 88 (London, 1887); Thomas Brampton, *A Paraphrase on the Seven Penitential Psalms*, ed. W. H. Black, Percy Society, 7 (London, 1843); monastic hours, Matins in particular, included psalms: an additional reason for the aptness of this prologue. See H. Phillips, 'Aesthetic and Commercial Aspects of Framing Devices: Bradshaw, Roos and Copland', *Poetica*, 43 (1995), 37–65.

[12] *Metrical Visions by George Cavendish*, ed. A. S. G. Edwards (Columbia, SC, 1980). Others include the *Libel of English Policy* (*c*.1436, IMEV 3491), *England's Trade Policy* (IMEV 2130).

[13] On Orléans, see D. N. DeVries, 'The Pleasure of Influence: Dunbar's *Golden Targe* and Dream Poetry', *SSL* 27 (1992) 113–27, esp. 119–21.

combinatorial inventiveness: components such as the complaint, seasonal frame, the debate, or envoy, can be arranged in endless permutations; new works can be made from old, by embedding existing poems (for example in Scogan's *Moral Ballade*, IMEV 2264, the *Ballade in Commendation of Our Lady*, IMEV 99, or *O Mercifull and O Merciable*, IMEV 2510), or by adding prologues, epilogues, or dream-frames (as in de Worde's *Fiftene Joyes of Maryage*, Pynson's *Letter of Dydo*, or Roos's and Pynson's *Belle Dame sans Mercy*), or by presenting extracts as independent lyrics.[14] *Troilus* and Lydgate's *Fall of Princes* were particularly subject to this kind of quarrying: an enterprising example is *The Tongue*, IMEV 3535, a lover's complaint against slander, based on four *Fall of Princes* stanzas and three *Troilus* stanzas.

More profoundly, the great Chaucerian poetry excels at using structure and style to carry meaning. This has only gradually won critical appreciation. Lydgate's *Temple of Glass*, whose poetic value its 1891 editor estimated 'very small, almost nil', emerges from Torti's 1991 study as a work of sustained original power, not just through its story of forced marriages and an extra-marital love thwarted by moral conscience, but through its manipulation of symbolic structural components, such as the initial seasonal description, which is of winter and windswept clouds, or its images of duality, especially the 'oxymoronic' images of *temple* and *glass*.[15]

2. The play of structure: frames and narrators

The Chaucerian framed narrative habitually exploits tensions—contrasts and parallels—between frame and core. It is a genre with almost built-in creative tensions: between lyric and narrative, between the narrator-self and others, and (a particular favourite with Chaucerian poets) between the reader's sense of the

---

[14] J. Boffey, *Manuscripts of English Courtly Love Lyrics in the Later Middle Ages* (Woodbridge, 1985), 69–71, 77–8, 91.
[15] *Lydgate's Temple of Glas*, ed. J. Schick, EETS ES 60 (1891), p. xiv. A. Torti, *The Glass of Form: Mirroring Structures from Chaucer to Skelton* (Cambridge, 1991), 67–86.

concrete, physical book or page and our abstract experience of fiction.[16] Three types of framing device contribute especially to the metafictional and self-reflexive virtuosity of Chaucerian literature: the 'eavesdropping' frame, 'transition' frames, and 'book' frames.

The eavesdropping frame, where a narrator overhears a lament, debate, or other event, which then forms a core of the narrative, appeared in *dits amoureux* from their thirteenth-century beginnings. It acts, to put its role at its simplest, as a divider, marking a detachment of the narrator from the experiences of the protagonist(s) of the core narrative. Late medieval poets developed both its metafictional and psychological potentialities with great inventiveness. In origin and operation the eavesdropping/observing frame is surely primarily narratological rather than psychological, though Spearing has pointed to its voyeuristic potential, and some Chaucerian works, including Dunbar's *Golden Targe*, support that theory.[17] The overhearing or watching narrator dramatizes a narratological structure usually hidden in fiction, the distinction between narrator and narrative. (It also offers a fictional answer to the question of how the story came to the author: a descendant of the Anglo-Saxon 'We have heard' formula, and the 'as I in toun herde' of *Sir Gawain*.) Early on, we find it in *chanson d'aventure* lyrics and dialogues, and a thirteenth-century pastourelle by Thibaut de Champagne is an example which economically illustrates elements which would remain central, like the link between the 'overhearing' motif and the poet's task of embarking on composition:

> J'aloie l'autrier errant,
> sanz conpaignon,
> seur mon palefroi *pensant*
> a fere une chançon,

---

[16] On poetics as a central theme in Chaucerian verse see L. A. Ebin, *Illuminator, Makar, Vates: Visions of Poetry in the Fifteenth Century* (Lincoln, Nebr., and London, 1988); Davidoff, *Beginning Well*, esp. 135–65; P. M. King, 'Chaucer, Chaucerians and the Theme of Poetry', in Boffey and Cowen (eds.), *Chaucer and Fifteenth-Century Poetry*, 1–14; DeVries, 'Pleasure of Influence'.

[17] A. C. Spearing, *The Medieval Poet as Voyeur: Looking and Listening in Medieval Love-Narrative* (Cambridge, 1993).

> *quant j'oï, ne sai conment,*
> *lez un buisson,*
> *la voiz du plus bel enfant*
> *q'onques veïst nus hom;*   (1–8; my italics)
>
> The other day, on my horse,
> I was wandering
> Alone, thinking
> Of writing a song,
> When I heard, I know not how,
> Next to a bush,
> The voice of the most beautiful child
> A man has ever seen.[18]

Overhearing and finding material for a composition are here paralleled, as are travelling out and progressing into the fiction. As so often later, the narrator is presented as an involuntary, passive channel (*ne sai conment*) for what occurs in the narrative.

The impulse to start writing and a fictional scene of overhearing are often directly linked in framed *dits*. The narrator of Machaut's *Fonteinne amoureuse* (c.1361) writes down a long lover's lament heard all night through a bedroom wall. In Cavendish's *Metrical Visions* the narrator announces that he took up his pen and immediately heard 'oon began to speke / With deadly voyce' (82–3). It is his first subject, coming to him.[19] *Chanson d'aventure* openings such as 'As I wandrede her bi weste', followed by seeing a lamenting figure or hearing an admonitory voice (as often that of a bird as a human in late Chaucerian verse), become very common in late medieval verse, courtly, religious, and moral. In more political examples the speaker-subject may approach more purposively the listener-narrator, rather than waiting to be overheard.[20]

This poet-as-observer frame is related to the poet-as-secretary, common in French and used in Lydgate's *Complaint of the*

---

[18] *Lyrics of Thibaut de Champagne*, ed. and trans. K. J. Brahney, Garland Library of Medieval Literature, ser. A, vol. 41 (New York, 1989), 150–1.

[19] *Metrical Visions*, 57–84. His next group of subjects walk towards him; the next, Anne Boleyn, he suddenly catches sight of, sobbing, while he himself is musing, a *chanson d'aventure* variant sometimes used for Marian laments, e.g. *Religious Lyrics of the XVth Century*, ed. C. Brown (Oxford, 1952), nos. 6, 9, 93. See also Kennedy's 'At matyne hours' (*IMEV* 429).

[20] e.g. *Metrical Visions*; *God Amend Wicked Counsel* (*IMEV* 372).

Black Knight, whose narrator calls himself 'a skryvener' (194).[21] Chaucer gave the detached narrator various guises: the mere translator, the unsuccessful lover, the ageing love-poet (the last used also by Gower, Charles d'Orléans, and in John Rolland's *Court of Venus*, c.1575[22]). In Chaucerian poetry, as in Chaucer, one effect of this relatively uninvolved, unassuming, or unpurposive narrator can be to leave the task of interpretation very much to the reader.

The detached narrator may hide: in the *Belle Dame* watching from behind a trellis, in Dunbar's *Golden Targe* behind leaves, in Lydgate's *Black Knight* among bushes. These hiding-places are the border between heterodiegetic and homodiegetic narrative levels, a border which the narrators of framed narrative often cross. Such devices, giving the narrator temporarily an external standpoint, reflect the sense in which the medieval first-person narrator (originating in an age of oral performance of texts) frequently represents an aspect of the mode of reception: a part written for the performer of the poem. Long into a period when reading was taking over from oral performance, Chaucerian frames often dramatize this ancient detachment of the narrator-presenter from the narrative: the unsought dream, the involuntary overhearing, the aimless wandering and so on. The *dit amoureux* narrator from the *Roman de la Rose* onwards plays many parts: *auctor*, *acteur*, protagonist, mere amanuensis, *persona*, or a direct representative of the poet. Whatever else s/he represents in a text, the narrator is above all the point of reception, combining writer and reader: an alter ego of the author certainly (as decades of debate about 'autobiographical' dream-narrators have exhaustively explored), but also, as dreamer, wanderer, and overhearer, passing through successive frames into scenes which gradually unfold their content to him or her, s/he is the alter ego of the reader or audience, experiencing the process of gradually entering the realm of fiction.

'Transition' frames take the narrator from one state into

---

[21] *Minor Poems of John Lydgate*, ed. H. N. MacCracken, EETS OS 192 (1934), ii. 382–410.

[22] John Rolland, *Ane Treatise callit the Court of Venus*, ed. W. Gregor, STS, 2nd ser. 3 (Edinburgh and London, 1884).

another and mirror a reader's progress into the central fiction. The most celebrated is the dream, a transition from waking to sleep. Just as common in Chaucerian verse is its converse, the 'I woke up' frame, a transition from sleep to waking. The 'I walked out' *aventure* frame is another transition: from indoors to outdoors and into a wider, less predictable, landscape, which will hold the work's main subject. Its converse is the frame where the narrator enters a building or enclosed place: palace, temple, court, island, or garden.[23] Roos and Douglas employ the waking frame to symbolize their decision to get on with the task of translating (*Belle Dame* prologue and *Eneados* prologue VII). There seems nothing random about whether a poet chooses to begin with a dreaming or a waking frame, or whether the main subject is immediately prefaced by a walking out into a landscape or a narrowing down of focus by entering a building. Chaucerian poets planned the selection and sequencing of frames carefully to match the core narrative. It always repays the reader to scrutinize the choice, ordering, and handling of frames: one of many respects in which we must learn to *read* the conventions in Chaucerian verse, not merely note them.

'Book' frames are of two kinds. One is the book read initially, before core events begin, that suggests a theme or poses an issue; this is one of the best-known Chaucerian devices, initiated, for English literature, by Chaucer's dream poems. Chaucerian poets also used book frames of another type, designed to turn attention outwards to the physical book, the completed volume the reader holds and peruses. Among these are references to the narrator's decision to write; requests to readers to receive or correct the book; 'Go Little Book' envoys; and 'self-begetting' devices, by which the text is presented as an account of how it was itself written.[24] Whereas transition frames mirrored a reader's progressive absorption into the abstract fictional realm, these other 'book' frames direct mental attention

---

[23] Enclosed gardens could function as private rooms, e.g. *Troilus*, II. 1114–15. The *Floure and the Leafe* narrator, 43–77, enters a *herber* with trellis sides and bough-roof, 'As a pretty parlour': an observation-post for the narrator, who can see out but is invisible.
[24] See S. G. Kellman, 'The Fiction of Self-Begetting', *Modern Language Notes*, 91 (1976), 1243–56.

in the opposite direction, outwards to the extrafictional world of the poem's consumers and the book as an object. Their late medieval popularity perhaps reflects the increasing prominence of reading.

Curious chronological tricks represent the mystery of the relationship between fiction and the written page that contains it. The *Assembly of Ladies* dream is presented both as a book the narrator wrote after her dream and an oral account requested before it by a sympathetic stranger-listener.[25] Skelton's *Bowge of Court* narrator, with a simultaneous dynamic, jumps out of a boat in his dream and 'even with that woke, / Caughte penne and ynke, and wroth this lytell boke' (532), a near-simultaneity of waking and writing, and an implicit identity of dreaming and composition, found in other works.[26] In Henryson's *Testament of Cresseid*, the *Testament* appears, completed already before the dream, as 'ane uther quair' (61) the narrator takes up after reading *Troilus and Criseyde*, seeming both to displace *Troilus* as *texte générateur* and also to be in existence before its own story is told, becoming its own *auctorite*. This is a novel twisting together of both types of book frame. It occurs in a prologue where, disconcertingly, other preliminary expectations are similarly laid down only to be whisked away: desolate seasonal opening gives way to warm comfort; expectations of an appeal for love to Venus are dropped; Troilus first hopes and then despairs; Chaucer's poem is full of pain, yet 'guidly' poetry, 'joly veirs'. Henryson in this prologue sets up contrasts (up/down, cold/fire, comfort/distress, among them) and avoids mediating them. The replacement of Chaucer's book by another, an event of analogous pattern, aptly introduces a question about where the basis for our judgements lies:

> Quha wait gif all that Chauceir wrait was trew?
> Nor I wait nocht gif this narratioun
> Be authoreist, or fenyeit of the new.   (*OBLMVP*, 290, 64–6)

---

[25] *The Floure and the Leafe, The Assembly of Ladies, The Isle of Ladies*, ed. D. Pearsall, TEAMS (Kalamazoo, 1990), 29–62; ll. 21–8, 740–56.
[26] John Skelton, *The Complete English Poems*, ed. J. Scattergood (Harmondsworth, 1983), 46–61.

The preface denies the reader any sense of sure foundations and standpoint, anticipating what Gray defines as the poem's enigmatic tensions between pity and horror, and between the narrator's role as poet and the emotional agony he recounts.[27]

The boldest examples of this second type of book frame are French: the *Chevalier des Dames* dreamer awakes to find the book of the dream completed, by his pillow.[28] *Le Messagier d'Amours* (1489) describes its own creation, a volume weighing a pound by the end of the story, as the narrator tiptoes round, constantly hides and overhears, copying down two lovers' words.[29] De Granson's *Livre Messire Ode* (1380s? a French work perhaps influenced by the *Book of the Duchess*) is presented as simultaneously a fictional journey taking a lover into and out of an assortment of traditional frame settings (a garden, dream, house, etc.), composing or hearing lyrics as he goes, and as the sequence of pages in a completed book containing those lyrics, which the reader is perusing.[30] It has multiple overheard lovers and frames within frames: fragmented reflections of a single emotional consciousness, with an allegory of infidelity and contrition at its centre, apparently representing the work's real-life subject, variously adumbrated throughout the text. Several framed narratives, including the *Book of the Duchess* and *Kingis Quair*, present their subject like this, reduplicated and fragmented in the text, only indirectly recorded there and never completely revealed: like an event reflected in pieces of a mirror.[31]

There are often significant parallels between the narrator and protagonist(s), and frame and core. In the *Belle Dame* the frame narrator's bereavement provides an ominous analogue to the core lover's disappointment in love. The *Quare of Jelusy* narrator's own 'suffraunce', typifying 'this worldis changeing and

---

[27] D. Gray, *Robert Henryson* (Leiden, 1979), 168–71.
[28] *Le Chevalier des Dames du Dolant Fortuné*, ed. J. Miquet (Ottawa, 1990).
[29] *Recueil des poésies françoises des xve et xvie siècles*, ed. A. Montaiglon and J. de Rothschild, 13 vols. (Paris, 1855–78), ix. 1–33.
[30] *Oton de Granson: Sa vie et ses poésies*, ed. A. Piaget, Mémoires et documents publiés par la société de l'histoire de la Suisse romane (Lausanne and Geneva, 1941).
[31] Gray, *OBLMVP*, 71, notes a critical turning away from 'autobiographical' interpretations to a more 'rhetorical' approach, and emphasis on the poem's ideas. In such *dits*, the rhetorical designs carry 'autobiographical' patterns.

his wo', for which he expects no comfort, prepares for its core narrative's subject of women defencelessly oppressed in cruel marriages.[32] The *Assembly of Ladies* narrator enters two gardens in the prologue, problematic variants on the Garden of Love, which prefigure its central subject of faithful lovers who encounter cruelty or betrayal. The first garden is a maze in which women, walking, experience confusion and setbacks; the second has a wheel and hidden water—images suggesting Fortune—but also flowers symbolizing virtue and constancy.

The *Kingis Quair* is a supreme example of meaning and unity created through repeated pattern. Like the *Book of the Duchess*, it uses recurrent parallel patterning (together with other Chaucerian devices, such as the book read before the dream), with equal sophistication but to different effect.[33] The *Book of the Duchess* is about mournful and tragic *impasse*, and its concentric frames and death-seeking parallel figures express this; the *Kingis Quair* is about progress and hope, and its repeated pattern of restless movement and summonses to action express that.

Its preliminary image of circling and progressing planets,

> Heigh in the hevynnis figure circulere
> The rody sterres twynklyng as the fyre;
> And in Aquary, Citherea the clere,
> Rynsed hir tressis like the goldin wyre,
> That late tofore in fair and fresche atyre
> Through Capricorn heved hir hornis bright,
> North northward approchit the mydnyght,— (1–7)

is a rendition of the traditional seasonal prologue which is patterned on movement. The beautiful movement upwards of a fair goddess (the moon, goddess of change), clad in her new 'fair and fresche atyre', as she advances, from crescent to full, across the sky, from December into the New Year and January,

---

[32] *The Quare of Jelusy*, ed. J. Norton-Smith and I. Pravda, Middle English Texts, 3 (Heidelberg, 1976).
[33] James I of Scotland, *The Kingis Quair*, ed. J. Norton-Smith (Leiden, 1981), pp. xvi–xvii. On structure see also D. Pearsall, 'The English Chaucerians', in D. S. Brewer (ed.), *Chaucer and Chaucerians: Critical Studies in Middle English Literature* (London, 1966), 201–39, esp. 227–8.

towards the meridian, is an appropriate opening picture for a work which will repeatedly present movement and newness as things to be welcomed, a narrative which presents its main subject, change, unusually in medieval literature, in a positive light.[34] The first line and the scene of Citherea-Cynthia progressing up through the sky prefigure central motifs of activity, progress, and the wheel: the culminating message of the dream will be that the hero can climb up optimistically on to Fortune's revolving wheel (1184–1204).

The vision of hope, authenticated by powers beyond man, that the world and change—Fortune—will be benevolent to an individual who has progressed to wisdom, self-control, and virtue, is conveyed also through James's audacious reworking of the message of *De consolatione philosophiae*, which is the frame's book read before the dream. Boethius, says James, is one

> That in himself the full recover wan
> Of his infortune, povert and distresse,
> And in tham set his verray sekernesse.
> And so the vertew of his youth before
> Was in his age the ground of his delytis. (33–7)
>
> He makith joye and confort that he quit is
> Of thir unsekir warldis appetitis. (39–40)

This selective reformulation (rather than actual betrayal) of the Boethian world-view in the frame presages the poem's unBoethian, positive attitude to worldly prosperity as a reward for integrity and temperance.

One after another, traditional prologue motifs, including the planetary opening, restless narrator in bed, and book read before the dream, appear, each shaped to prefigure the theme of optimistic movement. The revolving planets give way to the narrator's revolving thoughts: 'This mater new[e] in my mynd rolling' (50), 'thir thoughtis rolling to and fro' (64); his turning body, 'Forwakit and forwalowit, thus musing' (71), to a Mattins

---

[34] Most critics take 'Citherea' to be Cynthia, but see Norton-Smith (ed.), *Quair*, 51 n. 3.

bell's summons to pick up pen and write 'sum new[e] thing' (89) about his own progress out of misery into happy future, 'my turment and my ioye' (133); the bird summoning the lovers to hail new beginnings:

> Worschippe, ye that loveris bene, this May,
> For of your blisse the kalendis ar begonne,
> And sing with us, 'Away, winter, away!' (232-4)

Weather-descriptions, a justly celebrated feature of Chaucerian frames, generally provide analogues, commentaries, and clues for the ensuing fictions. The weather of the *Temple of Glass* has already been mentioned. Douglas's *Palice of Honour* begins with parallel references to the depressed poet's 'barrant wit, ovirset with fantasyis . . . thy dull, exhaust Inanitie' (127-35), and to a grim, storm-swept 'desert terribill', an analogy reminiscent of the *House of Fame*.[35] The mingling of springtime cheer with tear-like frost, dew, and hoary trees in the Valentine's dawn prologue in the *Flour of Curtesye* matches the text's contrast between the human lover's anxieties and the birds' simple joys.[36] Douglas used seasonal prologues, as he also used the dream-frame, for some *Eneados* prologues. They symbolize his role as Christian translator of Virgil, evoking the circle of the sun's year as a mirror of the achievement of his book.[37] Nevill's *Castle of Pleasure* enterprisingly relocates the weather passage to the waking, epilogue section of his frame, after the dream ends: a description of a thunderstorm, together with a look by the narrator out of his window—another kind of frame-motif —which shows the transitory vanity of life in the world outside.[38] Before his dream, this motif of mutability appeared only as literature: Ovid's *Metamorphoses* was his pre-dream book.

---

[35] *The Shorter Poems of Gavin Douglas*, ed. P. J. Bawcutt, STS, 4th ser. 3 (Edinburgh and London, 1967), p. xl.
[36] *Minor Poems of Lydgate*, ii. 410-18.
[37] Prologues VII, XII, and XIII, *Virgil's Aeneid, Translated into Scottish Verse by Gavin Douglas*, ed. D. F. C. Coldwell, 4 vols., STS, 3rd ser. 25, 27, 28, 30 (Edinburgh and London, 1957-64).
[38] William Nevill, *Castell of Pleasure*, ed. R. D. Cornelius, EETS OS 179 (London, 1930), ll. 855-94; there is a nice pre-storm urban evening scene before he sleeps, 98-109.

The *Testament of Cresseid*'s 'doolie sesoun' prefigures the 'cairful dyte' (1) and themes of decline, mutablity, and penitence: Lent hail-storms descend (5–6); Phoebus also descends (10, 14); coldness, and the passage of time it represents in medieval thought, including human age, detach the narrator from thoughts of love (20–35); the contrastive warmth of drink and fire replaces discomfort with bodily and literary comfort (36–42; a version of the topos of books rather than experience), yet also symbolizes the twinned fevers of desire and leprosy, and the reduction by time of human youth and glory to abject physical suffering.[39]

The *Floure and the Leafe* frame begins with repeated *new, fresh, bright, light, good, pleasaunt, wel*: 'sweet' rain, 'wholesome' air, 'wholesome' showers, 'glad' humans, 'glad' green, 'season swete', 'pleasaunt grove', (1–126). These anticipate its vision of a world filled with benign purpose, where adversity is merely beneficial learning-experience. Reversing conventions, its narrator is anxiety-free and its nightingale has a 'merry' note (99): no 'ocy, ocy'. There lies the clue: here sobriety yields happiness. The poem's nightingale and goldfinch are an *Owl and Nightingale*-like pair, without the squabbling, the nightingale being the sober Owl-figure. The nightingale is benevolent (99–105) towards the more pleasure-loving (= flower-eating) goldfinch, who eventually, like the company of the Flower, learns virtuous caution (442–8). Within the core-narrative, symbolic weather reappears, providing a symbolic test. Its storm is brief: enclosing all is the benign weather of the frame. Those with the virtues of perseverance and chastity flourish; those who love idleness fail—and then need succour. After this test the nightingale, having prudently spent the day's heat in the laurel's shade, perches on Diana's hand, queen of virtuous and prudent lovers, while the greenfinch, fleeing the unwisely chosen heat of a medlar, sits and sings on the Lady of the Flower's hand. The Flower company ends chastened, curbed, but also comforted. The poem perhaps consciously reformulates the imagery and message of the early Chaucerian *Book of Cupid*, to celebrate

---

[39] See Gray, *Henryson*, 165–71.

typically fifteenth-century themes of virtuous love and respect for women.

Female voices are fairly prominent in Chaucerian verse. There are female narrators in the *Floure and the Leafe* and *Assembly of Ladies*; female allegorical rulers such as Venus, Sapience, or Loyalty; women's laments besides men's, including the *Lay of Sorrow* and Lydgate's *Gentlewoman's Lament*.[40] Robbins dismissed the idea that any first-person female narrators could indicate real-life female authorship.[41] Yet it seems as likely that some do as that all are male authors 'ventriloquizing', though that was an established tradition from Ovid's *Heroides* on. The emotional experiences of suffering women was a subject Chaucer made peculiarly his own, with Alcyone, Anelida, Venus, Dorigen, and the *Legend of Good Women*; and lists of faithful women are common in Chaucerian verse, often specifically recalling Chaucer's handling.[42]

Questions of authorship apart, there is a literary aptness in female voices for texts about virtuous love, in view of the transformation by Christine de Pizan, Martin le Franc, and Chaucer's *Legend*, of Cupid into both a feminist and teacher of chaste, monogamous love, against sensuality, deception, and misogynist slander. The *Assembly* and the *Floure and the Leafe* depict mini-worlds dominated by women, with female narrators and companies ruled by ladies. All the court functionaries in the *Assembly* are female.[43] So is the authority figure who comes foward near the end of the *Leafe* to explain the allegory. Like the *City of Ladies* or *Academy of Women*, the *Assembly* is a

---

[40] Schmitz, *The Fall of Women*; J. Kerrigan, *Motives of Woe: Shakespeare and the 'Female Complaint'* (Oxford, 1991), 1–51 (includes texts).

[41] 'The Chaucerian Apocrypha', in *Manual*, iv. 1080, 1094, 1095.

[42] e.g. *The Nine Ladies Worthy* (IMEV 2767), *Assembly of Ladies*, 258–69; *Flour of Courtesy*, 190–217, *Ballade of Her that hath all the Virtues*, 8–26, *Palice of Honour*, 562–97, *Court of Love*, 230–2, 872–3. *Letter of Cupid*, 302–22, links Dido and Medea's faithful reputation to Chaucer. On *Temple of Glas*, see Torti, *The Glass of Form*, 68. Chaucer influenced the generally positive images of figures such as Cleopatra, Medea, or Dido, who had previously a mixed literary reputation.

[43] Perhaps Christine de Pizan's *Dit de la Rose*, where Loyalty is foundress of the *Order of the Rose*, was a source: see *Poems of Cupid, God of Love: Christine de Pizan's 'Epistre au dieu d'Amours' and 'Dit de la Rose', Thomas Hoccleve's 'The Letter of Cupid'*, ed. T. S. Fenster and M. C. Erler (Leiden, 1990), 16–17.

women-centred apologue, a narrative where one segment of society, here women, is deployed as if it constituted the whole. Is the *Assembly* a feminist vision, granting women wider scope than in normal society? Or a critique of normal society? Or a fantasy projecting a man-free sisterhood? Its delight in the female group, its predilection for referring to *we*, *us*, and *oure* shared experiences, are as marked as its concentration on women.[44] The final frame-stanza reinforces this with the title: not a Court of Loyalty (say) but *Assembly of Ladies*.

The *Isle of Ladies*, that irrepressibly optimistic and confident projection of what Pearsall calls 'the dream of male desire', treats the all-women kingdom as a joke, a temporary state—with its own interest for the male observer.[45] It only takes the would-be abductor to swoon (a scene recalling *Troilus* III. 939–1134) for the women to flutter round him, and his victim to succumb to *pytye*. Soon the God of Love and the masculine navy have captivated them. The all-woman realm also initially supplies the narrator-protagonist with a wish-fulfilment setting —lone man marooned amid women—and the brief *frisson* of the accused abductor in the hands of judgemental women.

This dream-narrator adventures through his own narrative as its chief protagonist, *Roman de la Rose*-style. Fittingly, motifs of hunting frame his dreams. Almost every detail embodies the impetus of desire driving through the whole work, right up to its unmistakably sanguine dedication to the object of his desire, aptly transforming 'Go little book' into 'Go furthe, myn owne trew herte'.

The *Letter of Dydo* is influenced by Chaucer, yet the result is not Chaucer-like. Its translator's prologue echoes the *House of Fame* and Chaucer's condemnation of Aeneas's 'untrouthe' in the *Legend of Good Women*. Boffey shows how the translator reshaped the original so that his Dido matched those works' sympathetic portrait of the heroine. Yet the Dido of the *Letter* misses the dignity and nobility which never leaves the *Legend*

---

[44] e.g. 'our' agreement about relaxing and dressing, 379–85, or 393–5, where 'We sawe' so many people 'we' could not number them.

[45] Edition in Pearsall, *Floure*, 63–142; see esp. 65, 66.

Dido. In her generosity, tenderness, and unsuspecting heart, Chaucer's Dido exemplifies his principle that *Pité* is a pre-eminent indicator of nobility.[46] Many Didos, from Ovid on, are sympathetically presented; only Chaucer's has undiminished dignity in her pain, innocent trust, and final despair. His Dido is a magnificently generous queen succouring a shipwrecked opportunist, an Amazon-like ruler over a land where women enjoy freedom (*Legend*, 971–1014); she ends disillusioned and destroyed but always superior—even in her dying words—to Aeneas. Chaucer's concept of the 'gentil' is the key to his conception of both Aeneas and Dido: the qualities that leave her vulnerable are *gentil*; his strengths, his invulnerability, are ignoble. Chaucer casts sneering doubts on Aeneas's status as a 'gentylman' (*Legend*, 1264–72). In contrast, the *Letter* sees his nobility as one of his attractive qualities; his only real fault is to hurt Dido by leaving her (52–3). This Tudor Aeneas retains more virtues, and still deserves a woman's admiration (46–54); it is the situation—that he decides to leave Dido—that is lamented. She is thus pathetic. Chaucer's Dido is never pathetic.[47] The *Letter* Dido exemplifies tender womanly devotion, still in love, worried about his safety.[48]

This Dido has become that Tudor instructive figure, the wronged but faithful wife: Griselda, Penelope, Susanna, and Lucrece were popular embodiments of the type (other undemure heroines who similarly dwindle into wives include Medea and

---

[46] Boffey, 'Richard Pynson's *Book of Fame*', and see D. Gray, 'Chaucer and "Pite"', in M. Salu and R. T. Farrell (eds.), *J. R. R. Tolkien, Scholar and Storyteller: Essays in Memoriam* (Ithaca, NY, 1979), 173–203.

[47] Her best argument is only that of a meek wife: even if you rule all Italy you will never find a *kinder* wife than me (Pynson, 103–6). This is not the voice of Chaucer's Queen of Carthage, leader of her exiled nation, founder of a great city. The poet manages neat parallels between love and pain: tears/blood on his sword, dart of love/sword of death; bleeding heart before consummation/real blood at death (Pynson, 79–93). There is a touch of Grand Guignol in the images of half-dead Dido, spotted with blood and hair pulled out, 'colde ymage of your disceyved wife', coming into Aeneas's mind as he drowns (*OBLMVP* 6D, 1–6), and Anna sifting the ashes with her hands to find the bone-powder to keep in her bedroom (ibid. 95–8).

[48] She still burns with fire, sees him always before her eyes (Pynson, 43–7). She cannot hate 'my swete Ene' or wish him harm (Pynson, 52, 92); she seems genuinely worried for his safety and comfort on the sea (perhaps because the poet could not manage, as Ovid could, a more complex tone of would-be manipulative but actually ineffectual solicitude). She lists his qualities: no woman could resist him (*OBLMVP* 6D, 47–54).

Boccaccio's Ghismonda). The translator's envoy to the *Letter* warns 'Ye good ladyes ... of tendre age / Beware of love' and lustful seducers promising marriage, cautioning against doing anything which could harm reputation. Archibald and Bawcutt both suggest that Chaucer, and specifically his warning to women in the Legend of Dido, inspired the appearance of such moralizing advice in Chaucerian framed texts, including the *Testament of Cresseid*, Douglas's Prologue to *Eneados* IV, and the *Palice of Honour*.[49]

Chaucerian taste prefers multiple voices and framed complaints. Pynson redesigned the *Letter* as a Chaucerian framed narrative: in a stanzaic prologue and envoy a masculine voice now encloses Dido's single-voiced complaint. This narrator says he chose Dido's 'rufull songe' as a vehicle to express his own love-melancholy.

The most aggressive use of a male narrator's frame to contain a female voice is the *Belle Dame sans Merci*.[50] Its core is a dialogue between a Lover, pressing traditional Courtly Love pleas, and a Lady arguing against them. The Lover proffers long-established coercive metaphors from the lyrics of male desire (his 'trouth' as entitling him to her acceptance, her eyes as wounds, a woman's sexual acquiescence as a duty of 'mercy', desire as death-threatening for him, etc.), to argue that she is responsible for what happens to him. She responds that he foolishly caused his own state, she wishes him no ill, and she wants to be free. She undermines his rhetoric: no one ever literally died for love; 'paynted' love-language is a trap to fool women into losing their honour; Love is a deceiver.

Indisputably the Lady wins the debate. Her arguments are fresh, intelligent, just, and calm, and Chartier's design focuses attention and sympathy on her replies, because his Lover's speeches remain love-lyric clichés, and attempt no serious engagement

---

[49] See E. Archibald, 'Gavin Douglas on Love', in McClure and Spiller (eds.), *Bryght Lanternis*, 244–57, and P. Bawcutt, 'Gavin Douglas and Chaucer', *RES* NS 21 (1970), 401–21; pp. 405–7.
[50] *The Poetical Works of Alain Chartier*, ed. J. C. Laidlaw (Cambridge, 1974), 328–78; *Chaucerian and Other Pieces*, ed. W. W. Skeat, supplement to *The Works of Geoffrey Chaucer*, 7 vols. (Oxford, 1897), vii. 299–326 (Roos); *STC* 5068 (Pynson).

with her points. They offer one casuistical metaphor after another, which she deconstructs. Chartier draws on the long medieval tradition of dialogues where women reject wooers and/or debunk the rhetoric of seduction.[51]

Chartier's frame narrative, however, reverses all that, unexpectedly tipping the balance back to favour the man. It reinforces the Lover's pathos with a parallel figure of much greater tragic status, the bereaved narrator. In contrast to the Lover's mere metaphors of dying, this frame contains literal death: in the prologue the narrator's bereavement, and in the envoy the statement that the Lover died. The dialogue left the Lady morally untainted, but the frame adds material which incites us to condemn her as merciless: she went back to dancing without a thought of him (807–8); he died of grief (810–12). It exhorts women readers not to imitate her (813–28), and finally labels her as 'la belle dame sanz mercy'.

The frame is emotional blackmail: women should not reject wooers like that, because—look—they might die. It reinstates the Lover's original metaphors, 'mercy' and 'death', metaphors the Lady had demolished in fair debate. The frame suddenly claims reality for them: he did die, she was merciless. The frame puts her into the cage the Lover's words failed to catch her in. Its naming of her, 'la *belle* dame *sanz merci*', repeats his first gambit: her beauty is cruelty. Chartier had found a structure that allowed the Lady's arguments first to be voiced and then damned. The frame acts as containment. It turns the feminist into an Aunt Sally.

Perhaps that explains why Chartier's poem generated so many responses, and why virtually all its French imitators and successors gleefully attack the Lady. Either they purport to be by women, disowning her views, or they expand on the Lover's pleas, or they stage a trial of the Lady (often very wittily), either as penitent or unrepentant, but always condemned.[52] What caused this excitement cannot have been her arguments— they are not new—but the feminist–antifeminist tension between

---

[51] e.g. in Capellanus' *De amore*, in Provençal *tençons*, in English and French pastourelles and dialogues (e.g. *Craft of Lovers*, IMEV 3761).

[52] Piaget, 'La *Belle Dame sans merci* et ses imitations' (1901, 1902, 1904, 1905).

the dialogue and frame, creating an endlessly unresolved conflict of sympathies, and also probably that slogan, 'la belle dame sanz merci', with its curious power to catch the imagination. While it encapsulates the medieval Lover's formula of 'merciless beauty', it also stirs other powerful notions: of *femmes fatales* and the attraction of a perilous absolute, those themes that link the poem to Keats and the 1890s.

There is another reading, in terms of poetics. On this reading, the main subject is voiced by the narrator, not the dialogue: the issue is words *versus* actuality. The actuality of death, for the narrator, removes his interest in mere words, poetry. Yet, paradoxically, he becomes the presenter of our poem and he sympathizes with forlorn lovers (53–6), specifically one who peddles poetic metaphors for his grief. Superficially, the frame-narrator represents real grief, and antagonism to mere rhetoric, while the Lover represents painted rhetoric and sexual desire dressed up as grief. Yet amid the Lover's metaphors occurs the statement that 'wordes' are proved by 'warkes' (340), and the concluding frame suddenly makes literal (*warkes*) the death which in the dialogue was mere metaphor (*wordes*).

The frame, then, poses the question of how poetry relates to sincerity, a theme expressed in the narrator's rejection of poetry (37–62), the Lady's deconstruction of the rhetoric of desire, and the Lover's difficulties with singing and speaking (119–32). The statement that the Lover died jolts the assumption behind these: contrary to the narrator's initial conviction that poetic words are incompatible with real grief, this death asserts the opposite. Through the figure of the Lady Chartier deflates love-sickness, but through the frame he asserts its affinity with death. It is a deeply dialectic poem.

Unlike other responses to Chartier's work, the English translator's frame eschews taking sides or alluding to the debate, apart from a final prayer for true lovers. It concerns rather his own task as translator, his commission from those (women?) who imposed the task as 'penaunce', in *Legend of Good Women*-style.

> Half in a dreme, not fully wel awaked,
> The golden sleep me wrapped under his wing;

> Yet nat for-thy I roos, and wel nigh naked,
> Al sodaynly my-selve remembring
> Of a mater, leving al other thing
> Which I shold do, withouten more delaye,
> For hem to whom I durst nat disobey.   (1–7)

Roos uses 'waking up' and *aventure* frames as metaphors for his writing. This is particularly clear if we read The translator's prologue and epilogue together. His mind emerging from unconsciousness (1–4), he clothes his naked self as he 'clothes' the narrative in words, both being arrayed in black (1–3, 22, also 831, 845), and sets out into scenery, 'a lusty green valey / Ful of floures', which can be read as the flowers of rhetoric his 'naked' writing needs (24–5, and 843–6) and as the core fiction itself into which he now enters. This appears as a rain- (tear- ?) swept 'playne' at the end (846). As *chanson d'aventure* translator, he now merges (22–9) into Chartier's original *chanson d'aventure* narrator: 'Nat long ago, ryding an esy paas...' (28). Pynson's 1526 epilogue condemns seducers: uniquely among responses to the *Belle Dame*, English Tudor moralization supports the Lady.

There is a strand in Chaucerian narratives, exemplified by the *Temple of Glass*, *Quare of Jelusy*, *Assembly of Ladies*, and *Complaint of the Black Knight*, which uses the *dit amoureux* to depict a sombre, settled, and hopeless sorrow, and uses the framed narrative to express a sense of a life imprisoned in unhappiness. The love sorrow these poems present is not the romantic yearning of young passion, with hopes that the poem itself may bring about a happy denouement, but the *impasse* of thwarted lives, adult sorrows to which neither hope nor a solution are conceivable. The *Assembly* and *Black Knight* seem tongue-tied even in voicing blame or protest. These poems look not to happiness or reward for devoted love, but only to the non-solutions of sympathy and continuance in virtue.

The *Quare*'s 1976 editors condemned its clumsy failure to integrate frame and complaint, and the writer's lapse into 'obsessional' intolerant denunciation of 'jelusye', lacking either the 'modest urbanity of Chaucer... or the good-natured moral earnestness of Lydgate' (p. 7). The *Quare*, however, is adapting courtly forms for grim uncourtly new topics. It is about not lovers but marriage, not amorous longing but marital cruelty. It belongs with the *Temple of Glass*: tragedies of imprisoning, loveless marriage, rather than with *dits amoureux*: tragedies of desire.

In May the narrator walks out, musing on a grief he knows no one can comfort, and overhears a woman sobbing for help to Hymenaeus. Her plea mentions Pluto, who carried off a bride to dwell in torment of 'body and soule'; she says she endures thraldom under Diana (because of her female sex?), and appeals to all-powerful Jupiter to see and redress her injustice. Another woman takes her away to comfort her. The narrator, puzzling over the nature of this 'jelusy' that causes cruelty towards innocent women, composes a *dyte* against 'jelusy', for women and all true lovers: a complaint in nine-line stanzas, enclosing a more sermon-like complaint in seven-line stanzas.

As a 'love aunter' this is a clear failure. The poet, however, is redeploying motifs such as the musing poet and the overheard complaint, and also the term 'Jelusy', so often wittily used in past courtly literature for those forces—often tedious moral constraints—which obstruct the path of romantic passion; now they convey the unromantic pain of abusive marriage. Seen in this light, the central *dyte* is well-structured: beginning with the argument (derived from the *Epistre au dieu d'Amours*) that women, generally uninclined to violence themselves, suffer violence; adding that bullying robs them of youth and beauty; that women in general are generous to men; that women have no means for resisting tyranny because duty dictates their passive obedience, and so on. The poet writes sharply about the double standard (290–9) and the psychological pathology of this 'maladye' of possessive bullying. He may perhaps be a Scottish manifestation of a trend seen also in late medieval French works for voicing religious and feminist protest against cruelty to wives, which focused attack on the famous figure of the *Jaloux mari* from the *Roman de la Rose*.[53]

---

[53] Philippe de Mézières criticized jealousy in marriage, and de Meun's *Jaloux Mari*: see J. M. L. Hill, *The Medieval Debate on Jean de Meung's 'Roman de la Rose* (Lewiston, Queenston, Lampeter, 1991), 20–1. Le Franc, *Champion des Dames*, 7325–8, links de Meun's *Jaloux* with condemnation of marital cruelty, and a prayer to Hymenaeus, 7561.

The *Assembly of Ladies* is built on a sequence of images of reticence and constraint: the women in the framing section walking in a maze, thwarted and confused; their presentation of petitions of complaint, reticent to the point of obscurity and resulting only in deferral of any remedy; an allegory which celebrates and reaffirms precisely those virtues of their own—perseverance, diligence, loyalty—which have already gained them nothing; the narrator's Fanny Price-like caution, propriety (222–6), and self-effacement, and her repeated refusal to give herself any identification (17–19, 309–15, 411). Here even the bright pictures of Chaucer's faithful women are behind a veil (470–2). The court's motto is 'A endurer' (489).

Lydgate's *Black Knight* is similarly understated, and undynamic in its lack of resolution of the lover's pain. It presents a sorrow which is habitual, without future or ambition: its protagonist is one who regularly visits a secluded 'logge' every May, year by year, to lament. It is a circular text, without impetus, rounded with sleep, coming out of settled misery, going back to it: the narrator emerges from the 'dreryhed' (9) of night and eventually retires again, 'werry wery', to sleep (647); day is a brief, painful illumination of true love blocked by vaguely defined enemies (Daunger, Fraude, the God of Love's favour towards false lovers). It is saturated with echoes of the *Complaint of Mars*, that bitter and hopeless protest of extra-marital and star-crossed love. Chaucer's Mars arraigned God himself for creating an emotion that causes such misery; Lydgate's lover—with typically fifteenth-century caution in questioning cosmic arrangements—attacks Love. The sharpest sensual experience in the poem is the almost surreally vivid description of the frame-narrator's morning walk: the occasional violence of language used for the advent of a summer morning's sun on night's dew, mist, and the rest of nature (e.g. 'al assaute of Phebus feuent fere', 55), seems a displacement of the lover's violently complex emotions and of Love's irresponsible power—a power which he attacks in 453–90 with a lament 'that I ever saugh the brighte sonne' (485).

Some earlier *dits amoureux*, including the *Fonteinne amoureuse* and *Book of the Duchess*, transmuted real-life tragedy into poignantly beautiful platonic yearning. Classic *dit amoureux* denouements include solutions to dilemmas pronounced by authority-figures, or auguries of the Lady's mercy. A feature of the fifteenth century, however, are these other forms, which acknowledge the numbing despair and inextricability of human emotional problems—rather as wintry or mixed weather comes often in Chaucerian framing fictions to replace perfectly *attempre* May. It is also typical of Chaucerian poetry that these compositions can seem banal to an unsympathetic critical approach, and original and thought-provoking to an optimistically sympathetic one.

5 The Verse Forms of Jon the Blynde Awdelay

ERIC STANLEY

1. Audelay; good and less good verse in MS Douce 302; the poet and his scribes

'It deserves mention here, since it is almost totally neglected by critics', says Douglas Gray,[1] writing of the alliterative 'De tribus regibus mortuis' (143 lines long in eleven thirteen-line stanzas), preserved only in Bodleian MS Douce 302 in which the poems of John Audelay have come down to us, poem 54 in the standard edition of his verse.[2] The mere suggestion that some poem may be undeservedly neglected soon leads to editorial and critical attention; and so it was with this poem, as by D. Pearsall:

and then the extraordinary poem of *The Three Dead Kings* (54). This is in a 13-line stanza consisting of genuine alliterative lines (usually alliterating *aa/aa*) rhyming alternately in the octave, with a 5-line wheel of loose alliterative three-stress lines rhyming *cdccd*. The *ab*

---

[1] D. Gray, *Themes and Images in the Medieval English Religious Lyric* (London and Boston, 1972), 209.

[2] E. K. Whiting (ed.), *The Poems of John Audelay*, EETS OS 184 (1931); references to it in this study take the form (23. 202) for poem 23 line 202 in the edition, or, for the poem alone, just Whiting's poem number. Her punctuation and other editorial details are not followed in quoting, and contractions are expanded silently; her emendations are not always followed. I have marked with an accent final é when it is syllabic.

See also *Manual*, for Audelay, so far vols. vi, vii, and ix. For the manuscript, see *Catalogue of the Printed Books and Manuscripts Bequeathed by Francis Douce, Esq. to the Bodleian Library* (Oxford, 1840), MS 302, 50–2, and cf. F. Madan (ed.), *A Summary Catalogue of Western Manuscripts in the Bodleian Library at Oxford*, iv (Oxford, 1897), 585–6 (no. 21876); Carleton Brown (ed.), *A Register of Middle English Religious and Didactic Verse* (Oxford, 1916), i. 113–18; and *IMEV* and *Supplement* to *IMEV*; the contents of the latter two are now made more accessible by R. Hamer (ed.), *A Manuscript Index to the 'Index of Middle English Verse'* (London, 1995), 46 for MS Douce 302.

and *cd* rhymes are themselves inter-connected by assonance, there is concatenation between octave and wheel, and furthermore the lines alliterate systematically in groups, *aabbccdd/ddeff*. Such pyrotechnics have only been seen before in the *Pearl* tradition and *The Awntyrs off Arthure*.[3]

In this study of the poetry of Audelay, 'De tribus regibus mortuis' (54) occupies a central place, for I can see little validity in the view, held widely it seems, that it is not by Audelay.

For biographical information about Audelay we are indebted to what is given in MS Douce 302. According to a note, dated 1426, at the end of 'An Exhortation II' (18), he spent at least part of his old age at Haughmond Abbey (about $6\frac{1}{2}$ kilometres east-north-east of Shrewsbury), a house of Augustinian Canons.[4] MS Douce 302 is well described by Whiting in the first section of her introduction. It is incomplete as we have it, consisting of thirty-five folios. Three hands wrote it in the second quarter of the fifteenth century; the first hand finishes at the end of the first column of fo. 34^v; the second hand is that of the corrector who made many alterations and corrections, sometimes adding whole lines, and on fo. 35^r he wrote the last poem of Audelay's collection, 'Sapiencia huius mundi stulticia est apud Deum' (55); a third hand wrote the Latin poem

---

[3] D. Pearsall, *Old English and Middle English Poetry*, The Routledge History of English Poetry, i (London and Boston, 1977), 250. See also T. Turville-Petre, '"Summer Sunday", "De Tribus Regibus Mortuis", and "The Awntyrs off Arthure": Three Poems in the Thirteen-Line Stanza', *RES* NS 25 (1974), 1–14. The first two of these poems are included in his *Alliterative Poetry of the Later Middle Ages: An Anthology* (London, 1989).

[4] See the convenient summary by Whiting, pp. xiv–xvi. What his status in that house was is uncertain; see E. K. Chambers and F. Sidgwick (eds.), 'Fifteenth Century Carols by John Audelay', *Modern Language Review*, 5 (1910), 473–91, 6 (1911), 68–84, at vol. 5, p. 474, for the view that 'he may have sought the abbey as a hospital, but he was evidently himself a secular *capellanus*, or chantry priest, probably serving a chantry in the immediate neighbourhood of Haghmond'. For the suggestion that we might look at Audley in north-west Staffordshire close to the boundary with Cheshire, see A. McIntosh, 'Some Notes on the Text of the Middle English Poem *De Tribus Regibus Mortuis*', *RES* NS 28 (1977), 385–92, 386 n. 1. It is difficult to determine how far that suggestion is based on his name rather than on his presumed spoken dialect. The dialectal evidence provided by spellings of the manuscript is likely to be that of the scribes who wrote the poems down for the blind poet. What information we have about his early life connects him with his services as chantry priest to Richard le Strange of Knockin Castle (about 9 km. south-south-east of Oswestry). See further A. T. Gaydon (ed.), *A History of Shropshire*, ii, The Victoria History of the Counties of England (Oxford, 1973), 64–5. See also n. 30, below.

The Verse Forms of Jon the Blynde Awdelay 101

'Cur mundus militat sub vana gloria' in the second column of fo. 34^v.[5]

The poetry of John Audelay is praised, if at all, chiefly for the composition of a substantial body of carols, all of them devout, on a wide range of subjects, usually religious subjects. The entire content of MS Douce 302 is devout even when the subject is primarily secular, as, for example, 'De rege Henrico sexto' (39).

In England, during the late Middle Ages, there appears to have been considerable interest in verse forms, and many works present a considerable variety. One thinks of *The Canterbury Tales*, earlier than Audelay; and the Towneley plays, later than Audeley, within which the thirteen-line stanza has been singled out by disintegrating critics as of higher quality and attributed to one called by them 'The Wakefield Master'. In MS Douce 302 the variety of form is great, usually stanzaic, and the degree of regularity in the number of syllables within the line is variable. Audelay is more regular in those poems, including his carols, that look singable, and probably were sung, than in the more sermonic or expository poems. The poems in this manuscript do not stand alone in their variety nor in their variable regularity. They do not stand alone in making use variously of alliteration, in some rhyming poems as an optional ornament, in others with a much higher degree of regularity. All the poems rhyme, though not always exactly. 'De tribus regibus mortuis' (54) is highly unusual in combining half-rhyme, full rhyme, and regular alliteration within a thirteen-line stanza, a stanza length much used by Audelay.

On the whole, Audelay has been and still is neglected; undeservedly so, especially since the variety of his verse forms has long been recognized.[6] Far from showering praise on Audelay, when

---

[5] No manuscripts from Haughmond Abbey have been identified, and though origination of MS Douce 302 in Shropshire might seem a reasonable inference, we only know that its subsequent ownership in the fifteenth century is connected with Coventry and with Laund, an Augustinian Priory of St John the Baptist at Loddington in Leicestershire. Two of those mentioned in the ownership inscriptions are described as 'minstrels', but the word is too imprecise in Middle English for us to be sure that these owners wanted the words to sing them. Madan's entry in the *Summary Catalogue* (see n. 2, above) prints the evidence.

[6] See J. E. Wülfing, 'Der Dichter John Audelay und sein Werk', *Anglia*, 18 (1896), 175–217. His useful analysis is, however, more mechanical, especially in counting syllables, than seems appropriate.

editors and critics find in MS Douce 302 poems to their liking, they doubt if compositions so good can really be wholly by Audelay; thus R. L. Greene on 'In die circumcicionis domini' (38):[7] 'The spirited rhythm is so much superior to Audelay's usual metres that his original authorship must be regarded as doubtful.'[8] Yet even if the superiority of this poem over his usual verse were granted, have not other poets in the history of English poetry achieved among their many verses some single poem that has delighted the anthologists and through them their readers? For example, could the smoother rhythm of *Gertrude of Wyoming*, III. xxviii, racked by tortured—dash-riven—syntax, prevent us from allowing Thomas Campbell to be the author of the much superior, spirited rhythm of 'Ye Mariners of England, A Naval Ode'—formerly much anthologized—in the same volume?[9]

> And tranc'd in giddy horror Gertrude swoon'd;
>   Yet, while she clasps him lifeless to her zone,
> Say, burst they, borrow'd from her father's wound,
> These drops?—Oh God! the life-blood is her own;
> And falt'ring, on her Waldegrave's bosom thrown—
>   'Weep not, O Love!'—she cries, 'to see me bleed—

---

[7] R. L. Greene (ed.), *The Early English Carols* (2nd edn., Oxford, 1977, the edition used in this study), 372 on his carol no. 117; similarly, Greene doubts Audelay's authorship of 'In die natalis Domini' (33), p. 344 his no. 7 A, and of 'De sancta Maria II' (45), p. 403 his no. 230b. Recognition of some merit, meritorious only when compared with two poems (Lydgate's 'Ballade to King Henry VI Upon His Coronation', *IMEV* 2211, and the anonymous *IMEV* 1224) regarded by Greene as even worse, is accorded by him to 'De rege Henrico sexto' (39), p. 475 his no. 428. In 'De puericia' (41) Greene, manifesting no sympathy with medieval devotional writing, praises Audelay's attitude to childhood, not the poetic art shown, p. 459 no. 412: 'The attitude of reverence for childhood expressed by Audelay in this carol is unusual and has been deservedly praised. Nevertheless, the expression of it is rather stiff and conventional with its systematic introduction of the Deadly Sins and is more probably inspired by the words of Jesus (Matthew xxviii. 3, Mark x. 15, Luke xviii. 17) than by sympathetic association with real children.'

[8] R. R. Raymo ('Works of Religious and Philosophical Instruction', *Manual*, vii. 2276) follows Greene in doubting Audelay's authorship of some of the poems he thinks best, but he has a quiet word in praise of Audelay's 'considerable technical virtuosity'.

[9] Thomas Campbell, *Gertrude of Wyoming; a Pennsylvanian Tale. And Other Poems* (London, 1809), 65 and 101. I have imposed on the unindented left margin favoured for both poems by T. Bensley, Campbell's elegant printer, the pedantic indentation that brings out better the rhyme scheme in both quotations, to accord with what is done for Audelay. In the ode, I have converted into a rhyming pair the internally rhyming five-syllable line 'And sweep through the deep'.

> 'Thee, Gertrude's sad survivor, thee alone—
> 'Heaven's peace commiserate; for scarce I heed
> 'These wounds;—yet thee to leave is death, is death indeed.'
>> Ye Mariners of England!
>> That guard our native seas:
>> Whose flag has braved, a thousand years,
>> The battle, and the breeze!
>> Your glorious standard launch again
>>> To match another foe
>>> And sweep
>>> Through the deep,
>> While the stormy tempests blow;
>>> While the battle rages loud and long,
>> And the stormy tempests blow.

Of course, MS Douce 302 includes some pedestrian verse, especially in the short versified directions to the reader, such as the request,[10]

> I pray yow, syrus, boothe moore and las,
> Syng these caroles in Cristemas.

Its verse form, the couplet, is employed at considerable length in only one poem in the manuscript, 'Ihesus Christus apparuit sancto Gregorio' (10). The first twenty-two lines of this are divided in the manuscript (but not in the edition) into two stanzas, each of five couplets, followed by a single couplet, all these twenty-two introductory lines underlined in red. These lines introduce the General Confession (10. 23–60). The poem ends with a couplet followed by another ten-line stanza in couplets. It seems quite possible that the General Confession, which is extant in other manuscripts too (*IMEV* 3233), is not by Audelay: the enclosing three stanzas and the two single couplets are probably by him.

Two couplets, the first line of the four with internal rhyme, introduce a prose text entitled 'De peccatis cordis':[11]

---

[10] See Whiting, p. 180.
[11] *IMEV* 2795; the lines are printed in the Douce *Catalogue* (see n. 2, above), p. 51, as well as in Whiting, p. x. The prose text, which is certainly not by Audelay (see L. Braswell (ed.), *A Handlist of Douce Manuscripts containing Middle English Prose in the Bodleian Library, Oxford*, IMEP iv (Cambridge, 1987), 70–1), is given the number

> Rede thys offt but rede hit sofft,
> And whatt thou redust foryeete hit noght;
> For here the soth thou maght se,
> What fruyte cometh of thy body.

Within the prose text (fo. 32^v) there is a triplet followed by a line not linked to it by rhyme:[12]

> Fore better hit were stil to be
> Then to say Godys servys undewoutly:
> Thai scornyn God ful sekyrlé
> And han his maleson.

These three short texts seem similar in character to the direction Audelay himself gives at the end of 'Prayer to St Winifred' (24. 117–20) and in the political allusion at the end of 'De rege Henrico sexto' (39. 59–66), that the carol be read or sung reverently, a direction to which Audelay attaches his name.[13] I presume, therefore, that they are by him, and that he was

---

XXXVI in the upper margin of the manuscript. These numbers are not without interest, but have not found a place in Whiting's edition, perhaps because their authority is doubtful. From her reference to these numbers (p. vii) it is clear, however, that she too attaches importance to them, at least as evidence of what is missing, though not, apparently, as evidence for what may have been thought to constitute a unit of composition at the time when the manuscript was compiled, either by the scribe who added the numbers, or perhaps even by Audelay himself. When his stanza forms are under consideration, Whiting's disregard for the way the poems are set out, the use of rubric, paraphs, and braces for couplets and triplets, leads sometimes to arbitrary deviation from the manuscript evidence; for example, 'An Exhortation II' (18) follows on directly from the preceding poem, but she says (p. 243), 'In the MS. this poem has no heading, and no number, but, because of the change in stanza form at this point, I have treated it as a separate poem.'

[12] *Supplement* to *IMEV* 813. 8; apparently unpublished.

[13] Another such piece of instructional verse comes at the beginning of 'De salutacione corporis Ihesu Christi' (8. 1–6); it is underlined in red in the manuscript, to indicate that this six-line poem introduces the poem that follows. Later in the poem (8. 63–70) an eight-line stanza (with identical rhyme scheme as the preceding seven stanzas forming the salutation to the Body of Christ) introduces the three six-line stanzas that follow (forming the prayer to God). A similar verse introduction (similarly underlined) precedes the sixty-six lines of 'An Exhortation I' (12); it has no Latin title, nor is it numbered in the manuscript, so that it may perhaps be regarded as following on from the preceding poem though that ends in a formal explicit. The rhymes of 'An Exhortation I' are continuative, and not every stanza is paraphed, so that perhaps the poem is not to be regarded as wholly stanzaic. 'De passione Domini . . . et de horis canonicis' (13) has a title and a number (XXIIII) in the manuscript. It is in eight-line stanzas, and the very unlyrical first stanza is underlined in red, forming a heading as well as a direction to the reader.

content to write pedestrian verse when giving directions to the reader. It is possible, however, that the couplet or the verses that go with the prose text are scribal, and indeed a similarly short scribal composition appears at the end of the first poem in the manuscript.[14]

The relationship of Audelay to his first scribe or scribes and to the scribes of MS Douce 302 (if that is not the book of the poet's dictation) is a subject of speculation. Being blind, Audelay himself could not have written down the poems.[15] Wülfing transcribed the poems in 1889,[16] and met Madan, who dated the manuscript as of 1430 to 1440. Madan persuasively argued, in view of the final prayer for Audelay's soul,[17] that when that was written the poet was dead (but he did not persuade Wülfing). If Audelay was dead by the time the scribe was copying the last poem, and perhaps also the two preceding poems (that is, everything after the prose text), their transmission cannot have benefited from direct checking with the poet: that may account for some of the textual problems. Wülfing argues further that Audelay, being deaf, may have mumbled. Wülfing does not enter into the difficulty experienced by the original scribe or his corrector in checking his scribal work by reading it back to the deaf poet. Some oddities of spelling, for example, those involving consonants (such as <c> for /g/ and <t> for /d/), may be a result of imperfect communication, rather than regional, phonetic peculiarities of Shropshire or East Wales. Not to be outdone by Wülfing, Chambers and Sidgwick suggest,[18] 'The whole of the poems may have been composed on Audelay's sick-bed in Haghmond Abbey.'

---

[14] Not in *IMEV*; but printed by J. Orchard Halliwell (ed.), *The Poems of John Audelay*, Percy Society, 14 (1844), 10, and by Whiting, p. vii.

[15] As far as I know, Henry Sweet was alone in thinking that Audelay himself wrote MS Douce 302, *A History of English Sounds* (Oxford, 1888), 155: 'the poems by Audelay... written in Shropshire in 1426, the ms being probably the author's autograph'.

[16] Wülfing, 'Der Dichter John Audelay', 175-8. For Madan's entry in the *Summary Catalogue*, see n. 2, above.

[17] Whiting, p. 224, last line.

[18] Chambers and Sidgwick (eds.), 'Fifteenth Century Carols', 474. See Audelay's lines quoted in n. 35, below.

2. Classifying the poems in MS Douce 302

A subjective, literary judgement that ventures to reject Audelay's authorship of any of the more substantial poems in Audelay's manuscript—Audelay's book, it seemed to the scribes who wrote it[19]—must have better reasons than those advanced by Greene and others. On the whole, Chambers's defence of Audelay's authorship against the doubts expressed by editors and critics 'on grounds which, where he [Greene] states them, seem to me rather hypercritical', has more to commend it than has recently been granted.[20] Chambers bases his defence even of the poems most often denied to Audelay on the fact that 'he is throughout an experimenter in metre'. That praise is implied in Raymo's words, that his compositions 'show considerable technical virtuosity'.[21] Turville-Petre's comment is more two-edged: 'his own, less accomplished, experiments with the thirteen-line stanza'.[22] Audelay's intellectual readiness to vary his verse forms explains sufficiently his varied uses of alliteration. The prosodic variety is not to be thought of as exercises, a despised category in any post-Romantic view, or as experiments, more favourably regarded in a post-Romantic view, but still perhaps prentice-work: Audelay's skilful display of the variety of metrical form available to his age is that of a master.

The prosodic variety of MS Douce 302 is matched by the generic variety of the poems. The manuscript itself has descriptive classifications in some of its Latin headings, which may well go back to the poet: the salutations, 'De salutacione corporis Ihesu Christi' (8), 'Salutaciones beate Marie virginis' (19), 'Salutacio composuit angelus Gabrielus' (21), 'Salutacio sancte Brigitte' (23), 'Salutacio sancte Wenefrede' (25), 'Salutacio in

---

[19] See the note at the end of 'An Exhortation II' (18), 'Iste liber fuit compositus per Iohannem Awdelay capellanum', and in the penultimate stanza of the last poem in the manuscript, 'Sapiencia huius mundi stulticia est apud Deum' (55. 32–3):

> Loke in this book: here may ye se
> Hwatt ys my wyl and my wrytyng,

followed six lines later by 'Thus counseles Jon, the blynde Awdelay.'

[20] E. K. Chambers, *English Literature at the Close of the Middle Ages*, Oxford History of English Literature, ii/2 (Oxford, 1945; corrected issue, 1947), 93.

[21] See n. 8 above.   [22] Turville-Petre, '"Summer Sunday"', 7.

honore sancte Anne' (26) with a prayer in Latin prose at the end, 'Salutacio in honore Saluatoris' (27) also with a prayer in Latin prose at the end; the narration, 'Narracio quo Michel duxit Paulum ad infernum' (16); the oration, 'Alia oracio de sancta Maria virgine' (20), but that could have been described as another salutation; the Magnificat classified as a psalm, 'Psalmus de Magnificat' (22); *in modum cantalenae* with *cantalena* apparently the same as 'carol',[23] 'Decem precepta in modum cantalene' (28), 'Cantalena de puericia' (41), perhaps 'De sancta Anna matre Marie' (43) by implication, 'Alia cantalena de Sancta Maria' (44), and 'Alia de Sancta Maria' (45) by implication, 'Cantalena de virginibus' (48).

Further, there are classifications within the poems such as Audelay himself found suitable: *Holy prayer*, 'De effusione sanguinis Christi' (4. 1); *oreso(u)n*, 'Ihesus reprobatus a Iudeis' (5. 38), 'Hore canonice passionis Ihesu Christi' (14. 74); *prayere*, 'Salutaciones beate Marie virginis' (19. 177), but in its heading a *salutacio*; *sauter of the passion*, 'De psalterio passionis' (6. 2), mainly in Latin; *sermon*, 'De meritis misse' (9. 408); *passion*, 'An Exhortation I' (12. 3), and 'De pasione Domini . . . et de horis canonicis' (13. 123); *pistil*, 'De epistola Domini nostri . . . in die Dominica' (15. 1, 131, 144); *remyssioune*,[24] 'Salutacio sancte Brigitte' (23. 199), but in its heading a *salutacio*; *carol* or *caral*,[25] 'Prayer to St Winifred' (24. 118), 'De rege nostro Henrico sexto' (39. 60), 'Timor mortis conturbat me' (51. 33), 'De sancto Francisco' (52. 53).

---

[23] For the couplet, introducing the carols for Christmas-tide, and making the equivalence of *cantalena* and 'carol' explicit, see p. 103 (and n. 10) above. The couplet refers to the carols for Christmas-tide following it, at least to (37) for 29 December (the tenth of the group), probably also (38) for 2 January, and conceivably the political prophecy 'De rege nostro Henrico Sexto' (39) described as a *carol* (39. 60). *Cantalenae* and carols are most likely to have been sung, but, MS Douce 302 itself having no music, music survives only when a poem is extant in another version together with the music. Cf. J. Copley, 'John Audelay's Carols and Music', *ES*, 39 (1958), 207–12, and 'A Popular Fifteenth-Century Carol', *N&Q* 204 (1959), 387–9; and J. Stevens (ed.), *Mediæval Carols*, Musica Britannica, IV (1st edn., London, 1958; 2nd edn., 1970), 8–9 and 20.

[24] 'Prayer for the remission of sins and perhaps also confirmation that remission is granted.'

[25] For the couplet preceding the carols, see p. 103 (and nn. 10 and 23), above. The modern sense of the word *carol* is usually thought to have developed after the Middle Ages. *OED*, s.v. *carol*, fails to cite Audelay, and *MED*, s.v. *carole* n., assigns the uses in 'Prayer to St Winifred' (24. 118) and 'Timor mortis conturbat me' (51. 33) to sense

Obviously, some of these categories describe the subject of the poem, rather than its form; thus prayer and orison, Magnificat, (Psalter of the) Passion, epistle, and remission. Others are more strictly of the form of the poems: carol and *cantalena*, salutation, narration, and sermon. Audelay has long been recognized as significant in the history of the English carol.[26] The salutation, with the opening word of each line *Hayle!, O Jhesu!* (19. 91–152), *O thou!* (19. 154–6), and the Latin *Gaude!* (26) or *Salue!* (27), is clearly identifiable as a form. Probably, though not so described in its title, 'In die natalis Domini' (33), with *Welcum, yole!* or *Welcum!* repeated at the beginning of each line, should be regarded as a salutation.[27]

3. The authorship of 'De tribus regibus mortuis'

Audelay's authorship is most often doubted for the penultimate poem in the manuscript, 'De tribus regibus mortuis' (54), the very poem Douglas Gray praises, in which alliteration is used consistently; and it is often doubted for the poem preceding it, 'Pater noster' (53).[28] On the former there appears now to be a consensus denying Audelay's authorship; thus T. Turville-Petre:

1(c): 'a religious poem or song; a psalm'. It may be, however, that Audelay had arrived at a usage for this word more specifically connected with singing, and closer therefore to the modern sense, than the lexicographers accept for late Middle English, a class that includes what Greene categorizes as a political carol (Whiting's 39, Greene's 428). For reasons why 'Prayer to St Winifred' (24) was not recognized as a carol before Greene's *Early English Carols* first appeared, see his note, p. 420 (1st edn., Oxford, 1935, pp. 408–9); a further reason why the burden was thought to be the heading may be that this poem has no (Latin) heading, unlike most of the other poems in the manuscript (unless acephalous).

[26] Cf. Greene, *Early English Carols*, 'The Carol as a Genre', pp. xxi–xlii, on Audelay at p. xxx; for Audelay's carols, see Greene's list, p. 317, under MS Douce 302; see n. 7, above. The importance of Audelay in the history of the English Christmas carol led to the early publication of 'In die natalis Domini' (33) by William Sandys in *Christmastide its History, Festivities, and Carols* (London, [1852]), 218–19, as a Christmas carol in the modern sense of the word. Sandys had earlier edited the variant version from MS Sloane 2593: *Christmas Carols Ancient and Modern* (London, 1833), 3–4, first edited by J. Ritson, *Ancient Songs, from the Time of King Henry the Third to the Revolution* (London, 1790), 81–2. The recognition of the importance of Audelay's carols led to the publication by Chambers and Sidgwick of the introductory couplet followed by twenty-five of Audelay's carols; see n. 4, above.

[27] This is different from the occasional initial *Welcum*, as in 'Salutacio sancte Brigitte' (23. 79), in the middle of a salutation using *Hayle* as its greeting.

[28] Cf. Whiting, pp. xxiv–xxviii; Bruce Dickins, 'The rhyme-schemes in MS. Douce 302, 53 and 54', *Proceedings of the Leeds Philosophical and Literary Society*, 2 (1932), 516–18; McIntosh, 'Some Notes', 386.

'De Tribus Regibus Mortuis' stands apart from its companions in its rhyme scheme, regularity of alliteration, and, most significantly, imaginative power and technical skill. It is therefore safe to say that it is not by the author of the other poems in the collection. Perhaps Audelay was attracted to it chiefly because of his own, less accomplished, experiments with the thirteen-line stanza. The date of the poem cannot be accurately determined, since it may have been composed many years before Audelay included it in his collection.[29]

Turville-Petre, referring to the poet of 'De tribus regibus mortuis', appears to labour under the impression that he is dealing with a linguistic fact when he avers, '*Kings* is . . . not by Audelay, for the poet's dialect is from further to the north; see Dickins (1932)';[30] but that is just an insecure philological deduction concerning the dialectal provenance of the poetical works in a manuscript, the alliterative verse of which may only appear more northerly because southern poets did not much *geeste rum, ram, ruf, by lettre*.[31] Other than MS Douce 302 and (about a century earlier) MS Harley 2253, little is known of the regionality of the poetry copied and, in Audelay's case, composed in Shropshire in the later medieval period: both these codices include alliterative

---

[29] Turville-Petre, ' "Summer Sunday" ', 7. Cf. R. Woolf, *The English Religious Lyric in the Middle Ages* (Oxford, 1968), 346 n. 5: 'It is most unlikely that this poem is by Audelay.' Earlier editors and commentators expressed no such doubt; thus Wülfing, 'Der Dichter John Audelay', 213–14, and W. Storck and R. Jordan (eds.), 'John Awdelays Gedicht "De tribus regibus mortuis." Eine englische Fassung der Legende von den drei Lebenden und den drei Toten', *Englische Studien*, 43 (1911), 177–88.

[30] Turville-Petre (ed.), *Alliterative Poetry . . . An Anthology*, 148, where he undertakes to restore what, he thinks, has been botched in transmission. For Dickins's article, see n. 28, above; Dickins says (p. 516) that the poems [(53) and (54)] 'are to be assigned to an area a good deal further north than Audelay's Shropshire and, in fact, belong to the alliterative school of which *Sir Gawain and the Green Knight* is the most splendid product'. McIntosh, 'Some Notes', 385–6, says (see n. 4, above, for the evidence of where Audelay lived), the scribe's 'task was not made easier by the fact that the original, if not the very text he copied, was almost certainly distinctly more northerly than his own'. It is not certain that the scribes and their dialect(s) are to be localized in Haughmond Abbey nor that Audelay's is to be localized in the area of Knockin Castle, which is not quite 20 km. north-west of the Abbey. If I understand Turville-Petre correctly (as he follows Dickins), he would place the dialect of the poem further north than Audelay's, which, so it has been thought, is further north than the dialect(s) of Audelay's scribe(s).

[31] The rhymes in MS Douce 302 are often inexact, and seem at times to rely on phonological and morphological doublets to make them more nearly exact; they are, therefore, not much use in establishing provenance of the poems. Whiting (p. xxix) rightly agrees with a doctoral dissertation, J. K. Rasmussen, *Die Sprache John Audelays, Laut- und Flexionslehre* (Bonn, 1914), that Audelay has many inaccuracies in rhyming. Rasmussen lists Audelay's rhymes at some length, and, disapprovingly, exemplifies the poet's inaccuracies and his preference for easy rhymes; see n. 47, below.

stanzaic poems. Those who speak of the more northerly feel of 'Pater noster' (53) and especially 'De tribus regibus mortuis' (54) make no mention of the geographical complication that MS Harley 2253 is associated with Ludlow (about 45 kilometres south of Shrewsbury) and not, as far as is known, with an area as far north as Audelay's part of Shropshire.[32] With the unrhymed Middle English alliterative short poems, 'A Complaint Against Blacksmiths' (*IMEV* 3227) and 'The Choristers' Lament' (*IMEV* 3819), both preserved in British Library MS Arundel 292,[33] the fact that they are unrhymed alliterative verse makes one 'feel', without hard evidence, that they must be more northerly in dialectal origin than Norwich, the provenance of the manuscript. Alliterative verse seems northern to us; and not only to us, for northern or southern seems to have been part of the dialectal self-awareness of the age, as the speech of the Cambridge scholars in *The Reeve's Tale*[34] and Mak's *sothren tothe* in the Second Shepherds' Play of the Towneley plays illustrate. At least some of the poets of alliterative verse appear to have thought it acceptable also *bi west*.[35] Poets conscious of poetic form are likely to have northernized or westernized the

[32] The dialectal origin of the Harley Lyrics is mixed. Cf. C. Revard, 'Richard Hurd and MS Harley 2253', *N&Q* 224 (1979), 199–202; but see also M. L. Samuels, 'The Dialect of the Scribe of the Harley Lyrics', *Poetica* (Tokyo), 19 (1984), 39–47 (repr. in M. Laing (ed.), *Middle English Dialectology* (Aberdeen, 1989), 256–63), which ends: 'The evidence for the dialect of the main scribe points clearly to Leominster rather than Hereford or Ludlow.' In some of the Harley Lyrics there are elements generally considered more northerly than Herefordshire, and perhaps more northerly even than Shropshire; cf. G. L. Brook, 'The Original Dialects of the Harley Lyrics', *Leeds Studies in English*, 2 (1933), 38–61.
[33] See the description of MS Arundel 292 by H. M. Wirtjes (ed.), *The Middle English Physiologus*, EETS OS 299 (1991), pp. ix–xv; the alliterative poems are her articles 23, added by Hand 4 of the middle of the fourteenth century, and 24, added by Hand 5 of the second quarter of the fifteenth century. F. L. Utley (ed.), 'The Choristers' Lament', *Speculum*, 21 (1946), 194–202, at p. 194, dates the addition of 'The Choristers' Lament' as about 1375 to 1390.
[34] Cf. J. R. R. Tolkien, 'Chaucer as a Philologist: *The Reeve's Tale*', *Transactions of the Philological Society* (1934), 1–70.
[35] For *bi west*, cf. the Vernon lyric 'Mercy Passes All Things' (*IMEV* 583), l. 1; in the Harley Lyrics, 'The Lover's Complaint' (*IMEV* 4194), l. 37, and 'Advice to Women' (*IMEV* 1504), l. 10; and, of course, the *Malverne hilles* on which Will fell asleep on a May morning. Audelay, in 'An Exhortation II', refers to the house in which he spent his years of sickness (18. 482–5):

> As I lay seke in my langure,
> In an abbay here be west,
> This boke I made with gret dolour
> When I myght not slep ne have no rest.

The Verse Forms of Jon the Blynde Awdelay

language of alliterative verse to make it chime with what they thought sounds good in the north or *bi west*. If there was among the poets themselves a degree of such self-aware northernizing and perhaps westernizing, the philological analysis of the language in terms of 'a good deal further north' or 'distinctly more northerly', whether applied to poet or scribe, must fail in terms of strict linguistic geography rather than in terms of deliberate regional colouring.

The scribe seems to have had greater difficulty with 'De tribus regibus mortuis' (54) than with all the other poems he had written in the manuscript; that could be explained perhaps as the result of unfamiliarity with its dialect, or regional colouring, yet the difficulty he had probably had other reasons. The greater density of scribal error in this poem than in the others in the manuscript may point to a greater complexity of transmission. There are errors in it that cannot be easily reconciled with a scribe mishearing the blind poet's dictation: the complex rhyme-scheme seems to have confused the scribe's eyes in copying; it is probably not a scribe's aural confusion.[36] The rhyme-scheme of this poem is a virtuoso's performance; thus the fifth stanza (54. 53–65):[37]

> The furst king he had care, his hert ovrcast,
>   Fore he knew the cros of the cloth that coverd the cyst;
> Forth wold not his fole, bot fnyrtyd ful fast,   55
>   His fayre fawkun fore ferd he fel to his fest:
> 'Nowe al my gladchip is gone, I gre and am agast
>   Of thre gostis ful grym that care me be gryst,
> Fore of have I walkon be wodys and be wast,

---

[36] For this poem, a course of frequent emendation to improve the rhymes (and the alliteration) seems justified to interventionist editors and annotators. Turville-Petre, often following suggestions made by others, has in the 143 lines of the poem no fewer than 48 emendations (29 to improve the rhyme, 7 to improve the alliteration, 12 for other reasons). Yet he denies that the poem is by Audelay, whose blindness and deafness might have provided him with more solid grounds for boldness in emending than he advances.

[37] 53 *ovrcast* 'troubled'.   54 *cyst* 'coffin'.   55 *fole* 'foal', *fnyrtyd* 'snorted'.   56 *ferd* 'fear'. For the doublets *fist* and *fest* see K. Luick, *Historische Grammatik der englischen Sprache* (Leipzig, 1921; repr. Stuttgart and Oxford, 1964), §409. 3. Such spellings as *ryst* for *rest* occur, for example, in 'De concordia inter rectores' (2. 179–81) *ryst / iblest / lest*, and cf. 'De sancta Maria I' (44. 17–20) *met / gret* ('greeted') / *set / wit*.   57, *gre* from *gruen* 'to be terrified'; thus McIntosh, 'Some Notes', 388.   58 For emendations of the line, see McIntosh, loc. cit., who has the correct reading *care me be cryst*, which he thinks stands for *gare me be gryst* 'made me be terrified' with the stop /g/ written <c> as often in this manuscript; that is the interpretation accepted here.   59 *of* for *oft*.

> Bot was me never so wo in this word that Y wyst: 60
> So wo was me never, I wene,
> My wit is away other wane;
> Certis, sone hit wil be sene
> Our connyg wil turne us to tene:
> Fore tytle, I troue, we bene tane. 65

The differently rhyming alternate lines are linked to those adjacent to them by half-rhyme, abababab in the first eight lines, cdccd in the last five; and the pairs of lines linked by half-rhyme are further linked by alliteration. Similarly complex rhyming, with rhyme and half-rhyme and with alliteration further linking pairs of lines in half-rhyme, is found in the preceding poem, 'Pater noster' (53), the only poem in the manuscript in eleven-line stanzas; thus its first stanza:[38]

> The *Pater noster* to expone, may no man hit prise,
>   That of prayers is pris and most fore to prayse.
> I rede thou rede hit aryght and out of syn ryse
>   That may restyng in heven unto thi soul rayse;
> Fore seven poyntis ther bene in e-set in asyse, 5
>   The lest salve hyt is to the synn, as the bok sayes:
> Oure Fader the wyche thou hart in heven—this orysoune thou yse;

60 *word* 'world', a very common spelling in this manuscript. 62 *away other wane* 'gone or deficient'. 63–5 *our connyg* 'our understanding; such wisdom as we have'; for /k/ alliterating with /t/ in this poem, see l. 18, 'Thre kyngys ther come trewlé itolde', unless that line is thought to have differing alliteration in its two halves, as is to be found elsewhere in the manuscript in alliterative poems (or with alliteration in the first half only), thus in 'De concordia inter rectores' (2. 59, 371, 694), and cf. 'Salutacione sancte Wenefrede' (25. 17). This alliterative licence is comparable with the rhyming licence as a result of which stops /p/ and /k/ occur occasionally in assonance, thus 'De epistola Domini nostri in die Domenica' (15. 119/21), and cf. 'De sancta Maria II' (45. 16/18) *fade / babe*. In l. 65, I accept Turville-Petre's interpretation of *for tytle*, and paraphrase the three lines: 'Indeed, it will soon become apparent that such wisdom as we have will make us change our position to sorrow: I think we have been taken as of right.'

[38] 4 *That may restyng in heven unto thi soul rayse* 'that may lift up thy soul to rest in heaven'. 5 *bene in e-set in asyse* 'are inserted in their proper place'. 6 *lest*, in *the lest salue hyt is*, is probably to be emended to *best*; some sense can be got out of the manuscript reading: 'the least (of those seven points) is a remedy'. That interpretation would, however, imply that the seven points to be expounded are of differing significance, so that one of them is the least; such a differential evaluation seems unlikely for The Lord's Prayer. 7 *yse*, as Whiting suggests, probably present subjunctive singular of *usen*, 'observe (as a rite)'. 8 *ayse* 'ease, freedom from annoyance or trouble'. 9 is a non-rhyming Latin line, as in other stanzas.

Ay e-halowyd be thi name, in angyr and in ayse.
Sanctificetur nomen tuum:
   Say whe the same, 10
   Oure Fader the wyche thou art in heven halowyd be thi
name.

Audelay had used rhymes with half-rhymes elsewhere: the third stanza of 'Salutacio in honore sancte Anne' (26. 9–12) has *broght / lyght / e-wroght / dyght*:[39]

> *Gaudé, felix Anna!* Oure blis to us thou broght.
> *Gaudé!* here that al the word, that lady heo gan lyght. 10
> *Gaudé!*, that maiden mercéful! Oure wele heo hath e-
> wroght.
> *Gaudé!* heo savyd al monkynd, fore syn to deth was
> dyght.

That variety of metrical form shown in the poems of MS Douce 302 and the metrical complexity of 'De tribus regibus mortuis' (54), in thirteen-line stanzas, a favourite form with Audelay, is sufficient to raise doubt in the current consensus that it is not by Audelay, and to reject even more firmly the view that 'Pater noster' (53), uniquely in eleven-line stanzas, is not by him either. The character of the former is rare in this manuscript, religious narration ending in prayer; not so, however, the character of the latter, which expounds the elements of the Faith, as Audelay does in many of his poems. 'Ihesus Christus apparuit Sancto Gregorio' (10) like 'De tribus regibus mortuis' is narrative, and it too ends in prayer; it has a verse form not found elsewhere in Audelay, couplets of short lines (usually of eight syllables, but Audelay is no exact arithmetician, and, for example, 'And grawntis xiij thousand yere of pardon' (10. 6) is eleven syllables long). 'De passione Domini . . . et de horis canonicis' (13) is also stanzaic, in fifteen eight-line stanzas, of the same rhyme-schemes as 'De misericordia Domini' (17)

---

[39] 10 *here that al the word that lady heo gan lyght* 'let all the world hear this, that lady shone in brilliance'; Audelay very frequently fills the metre by adding an unstressed subject (or object) pronoun in apposition to its preceding noun, *thou* in l. 9, *heo* in ll. 10 and 11; cf. T. Mustanoja, *A Middle English Syntax*, Mémoires de la Société Néophilologique de Helsinki, xxiii (1960), 137–8, on 'Pleonastic Use of the Personal Pronoun'. 12 *Fore syn to deth was dyght* 'because Sin was put to death'.

and as 'Magnificat' (22), all three with burdens varied to different degrees;[40] 'De passione Domini ... et de horis canonicis' is followed by a quatrain in which the poet names himself. That poem, like the poem after it, 'Hore canonice passionis Ihesu Christi' (14), related in subject but different in stanza form and with more alliteration, is narrative, and both end with a direction to the reader, to pray or to observe the Canonical Hours. There is no valid reason for doubting Audelay's authorship of any of these poems: on what hard grounds then doubt his authorship of 'De tribus regibus mortuis'?

4. Line-length, rhymes, stanza-length, and burdens

Thirteen lines is the most common stanza-length in MS Douce 302, used in nine poems.[41] Audelay has three poems in nine-line stanzas: 'Hore canonice passionis Ihesu Christi' (14), 'Salutacio sancte Brigitte' (23), and 'Salutacio sancte Wenefrede virginis' (25). All three are, to a varying degree, alliterative. In all three, the four long lines, with which the nine-line stanza opens, have a strong caesural break. In Audelay's verse stanzas of nine lines have a prosodic affinity with stanzas of thirteen lines, though the length of the lines and the lack of rhymes in some of them (when such poems are edited as thirteen-line stanzas by breaking the long lines at the caesura) makes the conformation of the resultant stanza look very different from stanzas of thirteen lines set out as such in the manuscript. A stanza of 'Salutacio sancte Brigitte' (23. 73–81), edited as of thirteen lines, exemplifies both the affinity and the difference:

---

[40] The refrain *Nolo mortem peccatoris* is not varied in 'De misericordia Domini' (17). Whiting (p. 242) gives as a biblical source Ezekiel 33: 11 with *impii* where Audelay's refrain has *peccatoris*. 'De misericordia Domini' (17) is not quite regular in form; the refrain is omitted three times after lines 72, 136, and 220, perhaps through scribal error since the rhyme in the stanzas is on -*is*, and the macaronic stanza (221–32) is twelve lines long, instead of the normal eight lines. Perhaps on account of its length (264 lines with a lacuna after l. 189 of one or more folios), the poem is not included among Audelay's carols by Chambers and Sidgwick nor by Greene in *Early English Carols*.

[41] See Wülfing's tabulation, 'Der Dichter John Audelay', 215–16.

The Verse Forms of Jon the Blynde Awdelay

Haile! to that perles prelat,
To the pope when thou come.
Haile! thou mendist thi mesage
In a meke manere.
Haile! faythfulli that fader
Ful reverenly at Rome,
Haile! he welcumd the worthelé
With a wonder chere
Into that holé place.
'Haile!' he said with myld steven,
'Welcum be ye fro the Kyng of heven.
Now blessid be thai that in the leven,
That ever thou borne was.'

In the manuscript, as in the edition, 'Salutacio in honore sancte Anne' (26) consists of six quatrains. Throughout, there is usually a very marked caesural break in the lines, and that break can be made conspicuous editorially by a mark of punctuation in the middle of the line, as in the stanza (26. 9–12) quoted at p. 113, above. In the manuscript there is nowhere, in this or any other poem, a mark of punctuation at the caesura. Converting Audelay's quatrains in long lines into eight-line stanzas in short lines (the odd lines unrhymed), and similarly, converting nine-line stanzas into thirteen-line stanzas receives no encouragement from the guidance given to metrical form by the scribes. For the nine-line stanza of 'Salutacio sancte Brigitte' (23. 73–81), here set out in thirteen lines, there is, as is usual in this manuscript, a brace linking the triplet rhyming on -*even*, but no virgule and no indentation.[42]

Post-medieval prosodic schematism, such as is found in many accounts of Middle English poetic forms, may misrepresent the poems analysed. The structures found pleasing by readers accustomed to modern printing of stanzaic verse may be the result of arbitrary decisions, of which the printing of the ballad-stanza in four lines, two of them unrhymed, is the most familiar, though it does not arise in Audelay. There is in Audelay a great

---

[42] The virgule is, of course, common in Middle English verse manuscripts, though never used in MS Douce 302; in printing Middle English verse, indentation is a modern editorial device.

variety of metrical structures, and a greater fluidity than lies in the strict count of lines.

Audelay was lax in his syllabic count. One recalls Furnivall's misguided critique of the metrical regularity of Audelay's contemporary, Thomas Hoccleve: 'Hoccleve's metre is poor. So long as he can count ten syllables by his fingers, he is content.'[43] A little more of what Furnivall thinks a fault in Hoccleve might have been a grace in Audelay. Within lines of varying syllabic count, the number of stresses is not fixed either, and is often difficult to determine. The last line of the thirteen-line stanzas of 'Narracio quo Michel duxit Paulum ad infernum' (16) varies in length from seven syllables and four stresses, for example, 'Joy and blis ther have ye schal' (16. 313), to eighteen or nineteen syllables and six stresses at the end of the next stanza, 'That we mow reyng with him in heven perpetualy' (16. 326).[44] Even within a single triplet within a single stanza Audelay varies the number of syllables and, as far as can be determined, the number of stresses; thus in 'De salutacione corporis Ihesu Christi' (8. 39–41):

> Hayle! I beleve faythfulé ye beth Fader omnipotent.
> Hayle! I beleve thou schalt me deme at thi jugement.
> Hayle! I beleve body and soule schal be ther present
>   Tofore thi gloryouse face.

In such cases it is usually possible for an emendator to bring about some metrical improvement, for example, by omitting *faythfulé* in the first line of the triplet, all the more so since the adverb 'faithfully' comes, especially with verbs of believing, so frequently in Audelay as to have lost much of its force; yet here it adds a touch of alliterative ornament, much as in the first

---

[43] In F. J. Furnivall and I. Gollancz (eds.), *Hoccleve's Works: The Minor Poems*, EETS ES 61 and 73 (1892 and 1925; repr. with some revision, by J. Mitchell and A. I. Doyle, 1970), p. xli.

[44] The poem was first edited by R. Morris, *An Old English Miscellany*, EETS OS 49 (1872), 210–22. Morris's edition, with paraphs, bold face (where the manuscript has red), and without indentation, gives a better idea of the appearance of the poem in the manuscript than Whiting's edition. Moreover he does not include in his line-numbering the Latin line (it goes back to Matthew 13: 30) translated in the next line (16. 62, in Whiting). Whiting's notes show how the Middle English poetic versions of *Visio Pauli* correspond to each other; Audelay's verse form is his own.

The Verse Forms of Jon the Blynde Awdelay 117

line of the preceding stanza (8. 23) the adverb 'loyally' adds alliteration, without, however, stretching the line: 'Hayle! I beleve lely in that lidy[45] ye lyght.'

Prominent among Audelay's verse forms is, as we have seen, the carol.[46] Audelay employs several stanza forms for his twenty-six carols. 'Prayer to St Winifred' (24) has, as is common in Audelay, a two-line burden in the form of a couplet, rhyming aa. The stanzas take the forms bbba, ccca, ddda, etc.; each stanza is marked with a paraph, even though the last line of each is on the same rhyme, to rhyme with and introduce the burden. Perhaps by chance, the triplet of the third stanza (ll. 9–11) is on the same rhyme as the eighth (ll. 29–31), ninth (ll. 33–5), eleventh (ll. 41–3), twelfth (ll. 45–7), and thirteenth stanzas (ll. 49–51): -el is the most common rhyme in this poem. The triplet of the first stanza (ll. 1–3) is on the same rhyme as that of the fifth (ll. 17–19) and comes close to the rhymes of the triplet of the twenty-fifth stanza (ll. 98–100) and to the rhymes of the fourteenth stanza (ll. 53–5): rhymes on -ene or -yne. Other rhymes are repeated less often.[47] Without claiming the greatest heights of prosodic art for Audelay, one could suggest that by repeated rhyming he does achieve some continuity even in poems of this very short stanza-length.

The use of repeated rhyme is not Audelay's only means of achieving continuity. 'De effusione sanguinis Christi' (4), a prayer but not in carol form, has no paraphs till line 19,[48] and the first eighteen lines are probably to be regarded as a single unit, the equivalent in length of three six-line stanzas; six lines is the stanza-length of lines 19 to 139 (each stanza marked with a paraph) except that the fourteenth stanza after the introduction,

---

[45] Whiting emends to L[a]dy. However, *levedi* and *ledy* occur in the the Harley Lyrics (the provenance of MS Harley 2253 is Shropshire); *lidy* might arise when a scribe not infrequently uses <i> for /e/, as in MS Douce 302.

[46] See pp. 107–8 and n. 26, above.

[47] This rhyming practice has been used to condemn the poet's art; thus Rasmussen (in general terms), in *Die Sprache John Audelays*, 16, §11: 'If we are to summarize everything [analysed in the dissertation], the result throws a very unflattering light on Audelay's art of rhyming: *he is an extraordinarily poor and very inexact rhymer*' ('Fassen wir alles zusammen, so wirft das Ergebnis ein sehr ungünstiges Licht auf die Reimkunst Audelay's: er ist ein ausserordentlich armer und recht ungenauer Reimer').

[48] The manuscript division into stanzas is reproduced in Halliwell's edition (n. 14, above).

the eighteenth stanza in Whiting's edition (4. 103–9), is seven lines long—for no apparent reason.[49] It has a triplet (4. 106–8) where there is normally a couplet, and that triplet rhymes on *-(si)on*, as in this position do several of the couplets (4. 4–5, 16–17, 70–1, 76–7, 94–5, 100–1; and, elsewhere in the stanza, lines 7–8 confirming the unity of lines 1–18, 21/24, 110–11, 130/3). In the same poem, the sentence begun in the antepenultimate stanza runs on into the penultimate stanza. There may be more to Audelay's stanza forms than appears at first sight, revealing poetic art, not merely varied but perhaps subtly so.

The burden of most of Audelay's carols is in the form of a couplet. Two carols have a different form for the burden. 'In die epephanis' (42) has the exclamatory 'Nowel! nowel! nowel!' (if that is strictly a burden), and that is outside the rhyme-scheme of the poem.[50] This Christmas jubilation is akin to Audelay's use of *Gaude!*, *Hayle!*, *Salue!*, and *O Jhesu!* in his *salutationes*, greetings that stand at the beginning of all or many of the stanzas and at the beginning of most of the lines within the stanzas. The burden of 'In die natalis Domini' (33) is

---

[49] In the case of the exceptional fifty-third stanza of 'De concordia inter rectores' (2. 677–88) there is a reason for it being only twelve lines long, whereas all other stanzas have thirteen lines. By making one stanza shorter by a line the total number of lines is exactly one thousand (in seventy-seven stanzas), followed by an autobiographical stanza of thirteen lines. It would be difficult for a blind poet to think of numerical perfection and to anticipate what is needed two-thirds of the way through a long poem, so that perhaps this poem may have been composed before Audelay became blind; that may account for its place early in the manuscript.

A different reason for exceptional length may account for the weighty seventeen-line stanza in the acephalous 'On the Vices' (1. 143–59). Audelay deviates from the normal thirteen-line stanza to accommodate the Ten Commandments in eleven lines followed by six lines of spiritual counsel, though a stricter versifier might have preferred the regularity of eleven lines on the Ten Commandments followed by only two of spiritual counsel.

[50] Not all agree that it is Audelay's work, or perhaps that only those stanzas are his that are not in the other versions; cf. Greene (ed.), *Early English Carols*, no. 122A (p. 67): 'By John Audelay?'. It seems that R. Dyboski (ed.), *Songs, Carols, and other Miscellaneous Poems, from the Balliol MS. 354, Richard Hill's Commonplace-Book*, EETS ES 101 (1908), p. xix, did not know Audelay's version when he commented on the version in Balliol MS 354, 'more purely narrative ... the framework is made up of lines from the hymn "*Veni, Creator Spiritus*," which gives the piece a somewhat striking, original aspect.' Chambers and Sidgwick (eds.), 'Fifteenth Century Carols', 476, comment on the fact that in most of Audelay's carols the burden consists of couplets, but in this poem 'of the Christmas jubilation "Nowell"'.

The Verse Forms of Jon the Blynde Awdelay

> Welcum, yole! in good aray
> In worchip of the holéday.

The last line of each of its five stanzas is 'Welcum, yole, for(e) ever and ay!' which rhymes with and introduces the burden.

The burden of 'De sancta Maria I' (44) is four lines long, in rhyming pairs of lines of varying length; it goes well with the six-line stanza form, the first four lines of which share the same rhyme. When the burden is added to the fourth stanza, but only to that stanza, the rhyme at the end of the stanza leads into the burden (italicized here):

> When that floure began to sprede
> And his blossum to bede,[51]
> Ryche and pore of everé lede
> Thai marvelt hou this flour myght sprede.   25
>   And kyngnys iij
>   That blesful floure come to se.
> *There is a Floure spr[u]ng of a tre,*
> *The rote ther-of is callid Jessé:*
> *A Floure of pryce,*
> *Ther is non seche in paradise.*

That Audelay[52] is not just stumbling into subtlety when matching stanza and burden is shown by 'In die circumcicionis' (38). In MS Douce 302, the phrase *ut supra* is to be expanded to *ye may here* (or *ye mow here*) within the stanza; at the end of

---

[51] Whiting's glossary suggests 'form a bead'; Chambers and Sidgwick (eds.), 'Fifteenth Century Carols', 83, give other suggestions and quote the variant reading from Balliol MS 354, for which see Dyboski (ed.), *Songs, Carols*, 6 (poem 10, l. 20) and nn. pp. 169–70. Greene's note, *Early English Carols*, 394, follows Whiting: 'form a bead or bud'. A more likely interpretation of *his blossom to bede* (MS *his his*) is perhaps 'to offer, present, show forth its blossom'. In the manuscript under ultra-violet light, the first word of Whiting's l. 26, *And kyngnys iij*, looks more like Whiting's *And* (written out) than Greene's *Til*.

[52] For Greene's view that this poem is too good to be Audelay's, see p. 102 and n. 7, above. His expansion of *ut supra* seems right; it follows Chambers and Sidgwick (eds.), 'Fifteenth Century Carols', 477 and 490–1 (nn.), based on the version in Trinity College, Cambridge, MS O. 3. 58. Assigning lines to the chorus and others to the leader and the burden to leader and chorus, as suggested by Chambers and Sidgwick, p. 477, may be fanciful. So too perhaps is my use of inverted commas; Whiting introduced inverted commas, but only in the first of the two stanzas quoted here, for the Virgin's salutation of the Child and for the Child's salutation of his mother. See also Stevens's note on his carol 27, *Mediæval Carols*, 125, discussing *ut supra* in the version of Bodleian MS Arch. Selden B. 26.

the stanza it indicates the burden. The lines of the burden end in *messangere* and *day*, and these are fitted into a comprehensive and varied rhyme-scheme; thus in the last two stanzas (38. 26–40, in Whiting), printed here with *ut supra* replaced within the stanza by the repetition (italicized), and at the end of the stanza replaced by the burden (italicized):[53]

> Thise lovelé ladé con grete her chylde,
> 'Hayle, sun! haile, broder! haile, fader dere!'
> 'Haile, doghter! haile, suster! haile, moder myld!'
> This haylsyng was on coynt manere.
> Seche wo[n]der tythyngis *ye may here*:
> This gretyng was of soche chere
> That mans pyne hit turnyd to play.
> '*What tythyngis bryngst us, messangere,*
> *Of Cristis borth this new eris day?*'
> 'That Lord that al thyng mad of noght
> Is mon becum fore mons love,
> Fore with his blood he schul be boght
> From bale to blys that is above.
> Seche wonder tythyngis *ye may here*,
> That, Lord, us grawnt now our prayoure
> To twel in heven that we may.'
> '*Seche wonder tythyngis bryngst us, messangere,*
> *Of Cristis borth this new eris day!*'

5. To Audelay: praise at the parting

It is good, at the end, at parting, to quote some of the best of Audelay's poetry. Yes, I think 'In die circumcicionis' (38) is Audelay's poem, and not the work of some greater anonym. It is easy to find in the Audelay manuscript pieces of theological exposition in verse, so unpoetic that no editor or critic would wish to deprive him of them. To some of the most didactic,

---

[53] It is perhaps a temptation to be resisted to seek to improve metrical imperfections; yet these are good stanzas, and they would sound even better with *mans* and *mons* read as two syllables, as is usual in early fifteenth-century verse for the genitive (and plural) of monosyllabic words. Disyllabic words do not always become trisyllabic, thus *tythyngis* is disyllabic. Perhaps *turnyd* may be read as a monosyllable, though that is unusual in early fifteenth-century verse. The word *prayoure* rhymes with *here* and *messangere*, in spite of the spelling *-oure* for *-ere*.

exhortatory, and remonstrative verse he attaches his name, and mentions his infirmities of body and soul. He is not a precisionist in the count of syllables and stresses, or in the sound of rhymes (made to look worse by scribal orthography); but he has a rare mastery of stanza form, and is subtle in prosodic linkings by rhyme, with alliteration a further mode. He uses other writers' verse in some of his poems, most obviously so in 'De meritis misse' (9) as his editor points out; yet even there the wording is turned by him to conform to his sermonic style in verse. His didactic narrative 'De tribus regibus mortuis' (54) combines several of his prosodic devices, seen elsewhere in the manuscript but nowhere else deployed together. In his *salutationes* and carols he often adopts a different voice in several different forms: if we had the music we could hear him sing.

6 Poetic Originality in The Wars of Alexander

PETER DRONKE

The title I have chosen may sound paradoxical. Can one really speak of the originality of a poetic text that is a translation—and for much of the time a close translation—of a Latin prose source? This Latin source, moreover—a variant, from around 1200, of the Alexander Romance that Leo of Naples had translated around 960[1]—is not one of the more compelling Alexander narratives that we possess: it is a compilation which is neither coherently shaped nor attractively written. How was it able to inspire sparkling, unpredictable writing in a vernacular poet-adapter some two centuries afterwards?[2]

---

[1] *Die Historia de preliis Alexandri Magni: Rezension J³*, ed. K. Steffens (Meisenheim am Glan, 1975). This is cited below as *Historia*, followed by page and line references. On the relation of this version to the complex tradition of Leo of Naples' *Historia* and its revisions, see esp. D. J. A. Ross, *Alexander Historiatus*, Warburg Institute Surveys, 1 (London, 1963), 47–61.

[2] On the basis of the carefully inconclusive observations of the editors, H. N. Duggan and T. Turville-Petre, *The Wars of Alexander*, EETS SS 10 (1989), pp. xlii–xliii, I assume for the poem a date of composition not too far from 1400. *MED*, when citing *The Wars*, gives the date of the Ashmole MS (*c*.1450), adding 'a. 1400?' in parenthesis. This would imply a date of composition around a century after the ME metrical *Kyng Alisaunder* (ed. G. V. Smithers, EETS OS 227, 237 (1952, 1957)), and one or two generations after the other ME alliterative Alexander fragments (1340–70): *The Gestes*, and *Alexander and Dindimus* (ed. W. W. Skeat, EETS ES 1 (1867) and 31 (1878)). *The Wars* would also be approximately contemporary with the *Prose Life of Alexander* (ed. J. S. Westlake, EETS OS 143 (1913)), and slightly earlier than the Scottish *Buik of Alexander* of 1438 (ed. R. L. G. Ritchie, STS NS 12, 17, 21, 25 (1921–9)); it would precede by several decades Sir Gilbert Hay's *Buik of King Alexander the Conquerour* (ed. J. Cartwright, STS 4th ser. 16, 18 (1986–)). It should perhaps also be recalled that there are already OE versions of two Alexander texts: A. Orchard, *Pride and Prodigies* (Cambridge, 1995), has just given new editions with translation of the OE *Wonders of the East* and *Letter of Alexander to Aristotle*. Finally, Aristotle's letter to Alexander, the *Secretum Secretorum*, enjoyed a vast fortune in England in the later Middle Ages: M. Manzalaoui (EETS OS 276 (1977)) has edited nine English versions from MSS ranging from *c*.1400 to the early Tudor period. I was unable to see Gerrit H. V. Bunt's *Alexander the Great in the Literature of Medieval Britain*, Medievalia Groningana, 14 (Groningen, 1994), before the completion of this essay; Bunt includes only a brief, mainly genealogical discussion of *The Wars*.

The English poet had an innate gift for vivacious, humorous and pungent language. Yet it is not just a matter of his infusing the jejune diction of his source with new life. At many key moments we can see that it is more: the poet fires his source with a sense of imaginative purpose. He uses two opposing but complementary strategies. One is to make the remote, exotic world of Alexander more familiar, to reinterpret its features reassuringly in terms of realities known to his audience. The other is deliberately to heighten the unfamiliar, increasing its fascination. It is with this second aim in view that he repeatedly enriches the narrative of his source with passages of *ecphrasis* that have no counterpart there—descriptive excursions in which language and imagery, while always rigorously controlled, give the effect of going 'over the top'. The characteristic technique here is an accumulative one, that is ideally well matched to alliterative versification. The cumulations make the monstrosities and the marvels, the beauties and the cruelties, inexorably larger than life—as if the poet's subject-matter itself impelled him to pile word upon word, image upon image.

In some of the poetically densest passages, the devices of accentuating the familiar as well as the unfamiliar are used in combination. The poet wants to ensure the acculturation of his material, yet he is equally concerned to outdo and surpass the realms of experience that his audience know. I shall analyse two episodes in which this double strategy seems to me particularly remarkable, and, at the close, shall hazard a suggestion about the underlying imaginative intentions. But first I shall touch more briefly on a few examples of the one device and of the other.

There is nothing in the Latin prose which deliberately evokes the Christian world of the writer's time; the English poet, by contrast, uses anachronism with knowing delight. When near the opening King Nectanebus (Anectanabus in the English text) makes his escape from Egypt, he *clede him all as a clerke* (121) and takes with him *astralabus, quadrentis* (128–9) and the full working kit of a medieval astrologer. When he wins the favour of Queen Olympias in Macedon, she summons him as *hire awyn clerke* (398). The temple of Ammon becomes *a synagoge*

(1182),³ as does that of Apollo's oracle (2309), whose priestess, Zacora, is *a semely nonn* (2306). The god Dionysus becomes *Sire Denys, a duke* (3684)—perhaps with a touch of playful euhemerism: since the Latin source explains that he is also called Bacchus and Father Liber,⁴ we may assume the poet knew who Dionysus was. On the other hand, when the Brahman Dindimus mocks Alexander's polytheism, the poet, who here had a faulty Latin text before him, failed to recognize Ceres, making her into *Serenon... sire of the wambe* (4639).⁵ A moment later, however, comes another flicker of Christian wit, as Dindimus derides Alexander for sending a wild boar *to Mars in his mynstir* (4651). Among the various pagan *mynstirs* in the poem, there is one of surpassing beauty and splendour: the palace of the Sun (5025). The poet makes the vestments and couch of the solar priest inseparably exotic and Christian: where the source knows merely that they were made of gold,⁶ in the poetry the hierophant has a blue mantle that

> Was browden all with brent gold full of bright aungels.
> The testre trased full of trones with trimballand wingis,
> The silloure full of seraphens and othire sere halows...
>
> was brocaded with burnished gold full of bright Angels,
> the bedhead carved full of Thrones with trembling wings,
> the canopy full of Seraphim and diverse saintly beings...
>
> (5040–2)⁷

The triple *full* and the *trimballand wingis* evoke no statuesque adornments but an image of consummate vital energy—as if

---

³ The editors, in their note *ad loc.* (*Wars*, p. 205), claim that '*synagoge* should be translated as "pagan temple or shrine", without special reference to Judaism'; similarly MED, s.v. *sinagoge*; none the less, the specific poetic point here, I would suggest, is analogous to that of filling Alexander's world with minsters, clerks, nuns, and the rest: a *synagoge*, even if not quite a minster, is less unfamiliar than a fane.
⁴ *Historia*, 104. 25.
⁵ The editors (*Wars*, p. 275) valuably cite a Latin MS variant—*Cerenon deum dicitis esse ventris...*—not given in the apparatus of *Historia*, 140. 9–10, which accounts for the error.
⁶ *Historia*, 156. 9–10.
⁷ With comparative and non-specialist readers in mind, I have offered translations for the verse citations here and below. These also help to indicate succinctly my way of interpreting certain nuances and problematic expressions, which would otherwise require more detailed discussion.

the pseudo-Dionysian hierarchies were coming alive and thronging the pagan shrine.

Another device the poet uses to give a sense of familiarity lies in his manipulation of point of view. Occasionally, but tellingly, he writes as if he were himself one of Alexander's men. At the siege of Tyre, Alexander's siege-towers are *all oure werke without the wallis* (1546). Alexander is *oure emperoure* (3572), *oure conquirour* (4024). At the sight of the immensity of King Porus' army, 'our company from Macedonia' (*oure meneyhe out of Messedone*) were perturbed (3732).

Familiarity is likewise achieved at the close of several of the poem's 'fitts', where moments of solemnity or horror or splendour are left lightly suspended as the final verse is given its tag-ending. Thus when the treacherous murderers of King Darius make their escape:

> Than dryfes furthe tha domesmen[8] and halfe-dede him levys,
> Famand out of fresch blod; and here a fitt endis.
>
> Then those justicers rush forth, leaving him half-dead,
> foaming out fresh blood—and here a section ends.   (3330–1)

The Latin has neither the getaway nor the foaming blood: merely 'they left him in the palace half-alive' (*dimiserunt eum in palatio semivivum*).[9] The poet first heightens the brutal scene, then brings it down to earth, with a hint of irony, as he slips back into his role as entertainer.

His most elaborate use of the jongleur's persona (which naturally has no counterpart in the source) comes with the wedding-feast of Alexander and Darius' daughter, *Rosan the riche*. It is as if to set an *entr'acte* between what the poet sees as the two acts of his drama: Act I, which concludes Alexander's triumph over the Persians with his marriage, and Act II, which depicts the adventures that lead him through the perils of India to Babylon and (if the poem was ever completed) to his own

---

[8] On *domesmen* (literally 'judges'), see *Wars*, p. 220, *ad* 1937, where it translates Latin *nuncios*; thus the editors suggest that the word 'may merely emphasise their social importance'; by my rendering, 'justicers', I imply that the poet does have the more specific sense 'judges' in mind, but here informs it with savage irony.

[9] *Historia*, 92. 3–4.

death through treachery. Then the death at the hands of base courtiers, such as Darius suffered as the first act closed, would have been echoed in Alexander's murder, making the two acts symmetrical.

In the four verses that conclude Passus XIV and the eight that open XV (3592–603), the poet turns directly to the *lordis* of his audience. There is humorous self-deprecation—even if his matter *be... bot mene*, he'd like to *tary for a time and tempire my wittis* (are they his instrument, or perhaps his weapons?)[10]—conjoined with a memorable devotional formula: 'May he that mounted to the stars station us in heaven!' After the *entr'acte*, the poet appeals to the *lordis* anew, stressing his fidelity to his source (*followand the lettir*), and asking that in their prayers they call to mind him 'that made you this mirth' (3601–3). In the last resort, the narrative that follows—of the grim ordeals and monsters of India—is mirth, re-created for the delight of a world in which God's in his heaven.

My next instance of familiarizing takes us also to the complementary device of outdoing. The poet several times mitigates the more extreme surges of brutality that Alexander displays in his source. At an encampment deep in India, the king and his army encounter a wild man (*homo agrestis*),[11] huge and hairy as a pig, whose speech consists only of porcine squeals. When Alexander tells his men to capture him, 'he did not show fear or flee, but remained intrepid before them all'. Even though the uncouth figure poses no threat, Alexander decoys him by sending a naked girl to 'that animal'; she arouses him and he grabs at her; then, at Alexander's order, the girl is taken away and the man bound and burnt alive.

The English poet had little taste for such gratuitous cruelty and contempt for human life, so he introduces some telling changes of detail. He invents an exuberantly grotesque description, making the wild man sinister and authentically bestial:

---

[10] MED, s.v. *tempren* 9d, glosses this passage '? to sharpen (one's wits), ? refresh'; the graphic quality of the poet's language, however, seems to me to admit the possibility of sense 7 ('to tune a musical instrument'), or 9a ('to work [metal . . .] to a proper degree of hardness and elasticity').

[11] *Historia*, 148. 35–150. 14.

A burly best and a bigge was as a [berne] shapen;
Umquile he groned as a galt with grysely latis
. . . .
And was as bristil[e] as a bare all the body ovire.
Dom as a dore-nayle and defe was he bathe,
With laith leggis and lange and twa laue eres.
A hevy hede and a hoge as it a hors ware,
And large was his odd lome the lenthe of a yerde.

A burly beast and a big was shaped like a man;
at times he groaned like a porker, with grisly cries
. . . .
and was as bristly as a boar all over his body.
Dumb as a doornail and deaf was he too,
with legs loathly and long and two low-hanging ears,
a heavy head and a huge, as if it were a horse,
and large was his outlandish tool, the length of a yard.

(4869–77)

Even more, when he sees the lovely naked girl (*that hend*), his impulse is murderous, rather than naturally lustful: he 'hisses like an adder: he'd have strangled her straight, had stout men not been near' (4884–5). To this extent the poet has extenuated Alexander's behaviour: even in his callous command, he remains someone whom the audience could recognize as a 'prince' (4887) rather than a mindless butcher.

The portrait of the wild man is one of the many examples of vivid, exciting *ecphraseis*, with their cascades of alliterating words, that reveal the poet's individuality of vision as well as of language. They serve a number of poetic purposes. Thus, soon after the burning of the wild man, where the Latin text says, baldly, that 'a very great abundance of dragons, serpents and lions came upon the army, which afflicted them with very great distress',[12] the poet conveys the experience of that distress by keenly specific details, to show that these men—'our men', he says, involving his audience more grippingly—faced the utmost limits of physical trials and dangers. Moreover, he adds sound-effects that set the ordeals in an atmosphere of uproar and elemental disorder:

---

[12] *Historia*, 150. 33–4: *venerunt super eos maxima copia draconum, serpentium et leonum qui angustia maxima afflixerunt eos.*

Thare was hurling on highe, as it in hell ware,
Quat of wrestling of wormes and wonding of knightis.
As gotis out of guttars in golanand wedres,
So voidis doun the vemon be vermyn[e]s schaftis.
At othir time of oure tulkis was tangid to dede
And slayn with tha serpents a sowme out of nounbre.
So hard thai hampird oure heere and herid oure erles,
Unneth it chansid thaim the cheke the cheffire to worthe.
Quen he sckonfet and skerrid all tha skathill fendis,
Then metis he doun of the mounte into a mirk vale,
A dreghe dale and a depe, a dym and a thestir;
Migh[t] thare na saule undire son see to anothire.

There was havoc on high as if it were in hell,
what with wrestling of serpents and wounding of knights.
As streams out of channels in howling weathers,
out pours the poison from vile creatures' jaws.
At times some of our men were stung to death
and slain by those serpents—a sum beyond number.
So harshly they hampered our host and harried our earls,
they had hardly the chance to prevail with their power.
When the king trounced and terrified those dangerous fiends,
he moves down from the mountain into a murky valley,
a mighty deep dale, a dim and darkling one,
no soul under the sun could there see another. (4921-32)

With the last two lines cited the poet rejoins his Latin source. Yet its dry statement, 'they came into a valley so dark that one could scarcely see another',[13] is not enough for him: with hyperbolic fantasy he continues:

> They were enveloped in that land by so thick a cloud,
> they could feel it with their fists as flapping cobwebs.[14]

The most frequent and abundant *ecphraseis* that the poet adds to the Latin are battle-descriptions. These can evoke, for instance, the exhilaration of Alexander's first chance to prove himself in combat, in his encounter with *Sire Nicollas* (894),

---

[13] Ibid. 152. 1-2: *venerunt in vallem obscuram ita, ut vix unus alium conspicere posset.*
[14] *Wars*, 4933-4:
> Thai ware umbethourid in that thede with slike a thike cloude
> That thai might fele it with thaire fiste as flabband webbis.

where the poet expands some four lines in his source to over forty, which begin (896 ff.):

> With that thai tuke up thaire trompes apon the twa sidis,
> Braidis banars abrade, buskis to mete,
> So knilid the clarons that all the cliffe rynges,
> The holtis and the haire [wode] and the hillis schenyn.
> . . . .
> Quat of stamping of stedis and stering of bernes,
> All dymed the dale and the dust ryses.
> With slik a bront and a brusche the bataill asembild,
> As the erth and all the el[e]mentis at anes had wrestild.
>
> With that they took up their trumpets upon the two sides,
> unfurl banners abroad, preparing to fight;
> so sounded the clarions that all the cliff rings,
> shattering the holts and hoar forests and hills.
> . . . .
> What with stamping of steeds and stirring of men,
> all the dale dimmed and the dust rises.
> With such racing and rushing the battle assembled
> as if earth and all elements had wrestled at once.

Here the interspersing of present-tense verbs in a narrative otherwise told in the past not only conveys the heightened vividness commonly associated with the historic present, but gives the very sense of a mêlée whose effects are still reverberating.

The descriptions can equally dwell on combat's harsher realities, as in one of the clashes of Greeks and Persians:

> Thare was stomling of stedis, stickinge of erles,
> Sharpe schudering of schote, schering of mailes,
> So stalworthly within a stond sterid thaim the Grekis,
> That of the barb[r]yne blod all the [bent] flowis.
>
> There was stumbling of steeds, stabbing of earls,
> sharp shuddering of shots,[15] cutting of coats of mail—
> so stalwartly soon did the Greeks show their mettle
> that with barbarian blood all the field flows. (2748–51)

---

[15] *Scharpe schudering of schote*: the editors (Glossary, pp. 367–8) render the words 'violent scattering of missiles'; MED, s.v. *shodering*, has '? movement; ? crashing, clashing' for this passage. In the light of the previous phrase *stickinge of erles*, however, I incline to picture *schote*—in the collective sense of 'discharges, shots', MED, s.v. *shot*, 2 (a)—entering bodies with a quivering impact (the first sense of *shodering* in MED is 'a shaking, quivering').

Poetic Originality in The Wars of Alexander

The graphic accumulations extend to a wide range of mood and tone. Where the Latin is perfunctory, the poet can choose to dwell on tender, as on savage, observation: for him the 'small and gentle bird'[16] that lays its egg in King Philip's lap

> thare hurkils and hydis as scho were hand-tame.
> Fast scho flekirs about his fete and fleytirs aboute,
> And thare it nestild in a noke, as it a nest were...
>
> crouches and hides there as if she were hand-tame,
> fast she flickers round his feet and flutters about,
> and there nestled in a nook as though it were a nest...
>
> (504–6)

Or again, the poet can feast on the macabre, as in his verses about Bucephalus, in whose cage there lie not only 'hands of men and feet and other limbs dispersed',[17] as in the Latin, but

> Tharmes thrist owt, thee-banes and shuldres,
> Som hanchyd of the heved, som the handez etyn,
> Som thair riggez owt rytte, and som thair ribbez rent.
>
> intestines thrust out, thigh-bones and shoulders,
> some with the head gnawed off, some with the hands eaten,
> some with their backs ripped out, and some with their ribs rent.
>
> (773–5)

With yet another spurt of invention, the poet can enrich the insults aimed at Alexander's puny size with all the verve of vernacular flytings and their pithy, often colloquial range of rudeness. Thus the Persians show Darius Alexander's portrait:

> Ane amlaghe, ane asalen, ane ape of all othire,
> A wirling, a wayryngle, a wawil-eyid shrewe,
> The cait[if]este creatour that cried was evire.
>
> a nobody, a little ass, an ape beyond all others,
> a dwarf, a butcher-bird, an odd-eyed shrew,[18]
> the most contemptible creature ever created. (1829–31)

---

[16] *Historia*, 12. 22.   [17] Ibid. 18. 15.
[18] The editors (p. 371) gloss *shrewe* as 'wretch'; but in view of the three other animal terms of abuse in these verses (*asalen*, *ape*, and *wayryngle*), I suspect that the literal sense, 'shrew-mouse', may be in the poet's mind. On the other hand, *OED* has no example of this literal sense between 900 and 1538, and *MED*, s.v. *shreue*, gives figurative senses only.

132   Peter Dronke

Darius, in his letter of defiance, capitalizes on this:

> And slike a dwinny[n]ge, a dwa[l]we, a dwerghe as thiselfe,
> A grub, a grege out of Gr[e]ce, ane erd-growyn sorowe...
>
> such a wizened one, a weakling, a dwarf like yourself,
> a grub, a gnat from Greece, an earth-grown disaster...
>
> (1876–7)

I should now like to try to adumbrate an imaginatively more profound use of both familiarizing and outdoing devices, in two episodes: Alexander's entry into Jerusalem, and his encounter with Candace.

In the poet's source,[19] both Alexander and the high priest, Jaddus, have dreams that reveal their destiny. An 'angel of the Lord' appears to Jaddus, commanding him to open the gates of Jerusalem and go without fear, with all his people robed in white, to greet Alexander. The King, instead of descending on the city as a destroyer, sees Jaddus' mitre, with the tetragrammaton, YHWH, inscribed in gold, and falls to the ground: he adores the name of God, and venerates the priest who bears it. Acclaimed by the Jews, he goes to sacrifice in the Temple, and there Jaddus shows him that he is the predestined victor over the Persians, he who had been foretold in the Book of Daniel.

The English poet invests the key moments of this episode with Christian associations: by his language and imagery, I would suggest, he presents the city's greeting of Alexander in a montage close to that of the Palm Sunday liturgy. First he conveys a blithe tumult and a sense of lavish welcome, Jerusalem and its high priest striving to be worthy of the King who is about to enter:

> Than rynnes he furth in a rase, arais all the cite,
> Braidis ovire with bawdkyns all the brade stretis,
> With tars and with tafeta thare he trede sulde,
> For the erth to slike ane emperoure ware ovire-feble.
>
> Then runs he forth racing, arrays all the city,
> braids over with baldachins all the broad streets,

---

[19] *Historia*, 34. 7 ff.

with Tharsian silk and taffeta where he should tread,
for the earth for such an emperor would be over-poor.

(1636–9)

The verses cannot but recall the garments that the populace in Jerusalem strewed upon Christ's route. Jaddus is called *oure bischop* (1629),[20] and he is robed in riotous episcopal splendour:

> And sithen he castis on a cape of kastand hewes,
> With riche r[y]b[an]s of gold railed bi the hemmes,
> A vestoure to vise on of violet floures,
> Wroght full of wodwose and othir wild bestes...
>
> Then he casts on a cope of coruscating hues,
> with rich ribbons of gold railed at the hems,
> a vestment to view of violet flowers,
> wrought full of woodsprites and other wild beasts...

(1660–3)

His mitre was

> Stight staffull of stanes that straght[en] out bemes,
> As it ware shemerand shaftis of the shire son.
>
> set surfeited with stones that sent out their beams
> like shimmering shafts of the sheer sun. (1666–7)

Where on Palm Sunday it is a liturgical procession of boys that sings the hymn of acclaim, *Gloria, laus et honor*, to the approaching Christ, here for Alexander

---

[20] In the Latin (34. 7 *et passim*), Iaddus is *pontifex Iudeorum*. The basis for this appellation may well lie in the Vulgate of St John's Gospel, where the high priest Caiaphas is several times called *pontifex* (John 11: 49 and 51; 18: 13). In her essay 'Alejandro en Jerusalén' (*Romance Philology*, 10 (1956–7), 185–96), María Rosa Lida de Malkiel pointed out that in various vernacular adaptations of the matter of Alexander Jaddus is designated bishop or even pope, and in particular in the thirteenth-century Spanish *Libro de Alexandre* there are a number of touches that show how 'the intention of making the source appear contemporary, without taking archaeological distance, gives the anachronisms their point' (p. 191 n. 7). Thus in the Spanish poem Jaddus puts on the vestment with which 'he said mass' (*la misa dizié*, 1137), and later not only a mitre but 'a dalmatic' (*una dalmática*, 1154). None the less, the Spanish poet does not invest the episode with any more pervasive *figura Christi* symbolism, nor does he have that element of 'taking sides' which the English poet once more indicates lightly by his expression '*oure* bischop'.

> Thare passis the procession a piple beforne,
> Of childire all in [c]halk-quyte, chosen out a hundreth,
> With bellis and with baners and blasand torchis,
> Instrumentis and ymagis within of the mynstire;
> Sum with sensours and so, with silviryn cheynes,
> Quareof the reke aromatike rase to the welken.
>
> In front of the people passes the procession
> of children all in chalk-white, a hundred chosen,
> with bells and with banners and blazing torches,
> instruments and images from within the minster,
> some with censers and suchlike, with silver chains,
> the spicy smoke of which rose to the skies.   (1684–9)

The poet expands the Latin acclamations of Alexander by the citizens—

> The wildire of all the werde and worthist on erthe!
> . . . .
> The gretest and the gloriosest that ever god formed...
>
> the wielder of all the world and worthiest on earth!
> . . . .
> the greatest and the gloriousest that ever God formed—
>   (1731–4)

the phrases coming close to the crowd's cries in Luke (19: 38): 'Blessed is the King who comes in the Lord's name: peace on earth and glory in heaven!' And in a sense Alexander entering Jerusalem *is* its saviour: he spares the city, even though previously the high priest, an ally of the Persians, had refused him tribute. But the paradox is that this sublime moment in Alexander's career, in which—for the medieval English poet, though not for his Latin source—Alexander becomes virtually *figura Christi*, comes about through his gesture of self-abnegation, prostrating himself in adoration of Yahweh. The poet makes the scene joyous and brilliantly coloured in ways that leave the Latin text far behind; at the same time, all the details by which he outdoes his source become ways of giving the episode a new foundation, in the Christian *imaginaire*.

The Candace episode is very different in tone: with its tricking and countertricking, it comes close to fabliau. Alexander arrives at the Queen's palace pretending to be a Macedonian courtier, but she, who had secretly ordered a portrait of him in advance, unmasks him, leaving him defenceless. While the battle of wits between Candace and Alexander is depicted in all the principal western versions of the Greek Romance, it would seem to be the twelfth-century German poet Lamprecht (or his lost Provençal source, Alberic) who first gave the scene a sexual dimension. In Lamprecht's poem, Candace, having taken Alexander to her chamber, says:

'I know well who you are. No cunning that you have, bold hero, will help you now: you are in my power. What use to you is your might, or your victories over many lands? ... Now a woman has vanquished you, without a fight ... Don't be angry, noble hero, put on a manly disposition ... I shan't give you away ...'
The lofty queen revealed her desire to me. Then in silence I made love with her. As I took her, she said I was her man; I was to leave off sulking, no evil would befall me.[21]

Whilst in every version Candace saves Alexander's life by keeping his identity secret, neither the English poet nor his Latin source tell that the pair become reconciled through lovemaking. Or rather, the English poet may imply it, though very discreetly, by way of another of his poetic feats in which, as in Alexander's entry into Jerusalem, the language of dazzling cumulations and that of familiar biblical echoes combine to create a surprising effect.

Both the Latin and the English tell that Candace's looks reminded Alexander of his mother, Olympias. Yet where the Latin has only the detached comment, 'the Queen was very beautiful',[22] the English poet launches into one of his most mettlesome evocations: he begins:

> Scho was so faire and so fresche, as faucon hire semed,
> An elfe out of anothire erde or ellis an aungell.
> Hire palais was full precious, thof parades [it] ware ...

---

[21] *Lamprechts Alexander*, ed. K. Kinzel (Halle am Saale, 1884), 6161 ff. (Strasbourg redaction).
[22] *Historia*, 166. 10 (*Erat autem regina formosa nimis*—at *Wars*, p. 292 the editors cite the MS variant *pulchra, formosa plurimum et decora*).

>   She was so fair and so fresh, like a falcon she seemed,
>   An elf out of another earth, or else an angel.
>   Her palace was all precious, as if it were paradise...
>
>   (5383-5)

This poet is fond of imagery of heaven and paradise, of which his Latin source knows nothing. For him, both the palace of Cyrus (3345) and the temple of the Sun (5032) are paradisal; Jerusalem, as Alexander is about to enter, *seems ane of the sevyn hevyns* (1651); in one of the loveliest lines in the whole poem, we learn that the Brahmans delight to walk in leaf-locked woods—

> Quen all is lokin ovire with levys, as it ware littill heven. (4512)

With Candace, the paradisal imagery colours the verse more and more. Of her summer hall: *Was nane so comly a close undire the cape of heven* (5392); it has precious stones *of paradise stremes* (5396); and at last, as Candace leads Alexander, all alone (5413), into her wondrous revolving chamber, comes a paradisal touch of a different kind from all the gold and gems that preceded: this *clochere*

>   Was sammed all of sipris and seder tables.
>   was assembled all of cypress and cedar tablets. (5416)

Even the excellent recent editors did not recognize that with this verse the poet takes us into the Song of Songs:

>   tigna domorum nostrarum *cedrina*,
>   laquearia nostra *cypressina*... (1: 16)
>
>   si ostium est, conpingamus illud *tabulis cedrinis*;
>   ego murus et ubera mea turris... (8: 9–10)
>
>   the beams of our dwelling are cedar,
>   our panelling is cypress...
>
>   If there is a door, let us adorn it with cedar tablets;
>   I am the wall, and my breasts are the tower...

It seems to me likely that for at least some of the poet's audience the secret room *all of sipris and seder tables* must have evoked the bridal bower of the Canticle and its erotic associations. The poetic subtlety is that here the erotic moment is conjured up *before* Alexander is humiliatingly identified by the Queen. Unlike Lamprecht, the English poet does not, after Alexander is outwitted, go on to tell of sexual consumation. Instead, by his fleeting allusion to the unique *thalamus* of the Song of Songs, before the King's exposure, he has delicately enhanced his narrative with a hint of a more blissful love, that looks beyond the fabliau situation, while still not troubling the narrative flow. Candace's palace is indeed a paradise—though a precarious one. We now see why at the outset she was evoked as falcon, as angel, and as elf: she is as dangerous as a bird of prey, but she is also the angel who guards the hero's life and the elf who routs him with her lovingly malicious teasing: 'Why splutter so, Sir Conqueror, and make your soul so crabbish?' (5449).[23]

We have noted the cumulative language of outdoing alongside the familiarizing language that anchors Alexander's world in the medieval Christian one; we have seen some instances of how what is rich and strange in Alexander's world can, through poetic syncretism, assimilate Christ's entry into Jerusalem, or pseudo-Dionysian angels, or the inner chamber of the Song of Songs. It remains to ask, can we discern an imaginative principle underlying such combination? Is it simply a heady, virtuoso delight in the gamut of expressive possibilities in late medieval alliterative poetry, or is there a further poetic secret?

It seems to me that the twofold orientation in language and content which is one of the distinguishing features of *The Wars of Alexander* reflects and reinforces a twofold perception of Alexander himself, that we can document far more widely in medieval literature, and that I shall try to characterize briefly in more general terms.

---

[23] 'Qui colkins thou, sire conquirour, and crabbis so thi saule?' *MED*, s.v. *colkenen*, relates this *hapax legomenon* to Danish *kulke* ('drink with a gurgling sound') and German dialectal *kolksen* ('burp'). The editors (*Wars*, p. 293) reject this on the ground that the Latin (*Historia*, 168. 13–14) has only '*Ut quid infra temet ipsum irasceris et turbaris?*' Thus they gloss *colkins* (p. 316) as 'become angry(?)'. But this is a dubious line of argument: examples of the poet's enlivening the language of his source are legion; in this verse alone, the sardonic addition of *sire conquirour*, and the rendering of *turbaris* by *crabbis so thi saule*, are sufficient indication that he was likely, too, to come up with something more piquant than 'Why do you become angry?'

The medieval Alexander was an *intrinsically* ambiguous figure —and it was precisely his ambiguity that made him seem so captivating. However diversely medieval writers and their audiences assessed Alexander, the stories about him catered to two contrary but complementary needs: they met the demands of wish-fulfilment and those of moral satisfaction. On the one hand, Alexander's career fulfilled a host of human longings. He seemed the nearest among men to have achieved unbounded existence: he broke every known confine of physical discovery, finding new realms of every kind and claiming them for himself —so many historical kingdoms, but also, in the legends, the heavens and the ocean's depths, and (almost) the earthly paradise. He is a visionary, driven within by a sense of destiny, a seemingly more than human force;[24] yet he is also a consummate trickster, often disguising himself as one of his own courtiers or messengers, even at the risk of his life. He becomes a fabulous Oriental potentate, whose every caprice, for good or ill, magnificently generous or wantonly cruel, is instantly fulfilled; yet he is likewise (*avant la lettre*) a Faust, a restless conqueror of knowledge as well as power, who never asks the passing moment to linger, but is forever impelled, unquenchably and sublimely, towards a moment that appears more perfect still.

On the other hand, against the stories of the intoxicating fantasies and the aspirations realized, are set again and again the cautionary tales, the *exempla*, the reminders: he was small, often weak, often afraid, often flawed in character, at times even pusillanimous. And this account too is welcome, for it is reassuring. Alexander was not in essence different from ourselves. If the mythical projection had been purely that of a superman, it would carry little meaning for common humanity. So it was important to stress that the impaired, vulnerable condition which we experience was his as well as ours, that even

---

[24] The poet, translating Alexander's words to the Gymnosophists ('*Vellem siquidem in pace consistere, sed alius spiritus, qui sensui meo dominatur, me hoc facere non permittit*', *Historia*, 124. 11–12), endows them with a sombre, incantatory splendour (4193–4):

'My will ware to riste,
Bot anothir gast and noght my gast thareof my gast lettis.'

a conqueror can be humbled, that even the mightiest of men can die young.

The Alexander of the great feats of outdoing is complemented by the Alexander of familiar human littleness. This complementarity is explored most profoundly near the close of the greatest of the medieval Alexander romances, Walter of Châtillon's *Alexandreis*.[25] Yet it is also, at least in some measure, manifest in a poetic presentation such as that of *The Wars of Alexander*. Here it is the language of outdoing and the language of familiarity, the flights of alliterative *ecphrasis* and the liturgical-biblical allusions, which, with notable aptness and power, suggest the ambivalence of this hero, who seems half to outstrip the poet's Christian cosmos and yet half to belong to it. It is especially in the 'ulterior motives' of the diction and the allusions that the originality of this poem lies.

---

[25] I have tried to show this in some detail in a longer essay, the 'Introduzione' to the forthcoming anthology of texts with facing Italian translations, *Alessandro nel Medioevo* (Fondazione Valla, Mondadori, Milan).

7 Counter-Romance: Civil Strife and Father-Killing in the Prose Romances

HELEN COOPER

... down into the dyke, and thare he felle, and was all to-frusched; and than Alexander said unto hym one this wyse. 'Fals wreche,' quothe he, 'that presumes to tell thynges that ere to com, reghte als thou were a prophete, and knewe the prevatés of heuen, now may thou see that thou lyes, and tharefore thou arte worthy to hafe swilke a dede.' And than Anectanabus ansuerd, and said: 'I wyste wele ynoghe,' quoth he, 'that I scholde die swylke a dede. Talde I noghte lange are to the, that myn awenn son schulde slae me?' 'Whi, ame I thi son?' than quoth Alexandire. 'Yaa, for sothe,' quoth Anectanabus, 'I gat the.' And with that word, he yalde the gaste.[1]

It is an accident of history, in the shape of a damaged manuscript, that the very first sentences to survive of what is probably the earliest English prose romance describe a son's killing of his father; but it is none the less a symbolic accident. The long-established tradition of metrical romances in English had occasionally allowed in ideas of family strife, but their general tenor was much more towards reunion, reconciliation, the due succession of father by heir—all the characteristics that are generally taken to be defining features of romance down through the Middle Ages to Shakespeare and beyond. The prose romance was the major contribution of the fifteenth century to the development of the whole genre in English, and its keynote is very different. Treachery and murder within the body politic or the kin group, the slaying of father by son, the failure to

---

[1] *The Prose Life of Alexander*, ed. J. S. Westlake, EETS OS 143 (1913), 7–8; from the Thornton MS, Lincoln Cathedral 91, fo. 1ʳ.

pass on good rule in a strong and righteous order of succession, and sometimes also incest, are repeated and urgent themes in these works. There are exceptions, of course, just as there are exceptions to the happy endings of metrical romances; but it is still true that the prose romances differ from the stanzaic ones not just in medium but in structure and content, to the point where they demand a rethinking of our conception of the genre.

The definition of genre as the conforming of a literary text to a certain horizon of expectation[2] has as its corollary that one has to bear in mind two sets of expectations: those contemporary with a work's composition and reception, and those of modern readers and scholars. There is an immediate problem with the prose romances, that the two sets may not be the same. Modern expectations have been shaped by the assumption that a prose romance is just a metrical romance in a different medium, and confirmed by their coexistence as an apparently authoritative single canon in such bibliographical compilations as the Romances volume of the *Manual of Writings in Middle English*.[3] But the modern plausibility of the volume's listings says nothing about whether the same categorization would have seemed plausible at the time the works were written. In the fifteenth century, there was more than just a change of medium involved in the writing of prose romance; a shift from verse into prose reflects a shift in association and literary context, a shift, therefore, of horizon. It seems that the very act of writing in prose, with its associations with genres such as chronicle history that made more direct claims to truth, brought with it different expectations for both authors and readers, and therefore also a shift in the centre of gravity of the romance genre. Furthermore, as Gabrielle Spiegel notes,

---

[2] Hans Robert Jauss, 'Theorie der Gattungen und Literatur des Mittelalters', in *Alterität und Modernität der mittelalterlichen Literatur: Gesammelte Aufsätze 1956–76* (Munich, 1977), 76–138 (p. 110).

[3] *Manual*, vol. i: *Romances* (1967). Its listings for prose romances are supplemented by George R. Keiser, 'The Romances', in A. S. G. Edwards (ed.), *Middle English Prose: A Critical Guide to Major Authors and Genres* (New Brunswick, 1984), esp. 284–6. The earliest prose 'romance' listed by Keiser (p. 284), a version of King Arthur, is in fact an extract from the Middle English prose *Brut*, so is excluded from consideration here.

The exact timing, location, and generic embodiment that give rise to prose composition are not necessarily the result of 'natural' linguistic process . . . The conditions under which prose narratives originate are as various as the cultures that produce them. In some cultures and at some times prose may represent a natural evolution of literary language, while in other places and periods it is socially generated by precise cultural needs and possesses ideological functions and meanings.[4]

The changes in content and ethos betwen English verse and prose romances suggest that there may be just such a cultural impetus behind the belated appearance of prose romance in England, over two centuries after the form had emerged in France.

Since the work of Johan Huizinga, the fifteenth century has often been accused of pursuing a fantasy of high chivalry that disguised the moribundity of its underlying ideology.[5] The abundance of copyings of metrical romances in this period, while war with France was briefly won and protractedly lost and England endured decades of intermittent civil war, could support just such an interpretation, though in the 1440s John Metham suggested rather that the increase in political unrest, 'encreasing of vexation', militated against new chivalric writing.[6] His own contribution to the genre, a rhyme-royal romance entitled *Amoryus and Cleopes*, is a version of the Pyramus and Thisbe story that incorporates a good deal of colourful chivalric action, and ends with a hermit resurrecting the dead lovers and baptizing them and their whole pagan society. The bulk of prose romances of the century, however, offer no such escape routes to a happy

---

[4] Gabrielle M. Spiegel, *Romancing the Past: The Rise of Vernacular Prose Historiography in Thirteenth-Century France* (Berkeley and Los Angeles, 1993), 2. The linguistic processes at work in the shift to prose are discussed by John H. Fisher, 'Chancery and the Emergence of Standard Written English in the Fifteenth Century', *Speculum*, 52 (1977), 870–99.

[5] Huizinga's *Waning of the Middle Ages* was first published in English in 1924, and continuing reprints testify to its continuing influence. Ironically, his faith in the rationalism of his own modern world and the unproblematic innocence of his references to male bonding make the book now appear itself the assertion of a dying ideology.

[6] *The Works of John Metham*, ed. Hardin Craig, EETS OS 132 (1916), *Amoryus and Cleopes*, l. 2189. For an argument that verse romance was itself perceived in the fifteenth century as an active defence against threats to religious and political order, see Helen Cooper, 'Romance after 1400', in David Wallace (ed.), *The Cambridge History of Medieval English Literature* (Cambridge, forthcoming).

ending, nor to any assertion of a providential ordering of human life. The testimony of these works indicates that their authors found a new literary form in which to express a more realistic and bleaker view of the world they lived in. The most famous of them, Sir Thomas Malory, makes the parallel explicit as he relates the civil war that marks the collapse of the Arthurian world to his own times, in his castigation of 'ye all Englysshemen' who have not yet lost the old custom of being discontented with their king.[7] The typical metrical romance ends with the succession of the true heir; the disrupted successions of the fifteenth century are much more accurately reflected in the prose romances.

I take as a working definition of prose romance those prose narratives with a primarily secular focus; aristocratic protagonists; a main concern generally with chivalry or love; and an exotic setting, far away or long ago, or both. The secularity distinguishes them from another genre moving more hesitantly into English prose in the fifteenth century, the saint's life, and it also excludes works such as the prose *Siege of Jerusalem*.[8] The exoticism of setting distinguishes them from histories such as the prose *Brut*, which may start long ago but which moves into the familiar present; and the distance of their subject-matter from the time or place they were written means that their contents are what we would broadly define as fiction, though much of the base material would have been taken in the fifteenth century as broadly historical. Six of the ten such works composed or translated before 1500 by authors other than Caxton, plus a seventh example from just after the turn of the century, illustrate this shift of generic centre, and form the focus of this essay. Of the other four pre-1500 romances, three are close translations of French originals that do not show the same tendency;[9] I largely exclude consideration of Caxton

---

[7] *The Works of Sir Thomas Malory*, ed. Eugene Vinaver, 3 vols. (3rd edn. rev. P. J. C. Field, Oxford, 1990), p. 1229 (XXI. 1 in Caxton's numbering).

[8] This is however included in the *Manual* (i. 163, #107); and see also Keiser, 'Romances', 276. There are two distinct fifteenth-century prose versions. Their content, which includes child cannibalism as well as the destruction of the city, would none the less fit well with my discussion here.

[9] These are *King Ponthus* and *Merlin* of the mid-century and *The Three Kings' Sons* of c.1500; the remaining work is the prose *Ipomedon* of c.1460, drawn from Hue de

since his own generic assumptions were formed so extensively by the Burgundian literary milieu where he spent so many years, and because the systems of commercial publication by print, commission, and patronage within which he made his translations tended to generate a different set of 'cultural needs and ideological functions'. The first six of the seven romances with which I am concerned—the stories of Thebes, Troy, Alexander, Charlemagne, Arthur, and Melusine—fall into the category of legendary history, though the last two in particular edge over into the implausible and overtly fictional; the seventh and latest, *Valentine and Orson*, makes no claims at all to be other than fantasy, but is all the more interesting in showing the same resetting of generic expectation as the others.

Both the choice of prose over verse for stories of disaster, even when they also recount chivalric and amatory material, and the selection of such material for adaptation or translation into English prose, show that shift in the centre of gravity away from the comforting ideologies of the verse romances, with their calamities avoided or redeemed and political and familial order restored, to narratives that precisely deny those comforts. The outlines of the stories of many of the 'disaster romances' often pre-date the emergence of romance in the twelfth century; their immediate sources range over widely differing generic and linguistic backgrounds. Lydgate's English verse *Troy Book* and *Destruction of Thebes* provide the immediate source for two of the earliest, the prose epitomes the *Siege of Troy* and the *Siege of Thebes*;[10] Lydgate's own versions already downplay the elements in the stories associated in the Middle Ages with romance, such as high chivalry and love, to emphasize treason and destruction. Hector may elsewhere be treated as a chivalric hero on the romance model (as in the metrical *Laud Troy*

Rotelande's verse *Ipomedon*. A fifth prose work of before 1500, the Dublin *Alexander* fragments, is largely based on Caxton's *Dicts and Sayings of the Philosophers*.

[10] They are edited by Friedrich Brie, 'Zwei mittelenglische Prosaromane: *The Sege of Thebes* und *The Sege of Troy*', *Anglia*, 130 (1913), 40–52, 269–85. The prose *Troy* draws on *Troilus and Criseyde* in addition to Lydgate's *Troy Book* (C. David Benson, 'Chaucer's Influence on the Prose "Sege of Troy"', *N&Q* 261 (1971), 127–30). The epitomes were made between the completion of Lydgate's source poems in 1420/1422 and their mid-century copying; they are therefore likely to be closely contemporary with the *Life of Alexander*, which was copied into the Thornton manuscript around 1440.

Book of *c*.1400), Aeneas's descendants may go on to found the nations of the West, but the story of Troy itself is one of catastrophe. The Oedipus story has notorious associations with the form that is almost the opposite of romance, tragedy, and no medieval narrative treatment altered its basic outline. The outlines of the story of Alexander were laid down by the facts of his own life as assimilated into Greek and Latin prose legendary biography. The very earliest, cryptic, reference to Arthur and Mordred is a bare note of their falling in battle; Malory's own sources lie in French prose romance, English metrical and alliterative romance, and probably English verse chronicle as well, but he makes the threat of disaster more of a constant presence than in any of them. The anonymous English prose Charlemagne romance is a translation, made probably before 1450, of the Latin *Pseudo-Turpin Chronicle*, which concludes with the death of Roland: the earliest version of the story is of course the *chanson de geste, Chanson de Roland*. Caxton's own romances include some with origins in chronicle (*Godfrey of Bouillon*) and, with prose intermediaries, *chanson de geste* (*The Four Sons of Aymon* and the end of *Charles the Great*, both on the Matter of France and both concerned with war or treachery within the polity). The English prose romance often therefore has more in common in terms of content and structure with the vernacular epic or the poems of the alliterative revival than with metrical romance. The bias towards disaster remains, however, even when the basic stories do belong to the age of romance, as in the instances of *Melusine* and, in particular, *Valentine and Orson*. The English versions of both are derived from French prose originals, but both stories also exist in metrical versions that show up just how uneasy is the generic relationship between prose and verse romance.

The episode quoted at the head of this essay, of Alexander's slaying of the magician Anectanabus—who had lain with his mother in the guise of a god, and who has just foreseen in the stars that his son will kill him—does not have any disastrous repercussions on Alexander's own triumphant career, though the number of figures he takes as in some sense fathers (Anectanabus,

Philip, the god Amon) gains a retrospective irony with his own early death without a lineal heir to preserve his vast conquests. The pattern suggested by the unwitting act of parricide emerges more strongly when it is set beside the other two texts that compete with it for the possible earliest dating of prose romance texts, the *Siege of Troy* and the *Siege of Thebes*. The prominence of kin-killing and civil strife in the history of Thebes is too familiar to require exposition, but it is striking how closely Edippes' slaying of his father in the prose *Thebes* agrees with the narrative outline of the parallel episode in the *Alexander*. In both, the father knows by prophecy how he will die; each son learns without any advance preparation that the king he imagines to be his true father is not so; each kills his real father in a temper and without knowing his identity. The consequences of Edippes' action—his marriage to his mother; their incestuous sons' hatred for him, 'putting him onder fote so, that he died in grete myschef' (p. 49); the civil war between those sons; their destruction of each other along with the kingdom—make up the rest of the story.

Fore hit preved well there of theym two, that weren so horribly gotten ayenst all nature and ordenaunce, for as clerkes seyn, blode to touche blode, bringeth forth corrupt frute. (p. 269)

Here, Edippes' initial parricide and incest initiates a cycle of kin-killing and political catastrophe that takes two generations to work itself out.

The history of the fall of Troy does not offer directly comparable models of incest and kin-slaying, but the prose *Siege of Troy* is none the less cast so as to emphasize the dark side of the war. The key word of the work, repeated in episode after episode, is 'treason'—destruction from within, from inside the family or the fellowship or the state. The epitome opens with an account of how Pelleus 'compassed tresoun' against his nephew Jason to prevent his succession to his father's crown, showing him 'hole love outeward, where there was ful dedely hate inward' (p. 273); it passes rapidly through Medea's betrayal of her homeland, abandonment by Jason, and her killing of her children; describes how Hecuba requites Achilles' 'fals tresoun' in mutilating Troilus' body with a further treacherous plot of her own to murder him (p. 284); finishes with the combined treachery of Calcas, Antenor, and Eneas in making the horse that brought the Greeks within the city; and signs off with the moral,

And alwey the ende of every tresoun and falsenes to sorowe and myschef at the last. Amen. (p. 285)

By this reading, the whole history of Troy is driven by jealousy, hatred, and division within successive kin groups; and here, as in the *Siege of Thebes*, it ends not in happiness and restored order, as one expects of romances, but in personal and political disaster.

Betrayal from within is similarly the keynote of the fifteenth-century prose Charlemagne romances. Most of the verse romances concerned with the Matter of France tell of chivalric exploits, combats against pagan champions who are eventually baptized, Christian princesses who fall in love with them, Saracen princesses who fall in love with the peers, marvels, miracles, and relics. Only two of the ten surviving metrical romances (the English *Song of Roland* itself, and *Otuel and Roland*) recount Ganelon's treachery and the disaster at Roncesvalles. That, however, constitutes the narrative of the anonymous prose translation of the *Pseudo-Turpin Chronicle*;[11] and the two other fifteenth-century prose romances on Charlemagne, both translations by Caxton, similarly focus on disaster, *Charles the Great* again concluding with Roncesvalles, *The Four Sons of Aymon* recounting the long blood-feud waged by Charlemagne against Renaud of Montauban and his brothers—a feud that feeds on divided loyalties and amounts to a protracted civil war.

The most famous medieval example of the realm brought down by internal faction fostered by incest is Malory's Arthuriad; and the downfall and destruction of the Round Table is

---

[11] See Stephen Shepherd, 'The Middle English *Pseudo-Turpin Chronicle*', *MÆ* 65 (1996), 19–34; an edition by Shepherd is in preparation. The work is not mentioned in the *Manual*; for the other Charlemagne romances, see i. 80–100, ##45–61. *Huon of Burdeux* (c.1534) is also a prose romance loosely attached to Charlemagne, but of a very different kind from the fifteenth-century examples.

not a matter of historical or narrative interest alone. A drawing together of the legendary past and disordered present seems to lie behind much of his shaping of his Arthurian material. What happens in the *Morte Darthur*, and the fact that it is written in prose, may seem now to be inevitable: it is, after all, a translation from French prose originals that already included the story of Arthur's fall and his death at the hands of Mordred.[12] But to Malory in the 1460s, the choices facing him were not provided with any obvious answers. All but one of the earlier English translations of Arthurian prose romances had chosen verse as their medium, from the early fourteenth-century *Of Arthour and Merlin*, down through the stanzaic *Morte Arthur* (*c*.1400) and the vast couplet versions of *Merlin* and the *History of the Holy Grail* produced by the Londoner Henry Lovelich in the 1420s; and writers after Malory were still making the same decision for verse, for instance the author of the Scottish *Lancelot of the Laik* (?1470s). The one exception to verse translation before Malory is the anonymous *Merlin* translated from the Vulgate cycle around the mid-century, which was apparently unknown to him (his own source for the equivalent material is the non-Vulgate *Suite du Merlin*). The English works he knew and used were all in verse of one kind or another: the stanzaic *Morte Arthur*, the alliterative *Morte Arthure*, even the substantial Arthurian section of John Hardying's mid-century rhyme-royal chronicle.[13] If P. J. C. Field is right, Malory himself may have tried his hand at composing Arthurian romance in verse too, as the prisoner author of *The Wedding of Sir Gawain*

---

[12] It is widely accepted that the prose *remaniement* of Arthurian material in French was similarly a response to a cultural moment, and this has been taken as an argument against reading Malory's appropriation of them in analogous terms: see e.g. William Calin, *The French Tradition and the Literature of Medieval England* (Toronto, 1994), 506, 'The cultural crisis of the fifteenth century exemplified in *Le Morte Darthur* proves also to be a cultural crisis of the thirteenth century.' But this overlooks both Malory's reshaping of his sources, and the new significances that traditional material can assume in different circumstances (a notable modern example would be Sophocles' *Antigone*, banned by the Greek colonels). See also Elizabeth T. Pochoda, *Arthurian Propaganda: Le Morte Darthur as an Historical Ideal of Life* (Chapel Hill, NC, 1971).

[13] See Edward D. Kennedy, 'Malory and his English Sources', in Toshiyuki Takamiya and Derek Brewer (eds.), *Aspects of Malory* (Cambridge and Totowa, NJ, 1981), 27–55 (pp. 42–8); and *The Chronicle of Iohn Hardyng*, ed. Henry Ellis (London, 1812), 118–49 (caps. lxxii–lxxxv).

and Dame Ragnell.[14] So prose was not the natural medium that it seems with hindsight: it was deliberately chosen, and, it would seem, chosen to accommodate just such a generic shift away from romance, to civil war, treachery, and murder within the fellowship and the kin-group.

Malory's selection and treatment of topics from across the corpus of Arthurian romance was similarly deliberate: he did not just rework what was in front of him. The sources he was using offered him a range of different traditions, some of them incompatible or contradictory; he selects from those to present a single coherent vision of Arthurian history such as overrides the radical differences of story and interpretation between the *Suite du Merlin* and Hardyng, the alliterative *Morte Arthure* and the *Queste del Saint Graal*. In Malory, the greatest chivalric fellowship ever known is brought down, not so much by the moral and religious shortcomings revealed by the Grail Quest, as happens in the French Vulgate cycle, but by the splitting of the kingdom into viciously hostile magnate affinities in a manner analogous to his own age of the Wars of the Roses. The process is begun in his *Tristram*, when Gawain and his brothers, Arthur's nephews, avenge their father King Lot's death by murdering Sir Lamorak, son of Lot's killer Pellinore; it is continued in their jealous hatred of Lancelot and therefore also of his kin-group, and carried through to disaster in the blood-feud that follows Lancelot's accidental slaying of Gareth. The final battle pits Arthur against the nephew who is also his own incestuous son, Mordred.

The tradition that makes Mordred Arthur's son is first found in the Vulgate cycle; his mother is Arthur's half-sister (daughter of Ygerne by her first husband Gorlois), wife of King Lot of Lothian, and named by Malory as Morgause. This is far more subversive than the 'historical' tradition founded by Geoffrey of Monmouth that makes Mordred the legitimate son of Lot by Arthur's ful sister, daughter to Uther and Ygerne, here named

---

[14] P. J. C. Field, 'Malory's *The Wedding of Sir Gawain and Dame Ragnell*', *Archiv*, 219 (1982), 374–81. Field acknowledges the difference of ethos from the *Morte Darthur* as a problem; but this could be accommodated within the shift from verse romance to prose.

Anna.¹⁵ Geoffrey's account was followed by the most widely known of the histories of England, the prose *Brut*; and Scottish historiographers from the late fourteenth through to the sixteenth century, keen to refute English claims over Scotland, go still further, making Mordred Lot's eldest son, and therefore, since they also argue that Arthur was begotten in adultery, Uther Pendragon's legitimate heir.¹⁶ Hardyng also makes Mordred legitimate despite his familiarity with the Vulgate tradition (but not surprisingly given his concern to cleanse the whole Arthurian narrative of sexual irregularity: even his Lancelot and Elaine are married).¹⁷ In the alliterative *Morte* too, more directly derived from Geoffrey than Hardyng's eclectic compilation, Mordred is Arthur's 'sister son', and if there is any hint of a closer relationship between them it is very muted indeed.¹⁸ Even on this issue, then, Malory had the freedom to choose an alternative tradition if he had wished. The 'historical' Arthur has no direct heir to ensure a safe linear succession; but in the prose romance versions, any possibility of rightful succession is disastrously compromised by the existence of an incestuous son.

In no version do Arthur and his sister know each other's identity when Mordred is begotten, but the Vulgate *Merlin* does not even ascribe deliberate adultery to Lot's wife: she believes

---

¹⁵ Geoffrey of Monmouth in fact varies between identifying Anna as the daughter of Uther and Ygerne, therefore Arthur's full sister, or occasionally as his aunt, sister of Aurelius and Uther, and married to Lot in both identities (*Geoffrey of Monmouth: The History of the Kings of Britain*, trans. Lewis Thorpe (Harmondsworth, 1966), 208–9, 221, 223 n. (*Historia*, viii. 20–1, ix. 9, ix. 11)). The *Brut* describes Anna as full sister and Mordred as nephew (*The Brut or the Chronicles of England*, Part I, ed. Friedrich W. D. Brie, EETS OS 131 (1906), 67, 83). See also Elizabeth Archibald, 'Arthur and Mordred: Variations on an Incest Theme', *Arthurian Literature*, 8 (1989), 1–27.

¹⁶ The tradition runs from John of Fordun (1385) to Hector Boece (1527) and his translators; for a summary, see Robert Huntington Fletcher, *The Arthurian Material in the Chronicles*, 2nd edn. expanded by Robert Sherman Loomis (New York, 1966), 241–9, modified by Flora Alexander, 'Late Medieval Scottish Attitudes to the Figure of King Arthur: A Reassessment', *Anglia*, 93 (1975), 17–34. Boece picks up the variant relationship of Arthur and Anna from Geoffrey to make Anna Aurelius' and Uther's elder sister (p. 247).

¹⁷ *The Chronicle of Iohn Hardyng*, 120, 137 (l. 27 requires the variant reading 'mordred' to make sense), and 131 (caps. lxxii, lxxviii, lxxvii).

¹⁸ *Alliterative Morte Arthure*, l. 645, in *King Arthur's Death*, ed. Larry D. Benson (Exeter, 1986). The only indication that Mordred might be Arthur's son is Gawain's comment on Mordred, 'Of such a engendure full little joy happens' (3743); but this could be no more than an analogue to the commonplace curse on the day an enemy was born.

that the man in bed with her is her husband, when it is in fact the young squire Arthur who has crept in beside her from his lodging in a corner of the chamber. Despite having been smitten (more in the adolescent than the god-of-love sense) by the beauty of the queen, he at first dares do nothing more, until

hit fill so that the lady awoke and turned hir toward hym, and toke hym in her armes as a woman slepynge, that wende verely it hadde ben her lorde. And that nyght was begete Mordred.[19]

Arthur tells her what he has done the next day while he kneels before her at table; but even when his true identity is discovered, she reacts with love (p. 181). Any sense of the enormity of the act is delayed until Merlin's later prophecy that 'the fader sholde sle the sone, and the sone sle the fader, and the londe of the grete breteigne abide withouten heir and lordles' (p. 579); and even that relates more to the broader context of civil war than to the specific act of incest.

In Malory and his immediate source,[20] Arthur and Morgause do not know they are related, but the act is one of deliberate adultery with none of the aura of adolescent innocence of the *Merlin* about it. Immediately afterwards, Arthur is given a dream in which he foresees the destruction of the country by griffins and serpents (Malory, p. 41 (I. 19)), and Merlin relates the prophesied doom to the guilt incurred by the act:

Ye have done a thynge late that God ys displesed with you, for ye have lyene by youre syster and on hir ye have gotyn a childe that shall destroy you and all the knyghtes of youre realme. (p. 44 (I. 20))

Malory's Arthur incurs further guilt in his next action. In the French, he orders all the children born in May to be sent to him, but the boat carrying Mordred to him is wrecked and he

---

[19] This is from the anonymous mid-century prose translation of the *Estoire de Merlin*: *Merlin*, ed. Henry B. Wheatley, vol. i, part II, EETS OS 21 (rev. edn. 1877), 181.

[20] This is the *Suite du Merlin* (also known as the 'Huth Merlin'; ed. Gaston Paris and Jacob Ulrich, *Merlin*, 2 vols., SATF (Paris, 1886)). For its relation to the Vulgate *Merlin*, see Alexandre Micha, 'The Vulgate *Merlin*', and Fanni Bogdanow, 'The *Suite du Merlin* and the Post-Vulgate *Roman du Graal*', in Roger Sherman Loomis (ed.), *Arthurian Literature in the Middle Ages* (corrected edn., Oxford, 1979), 319, 325–35.

is the sole survivor. Arthur considers killing the children he has collected, but instead obeys a visionary instruction to set them adrift in a pilotless boat so that Christ may save or destroy whom He wishes; in the event, all of them come ashore safely, and are raised by Arthur's own care.[21] Malory conflates the two sea journeys into a single one: the boat carrying all the babies is wrecked, and Mordred is the only one to survive. All the innocent children therefore die as the direct result of Arthur's own action, in an episode that notoriously casts Arthur in the role of Herod. There is an additional irony in this, however, since it is the baby who will be most guilty who is the only one to survive. Malory is here rewriting, not just his Arthurian source, but the whole tradition of stories of setting adrift in which God preserves the innocent or the future hero: saints such as Mary Magdalene or the infant Gregorius, falsely accused women such as Constance, heroes such as Perseus or the Anglo-Norman Horn.[22] The child of incest may elsewhere grow into a saint, as Gregorius does; but I know of only one survivor of casting adrift apart from Mordred who brings disaster on his community, and that is Judas, who himself grew up to commit the worse incest with his mother, and to make the ultimate betrayal.[23] Malory's redrafting of his source rewrites it as if to make Judas the only survivor of the Massacre of the Innocents.

Malory's selection and rewriting of the various traditions of Mordred's parentage, birth, and upbringing extend to his account of Mordred's treachery and death. The historical tradition, exemplified among his known sources by the alliterative *Morte*, makes Guinevere a willing adulteress with Mordred: she betrays both her husband and her king as Mordred betrays his uncle and his king, in a relationship defined in the Christian world as itself prohibited (Mordred being her husband's

---

[21] *Merlin*, ed. Paris and Ulrich, 203–12.
[22] On the tradition, see J. R. Reinhard, 'Setting Adrift in Medieval Law and Literature', *PMLA* 56 (1941), 33–68, and Helen Cooper, 'Prospero's Boats: Magic, Providence, and Human Choice', in Sukanta Chaudhuri (ed.), *Renaissance Essays for Kitty Scoular Datta* (Oxford and Calcutta, 1995), 160–75.
[23] The medieval legend of Judas has him cast away in the sea in a barrel at birth as the result of his mother's prophetic dream; he kills his foster-brother, then his own father, and unwittingly marries his mother (see e.g. *The South English Legendary*, ed. Charlotte d'Evelyn and Anna J. Mill, EETS OS 235–6 (1956), 692–7).

nephew). This displacement of the incest motif further blackens Mordred, but it diverts the sense of retributive destiny from Arthur himself. In the stanzaic *Morte Arthur*, based on the Vulgate tradition, the fact that Mordred is Arthur's own son is mentioned only at the point when he is pursuing Guinevere, intensifying Mordred's incestuous intentions but insulating Arthur himself from either blame or retribution.[24] The Guinevere of the romance tradition, however, remains faithful to Arthur even after Mordred spreads a false rumour of his death: when he demands her in marriage, she escapes to the Tower of London and faces a siege by him. This whole issue of feudal loyalty, with its associated principle of the upholding of the common weal, seems to matter far more to Malory in the apportioning or withholding of blame than the problematics of adultery, or indeed of incest. Lancelot's adultery may worry the hermits on the Grail quest, but Malory, in a passage without parallel in the Vulgate, has God express His approval of Lancelot on his return to court by allowing him his own personal miracle, the healing of Sir Urry. The whole weight of blame can therefore be thrown, first on to the jealousies and hatreds of Gawain and his brothers, then on to the 'unhappy' Mordred—and the word is a strong one, carrying the sense of being doomed to misfortune, almost accursed.[25] At the moment when Arthur and Mordred meet in their final combat in the French *Mort*, the primary syntactic and rhetorical emphasis falls on God's anger (possibly, though not explicitly, for Arthur's act of incest), and only secondarily on the killing of father by son and son by father.[26] To Malory's Arthur—and there is no indication of authorial dissent—Mordred is 'the traytoure that all thys woo hath wrought' (p. 1236 (XXI. 4)); and here it is emphasized that the greatest treachery and sin is Mordred's deed of parricide,

---

[24] *Stanzaic Morte Arthur*, ll. 2954–61, in Benson (ed.), *King Arthur's Death*.

[25] Malory uses it at two key moments, once to blame Mordred and Agravain together for causing Arthur's fall through their hatred of Lancelot, once when Lucan tries to dissuade the King from attacking him when Mordred alone of all his army is left alive at the end of the final battle—'for he ys unhappy': Malory, *Works*, 1161 (XX. 1), 1236 (XXI. 4).

[26] *La Mort le roi Artu*, ed. Jean Frappier, Textes littéraires français (2nd edn., Geneva, 1954), 245 (caps. 190–1), and the preceding prophecy, 211 (cap. 164); trans. James Cable, *The Death of King Arthur* (Harmondsworth, 1971), 220, 192.

not the initial sexual transgression that made it possible. Malory, moreover, gives Mordred the most gruesome death of his entire work, and of all versions of the final combat.

And there kynge Arthur smote sir Mordred undir the shylde, with a foyne of hys speare, thorowoute the body more than a fadom. And whan sir Mordred felte that he had hys dethys wounde he threste hymselff with the myght that he had upp to the burre of kyng Arthurs speare, and ryght so he smote hys fadir, kynge Arthure, with hys swerde holdynge in both hys hondys, uppon the syde of the hede, that the swerde perced the helmet and the tay of the brayne. And therewith Mordred daysshed downe starke dede to the erthe. (p. 1237 (XXI. 4))

'Hys fadir, kynge Arthure': it is the only time in the work that Malory uses the dual formulation, and he holds it back until the stroke that cuts down the whole Arthurian world.

The closing sections of Malory's work that recount the collapse of the Round Table show a qualitative shift in the generic character of the work, not only in their emphasis on civil war and destruction, but in their avoidance or rejection of magic and the supernatural. Nothing intervenes to save Arthur: Excalibur's marvellous properties are never mentioned in the final battle, and the arm that draws the sword back into the lake withdraws whatever magic it may have had from the world. The possibility of Arthur's healing and return suggested by his departure in the barge to Avilion is frustrated by Bedivere's discovery of his tomb, and by Malory's refusal to endorse the idea that he may yet be *rex futurus*. Although romances frequently contain some kind of symbolic resurrection—lost children and wives restored after apparent death, Gawain returning home alive after his encounter with the death-dealing Green Knight—they seldom offer their protagonists perpetual life, though having a fairy mistress may, as in *Sir Launfal*, be a good way to set about it. That mortality might itself be an object of desire runs deeply counter both to the preference of romance for happy endings and to the escapism inherent in the supernatural. Yet in *Melusine*, the half-fairy nature of the heroine and her consequent immortality are a cause more of calamity than celebration.

Her dual nature is responsible for the deformities and birthmarks of her various children, including the diabolic temperament of the aptly named Horrible, who is put to death on his parents' orders while still a child after he has killed two wet-nurses. And after her husband, Raymondin, breaks her prohibition on seeing her on Saturdays (when she is condemned to turn into a serpent from the waist down), she has to leave the castle and family of Lusignan that she has founded, to endure torment until the Day of Judgment in the shape of a flying serpent. For Melusine, the greatest blessing would have been ordinary mortality: without Raymondin's breaking of his oath, she

> hadd lyved the cours natural as another woman; and shuld have be buryed, aftir my lyf naturel expired, within the chirche of Our Lady of Lusynen, where myn obsequye and afterward my annyversary shuld have be honourably and devoutely don.[27]

Raymondin, like the lovers of fairy mistresses in the Breton *lais*, may derive both his personal happiness and his wealth from his wife, but her own supernatural status, in contrast to theirs, is ultimately a source of disempowerment and disaster that condemns her to perpetual life.

Melusine is translated from a French prose original made about a century earlier, but the legends on which it is based go back much further.[28] It too contains elements of family violence that are deeply disturbing. Melusine's fairy mother has been betrayed by her own husband in a manner that foreshadows Raymondin's betrayal of her; Melusine takes revenge by shutting her father inside a mountain, where he eventually dies. Her shape-shifting into a serpent is the result of her mother's curse for that act. Raymondin too commits an act analogous to parricide, in a scene apparently modelled on the story of Alexander. His uncle and foster-father, like Anectanabus, can read the stars; when he and Raymondin are benighted in the course

---

[27] *Melusine*, ed. A. K. Donald, EETS ES 68 (1895), 316 (ch. XLIII). The French original is edited by Louis Stouff, *Jean d'Arras: Melusine* (1932; repr. Geneva, 1974).

[28] See Jacques Le Goff, 'Melusina: Mother and Pioneer', in his *Time, Work and Culture in the Middle Ages*, trans. Arthur Goldhammer (Chicago, 1980), 205–22.

of a boar-hunt, he looks up to them and reads there both his own imminent death at the hands of a subject and the future prosperity of the murderer. Moments later, the boar reappears, and Raymondin accidentally kills his uncle as they fight it. Raymondin does indeed prosper, through the help of Melusine; but he participates too in her 'unhappiness', both in losing her and in family disaster. Most of their children make good, becoming leaders of the Christians against the Turks and winning kingdoms and dukedoms; but when the seventh son, Froimond, takes his vows as a monk, his brother, the violent Geoffrey with the great tooth, is so angry that he burns the monastery, with Froimond and his fellow monks inside it. Melusine's more distant descendants incur further trouble. When one breaks the terms of an adventure at the 'sparrow-hawk castle' and asks as his reward the lady who governs it, she declares herself to be Melusine's sister, his request incestuous, and that the consequences will be that his heirs will suffer 'grete myschief' and exile to the ninth generation: 'and wete it wel that his heyres after his decesse were not fortunat, but unhappe in al their actes'.[29]

Interestingly, the metrical versions of *Melusine* in both French and English markedly soften the elements of violence and family murder, to bring the story into closer conformity with the generic expectations of verse romances. Raymondin's responsibility for his uncle's death extends only to shouting him a warning that angers him into standing his ground against the boar, which gores him fatally; the monks are claimed to have brought their own destruction on themselves by corrupt living; and Melusine's disposal of her father is held over to the end of the story, and then, in a loss of leaves as symbolic as that of the Prose *Alexander*, the folio that should contain it in the English is missing.[30]

It is none the less a strange story for any house to take as its

---

[29] *Melusine*, 367–8 (chs. LXI–LXII).
[30] *The Romance of Partenay*, ed. W. W. Skeat, EETS ES 22 (rev. edn, 1899): see ll. 225–63, 3669–90, 4550 ff. This is based on the shortened octosyllabic version of the French prose: *Le Roman de Mélusine ou Histoire de Lusignan par Coudrette*, ed. Eleanor Roach, Bibliothèque française et romane (Paris, 1982).

founding legend, even though here enough sons remain for the dynasty to be carried forward; genealogical romances are usually more unequivocally laudatory. Yet the disturbing qualities that mark these romances cannot all be ascribed to fifteenth-century rewritings of early legends. *Valentine and Orson* is a late-medieval invention that made its way into English only at the start of the sixteenth century,[31] and is made up of most of the motifs found across the whole corpus of romance: an accused queen, twins separated at birth, one of them reared by bears, a 'green knight' equipped with a miraculous balm that can heal the most mortal of wounds, battles against the Saracens, a magician, a mechanical horse controlled by a pin, a lion that will not hurt a king's son, a dragon-fight, ladies to be won and an empire to be inherited. It is as implausible a romance as any that appeared in English before the translations of Italian and Spanish chivalric romances. Yet even here, the expectations of romance are set up only to be baffled at the end, in a symmetrical weaving and unravelling of the whole ethos of the genre.

The decisive moment in this unravelling is Valentine's killing of his father. The other parricides I have described do not obviously invite discussion in Freudian terms; with *Valentine and Orson*, such associations are hard to avoid. The Freudian model, however, is not so much that of primal jealousy as of the family romance, and of the infinity of desire beyond its ostensible object.[32] Valentine, separated from his mother at birth, is driven by the urge to discover her identity; from finding his mother he extends his quest to finding his father.

I am purposed never for to reste unto the time that I have knowledge of my nativite. (p. 85)

---

[31] It was first printed in French in 1489, and probably composed in its prose form only shortly before that; the *Manual* suggests a date of *c.*1502 for the earliest surviving English fragment, which would suggest a date a year or so earlier for Henry Watson's translation; it is however dated *c.*1510 by the *STC* (24571. 3). Arthur Dickson suggests a date of ?1503–5 in his edition (*Valentine and Orson*, EETS OS 204 (1937), p. xiv).

[32] See e.g. Sigmund Freud, 'Family Romances', in *On Sexuality*, Penguin Freud Library, 7 (Harmondsworth, 1977), 221–5; 'Group Psychology: Postscript', in *Civilization, Society and Religion*, PFL 12, pp. 168–70; 'On Transience' and 'Those Wrecked by Success', *Art and Literature*, PFL 14, pp. 287–90, 299–316.

But he does not cease from questing when he has discovered his parents: his insatiable pursuit of chivalry takes over from its initial motivation, until it arcs into disaster. The deep psychoanalytic desire for origins and the historical desire for stable succession are disrupted together, in a direct inversion of those conventions of the romance regarded as central by both modern and medieval analysts.

The earliest form of the narrative, which was in verse rather than prose, seems to have consisted only of the first, more 'romance', half of the story.[33] It is built on a series of major episodes interspersed with innumerable minor adventures: the birth and separation of Valentine and Orson, and their eventual discovery first of their mother, King Pepin's sister, and later of their father, the Emperor of Greece; Valentine's vowing of faith to Pepin's daughter Eglantine, and the unsuccessful plotting of Pepin's illegitimate sons Haufray and Henry against Valentine; Orson's marriage to Fezonne; the brothers' enlisting of the dwarf magician Pacolet, who can get them out of the most life-threatening situations. Every one of these episodes could be described as quintessentially romance; but each one is countered or reversed by the end of the prose extension of the work.

The process starts with some uncomfortable elements even within this first part of the story. Orson decides to test Fezonne's faithfulness, on the grounds that 'women were of suche a nature that for a lytell thynge they chaunged theyr thoughtes and promyses, and broke them falsly' (p. 163). Fezonne passes the test safely; but later in the work Orson himself turns out to be a promise-breaker, when he 'acquainted him with the faire Galazye, for he knewe not whether Fezon was dead or not' (p. 300; it has to be noted that he has made no attempt to keep up with news of his wife), gets her pregnant, and then reveals that he cannot marry her because he is married already. Galazye retreats into a convent; when Fezonne hears that Orson 'had

---

[33] See Arthur Dickson, *Valentine and Orson: A Study in Late Medieval Romance* (New York, 1929), 4–21. The earliest surviving version of the story is represented by a few fragments in Middle Dutch; these, and similar versions with happy endings in other languages, are probably based on a lost metrical French original.

another ladi in love that he had gotten with child', she is so grieved that she dies. This frees Orson to marry Galazye, but it is still a very strange way of achieving a happy ending to a crossed love affair. Valentine does no better: despite the oaths he has exchanged with Eglantine, he falls in love with another lady, Clerimond, spends most of the romance pursuing her, and eventually marries her.

The romance initiation of the story sets up strong expectations on the part of the reader for a happy ending, fulfilled in the original metrical version, but increasingly and aggressively thwarted in the prose. The faithful Pacolet is stabbed to death by one of the Saracen kings he has tricked; Valentine inherits his magic tables, 'in whych was wryten all the secretes of hys arte' (p. 282), but that does not prevent him from the entirely natural catastrophe of his killing of his father. From this moment on, there is no question of this story's being just an unusually capacious romance: it has turned into something actively opposed to the genre. Haufray and Henry have likewise killed their father Pepin and his queen by poison, a form of murder that was regarded in the Middle Ages with particular abhorrence as being close to witchcraft. The magic of the romance is tainted by the same idea, becoming an evil to be renounced:[34]

> Never please it God that I plaie more with suche arte, for it is dampnable. And he that tought it me dyed unhappely at the laste, and I beleve that for this sinne I have slain my father. (pp. 310–11)

Valentine's killing of the Emperor is in fact a chivalric act that goes wrong (both are disguised as Saracens); but whatever his motives may be, the action itself replicates that of Haufray and Henry. Orson, who had been fighting alongside the Emperor, realizes from hearing Valentine's battle-cry

> that it was his brother that hade slayne his father, so he threw downe his shelde and hys spere, and lyfte up hys helme. After he cryed in

---

[34] This is also an important motif in the *Four Sons of Aymon*, published by Caxton in 1489, in which the sons' magician cousin Maugis renounces his magic (*The Right Pleasant and Goodly History of the Four Sons of Aymon*, ed. Octavia Richardson, 2 vols., EETS ES 44, 45 (1884–5), 503).

weping, brother Valentyne evill prowesse have you doone, for to daye you have slayne the father that engendred you. (p. 308)

The succession to the throne, which usually seals the happy ending of a romance, is therefore impossibly compromised. At first Valentine alternates in ruling the empire with his brother Orson, but then he leaves to embark on a life of penance. Only a few pages after he has married Clerimond, Valentine breaks in half their wedding ring—ostensibly to serve as a recognition token, but they never meet again as husband and wife. Part of the penance prescribed for him is that he is not to speak for seven years: Orson's wild dumbness of the opening of the story is now imposed on his brother as punishment for sin. After Valentine's pious death, Orson receives a vision of heaven and hell, and he too abandons his office of emperor to become a hermit in the woods, so retreating to the wilds into which he was first born. The Emperor of Greece had rendered himself heirless by his casting off of his wife; the story ends, not with the safe succession from father to recovered son, but with both the empire and the kingdom of France in the hands of regents while the infant heirs are incapable of government—perhaps the most unstable of all political conditions.

The story of *Valentine and Orson* enjoyed a continuing popularity in England in various versions, but when it was recast in metrical form in the seventeenth century its betrayal of expectations proved too radical for the unhappy ending to be maintained. The short rhymed version of *c*.1600 contained in the Percy Folio Manuscript, entitled *The Emperour and the Childe*, ends, as the early Continental metrical versions of the story also seem to have done, with Valentine's marrying Clerimond and discovering his mother and father, and the Emperor's reconciliation with his calumniated wife[35]—the same pattern as

---

[35] *Bishop Percy's Folio Manuscript: Ballads and Romances*, ed. John W. Hales and Frederick J. Furnivall, 3 vols. (London, 1868), ii. 390–9. The story was also dramatized by Richard Hathway and Antony Munday in 1598 for the Admiral's Men; there are also entries for a play of the same name in the Stationers' Register in 1595 and 1600, which cite the Queen's Men and may refer to a different, anonymous dramatization: see E. K. Chambers, *The Elizabethan Stage*, 4 vols. (Oxford, 1923), iii. 333, 448, iv. 403–4. Neither play survives, so it is impossible to know whether they followed the disaster model of the prose version of the story or the happy ending of the verse.

is found, for instance, in Shakespeare's near-contemporary romance *The Winter's Tale*. The poem concludes cheerfully, and, in terms of the whole textual tradition of the work, with maximum inaccuracy,

> and soe att lenght, in spight of ffortunes happ,
> they lived in joy, and ffeared noe after clappe.

It is true (and important) that in the prose version Valentine is allowed redemption for his act of parricide in his final years of piety; but the deed itself cannot be reversed, and his curse on himself when he discovers what he has done is almost biblical in its intensity.

I am above all the other the moost cursed, unhappy, and evil fortuned. Alas, death, where arte thou that thou comest not and take me, for I am not worthy that the earthe susteyne me, nor that none of the elementes lende me nourisshinge whan that I have commytted suche a dede before god detestable, and to the men abhomynable... It is not reason that I live ani more upon the earth, nor that I be put in the nombre of knightes. (pp. 308–9)

He, like Mordred, is an 'unhappy' knight; his commitment to chivalry may seem exemplary compared with the traitor of Arthur's court, but he is betrayed by that ethos into an act of 'evill prowesse' just as much as is Edippes. That is not a note that is sounded in the metrical romances of the fourteenth century, nor in the dramatic romances of the Renaissance; but it is one that carries a particular resonance at the troubled close of the Middle Ages.

8 The Ballad and the Middle Ages

RICHARD FIRTH GREEN

In the mid-1980s, when John Fyler undertook to update the explanatory notes to the *House of Fame* for the new Riverside Chaucer, not only could he find nothing new to add to Robinson's forty-year-old comments on 'The Bret Glascurion' (III. 1208)—a figure usually identified with the traditional ballad hero Glasgerion (Child 67[1])—but he even felt it necessary to abridge them slightly.[2] This recent example of a prominent medievalist's indifference to earlier ballad scholarship is a sign of the times. Twenty years before, when Edward Vasta had published a collection of scholarly essays under the title *Middle English Survey*, he had felt himself obliged to include a piece by Arthur K. Moore on 'The Literary Status of the English Popular Ballad',[3] and three years later, when William Matthews compiled a highly selective bibliography of Old and Middle English Literature he still managed to find space in it for a couple of pages on the ballad.[4] In the 1960s Moore, better known for an anthology of Middle English lyrics, was only one of a number of medieval scholars who took a professional interest in the traditional ballad (among others were Bertrand H. Bronson, the noted Chaucerian, Albert B. Friedman and MacEdward Leach, both editors of Middle English romances for the Early English Text Society, and the distinguished Harvard

---

[1] Unless otherwise noted all ballads are quoted from Francis James Child (ed.), *The English and Scottish Popular Ballads*, 5 vols. (Boston, 1882–98; repr. New York, 1965), and referred to, as here, by their number in Child's edition, given in parentheses.
[2] Geoffrey Chaucer, *The Riverside Chaucer*, ed. Larry D. Benson, 3rd edn. (Boston, 1987), 986.
[3] Notre Dame, Ind., 1965, 309–36.
[4] *Goldentree Bibliographies: Old and Middle English Literature* (New York, 1968), 50–1.

medievalist B. J. Whiting), yet, thirty years later, it is hard to think of a single medieval scholar who is willing to offer the traditional English ballad so much as house-room.[5] Douglas Gray's inclusion of a section of 'Ballads and Verse Romances' in his anthology of *Late Medieval Verse and Prose*, then, is a notable exception to a recent and, as I shall seek to argue, regrettable trend.[6]

There are, no doubt, many reasons why the study of the traditional ballad should have fallen out of favour among present-day scholars of medieval literature, but one important factor has certainly been the success of David C. Fowler's *Literary History of the Popular Ballad*,[7] which presents a powerful case for regarding the eighteenth century, rather than the Middle Ages, as the major creative period in the history of English and Scottish balladry. Fowler is strongly opposed to what he calls, 'the supposed autonomy of oral tradition'—the belief that, as G. L. Kittredge put it in 1904, 'nothing has less significance for the date of any ballad than the precise moment at which it first excited the interest of some collector who reduced it to writing'.[8] Fowler, by contrast, starts from the assumption that 'a given ballad took the particular shape it has about the time that it was written down unless there is specific evidence to the contrary' (p. 5), and since only some twenty-five of Child's 305 ballads can be shown to have been written down prior to the

[5] The only exceptions that come to mind are Douglas Gray's own article 'Medieval English Ballads', in Patricia Shaw et al. (eds.), *Actas del Primer Congreso Internacional de la Sociedad Española de Lengua y Literatura Inglesa Medieval* (Oviedo, 1989), 129–54, and Thomas J. Garbáty's 'Rhyme, Romance, Ballad, Burlesque, and the Confluence of Form', in Robert F. Yeager (ed.), *Fifteenth-Century Studies: Recent Essays* (Hamden, Conn., 1984), 283–301. The Robin Hood ballads have been the subject of studies by Douglas Gray ('The Robin Hood Poems', *Poetica*, 18 (1984), 1–39), and Stephen Knight (*Robin Hood: A Complete Study of the English Outlaw* (Oxford, 1994), 44–97), and Knight has also written on 'Lady Isabel and the Elf Knight' (Child 4) in Stephanie Trigg (ed.), *Medieval English Poetry* (London, 1993), 272–88.

[6] (Oxford, 1985), 179–203. There is, however, a selection of ballads in at least one other recent anthology, *Medieval English Literature*, ed. Thomas Garbáty (Lexington, Mass., 1984), 479–504; Garbáty was a pupil of MacEdward Leach.

[7] Durham, NC, 1968.

[8] In the introduction to the one-volume edition of F. J. Child's *English and Scottish Popular Ballads*, edited by Helen Child Sargent and by Kittredge himself (Boston, 1904), p. xv.

compilation of the Percy Folio Manuscript (c.1650),[9] this premiss requires him to redirect his focus from the middle ages to the great eighteenth-century collectors of ballads such as David Herd, Joseph Ritson, and, of course, Bishop Percy himself. The thrust of his study was to uproot the ballad from the untidy profusion of medieval popular culture and transplant it into the more orderly garden of gothic antiquarianism, so that medievalists suddenly found themselves freed of responsibility for what had already begun to seem an uncomfortably unruly genre.[10] Though I very much doubt that Fowler himself expected his admirable book to have this unfortunate effect, a brief glance at W. Edson Richmond's recent *Bibliography of Ballad Scholarship*[11] will confirm that the field has now been almost entirely abandoned to folklorists and musicologists.

In this chapter I want to challenge Fowler's conviction that it is fruitless to speculate about an oral tradition anterior to the earliest appearance of any given ballad in print, and hence that the medievalist has little to learn from the study of traditional ballads first copied down in more recent times. Whilst we must always be alert to the possibility of contamination and sophistication in the received version of any ballad, this should not blind us to the remarkable conservatism of oral transmission in general nor to its ability to preserve certain aspects of traditional culture rather more effectively than the manuscript rooms of our major libraries. Fowler devotes the whole of the last chapter of his book to one of Walter Scott's informants, Mrs Anna Brown of Falkirk, whom he calls, with only slight exaggeration, 'the most important single contributor to the canon of English and Scottish ballads' (p. 294). A native of Aberdeen, Mrs Brown seems to have acquired her stock of ballads from her mother's Highland family, but there is no doubt that she herself, as the daughter of a university professor and the wife

---

[9] See David C. Fowler, 'Ballads', in *Manual*, vi. 1759–81.
[10] To some extent, Fowler's position is anticipated in E. K. Chambers, *English Literature at the Close of the Middle Ages* (Oxford, 1945), 122–84, and in M. J. C. Hodgart, *The Ballad* (London, 1950).
[11] New York, 1989.

of a minister, was an educated and cultivated woman, far more at home in a drawing-room than a croft. Such a person is easily suspected of polishing, adapting, or even inventing ballads,[12] but we should not be deceived into supposing that she was typical of Scott's informants nor into imagining that many of the others would have inhabited his literary milieu with equal assurance. Had his agenda been otherwise, Fowler might quite as well have chosen to conclude his book with a very different example of one of Scott's sources, Margaret Hogg (the mother of 'the Ettrick Shepherd'): Mrs Hogg is reported to have complained to the collector, 'there war never ane o' my songs prentit till ye prentit them yoursel', an' ye hae spoilt them awthegither. They were made for singin' an' no for readin'; but ye hae broke the charm noo, an' they'll never be sung mair. An' the worst thing of a', they're nouther richt spell'd nor richt setten down.'[13] He might, however, have found it rather more difficult to convince us of the presence of an affected antiquarianism in the ballads of the rebarbative Mrs Hogg than in those of the genteel Mrs Brown.

The most obvious place to start this discussion is with a group of ballads that appear to derive in some fashion from medieval romances that are still extant in manuscript: 'Hind Horn' (17), 'King Orfeo' (19), 'The Marriage of Sir Gawain' (31), and 'Thomas Rymer' (37).[14] For only one of these ballads, 'The Marriage of Sir Gawain', is there no real possibility of literary contamination from a printed text: its counterpart, the fifteenth-century romance *The Wedding of Sir Gawain and*

---

[12] Mrs Brown's precise role in the transmission of ballads has been the subject of much speculation; the most balanced appraisal seems to me that of Flemming G. Andersen and Thomas Pettitt ('Mrs Brown of Falkland: A Singer of Tales', *Journal of American Folklore*, 92 (1979), 1–24): 'That she was capable of changing, or even improvising, individual phrases, lines, or stanzas can hardly be denied, and is even indicated by the evidence: but the instances are few and scattered, and the process involved in her transmission of ballads is overwhelmingly the memorization of a fixed text' (p. 23).

[13] Quoted in Edgar Johnson, *Sir Walter Scott: the Great Unknown*, 2 vols. (London, 1970), i. 192.

[14] The question of the general priority of romance to ballad is certainly more complex than this statement implies (as Thomas Garbáty has shown); nevertheless, where detailed comparison between two versions is possible it generally points to the ballad's being the later one, as is the case with Garbáty's own analysis of *The Weddynge of Sir Gawen and Dame Ragnell* and 'The Marriage of Sir Gawain' ('Rhyme, Romance, Ballad, Burlesque', 291–7).

Dame Ragnell, was first printed by Sir Frederick Madden for the Bannatyne Club in 1839, almost two hundred years later than the earliest record of the corresponding ballad in Bishop Percy's Folio Manuscript (c.1650). Unfortunately this particular narrative seems to have held little appeal for later performers, and if we except a fascinating variant called 'The Half Hitch' recorded in Shrewsbury, Vermont in 1932,[15] the ballad appears to be almost extinct in modern tradition.[16] By contrast, the Breton lay of *Sir Orfeo* was first printed in Joseph Ritson's *Ancient Engleish Metrical Romancees* in 1802, so that the ballad of 'King Orfeo', first recorded in the Shetlands in 1865, over sixty years later (and still alive in local tradition as recently as 1947),[17] might quite plausibly be regarded as an adaptation of it, were it not for an absence of obvious verbal echoes or any other sign of deliberate imitation. In fact, the recent recognition of a fragmentary Scottish romance of *King Orphius* in a late sixteenth-century manuscript, discovered by Marion Stewart in the Scottish Record Office,[18] strongly suggests that the Shetland ballad is the last survival of an ancient and remarkably durable indigenous tradition, only tenuously related to the English romance.[19] In the case of 'Hind Horn' there is a twenty-five-year gap between Ritson's edition of the Middle English romance (which comes down to us in two quite distinct versions), and the first printed record of the ballad in William Motherwell's *Minstrelsy* (1827); again, the claim that the ballad might have been fabricated by an early reader of the printed romance looks plausible enough on the surface, but in this case

---

[15] Bertrand H. Bronson (ed.), *The Traditional Tunes of the Child Ballads*, 4 vols. (Princeton, 1959–72), i. 318–19.
[16] An Appalachian version, compressed to the point of near unintelligibility, called 'Sir Gaunie and the Witch', is printed in *The Ballad Book of John Jacob Niles* (Boston, 1961), 106–8.
[17] Patrick Shuldham-Shaw, 'The Ballad of "King Orfeo"', *Scottish Studies*, 20 (1976), 124–6.
[18] Marion Stewart, '"King Orphius"', *Scottish Studies*, 17 (1973), 1–16.
[19] Unfortunately, for the purposes of comparison, the most intact section of the text of *King Orphius* (the return of Orphius to his kingdom) is only briefly sketched in 'King Orfeo', while there is a major lacuna in the manuscript just at the point where the ballad narrative is fullest (the visit of Orfeo to the King of Fairies' hall). Nevertheless, two important details attest to an independent Scottish tradition: the fact that Orphius/Orfeo's wife is called Isabel (or more recently Lisa Bell), and that his kingdom is left in the care, not of his steward, but his nephew.

there are clear signs that 'Hind Horn' incorporates specific details only to be found in an Anglo-Norman *Romance of Horn*,[20] a text that was not to be edited until 1845.[21]

The final ballad in this group, 'Thomas Rymer', first reported by Mrs Brown of Falkland in 1800, is worth dwelling on at a little greater length, for it is one that Fowler at one time claimed unequivocally to be an eighteenth-century composition: ' "Thomas Rymer" is composed directly from the romance rather than from a generalized conception of the story' (p. 321). The dating here is rather tricky, for, apart from a somewhat obscure seventeenth-century printing in *Sundry Strange Prophecies of Merlin, Bede, Becket, and Others* (London, 1652), the first appearance of the romance of *Thomas of Erceldoune* in print was in Walter Scott's *Minstrelsy of the Scottish Border* in 1803. Since Mrs Brown's version had been communicated to Robert Jamieson three years earlier, only some kind of hypothetical conspiracy between Brown and Scott could explain how she might have been able to fabricate her ballad from the hitherto unprinted romance. In fact such an elaborate hypothesis is quite unnecessary for there can be little doubt that there is no direct connection between 'Thomas Rymer' and *Thomas of Erceldoune* of the kind that Fowler imagined. The proof of this will also serve to demonstrate the remarkable conservatism of oral transmission. The D text of 'Thomas Rymer' in Child's edition (iv. 454) appears in a collection of notes and papers assembled by Walter Scott in preparation for his *Minstrelsy of the Scottish Border* and now in the National Library of Scotland; it is in the handwriting of John Leyden, a fellow enthusiast whom Scott first met in the summer of 1799,[22] and is claimed to have been collected from a J. Ormiston of Kelso. This variant concludes with the lines, 'Gin ere ye want to see me again, / Gang to the bonny banks o Farnalie' (Child iv. 454). Scott was puzzled by this place-name and thought it might be

---

[20] See *Horn Childe and Maiden Rimnild*, ed. Maldwyn Mills, Middle English Texts, 20 (Heidelberg, 1988), 47–8.
[21] William Henry Schofield, 'The Story of Horn and Rimenhild', *PMLA* 18 (1903), 3 n. 3.
[22] Johnson, *Scott*, i. 167–8.

connected with Fairnalie in Selkirkshire. However, since the setting for Thomas's first meeting with the Queen of Elfland in all of Child's versions (except Mrs Brown's) is 'the Eildon tree' (a detail also to be found in the medieval romance),[23] there can be little doubt that the place is in actuality the *farnalie* referred to in a document of 1208 defining a disputed boundary in Roxburghshire's Eildon Hills between two estates owned by the rival monasteries of Melrose and Kelso.[24] It is frankly incredible that a ballad composed by Mrs Brown in Falkland, north of the Firth of Forth, should have been recorded on the English border within three years, having acquired in the process authentic local colouring that mystified even Scott himself. To his credit, Fowler has since withdrawn his original hypothesis about the composition of 'Thomas Rymer'.[25]

Of course, the fact that all four of these ballads can be shown to contain links with extant medieval romances, for which continuous oral transmission is the only credible explanation, cannot be used to justify the use of ballad texts to reconstruct hypothetical romances for which we have no manuscript evidence. Counter-examples, such as the ballad of 'Blancheflour and Jellyflorice' (Child 300), which shares almost nothing of substance with the romance of *Florice and Blancheflour* beyond the names of the main characters, could easily be adduced to support the opposite position. In a few cases, such as the Percy Folio's 'King Arthur and King Cornwall' (Child 30), a medieval original, such as it was, might be reconstructed with some degree of confidence; in others, such as 'Sir Aldingar' (Child 59), which employs the common medieval romance motif of the falsely accused queen,[26] the problems are more complex. Christophersen has argued for its twelfth-century origin in a

---

[23] The Thornton Manuscript has, '"Now sall I go with all my myghte, / Hir for to mete at Eldoune tree"' (ll. 79–80; cf. 168, 280, 298, 508, etc.); versions of this name appear in all four of the other manuscripts. *Thomas of Erceldoune*, ed. Ingeborg Nixon, University of Copenhagen, Publications of the Department of English, 9/i–ii (Copenhagen, 1980–3).
[24] E. B. Lyle, 'A Reconsideration of the Place-Names in "Thomas the Rymer"', *Scottish Studies*, 13 (1969), 66.
[25] *Manual*, vi. 1803.
[26] See Margaret Schlauch, *Chaucer's Constance and Accused Queens* (New York, 1927).

story first told by William of Malmesbury of how a dwarf called Mimecan successfully exonerated Gunild, the daughter of King Canute, from a charge of adultery by defeating her burly accuser in a judicial combat. A form of the name *Rodingar*, by which this accuser is known in most medieval sources, can be found as early as Matthew Paris's *Chronica Maiora*,[27] and it bears so obvious a resemblance to both *Aldingar* (the Percy Folio form) and *Rodingham* (its form in a version collected by Scott) that the general justice of Christophersen's hypothesis can hardly be doubted. Whether this further justifies us in postulating a lost medieval ballad, or even romance, on the subject is obviously more problematic, however, for scholars have been understandably reluctant to speculate about the existence of genuine ballads before the late Middle Ages. Though a thirteenth-century poem on Judas is sometimes claimed to be the earliest extant ballad,[28] this claim has been challenged a number of times—not least by Fowler himself, who seems inclined to deny that anything that can be truly termed a ballad existed before the sixteenth century.[29]

At least one popular ballad, however, is recorded in the late Middle Ages and has been preserved by oral tradition in most of its essential details right down to the present day. 'The Fox and the Goose', written on the flyleaf of a French *Dits moraulx des philosophes* in the second half of the fifteenth century,[30] is the unmistakable ancestor of a ballad, often called 'Old Daddy Fox' (and still popular on both sides of the Atlantic), describing a fox's daring midnight raid on a local farmyard and his triumphal return to the bosom of his family with a prize goose (or duck).[31] It may be that scholars have generally ignored 'The Fox and the Goose' because of a feeling that its subject is too

---

[27] Paul Christophersen, *The Ballad of 'Sir Aldingar': Its Origin and Analogues* (Oxford, 1952), 23–4.
[28] See especially Karin Boklund-Lagopoulou, '*Judas*: The First English Ballad?', *MÆ* 62 (1993), 20–34.
[29] *Manual*, vi. 1757; for a defence of the opposing position see Gray, 'Medieval English Ballads'.
[30] Rossell Hope Robbins (ed.), *Secular Lyrics of the XIVth and XVth Centuries*, 2nd edn. (Oxford, 1955), 43. 'The Fox and the Goose' is also printed by Gray, *OBLMVP*, pp. 164–5.
[31] Peter Kennedy (ed.), *Folksongs of Britain and Ireland* (London, 1975), 656–7.

slight, or even childish, to warrant serious attention (a similar prejudice has probably inhibited academic interest in the ballad of 'The Frog and the Mouse', often known as 'Froggy Went A-Courting', which can be traced back to the sixteenth century).[32] In recent times, its inclusion in R. L. Greene's collection of carols seems further to have discouraged medievalists from thinking of it as a ballad (it is not mentioned in Fowler's chapter on ballads for the new *Manual of Writings in Middle English*, for instance),[33] yet the distinction between these two genres is not always obvious in practice, and certainly should not be determined solely on the presence or absence of a 'external' refrain.[34] 'The Fox and the Goose' has a clear narrative line, and most modern singers who bother to consider the question of genre at all would probably describe its descendant, 'Old Daddy Fox', as a ballad. A cursory comparison of the two reveals an obvious parallelism, not only in their central plots, but in a number of their narrative details (the feasting of the cubs back home in the fox's den, for instance).[35]

Other medieval 'outcroppings', as R. L. Greene calls them, 'of an underlying layer of stanzaic popular poems on the central theme of a farmyard foray by a fox' (p. 466) help to confirm the ancient ancestry of 'Old Daddy Fox'. 'The False Fox',[36] one of the poems in Cambridge, MS Ee. 1. 12 (a collection of English songs and translations made by a late fifteenth-century Franciscan called James Ryman),[37] is clearly derived from a somewhat fuller version than 'The Fox and the Goose'—one that evidently made more of the consternation of the farmer and his wife on finding their goose gone and of their vigorous pursuit of the fleeing fox (motifs which survive to the present day in the antics of 'old mother Slipper-Slopper' and her husband).

---

[32] Ed. Kennedy, p. 649; see Chambers, *English Literature at the Close of the Middle Ages*, 184.
[33] Richard L. Greene (ed.), *The Early English Carols*, 2nd edn. (Oxford, 1977), 249.
[34] An 'external' refrain of the type found in the 'The Fox and the Goose' is indeed common to almost all carols, but, though relatively rare, it is not unknown to the ballad (see Greene (ed.), *Early English Carols*, pp. lxvi–lxviii).
[35] For a full comparison between the two, see George Perkins, 'A Medieval Carol Survival: "The Fox and the Goose"', *Journal of American Folklore*, 74 (1961), 235–44.
[36] Robbins (ed.), *Secular Lyrics*, 44–5.
[37] See Greene (ed.), *Early English Carols*, 321.

Rather more distant medieval traces of the same motif can be detected in a political lampoon on the fall of the duke of Suffolk (1450),[38] and in the hue and cry that is raised for Daun Russell in Chaucer's *Nun's Priest's Tale* (VII. 3375–401). Moreover, Ryman's poem seems to anticipate not only narrative motifs but actual verbal details that will crop up again in nineteenth- and twentieth-century versions of the ballad. One might compare, for instance, Ryman's lines,

> He toke a gose fast by the nek,
> And the gose thoo began to quek.
> . . . . . .
> He threw a gose upon his back,
> And furth he went thoo with his pak,   (16–24)

with the following stanza from a nineteenth-century American version,

> He seized the black duck
> And swang it o'er across his back,
> Which made the old duck go quack, quack, quack,
> For its legs hung dangling down O.[39]

Even more intriguing is the parallel between Ryman's rendering of the goose's squawking, '[he] made her to say "wheccum-quek"' (36), and similar imitative renderings in some modern versions: 'I heard her go quink quankeo'.[40] The real question is whether such verbal echoes provide genuine evidence of the durability of oral tradition, or are merely the kind of coincidences we might expect to find in two independent works dealing with identical subject matter.

There is no question that some details in the verbal fabric of traditional ballads have proved remarkably durable. Predictably enough, opening lines, which doubtless served as mnemonic cues in the singer's mental inventory, remained particularly stable.

---

[38] Rossell Hope Robbins (ed.), *Historical Poems of the XIVth and XVth Centuries* (New York, 1959), 186–7.
[39] George Perkins, 'A Pre-Civil War American "Fox and the Goose"', *Journal of American Folklore*, 77 (1964), 264.
[40] Florence Truitt, 'Songs from Kentucky', *Journal of American Folklore*, 36 (1928), 378 (st. 7).

An early example of this is the well-known catch-phrase 'Robin Hood in Barnsdale (or Greenwood) stood'—though, strictly speaking, in 'A Gest of Robyn Hode' (Child 117), the earliest of the Robin Hood ballads to have come down to us, it corresponds, not to the very first line of the poem, but to the point (the beginning of the third stanza) at which the action proper begins, 'Robyn stode in Bernesdale / And lenyd hym to a tre'. As early as 1429 the phrase 'Robin Hode en Barnesdale stode' had been used by lawyers in court to represent an unprovable assertion,[41] and in 1432 an ingenious clerk had arranged the names in a list of fictional sureties for the members of parliament for Wiltshire in such a way that they formed an acrostic that read (in part), 'Robyn, hode, inne, Grenewode, Stode, Godeman, was, he'.[42] In *The Interlude of the Four Elements* (c.1526), attributed to John Rastell, a character called Yngnoraunce delivers a comic cento stitched together from various ballads and popular songs that begins, 'Robyn Hode in Barnysdale stode / And lent hym tyl a mapyll thystyll', and the phrase appears once more a few years later in Nicholas Udall's translation of *Erasmi Apothegmata*.[43] Finally, it makes a late appearance in the second stanza of the ballad of 'Robin Hood and Allen a Dale' (Child 138), first recorded in broadside copies from the second half of the seventeenth century:

> As Robin Hood in the forrest stood,
>   All under the green-wood tree,
> There was he ware of a brave young man,
>   As fine as fine might be.   (Child iii. 173)

These intermittent occurrences over a period of more than two hundred years attest to the durability of such oral incipits, but what of lines, such as those we noted in Ryman's 'False Fox', that appear further along in the course of the action?

Sometimes, such lines appear to have acquired a particular

---

[41] William Craddock Bolland, *A Manual of Yearbook Studies* (Cambridge, 1925), 107 n. 2. It was still being invoked as a legal catchphrase (though somewhat corrupted) as late as 1772; see Joseph Ritson, *Robin Hood* (London, n.d. [c.1820]), 23.
[42] J. C. Holt, *Robin Hood* (London, 1982), 69.
[43] See Fowler, *Literary History*, 69–70. The Rastell passage is also discussed in Ritson's *Robin Hood* (p. 24) and in Child (ii. 240 and iii. 42 n.).

resilience from seeming in some way to epitomize or encapsulate the essence of the ballads in which they occur. A postmedieval ballad, 'The Gypsy Laddie' (Child 200), furnishes a particularly clear example of the kind of lines I am thinking of. Almost all versions of this story of a noblewoman's elopement with a band of gypsies contain some version of the following vivid contrast:

> Last night I lay in a weel-made bed,
>   And my noble lord beside me
> And now I must ly in an old tenant's-barn,
>   And the black crew glowring owre me.   (Child iv. 66, st. 8)

It hardly matters in detail whether the lady exchanges 'a weel-made bed' (or 'a goose-feather bed') for 'an old tenant's-barn', 'the cold, cold, ground', or even, in one American version, 'Pittsburgh jail'; this essential contrast remains closer to the heart of the ballad than even the climax of the story, where we encounter a far greater range of variation—some versions ending with the savage butchery of the gypsy band, some with the loving reconciliation of the lady and her lord, and some with her successful escape to the open road.[44]

It seems possible that the apparent echoes in the modern ballad 'Old Daddy Fox' of Ryman's poem 'The False Fox' furnish an instance of this kind of survival, but there is an even clearer illustration in its companion piece, the 'Fox and the Goose'. The fox's boast in the fifteenth-century ballad,

> I shall macke some of yowre berde,
> or that I goo from the toowne,   (7–8)

---

[44] Such lines are closely related to proverbial sayings and, as Helen Cooper has pointed out to me, might be compared with expressions like, 'He that will not when he may when he will shall have nay', whose long history has been traced by Archer Taylor (Stanley B. Greenfield (ed.), *Studies in Old English Literature in Honor of Arthur G. Brodeur* (University of Oregon Press, 1963), 155–61). Ironically, Taylor says of an example he finds in Robert Louis Stevenson that he suspects it 'may be referring to a song that I have not identified' (p. 160), but any student of the ballad would instantly recognize Stevenson's reference as being to 'The Baffled Knight' (Child 112), most versions of which end with some form of the stanza, '"And if you meet a lady gay, / As you go by the hill, sir, / If you will not when you may, / You shall not when you will, sir"' (B. 8; ii. 484).

The Ballad and the Middle Ages 175

resurfaces in a version printed in Baltimore in 1837 as,

> Ah! the best of you shall grease my beard
> Before I leave the town O.   (Perkins, 1964, p. 265)

Though the medieval expression *to make one's beard*, meaning 'to make a fool of' (as in Chaucer's *Reeve's Tale*, 'Yet kan a millere make a clerkes berd, / For al his art' (I. 4096–7)), was plainly no longer current by the early nineteenth century, traditional singers had evidently managed to preserve, not only the jaunty swagger of the original boast, but even something of its verbal texture. Almost all modern versions of 'Old Daddy Fox', from both sides of the Atlantic, contain a recognizable variant of these ancient lines.

'The Fox and the Goose' was first published in 1952, so there can be no question of 'Old Daddy Fox' not representing a genuine oral survival or of its verbal echoes being the product of literary sophistication, but an even more dramatic example occurs in 'The Grey Cock' (Child 248). Child, in fact, printed only one rather uninteresting version of this powerful story of a lover who returns from the grave to spend one last brief night in his mistress's arms, but a far more coherent version from Ireland was published by P. W. Joyce seventeen years later,[45] and many others have since come to light.[46] In 1905 a version was recorded from the singing of Farmer Mills of Beaminster, Dorset, which included the stanza:

> The wind it did blow, and the cocks they did crow,
> As I tripped over the plain, plain so very, plain so very, plain—
> So I wished myself back in my true love's arms,
> And she in her bed again.[47]

When I first encountered these lines I assumed that Farmer Mills must have come across the celebrated late fifteenth-century lyric,

---

[45] *Old Irish Folk Music and Song* (Dublin, 1909), 219.
[46] Bronson (ed.), *Traditional Tunes*, iv. 15–23, gives sixteen versions (including Joyce's).
[47] Cecil Sharp House, Hammond MS D538 (I am grateful to Mr Malcolm Taylor, the librarian at Cecil Sharp House, for sending me a xerox copy of this version). An inaccurate text, conflated with another Somerset version collected by Hammond, is printed by Frank Purslow in *Marrow Bones: Songs from the Hammond and Gardiner MSS* (London, 1965), 52.

'Westron Wynde', in some anthology[48] and decided to work it into one of the ballads in his repertoire:

> Westron wynde, when wyll thow blow,
> The small rayne downe can rayne—
> Cryst, yf my love wer in my armys
> And I yn my bed agayne![49]

The verbal echoes seem far too close to have survived intact across four hundred years of oral transmission, yet there is compelling evidence to suggest that this is indeed the correct explanation of their presence. In Henry Bold's *Latine Songs* (1685) occurs what is unmistakably a drollery version of 'The Grey Cock' with the following concluding stanza:

> Then up I rose, and donn'd my Cloaths,
>   And walk'd over the plain;
> Wishing my self on my true Love's Bed
>   And her in mine arms again.[50]

Not only does this striking sequence demonstrate the remarkable durability of oral tradition,[51] but it forces us to recognize the possibility that the fifteenth-century quatrain may be a fragment of a lost ballad and to ask ourselves whether other such lyrics might not sometimes represent similar ballad fragments.[52]

There are, however, far more mundane instances of oral continuity that in some ways are even more impressive. The 'Westron wynde' quatrain is, after all, a particularly evocative one, likely to live long in the memory, but other examples show that verbal

---

[48] 'Westron Wynde' was printed twice in the eighteenth century—by Stafford Smith in 1779 and Joseph Ritson in 1790—and appeared in William Chappell's *Popular Music of the Olden Time*, first printed in 1853, reprinted in 1859, and reissued in 1893. See Rossell Hope Robbins and John L. Cutler (eds.), *Supplement* to *IMEV*, 444 (no. 3899. 3).

[49] *OBLMVP*, p. 178.

[50] Albert B. Friedman, '"The Grey Cock"—A Drollery Version', *Journal of American Folklore*, 67 (1954), 287.

[51] For a motif study of the antiquity of such revenant ballads, including 'The Grey Cock', see Peter Dronke, 'Learned Lyric and Popular Ballad in the Early Middle Ages', *Studi Medievali*, 3rd ser. 17 (1976), 1–40 (esp. pp. 33–6).

[52] One might, for instance, compare the thirteenth-century fragment, beginning 'I ne may cume to mi lef but by the watere' (J. A. W. Bennett and G. V. Smithers (eds.), *Early Middle English Verse and Prose* (Oxford, 1966), 128), with the first line of 'O Waly Waly' (a version of 'Jamie Douglas' (Child 204)): 'The water is wide and I can't get over' (*Cecil Sharp's Collection of Folk Songs*, ed. Maud Karpeles (London, 1974), i. 173).

details can be passed down almost intact even in quite unremarkable contexts. What made Fowler most suspicious of Mrs Brown's 'Thomas Rymer', apparently, was the presence of just such verbal echoes of *Thomas of Erceldoune*, echoes he could only imagine as being due to literary sophistication,[53] yet, as we have seen, Fowler's explanation can be shown on other grounds to have been wrong in this case, and in fact quite similar verbal echoes are easily demonstrated in other cases. For instance, though Child speculated that the ballad of 'Sir Cawline' (61)—which is found in the Percy Folio Manuscript (*c*.1650) and was printed, with considerable editorial interference, in the *Reliques* (1765)—was based on a lost medieval romance, he was plainly unwilling to extend this hypothesis to cover a version called 'Sir Colin', said to have been learned by a Mrs Harris of Perthshire about 1790 and written down by her daughter in 1859. The Harris version he characterizes as 'a fabrication of recent times', suggesting that it was 'most likely . . . put together by some one who was imperfectly acquainted with the copy in the Reliques' (ii. 61). Child's hypothesis about 'Sir Colin', however, can now be shown to be no better founded than Fowler's about 'Thomas Rymer'.

The sixteenth-century Scottish manuscript of *King Orphius* discovered by Marion Stewart also contains a romance version of *Sir Colling*, and as Stewart herself points out there are several places where the verbal texture of this version is far better represented by Mrs Harris's ballad than by the one given nearly a century earlier in Percy's *Reliques*.[54] Here, for example, is an unremarkable moment early in the narrative as it occurs in Mrs Harris's ballad:

> 'Win up, win up, my dochter Janet,
> I wat ye are a match most fyne;
> Tak the baken bread an wine sae reid
> And to Sir Colin ye maun gieng.'

---

[53] For a detailed comparison of the two see E. B. Lyle, 'The Relationship between *Thomas the Rymer* and *Thomas of Erceldoune*', *Leeds Studies in English*, NS 4 (1970), 22–30.
[54] Marion Stewart, 'A Recently-Discovered Manuscript: "ane taill of Sir colling ye kny^t"', *Scottish Studies*, 16 (1972), 23–39.

> Up she rase, that fair Janet,
> An I wat weel she was na sweer [reluctant].
> An up they rase, her merrie maries,
> An they said a' they wad gae wi her.
>
> (Child ii. 61, sts. 3-4)

If Child were right these verses should derive in some way from the following lines in Percy's *Reliques*:

> 'Fetche me downe my daughter deere,
> She is a leeche fulle fine:
> Goe take him doughe, and the baken bread,
> And serve him with the wyne soe red;
> Lothe I were him to tine.'
> Fair Christabelle to his chaumber goes,
> Her maydens followynge nye. (29-35)[55]

However, it is quite clear from even the most cursory comparison that Mrs Harris's version has far more in common at this point with the sixteenth-century romance:

> he sayis get up my dochtar deir
> yow art ane leiche ful fyne
> tak bakin breid and wyne sa reid
> and beir to sir colyne
> w^t yat ye ladie was no^t sweir
> hir madinis schon it syne. (36-41)[56]

Though the version printed in Percy's *Reliques* does preserve the word *leeche*, in almost every other respect it is much further removed from the older *Sir Colling* than Mrs Harris's maligned 'Sir Colin'.

I would not wish to over-stress this point. Most modern versions of ancient ballads (including Mrs Harris's no doubt) are capable of taking at least as great liberties with the phrasing of their sources as they are with narrative detail and storyline.

---

[55] *Reliques of Ancient English Poetry... by Thomas Percy*, ed. Henry B. Wheatley, 3 vols. (1885; London, 1927), i. 63-4; Stewart's own analysis of these passages (p. 37) weakens the contrast somewhat in quoting, not from Percy's *Reliques* (which Mrs Harris might have known), but from the Percy Folio Manuscript, which could not possibly have been available to her.

[56] I cannot make anything out of 'schon it syne'; I suspect that the correct reading is either *schouit syne*, i.e. 'crowded after,' or (as Sally Mapstone has suggested to me) *shonkit* 'burst out'.

Nevertheless, I hope that I have by now adduced enough such ancient survivals to show that it is unwise ever to dismiss out of hand the possibility that any given traditional ballad might incorporate some detail of great antiquity. This insight will rarely be of much help to the medieval editor, who is unlikely, for instance, to find Mrs Brown of Falkirk a valuable witness to the original text of *Thomas of Erceldoune*, but it can be of far greater significance to the student of medieval popular culture, who should always be prepared to recognize the traditional ballad's potential for preserving clues, however opaque and dispersed, to unofficial attitudes and beliefs that might otherwise have disappeared from view.

The story of the miraculous harvest, as it appears in the ballad of 'The Carnal and the Crane' (Child 55), offers a case in point. Two versions of this story can be found in the apocryphal gospels: the older, appearing first in the A-text of the Greek *Infancy Gospel of Thomas* (12: 1–2), and again in the later *Gospel of Pseudo-Matthew* (34) and the Latin *Gospel of Thomas* (10: 1–2), tells of the 8-year-old Jesus sowing a tiny quantity of Joseph's wheat and later harvesting a crop sufficiently abundant to feed the poor of the whole village;[57] the second, found only in the Latin *Gospel of Thomas* (1: 2), and apparently dating from the high Middle Ages, describes an incident on the flight into Egypt when the infant Jesus, having eaten a handful of grain from a field he was passing, makes this field repay the loan in later years by yielding its owner as many measures of wheat as the number of grains taken from it.[58] Neither of these versions, however, prepares us for the charming story found in 'The Carnal and the Crane', a traditional ballad first written down in the middle of the eighteenth century (Child ii. 7). In the ballad the infant Jesus makes a freshly sown field ripen instantly so that, having learnt from a helpful farmer that he has not seen Jesus since sowing time, Herod and his men are tricked into assuming that the trail has gone cold:

---

[57] See *Evangelia Apocrypha*, ed. C. Tischendorf (1876; Hildesheim, 1966), 151, 104, 175; the first and last of these are translated in M. R. James, *The Apocryphal New Testament* (Oxford, 1924), 52, 63.

[58] Ed. Tischendorf, 164, and trans. James, 58; some texts omit the repaid-loan motif.

> 'Turn back,' says the captain,
> 'Your labour and mine's in vain;
> It's full three quarters of a year
> Since he his seed has sown.' (Child ii. 9, st. 27)

This tale is widely distributed in the European ballad tradition (post-medieval versions have been recorded in Denmark, the Low Countries, Germany, France, Provence, Catalonia, and Spain), yet it is almost completely absent from the obvious medieval sources, such as poems on the childhood of Christ.

It would be easy to be sceptical about a putative medieval origin for 'The Carnal and the Crane', were it not for two obscure medieval survivals. In the *Geu des trois roys*, a play (possibly as early as the mid-fourteenth century) from the mystery cycle of the Abbey of St Geneviève in Paris, a sower agrees to Joseph's request that he tell Herod's soldiers that he has seen no one pass him by.[59] After a brief interlude in which the soldiers are shown massacring the innocents, the scene shifts back to the sower, who discovers that his wheat has miraculously ripened and that he can now tell the soldiers in good conscience:

> Certes, seigneurs, je vous convant
> C'onques puis que mon blé semay
> Personne vu venir n'aler n'ay,
> Ne creature petit ne grant. (1380–3)

Indeed, sirs, I certify to you that I have never seen anyone come or go, no creature great or small, since I sowed my wheat.

There is, however, a significant difference between this story and the form it takes in the later ballad, a difference that offers a valuable clue as to why this 'pretty and clever legend', as Child called it, should have been so popular in post-medieval tradition yet so poorly represented in medieval sources. In the play, the sower is already prepared to lie on behalf of the holy family even before the miracle of the wheat has been performed; the miracle therefore provides him with a kind of retroactive

---

[59] *La Nativité et le geu des trois roys*, ed. Ruth Whittredge (Bryn Mawr, 1944), 190–3.

remedy against perjury. It does not, as in the ballad, offer him a deliberate incentive to equivocate:

> So Herod was deceived,
> By the work of God's own hand,
> And further he proceeded
> Into the Holy Land. (st. 28)

Such equivocation was common enough in the medieval secular tradition (Béroul's account of the trial of Isolde furnishes a particularly well known example),[60] but the Church strongly disapproved of it and could scarcely be expected to have condoned a story that showed Christ himself stooping to its use.[61] In fact, apart from the watered-down version in the *Geu des trois roys*, there seems to be only one clear medieval survival of this story of the miraculous harvest (in a single thirteenth-century manuscript of the so-called *Romanz de Saint Fanuel*),[62] but this is enough to suggest that the ballad of 'The Carnal and the Crane' preserves the story in its original form (perhaps even the form lying behind the Latin *Gospel of Thomas*) and that this was later suppressed or modified to try to make it conform with official attitudes.

There are several other areas in which the traditional ballad seems to offer us an authentic glimpse of a popular culture that was almost entirely silenced by the official voice of the medieval church and state. We can learn much about the workings of the unwritten local custom of earlier times, for example, from ballads such as as 'Sir Aldingar' (Child 59), which depicts a trial by battle, or 'Young Hunting' (Child 68), which shows us a kind of trial by ordeal. One could hardly do better as a demonstration of the remarkable longevity of such customs in

---

[60] See Brian Blakey, 'Truth and Falsehood in the *Tristran* of Béroul', in F. J. Barnett et al. (eds.), *History and Structure of French: Essays in Honour of T. B. W. Reid* (Totowa, NJ, 1972), 19-29.

[61] See *Decretum Magistri Gratiani*, Pt. 2, Ca. 22, Qu. 5, C. 11, in *Corpus Iuris Canonici*, ed. Emil Friedberg (Leipzig, 1879), i. 885-6.

[62] See C. Chabaneau, 'Le Romanz de Saint Fanuel', *Revue des langues romanes*, 32 (1888), 378 (n. 2204). The relevant passage, which makes no bones about Jesus's setting up the grounds for the equivocal oath (sworn, ironically enough, 'si m'ait Diex, qu'i ne menti'), is printed in Robert Reinsch, *Die Pseudo-Evangelien von Jesu und Maria's Kindheit* (Halle, 1879), 60-6.

the popular imagination than to compare the so-called 're-
paired rape' in the ballad of 'The Knight and Shepherd's Daughter' (Child 110),

> It's if he be a married knight,
> It's hanged he shall be;
> But if he be a single knight,
> It's married ye sall be,   (Child ii. 471, st. 12)

with the following passage from the early thirteenth-century
Très ancien coutumier de Normandie: 'and if he has been earlier convicted of that crime, should the girl wish to marry him,
he shall take her as his wife; as long as she and her family wish
it, this shall be lawful'.[63] Another obvious area where traditional ballads can frequently reveal attitudes and beliefs that
have been generally excluded from the records of official medieval culture is magic and enchantment. Not even in Walter
Map or Gervase of Tilbury, for example, do we find any hint
that there might have been a medieval English precursor of the
shape-shifting duel that occurs in the ballad of 'The Twa
Magiciens':

> Then she became a gay grey mare,
> And stood in yonder slack,
> And he became a gilt saddle
> And sat upon her back.   (Child i. 403, st. 11)

Yet, as Thomas Hill has recently pointed out, just such a precursor does survive from pre-conquest England in the obscure
Prose Solomon and Saturn: here is one round from its description
of a battle between the Devil and the Pater Noster: 'Dreoteoðan
siðe bið ðæt deoful on sweordes onlicnesse. Feowerteoðan siðe
bið se Pater Noster on gyldenre byrnan onlicnisse' ('The thirteenth time the devil is in the likeness of a sword; the fourteenth
time the Pater Noster is in the likeness of a golden corslet').[64]

---

[63] *Coutumiers de Normandie*, ed. Ernest-Joseph Tardif, 2 vols. (Rouen and Paris, 1881–96), i. 41 (my translation). For evidence of this ethos from a medieval Scottish legal text see *Regiam Majestatem*, ed. Lord Cooper, Stair Society (Edinburgh, 1947), 256–7.

[64] Thomas D. Hill, 'The Devil's Forms and the Pater Noster's Powers: The Prose Solomon and Saturn *Pater Noster* Dialogue and the Motif of the Transformation Combat', *SP*, 85 (1988), 166–7.

Elsewhere, Hill has shown how an allusion to journeying 'ofer grenne grund' in the Old English *Exodus* can be explained by reference to an apparently pre-Christian belief preserved in a nineteenth-century version of 'The Wife of Usher's Well' (Child 79).[65]

What, finally, has been the value of this extended demonstration of the antiquity of some features of the traditional ballad? I should like to conclude by suggesting how study of the humble ballad can sometimes throw an interesting light on far more elevated literary works. In Chaucer's *Wife of Bath's Tale*, to cite just one example, the loathly hag reads her recalcitrant husband a long lecture on the virtues of *gentilesse* (1109–218) on their wedding night. Little in what we have been told of the Wife of Bath herself has led us to suppose that such a subject would hold much interest for her, and the discourse might easily strike a modern reader as being, if not psychologically and dramatically misplaced, at least a striking intrusion into the story: Helen Cooper, for instance, has called it 'the most astonishing' of the developments in the *sentence* of the tale, effectively shifting its emphasis 'from the magic of *fayerye* to inner virtue'.[66] Yet a glance at the ballad analogues of the *Wife of Bath's Tale* may in fact serve to convince us that a concern with gentility lies very close to the heart of the story itself. The ballad of 'King Henry' (Child 32), like the Vermont ballad, 'The Half Hitch', that I alluded to earlier, is a courtship ballad in which a suitor's credentials for marriage are put to the test.

> Lat never a man a wooing wend
> That lacketh thingis three,
> A routh o gold, an open heart
> Ay fu of charity.   (Child i. 298)

Henry passes the test when his courteous behaviour proves him to have learnt the vital lesson that inner worth is of more lasting value than external beauty:

---

[65] '"The Green Path to Paradise" in Nineteenth-Century Ballad Tradition', *Neuphilologische Mitteilungen*, 91 (1990), 483–6.
[66] *Oxford Guides to Chaucer: The Canterbury Tales* (Oxford, 1989), 162.

> When night was gane, and day was come,
> An the sun shone throw the ha,
> The fairest lady that ever was seen
> Lay atween him an the wa.
>
> 'O well is me,' says King Henry,
> 'How lang'll this last wi me?'
> Than out it spake that fair lady,
> 'Even till the day you dee.
>
> 'For I've met wi mony a gentle knight
> That's gien me sic a fill,
> But never before wi a courteous knight
> That ga me a' my will.'   (Child i. 299, sts. 18–20)

Homespun and naïve it may be, when set alongside Chaucer's learned quotations from Dante, but this passage draws none the less on a rich storehouse of traditional lore that makes *gentilesse* an indispensable quality in a happy marriage. Is it out of place to wonder, not merely whether such lore might not have been particularly congenial to Alice of Bath, but whether it might not also have enriched the vision of her creator?

9 'Send thine heart into purgatory': Visionaries of the Other World

ROBERT EASTING

In 1492 Columbus found another world if not the other world. He had sailed partly in the wake of St Brendan's search for the 'Land of Promise', and on his third voyage, in May 1498, he believed that the waters flowing from the mouths of the Orinoco descended from the Earthly Paradise.[1] With God's grace, the Earthly Paradise was still potentially accessible in the flesh, as it had been for Alexander, who had supposedly approached its mossy walls.[2] However, even as adventurous an armchair-traveller as Mandeville confessed, 'Of paradys ne can I not speken propurly for I was not there; it is fer beyonde and that forthinketh me. And also I was not worthi.'[3] Worthy or not, many visitants, religious and lay, claimed to have journeyed to the Earthly Paradise while rapt in spiritual vision, but their sojourn there was usually brief, and preceded by a long and arduous traverse of purgatory. Accounts of such visions retained their popularity throughout the fifteenth century, and well into the seventeenth century in Catholic Europe.

What Douglas Gray calls the 'traditional and "cumulative" quality' of the literature of medieval spirituality[4] is well illustrated by the genre of other-world visions, of which over seventy European examples survive from the third to the fifteenth

---

[1] See *OBLMVP* 7F, and Cristóbal Colón, *Textos y documentos completos*, ed. Consuelo Varela (Madrid, 1982), 218, 220.
[2] See Mary Lascelles, 'Alexander and the Earthly Paradise in Medieval English Writings', *MÆ* 5 (1936), 31–47, 79–104, 173–88, at 99–100.
[3] *Mandeville's Travels*, ed. P. Hamelius, EETS OS 153 (1919), p. 202/10–12.
[4] *OBLMVP*, p. 94.

century.⁵ Such visionary material fed the enduring human appetite for news of the afterlife. Late, vernacular texts were clearly aimed at the devout laity, as well as created by them, and also prepared by and for female religious, and the lines of transmission for these different audiences overlapped. Pious layfolk in the fifteenth century sought many domestic equivalents to the offices and devotional practices of religious, and other-world visions dealt with issues of interest to all, including the fate of the individual soul, the shape of the other world, and practices of penance and intercession. They are allied with *contemptus mundi*, and, in the late Middle Ages, with arts and crafts of dying, books of consolation, and other reflections and intimations of physical mortality and spiritual immortality, from *transi* tombs to Doomsday paintings. On the other side, they link with debates of the body and the soul, and the wider world of visions—of saints, the Virgin, Christ, and the Passion; literary visions, for example, Deguileville's *Pèlerinage de l'âme* (1355–8);⁶ and, a little more distantly, contemplative or mystical experience.

Properly, we should distinguish at least two main kinds of other-world vision. In one, the seer's soul goes on a journey. The principal early Christian text is the *Vision of St Paul* (third century). Highly influential examples, Drihthelm (*c.*690) and Tundale (1149), would nowadays be called 'near-death experiences': while the body of a sick or apparently dead person lies inert, the soul is led on a guided tour of the other world by a guardian angel or saint, instructed on what is seen or suffered, and told to report its experiences on returning to the body.⁷ A variant form, which claims to take the journey literally, has the seer go bodily, as in Aeneas's experience of Hades in *Aeneid* VI, or Owein's visit to St Patrick's Purgatory (1146–7). In the other kind, a purgatorial spirit appears to the seer, vividly

---

⁵ See the tables in Peter Dinzelbacher, *Vision und Visionsliteratur im Mittelalter* (Stuttgart, 1981), 13–23, and Alison Morgan, *Dante and the Medieval Other World* (Cambridge, 1990), 197–9 and App. 2. Eileen Gardiner, *Medieval Visions of Heaven and Hell: A Sourcebook* (New York, 1993), should be used with caution.

⁶ See *OBLMVP* 7C, and *IPMEP* 75.

⁷ See Carol Zaleski, *Otherworld Journeys: Accounts of Near-Death Experience in Medieval and Modern Times* (New York, 1987).

describes his or her sufferings, and usually requests, or sometimes, indeed, demands, suffrages to alleviate them. An example is *The Gast of Gy*, the title of Middle English verse and prose versions of *De Spiritu Guidonis*, concerning an apparition in 1323.[8] Sometimes the two kinds overlap: the visionary not only hears of the other world from a spirit but sees it too, with or without the guided tour. An interesting Anglo-Latin example, unnoticed by recent writers on visions, is Peter of Bramham's account, found in Balliol College, Oxford, MS 228, with a variant version in the third person in the Bodley MS 462 copy of the St Albans Chronicle.[9] About 1343, Peter reports, a priest encounters the purgatorial spirit of his father on horseback who is nearly free of his pains except that he must lead the suffering spirits of his master's wife and her illegitimate child, because he permitted her adultery while entrusted with her care when his master journeyed to Jerusalem. The priest is allowed to see some of the sufferings of souls in purgatory and is instructed on its precise subdivisions according to the degrees of sin and penance performed. Importantly, this vision reminds us that purgatory was not necessarily thought of as one place, but that souls suffered purgatorial punishment in many places, including 'near London', 'on the hill of Monseya' (unidentified), on the island of May in the Firth of Forth, and in Derbyshire (possibly in the cavern at Castleton, that Drayton later calls 'the Divels-arse in the Peake'),[10] as well as near Bramham, Yorkshire [?], where the vision takes place. Similarly in the Middle English translation of Deguileville, *The Pylgremage of the Sowle*, purgatorial spirits suffer in a variety of locations: 'somme in the places where they were born Some in stedes / where they had before hand lordshyp and soveraynte had in theyr lyves / Somme in howses / somme in feldes / Somme in the see / somme in Ryvers / somme in the erthe / somme in deserte /

---

[8] *Manual*, iii. VII [22].
[9] V. H. Galbraith (ed.), *The St Albans Chronicle 1406–1420* (Oxford, 1937), 128–31, prints the latter without reference to the former. For an edition of Peter of Bramham, see my 'Peter of Bramham's Account of a Chaplain's Vision of Purgatory (*c*.1343?)', *MÆ* 65 (1996), 211–29.
[10] *Poly-Olbion*, song XXVI, ed. J. W. Hebel (Oxford, 1933), IV. 531, ll. 397 ff.

somme in wyld forestes...'.[11] The Earthly Paradise was small and certainly remote, but purgatory was thought by many to be ubiquitous.

It is not surprising, therefore, that much of the structure of the late medieval Church was founded on belief in the close interrelationships of the living and the dead. The virtual inevitability of a period in purgatory for Everyman and Everywoman before attaining paradise, entailed indulgences, masses, chantries, hospitals, colleges, obits, lights, anniversaries, and other intercessory institutions, with associated funerary arrangements, wills, and bequests.[12] Accordingly, the devout Christian was widely encouraged via sermons and other didactic material to consider inwardly, to meditate, not only on the Passion but also on the state of souls in the afterlife, as part of a spiritual programme of learning how to live well and die well. In the *ars moriendi* chapter of the *Orologium Sapientiae* (II. 2) of Henry Suso (d. 1365), the Disciple inwardly imagines the likeness of a fair young man on the point of death, who says, 'Putte in thy herte as they [though] thy soule were now in purgatorye and hadde in penaunce for thy trespasses X yeere in the fourneys of brennynge fyre'.[13] In 'A Treatise of Ghostly Battle', we are instructed, 'sende thyne herte in to helle... purgatory... hevyne', with extensive descriptions of each.[14] The Lollard 'Sermon of dead men', on the text 'Memorare nouissima tua' (Ecclus. 7: 36) (which Thomas More considered above 'many whole and great volumes of the best of old philosophers'),[15] after recounting the ten pains of hell (ll. 845–957), advises that 'every man, and specialy men in her myddil age' should 'make a jornay in her thought to the yatis of helle' (citing Isaiah 38: 10), just as

---

[11] *The Pylgremage of the Sowle* [facsimile], The English Experience, 726 (Amsterdam, 1975), cap. lv, fo. 44ᵛ.

[12] See Eamon Duffy, *The Stripping of the Altars: Traditional Religion in England c.1400–c.1580* (New Haven, 1992), esp. chs. 9 and 10, and for a useful collection of (translated) texts, and further bibliography, R. N. Swanson, *Catholic England: Faith, Religion and Observance before the Reformation* (Manchester, 1993).

[13] K. Horstmann, 'Orologium Sapientiae or The Seven Poyntes of Trewe Wisdom aus MS Douce 114', *Anglia*, 10 (1887), p. 361/25–7. For the ME translation, see *IPMEP* 465 and *Manual*, ix. XXIII [80].

[14] *Yorkshire Writers*, ed. C. Horstman, 2 vols. (London, 1895–6), ii. 428–33 (cf. ii. 36–45 (*IMEV* 244)).

[15] 'The Four Last Things', *The English Works of Sir Thomas More*, ed. W. E. Campbell (London, 1931), p. 72c.

they should ever have in mind the joys of heaven, which are subsequently explicated.[16] *The Book of Vices and Virtues*, one of nine complete or partial Middle English translations of the thirteenth-century *Somme le Roi*, recommends such meditation daily: 'departe thi soule fro thi body bi thinkynge; sende thin herte in-to that other world, that is in-to hevene or in-to helle or in-to purgatory, and ther thou schalt see what is good and what is yvele ... Foryet thi body ones a day, and go in-to helle while thou lyvest, that thou come not there whan thou art ded.'[17] Walter Hilton also says that 'for to seen with the gastly eiye the peynes of reprofed and the joye and the blis of chosen soules, it is ful confortable'.[18]

Such encouragements to remembrance of things to come made an explicit appeal to the emotions of fear and hope, the former much sharpened by descriptions of the afterlife which give a detailed sense of its spiritual/physical actuality, conveyed in language of the senses as acute and as concrete as that used to describe the immediacies of earthly life. For instance, when in *The Holy Boke Gratia Dei* 'Drede', like Fearlac in *Sawles Warde*, tells what he saw in Hell, he includes 'Slike mirknes ... that I might it grape [grasp]'[19] and smoke so bitter it made the wretches weep glowing tears. This text is aimed at more potential denizens of hell, from 'Werkmen that falsli swynkis: and takis ful hire' to rich, false judges, and 'Prelates that has cure of mannes saulis: that noither chastis ne techis thaim' by giving them this very kind of instruction. 'Hope', conversely, tells of joy in heaven so great that whoever 'might taste of it a cely drope' should be overtaken by so great a love in yearning to win that bliss that 'a hundreth sithes it suld mare stere him to luf vertuz and flee syn / then ani drede he might have of the payne of hell'.[20]

Among the writings of mystics are moments which show the results of such meditation. For example, St Bridget, whose voluminous revelations circulated in Middle English prose translations, witnesses, often in horrifying detail, the pains of souls in

---

[16] *Lollard Sermons*, ed. Gloria Cigman, EETS OS 294 (1989), p. 234/960–7.
[17] Ed. W. Nelson Francis, EETS OS 217 (1942), pp. 70/33–71/2, 71/14–16.
[18] *Scale of Perfection*, II. 45.
[19] Reactivating Job's 'tenebras palpabunt', cf. Exod. 10: 21 and the *tenebrae palpabiles* of Honorius of Autun's *Elucidarium*, III. 14.
[20] *Yorkshire Writers*, i. 153–4.

hell and purgatory. But these are isolated, usually short, revelations of the judgement and/or sufferings of certain individuals.[21] Bridget does not undergo any extended soul journey. Most of her revelations take the form of addresses by or dialogues with Christ or Mary, experienced while 'suspendid in extasy of gostely contemplacion'.[22] Indeed, the tradition of other-world visions is generally distinct from the contemplative, mystical, ecstatic model, which seeks union with the Divine. Julian of Norwich 'desyeryd as I durste that I myght have had som syght of hel and of purgatory',[23] but her prayer was not answered.

Given the emotional incentive to imagining the other world, and the large number of related exempla which survive,[24] it might be expected that Margery Kempe, attuned to so many strains of contemporary spirituality, would recount such visions. Perhaps she did, but not to us. 'Why speke ye so of the myrth that is in Hevyn; ye know it not and ye have not be ther no mor than we' (11/30-2) was one of many kinds of rebuke she faced.[25] Indeed, she was assured that she should have 'noon other Purgatory' herself 'than slawndyr and speche of the world' (51/14-15, cf. 16/36, 157/6), as when her 'gret wepyngys and boystous sobbyngys' made some wish 'sche had ben in the se in a bottumles boyt' (69/25-6). But there is, after all, a significant difference between describing imaginatively a scene unseen and claiming to have had direct visionary experience of it. There is always the problem of authentication if a real person rather than a personification undertakes to tell a vision. And Margery Kempe was only too well aware of the difficulty in being assured of the divine authenticity of her own visions: 'revelacyons

---

[21] *The Liber Celestis of St Bridget of Sweden*, ed. Roger Ellis, EETS OS 291 (1987), Bk. I, ch. 50, IV. 7-9, 34, 51-2, 102, VI. 16, 31, 35, 39-40, 52, VII. 14, and *The Revelations of Saint Birgitta*, ed. William Patterson Cumming, EETS OS 178 (1929), VIII. 48, 58.

[22] EETS OS 291, p. 366/11-12.

[23] *A Book of Showings to the Anchoress Julian of Norwich*, ed. Edmund Colledge and James Walsh (Toronto, 1978), p. 427/1-2.

[24] Frederic C. Tubach, *Index Exemplorum: A Handbook of Medieval Religious Tales*, FF Communications, 204 (Helsinki, 1969), lists at least 70 exempla concerning visions of the dead, hell, purgatory, and heaven, and over 175 dealing with return of the dead.

[25] Quotations with page and line numbers from *The Book of Margery Kempe*, ed. S. B. Meech and H. E. Allen, EETS OS 212 (1940). Cf. the story of the peasant who sneered at the preacher's account of hell's pains for the latter had not been there to see for himself: Tubach 4237.

'Send thine heart into purgatory'   191

be hard sum-tyme to undirstondyn. And sumtyme tho that men wenyn wer revelacyonis it arn deceytys and illusyons, and therfor it is not expedient to yevyn redily credens to every steryng but sadly abydyn / and prevyn yf thei be sent of God' (219/33–220/1). As Hilton pointed out, with his customary caution, there are dangers for anyone who 'overtravells by ymaginaciouns his wittes and... turnes the braynes in his hevede'.[26] Like Julian of Norwich, Margery never recounts directly any vision of the other world. '[H]yr mevynggys and hyr steringgys', 'hyr felyngys and hyr revelacyons' (3/19, 25) are of the affective kind and, like St Bridget's, nearly all centre on Christ or the Virgin, though she does tell Bishop Philip of Lincoln 'secret thyngys bothe of qwyk and of ded as owyr Lord schewyd to hir sowle' (34/1–2). She also tells two widows that their husbands are in purgatory (46), and when she is in grief at the thought of damnation, and God sends her evil thoughts for twelve days, He tells her, 'Dowtyr, thu must as wel heryn of the dampnyd as of the savyd' (144/22–3).

There survive, however, four fifteenth-century Middle English other-world visions. Two were seen by laymen—*The Vision of William of Stranton* (1406/9), and *The Vision of Edmund Leversedge* (1465)—and two by Benedictines, a nun, *A Revelation of Purgatory to an unknown woman* (1422), and a monk, *The Revelation to the Monk of Eynsham*, printed in London c.1482 by the Belgian printer William de Machlinia and surviving in two slightly variant copies. This latest text is a translation into a NE Worcestershire dialect of a C-text[27] of a Latin account by Adam of Eynsham of his brother Edmund's vision, which occurred in 1196. The translation probably does not pre-date the print by many years. These four texts all deal with purgatory and paradise, but not hell.[28]

---

[26] 'Of Angels' Song', *Yorkshire Writers*, i. 179.
[27] As defined by H. E. Salter, 'Vision of the Monk of Eynsham', *Cartulary of the Abbey of Eynsham*, II, Oxford Historical Society, 51 (1908), 257–371, at 280–3.
[28] Morgan claims that 'All visions up to and including the twelfth-century texts present hell and purgatory jumbled together as one realm of the other world' (*Dante*, 132), but from the time of H[enry] of Sawtry's *Tractatus* in the 1180s, and *Visio monachi de Eynsham* in 1196–7, purgatory as a clearly separate domain dominates other-world vision literature; see my 'Purgatory and the Earthly Paradise in the *Tractatus de Purgatorio Sancti Patricii*', *Cîteaux* 37 (1986), 23–48, one of many responses to Jacques Le Goff's influential *La Naissance du Purgatoire* (Paris, 1981).

Middle English verse versions of earlier Latin visions—of St Paul, Owein at St Patrick's Purgatory, and Tundale[29]—were copied throughout the fifteenth century, but the three new accounts, and the *Eynsham* translation, are in prose.

Stranton recounts an extended soul-journey, consciously prepared for, as it takes place in St Patrick's Purgatory, Lough Derg, which had been widely regarded since at least the mid-twelfth century as a physical entrance to the other world. Unlike his prototype Owein, who claimed to have visited the other world in the flesh, Stranton experiences his vision during sleep within the 'cave' of the Purgatory. Whereas Owein was dragged round purgatory by devils, Stranton, a northerner, is led by one northern saint to whom he is especially devoted, St John of Bridlington, and periodically both scolded and encouraged by another, St Hild of Whitby. He reaches the Earthly Paradise thanks to a cord which he once gave to a merchant who was robbed; this helps him mount a ladder which crosses a river to a high tower on the farther shore. In the Earthly Paradise he is guided by a bishop, and witnesses the judgement of the soul of a vain and idle prioress. About five-sevenths of the vision is devoted to purgatory, which is subdivided into nine fires and five further places of torment, including rocks, towers, a walled enclosure, and a river. Fiends are the agents of God's will. St John of Bridlington explains the sins punished in each torment; St Hild reminds Stranton of Christ's saving Passion and a prayer that he has been given to protect him.

Stranton's vision, like the other three, is a matter-of-fact record of claimed spiritual experience, distinct from literary dream visions, and with no allegorical or verbal pretensions. It is principally a means to attack a wide range of sins and social abuses, mostly committed by religious, for example, lechery, backbiting, and neglect of divine service. Each failing is punished with an inventive but befitting grisliness: the 'stynkyng

---

[29] See *Manual*, ii. V [320] d; [321] c, d; [322]. After mentioning Gy, Owein, St Bridget, and *Tundale* (which he mistakenly states is 'concerned with St Patrick's Purgatory'), Duffy claims that 'there were innumerable less well-known revelations' of the afterlife in late medieval England, and notes *A Revelation of Purgatory* and *Eynsham* (*The Stripping of The Altars*, 338). Unless he is referring to short accounts, such as the numerous exempla noted above, this is misleading. He does not discuss *Leversedge*.

synne and unklene levyng' (104/468) of priests and vicars, who gave their charges no fruit of teaching and good example, is rewarded by 'fendes turnyng here arses toward [them], shytyng uppon hem' (102/449–50).[30] We might consider that there is little gradation of horrors: those who swore by God's members are dismembered as cruelly as the murderers. The vision allows the limbs of the former to protest that 'we have natt deservyde thys horrabyll penance that we suffyr, bott owre herttys and owre tongys, thay dyde the tryspasse' (91/232–4), but this buck-passing is, of course, to no avail. Though the sin may have been a metaphorical murder, the penance is not. The text presents a fully infernalized purgatory, in the sense that the pains of purgatory look just like those of hell, except that they will last 'during the will of God', and may be mitigated by suffrages. The vision is a call to 'worldly men' to repent, and a reminder of the ways both clergy and laity can assist the souls in purgatory: 'as to lernyd men, as bi masses singyng, saing of sawters, Placebo and Dirige; commendacions, .vij. salmes and the .xv. psalmes with the letenye; bi almes-dede, and bi pilgrimage; and also bi lewid men with the Pater noster, the Ave Maria, and the Crede; almes-dede, fastyng, and pilgrimage; and bi many other good dedis' (106/520–5).

Of Stranton himself we are told little directly. He had been on repeated pilgrimages from his home near Hartlepool to Bridlington and Whitby before his visit to Lough Derg in Ireland. His uncle, dead eleven (or sixteen) years, had been a lax and worldly parson, who still suffers with his kind. Stranton is thanked in paradise for all his good works, however small, such as lighting a candle before a saint's image in a church. His conscience, as well as St John of Bridlington, clearly condemns him for forbidding his sister's love-match. This is the one explicitly personal moment in the text. His sister's spirit accosts and accuses him, declaring that she and her lover had wanted three children, yet Stranton had told them they would 'nothir have joye of other' (84/129–30), and for that cause they abandoned

---

[30] Quotations with page and line numbers from *St Patrick's Purgatory*, ed. Robert Easting, EETS OS 298 (1991).

their marriage plans. If he was responsible for the original text of his vision, he was familiar with some version of the *Tractatus de Purgatorio Sancti Patricii*, and possibly the Middle English *Vision of Tundale*, as well as with the complaints of sermon literature. A devout, sober, even sombre citizen, Stranton gives a plain-spoken and orderly account of the fate awaiting disorderly clerics and other worldly men. Be 'a good man in thi levyng' (112/646), he is enjoined in paradise; 'live rightfully and thow shalt come to everlestyng joy' (116/702-3). He enters St Patrick's Purgatory on Friday after Holyrood day, with proper recognition of the saving power of the Passion. The alternative manuscript reading, Easter Day, looks (in the context of other mistakes) like a copyist's devout improvement—Edmund of Eynsham's vision, for instance, took place between Good Friday and Easter Eve. Stranton is to recount what he has seen 'to them that this bilongith to' (116/702) and prays for the prayers of those that hear or read his text. The two surviving manuscript copies indicate that it reached from Hartlepool to Leicestershire and Warwickshire at least, if not further south, given the substitution of the Cornish St Ive of Quethiock for Hild of Whitby in the Warwickshire copy.

The Leicestershire copy is bound up in BL MS Additional 34193 with the unique Leicestershire copy of *The Vision of Edmund Leversedge*. This manuscript contains further otherworld material, *The Pylgremage of the Sowle* and *De Spiritu Guidonis*. Leversedge, a 'gentilman' according to his will, was lord of the manor of Frome Falaise in Somerset, of a class not otherwise represented among other-world visionaries.[31] His vision conforms to many of the standard patterns of the genre. It recounts his apparent three-hour death from 'the plage of pestylence' (22-3)[32] in May 1465, his soul's journey guided by his 'good angel', his encounter with demons, a dispute concerning his good and evil deeds, his meeting with a Lady (possibly, even probably, the Virgin, though this is never made explicit),

---

[31] *Leversedge* has recently been discussed in Andrew D. Brown, *Popular Piety in Late Medieval England* (Oxford, 1995).

[32] Quotations with line numbers from *The Vision of Edmund Leversedge*, ed. W. F. Nijenhuis (Nijmegen, 1991).

his good angel's instructions about seeking spiritual advice from his local clergy, and his return to the body. But this short text has a marked individuality. It eschews much of the machinery of other-world descriptions.[33] There is no tour of the places of punishment or purgation, and, apart from a hill and ladders, no attempt is made at an other-world topography. It focuses less on pains and pleasures and more on what is heard than seen, the judgements and instructions of God, the Lady, and his good angel, who all seek to redirect the future course of his life. Whereas Stranton is reticent about himself, Leversedge is almost wholly self-centred: he is concerned with his personal circumstances to a degree unmatched by other such visions.

After his death in 1496, the memory of his vision was 'handed down by oral tradition, with a sort of sacred carefulness', and versified by the local poet Elizabeth Tuck, who recounted his passage to 'that amazing scene / Where ... souls in endless freedom range',[34] and his subsequent conversion from a life of Pleasure and Vice to plain dressing and pious good works. Edmund's vision and its impact on his wayward youth were known to the contemporary continuator of the 'Compilacio de gestis britonum et anglorum' in Lambeth Palace Library, MS 22, who writes that Leversedge 'adolescentiam suam insolenter consumpserat' (fo. 148^v).[35] His besetting vice was indulgence in high fashion and it seems his vision cured him of it. Extravagant, wasteful dress, 'inordinate aray' (145, 287–8, 292, 388), was lambasted from the pulpit in the fourteenth and fifteenth centuries, and is the object of attacks in *Stranton*, which Edmund seems to have known, but whereas Stranton speaks in the common voice of advocate for the poor and needy, Leversedge speaks as a reformed devotee of *haute couture*. He is convinced that pride, vanity, and excess in dress 'wyl be the cause of uttire distruccion of this seyd realme' (11–12) and his first intended audience is very specific: 'thees prowde men namyng themselfe

---

[33] See Wiesje F. Nijenhuis, 'Truncated Topoi in *The Vision of Edmund Leversedge*', *MÆ* 63 (1994), 84–97.
[34] 'Vallis Vale. Part II', *Vallis Vale, and Other Poems* (London, 1823), 28, and Preface, p. vi. A long extract is cited in Nijenhuis' edn (misreading 'rage' for 'range', p. 133), and see pp. 56–7.
[35] Cited in Nijenhuis' edn, p. 56.

galandis' (96-7). The expression 'galants' (see also 141, 158, 290) was fairly recent—*MED* first records it as a noun meaning a 'man of fashion' from the Paston Letters in 1448. The cockiness of these self-styled 'galants' and his own previous behaviour clearly vexed Edmund bitterly. One of the most startling moments in the vision is his discovery that the horde of devils who come to torment his soul, four or five thousand of them, 'were non otherwise arayd to my aperyng but aftire the aray that theese galantes, thes proud peeple, nowondayes usune' (140-2); they were clad 'in schort gownes and dowblettes, closse hosyn, longe heere upon here browes, pykes on ther shon of a foot in lengh and more, hyghe bonettes as I myselfe sumetyme usid, and thes prowid peple that callis themselfe galantes yit usid' (154-8). These over-dressed devils later cry out to the Lady against Edmund's release from their clutches. To urge their complaint they make what appears to be a model of Edmund and brandish it in her direction (373-7). The Lady imposes on Edmund a personal set of sumptuary laws—specifying price limits on his tailoring—and tells him to get his hair cut; he is an icon of pride humbled.[36] Edmund's achieved sobriety befits his later Carthusian connections.

Despite the monetary and social niceties—the Lady also condemns his 'liberte of kissyng' ladies—Leversedge's vision does show a fundamental concern for his spiritual welfare. His steadfast faith in the sacrament of the altar and the mercy of God are insufficient for salvation without good works and the Lady requires of him a major change of life. She commands him to leave Frome and study divinity for eight years at Oxford under the alias William Wreche. Oxford records are incomplete and do not record his presence there under either name. That he had some familiarity with the city is suggested by the Lady's showing his soul 'the towne and wallis of Oxforth, with the

---

[36] Cf. e.g. the 'Grasless [graceless] galante in all thy luste and pryde' in the verses for the Hungerford Chantry, Salisbury Cathedral (*Manual*, v. XIII [163]), cited M. A. Hicks, 'The Piety of Margaret, Lady Hungerford (d. 1478)', *Journal of Ecclesiastical History* 38 (1987), 19-38 (p. 28), and the figure of pride in the Carthusian BL MS Additional 37049 fo. 47ᵛ, and see further Wendy Scase, '"Proud Gallants and Popeholy Priests": The Context and Function of a Fifteenth-Century Satirical Poem', *MÆ* 63 (1994), 275-86.

ryvers and medeues perteining therto' (528–30), and also by his likening the debate at his judgement to a dispute of 'docturs in ther scolis' (316–17). It is characteristic of the domestic practicalities of his vision that the Lady also warns him while in Oxford not to visit the 'lavender howse, ne lett her [i.e. the laundress] com in thi chambir' (531–2). Did he call himself William Wreche? He constantly reiterates the epithet 'wrechid' to describe himself (145, 433, 469, 520, 634) and the world (686), a common enough word in such a text as this. But he also refers to himself as 'I, synful wrecche' (417–18, cf. 649, 652), and the opening paragraph introduces him as 'I, a wrechid creature and a synfulle, namyd sumetyme Edmunde Leversegge' (5–6, cf. 145–6), where 'sumetyme' may carry a specific charge, indicating his name before and after residence in Oxford. Could all this be a play on his alias, assumed or intended, or is it just a commonplace expression of penitence? At any event, Leversedge's other-world vision aims to show one 'wretched', that is miserable as sinner and exiled from his true God-given shape by pride of array (378–82), converted and re-formed by penance, which, like Stranton, he enjoins on his readers and hearers.

Stranton and *Leversedge* give us valuable access to the spiritual anxieties and aspirations of middling to well-to-do layfolk. The other two visions concern religious. *A Revelation of Purgatory* (1422), or 'A Revelacyone schewed to ane holy womane now one late tyme' (as the Thornton MS copy heads it), records a vision seen most likely by a sister of Nunnaminster, Winchester, and is couched in the form of a letter addressed to her spiritual father. She recounts how she was 'ravyshed into purgatory' (13)[37] on the night of St Lawrence, the grid-iron saint. On the same anniversary (10 August), the 'full merveylous dreme' of the Middle English *Pylgremage of the Sowle* takes place. On three successive nights she sees the purgatorial progress of the soul of one Margaret, 'a sustre of a house of religious' (43–4), likewise, it seems, Nunnaminster.

Purgatory here is complex and threefold: the first purgatory

---

[37] Quotations with line references from *A Revelation of Purgatory by an Unknown, Fifteenth-Century Woman Visionary*, ed. Marta Powell Harley (Lewiston, 1985).

is the general Purgatory of Righteousness; the second is the Purgatory of Mercy; the third, the Purgatory of Grace. The general Purgatory of Righteousness is the equivalent of the usual purgatory seen by visionaries. Here it comprises three fires along with the torments of various categories of sinners, religious and secular men and women, married and single.[38] In *A Revelation* the first fire is the immediate destination of those who have not completed penance for deadly sin and those who delay being shriven till the last possible moment. They must subsequently pass through the other two fires. The middle fire immediately receives a wide spectrum of intermediate sinners with unshriven venial sins, or sins forgotten, 'or lyght penaunce or over-lytell, or over-negligently done that was enjoynet ham to do, or overlytell repentaunce, or penaunce joynet and noght fulfilled ar thay deyed' (737–41). These also pass through the third, 'cler fyr', whither go straightaway innocents, religious, anchoresses and anchorites 'and al holy closed peple', martyrs and confessors and 'all maner of Cristen men and wommen in the world what syn that ever thay have done if har penaunce be fulfilled ar thay deyed' (751–4). This careful enumeration of categories befits the religious background of the visionary and is unlike anything found in *Stranton* or *Leversedge*. The Purgatory of Mercy is the experience of 'sekenesse and grete tribulacions in this wor[l]de' (765–6), and the Purgatory of Grace (774–89) is where souls suffer in the places in which they sinned and appear to men and women waking or sleeping and 'telle whate may helpe tham, and so thay ere delyvered of thair paynes' (783–5), as in the vision recounted by Peter of Bramham.[39]

The seer in *A Revelation of Purgatory* had clearly had many previous such experiences: 'sodeynly I saw al the peynes whiche wer showed to me many tymes before—as ye, fadyr, knew wel

---

[38] Eynsham also divides purgatory into three places (see below), as does one vision seen by St Bridget (Bk. IV, ch. 7), who may be a model for this anonymous nun.

[39] This idea is found in *Legenda Aurea*, cap. CLXII, ed. Th. Graesse, 3rd edn. (Bratislava, 1890; repr. Osnabrück, 1965), 730–1, and thence, e.g., in *The Early South-English Legendary*, ed. Carl Horstmann, EETS OS 87 (1887), pp. 422–3/79–94, and *The Pricke of Conscience*, ll. 2876–89, where *Legenda Aurea* 'per divinam dispensationem' is rendered '[t]hurgh speciel grace' (2885). On earlier examples, see Franz Neiske, 'Vision und Totengedenken', *Frühmittelalterliche Studien*, 20 (1986), 137–85.

by my tellynge' (13–15, cf. 212). This is characteristic of many of the women visionaries of the later Middle Ages, and is distinctly different from the one-off visions of the other world recorded of men, like Stranton and Leversedge. None the less, at the initial threatening (65–6) appearance of Margaret's spirit, the visionary is as uncertain of what faces her as Hamlet is before his father's ghost, and asks 'whether thou be a spirite of purgatory to have help of me other a spirite of helle to overcome me and trowble me' (82–4). Margaret proves herself an honest ghost by identifying herself as one known in life to the visionary (89–91), and by her immediate request that masses be said for her. Like the ghost of Gy, who expatiates on the merits of masses of the Trinity and of the Holy Spirit, and the Seven Psalms with the Litany, the ghost of Margaret is meticulous in detailing the exact combinations of masses and recitations of the psalm *Miserere mei deus* and the hymn *Veni creator spiritus* which will release her and other souls from their pains (94–191).

As in *Stranton*, the pains in *A Revelation* are particularly violent. It is some reassurance, no doubt, to the souls of the lecherous unmarried to be told by tormenting devils, 'wit ye welle this is noght helle—this is an instrument of Goddis ryghtwisnesse to purge yow of your syn in purgatory' (574–7), for in these visions we are (literally) a world away from the positive spirit of Dante's antipodean Purgatorio. In *A Revelation* lecherous priests have the most pain, and Margaret is tormented by the devil of pride for extravagant dress (like Leversedge, and the prioress in *Stranton*), and by six further devils for the other deadly sins (247–332). Her arms and legs are also eaten by a dog and cat (74, 193, 197, 265) for 'thay wer hir mawmettes the whil sho was on lyve, and sho sett hyr hert to mych on such foul wormes' (628–30—Madame Eglentyne, beware!). But by the prayers and masses she requested, Margaret is released from purgatory, and the visionary briefly witnesses her being bathed in a well, presented with a crown and sceptre in token of her defeat of her spiritual enemies, and brought in procession to the golden gate of paradise.

It is the Easter bells pealing in paradise which awaken Edmund of Eynsham from his vision in 1196. The original Latin *Visio* was a monastic production; the Middle English *Eynsham* is adapted for a lay audience: certain monastic expressions are explained, for instance, and all embedded scriptural citations in Latin are also translated. *Eynsham* omits Adam's prologue but is otherwise a fairly faithful, though not particularly elegant, translation. Like Edmund Leversedge 269 years later, Edmund of Eynsham experiences his vision while apparently dead or close to death. Following more than a year of a debilitating illness, in a heightened emotional atmosphere of bodily mortification, and feeling himself near death, Edmund prays for a vision of the other world, that 'our lord god ... wolde white safe [vouchsafe] to revele and shewe to me in some manner of wise the state of the worlde that is to come and the condicion of the soulys that byn past her bodyes after this lyfe' (29),[40] so that he might 'stabylle' himself in the dread and love of God. Unlike Julian of Norwich, he finds this prayer successful. At the beginning of Lent, in a dream vision, he is told that his petition will soon be granted if he prays and asks for the prayers of certain devout persons on his behalf, including, it seems, the nuns of nearby Godstow. He collapses on the eve of Good Friday and recovers on Easter eve, during which time his vision takes place.

Eynsham presents yet another different picture of the other world. Led by St Nicholas, Edmund sees purgatory,[41] which has three divisions: the first, a wide region of miry, thick clay; the second, a high hill, the near side cold and stormy, the far side fiery, with a deep dark valley and a stinking pond; the third, a great, low, isolated, cloudy field. The torments in each are commonplace in such visions—for example, souls are roasted, fried, and 'gnawyn with the venummys teth of wondyrfull wormys' (38). Thereafter Edmund passes through the flowery field of the Earthly Paradise, where souls enjoy a vision of the Crucifixion, to a crystal wall. Here a gate bearing another cross

---

[40] Quotations with page numbers from *The Revelation to the Monk of Evesham* [sic], ed. E. Arber (Westminster, 1869; repr. 1901). I am preparing a new edition of *Eynsham* for EETS.

[41] Not hell, *pace* Morgan, *Dante*, 223.

descends and parts him temporarily from his leader before he enters and beholds a brilliant light, which unlike most such encounters does not dull a man's sight, but 'rathyr scharpyd hyt' (108). Stairs lead up to Christ seated on a throne, but this is 'not the hye hevyn of hevyns where the blessid spiritis of angels and the holy sowlys of ryghtwys men joyin yn the seyghte of god seyng hym yn hys mageste as he ys' (108). He returns to his body as the bells in paradise ring for Easter. The parallel timing of Edmund's vision and Christ's Harrowing of Hell is matched, as we have seen, in one copy of *Stranton*, and, of course, in Dante's traverse of the Inferno.

Though Edmund's vision is the earliest of those under consideration here it is also in many ways the most modern in its exploration of the inner life. The souls of a range of sinners known to Edmund recount their confessional stories as they are encountered in purgatory. These testimonies are more extensive and personal than in any other of the visions preceding Dante. They show an interest in the moral life and conscience of the individual which was developing rapidly in the twelfth century and encouraged by more searching confessional practices. One remarkable case is that of the alcoholic goldsmith, which takes up five chapters.[42] Whereas Leversedge's vision truncates the expected topoi, Edmund of Eynsham's builds upon them in novel ways. For instance, though anonymous, the goldsmith is not merely an example of the sin of drunkenness, as he might have been in any number of earlier visions or other didactic texts; we learn of his personal struggles to control it, and his relapses, encouraged by 'the importunyte of feleshyppe that y dranke with' (48). He not only exemplifies the benefits of serving the saints, but we learn much personal detail of his devotion to St Nicholas as 'hys famylyar servante and mawncypylle' (49). He tells of his encounter with the devil who comes for his soul, following a pattern found in many another death-bed scene, but here enlivened with an idiosyncratic image, 'Trewly I felte him [the devil] like an owle goo in to my mowthe'

---

[42] Discussed also by Morgan, ibid. 69–70, and see Kim Dian Gainer, 'Prolegomenon to *Piers Plowman*: Latin Visions of the Otherworld from the Beginnings to the Thirteenth Century', Ph.D. thesis (Ohio State University, 1987), 178–93.

(51). He subsequently appears thrice to his wife 'wakingly' to encourage her to continue his devotions to St Nicholas, but she 'excused her that for the on-certente of vysyons sche dyfferde hyt leste that hyt sculd have bene supposyd that sche hadde be dysceyved and begylde' (55). (Margery Kempe had similar doubts.) *Eynsham* suggests how Edmund imagines that the spiritual lives of this devout layman and his family and others were shaped by the commonplaces of other-world literature and iconography, at the same time as the scope of that literature is itself modified and extended by their personal stories.

Edmund of Eynsham's vision is one of the longest and the latest of the great series of twelfth-century Latin other-world visions, of Alberic, Tnugdal (Tundale), Gunthelm, Owein, and Godeschalc, among others. Morgan has claimed that 'No new visions are recorded after that of Thurkill in 1206'.[43] True, there were no new major visions of the other world recorded between that of Thurkill and Dante's literary summation and re-creation of the genre, and the visionary impulse shifted towards the affective, contemplative, mystical, and ecstatic from the mid-twelfth century onward, but as we have seen there *were* new other-world experiences and texts recording them in fifteenth-century England, and earlier visions continued to be widely copied and translated into both verse and prose, and transmitted alongside everything from legal documents to romances and devotional material. In a century when vernacular religious writing was suspiciously scanned for traces of Lollardy, the experience, composition, copying, and printing of visions of purgatory were sure signs of orthodoxy.

Visions of the other world are traditional and cumulative. They rehearse well-known images of pain and joy, not only because the visionaries themselves are familiar with earlier texts or descriptions and their imaginations are necessarily prompted by such accounts, but also because such images are a means of claiming authority for a vision by its likeness to previous reports. Nevertheless, as we have glimpsed, there remained much scope for personal variations on central themes, not least because

---

[43] Morgan, *Dante*, 3, and see also p. 112.

there was no official Church doctrine on the details of the topography and content of the other world. Theologians tended to be cautious rather than speculative about 'that unknowen cuntrey' of the dead;[44] visionaries filled in the gaps.

Before it was thrown out as 'trash' in the 1530s, purgatory was pivotal in the post-mortem hiatus before Doomsday: it swung the soul from fear to hope, the arc of the faithful Christian's story being a divine comedy. One of the few additions in the late Middle English *Eynsham* emphasizes that 'some that were in peynys knew a certente of her delyverans and that was to hem a grete solace'.[45] These visions were practical aids to achieving the solace of paradise and entry to the 'holy universite of hevene'.[46] They are not presented as the fruits of divine contemplation. They skirt the metaphorical, metaphysical, and mystical quicksands of the difficulties of seeing and understanding 'gostely', which frequently concern contemplatives, such as Hilton. Their goals are instruction, amendment, and penance, as with the most copied of all Middle English texts on the last things, *The Pricke of Conscience*. They give us immediate access to some of the ways in which the injunctions of handbooks of penance and the pulpit impinged on the consciousness and consciences of certain individuals, and, whether consciously or not, they reveal the seer as well as the seen.

---

[44] *Anglia*, 10 (1887), p. 362/44–5.   [45] Arber (ed.), *Revelation*, 81.
[46] *Speculum Sacerdotale*, ed. Edward H. Weatherly, EETS OS 200 (1936), p. 200/3–4.

10 Fleshly Monks and Dancing Girls: Immorality in the Morality Drama

MALCOLM GODDEN

The morality play *Wisdom*, usually dated around 1460, survives in two early manuscripts, a rare thing for medieval English drama and presumably testifying to some degree of interest, if not popularity, in its own time.[1] Yet though it has received a fair degree of attention in recent years, compensating for earlier neglect in favour of the racier *Mankind* and the better-known *Everyman*,[2] its place in late medieval dramatic and theatrical tradition remains a puzzle. Linguistic and codicological analyses have now firmly located it within the rich tradition of fifteenth-century East Anglian drama, alongside the N-town cycle of mystery plays, *The Castle of Perseverance*, *Mankind* and a number of other individual plays.[3] But ideas about its origin and theatrical context remain remarkably varied, moving on from E. K. Chambers's suggestion that it 'was intended for school performance' to a whole series of alternatives: that it was part of a professional troupe's repertoire; or designed for

---

[1] The two versions (which are very similar) are edited in *The Macro Plays*, ed. M. Eccles, EETS OS 262 (1969), and *The Digby Plays*, ed. D. C. Baker, J. Murphy, and L. B. Hall, EETS OS 283 (1982). Of the other medieval morality plays, *The Castle of Perseverance* and *Mankind* survive only in the Macro manuscript, and *Everyman* (OBLMVP 21) only in sixteenth-century prints. The fragmentary *Pride of Life* now survives only from a nineteenth-century print, the sole manuscript having been destroyed (in *Non-Cycle Plays and Fragments*, ed. N. Davis, EETS SS 1 (1970)).
[2] Note especially the collection of essays prompted by a production of the play in 1984, Milla Cozart Riggio (ed.), *The Wisdom Symposium: Papers from the Trinity College Medieval Festival* (New York, 1986).
[3] See especially Gail McMurray Gibson, *The Theatre of Devotion: East Anglian Drama and Society in the Late Middle Ages* (Chicago and London, 1989), and J. C. Coldewey, 'The Non-Cycle Plays and the East Anglian Tradition', in *The Cambridge Companion to Medieval English Theatre*, ed. R. Beadle (Cambridge, 1994).

performance in a baronial hall or court; or written by a monk for performance in his abbey; or performed 'by the men and women of a town or guild for a general audience'; or produced for a Cambridge college.[4]

One of the particular puzzles of this play is the use of dance. The play's central characters are three male figures, Mind, Will and Understanding, who represent the active mental faculties belonging to Anima the soul, represented as a virgin: Lucifer successfully tempts them into the sins of the world, causing Anima to lose her beauty and innocence, but Wisdom intervenes to prompt the three faculties to repent and thus restore all four to their original purity. At the critical stage of their corruption, the three central characters call up three sets of dancers in turn to show the vices which accompany their new concerns. For Mind there are six yeomen or retainers, identified with violence and oppression, and called Indignacyon, Sturdynes, Males, Hastynes, Wreche, and Dyscorde; they have trumpeters as their accompaniment, and Mynd rechristens himself Mayntennance to be their leader. For Understanding there are six jurymen, named Wronge, Sleyght, Dobullnes, Falsnes, Raveyn, and Dyscheyit; their musician is a bagpiper, and Understanding becomes their leader as Perjury. Finally for Will we have the following stage-direction, at line 752 in the Macro version:

Here entreth vi women in sut dysgysyde as galontys and iii as matrones wyth wondyrfull vysurs conregent here mynstrell a hornepype.

The Digby copy has essentially the same stage-direction (and promptly breaks off incomplete at that point). Will has called them on to the stage as the company or offspring of Lechery, identifying them with the brothel—'Here forme ys of the stewes

---

[4] See for instance E. K. Chambers, *English Literature at the Close of the Middle Ages* (Oxford, 1945), 61; David Bevington, 'Political Satire in the Morality *Wisdom who is Christ*', in *Renaissance Papers 1963* (Durham, NC, 1964), 41–51, at 51; Alexandra Johnston, '*Wisdom* and the Records: Is There a Problem?' in Riggio (ed.), *The Wisdom Symposium*, 87–101; Gail McMurray Gibson, 'The Play of *Wisdom* and the Abbey of St Edmund', ibid. 39–66; Eccles (ed.), *The Macro Plays*, p. xxxv; Milla Riggio, '*Wisdom* Enthroned: Iconic Stage Portraits', in Clifford Davidson and John H. Stroupe, (eds.), *Drama in the Middle Ages: Comparative and Critical Essays. Second Series* (New York, 1991), 249–79, at 276 n. 8.

clene rebaldry'— and names them as personifications of sensuality and sexual licence:

> Cum slepers, Rekleshede and Idyllnes,
> All in all, Surfet and Gredynes,
> For the flesche, Spousebreche and Mastres,
>   Wyth jentyll Fornycacyon.

The stage-direction seems to indicate nine women dancers, but the editors of both versions emend the text to read 'six women in sut, thre dysgysyde...', making six dancers in all, perhaps rightly since the other two characters in this very symmetrical play each have six dancers and only six or seven names are given for Will's set (Eccles suggests that 'Surfet and Gredynes' represent one character). The 'galauntes' are presumably presented as fashionably dressed young men about town of the kind that frequent brothels. In the N-town play (from the same region as this play) Raise-Slander suggests that Mary has been made pregnant by 'some fresh young gallant' who has cuckolded Joseph,[5] while in the Digby play *Mary Magdalen* a finely dressed 'gallant' is introduced as the agent of Lechery to seduce Mary.[6] Their vices are not simply the sins of the flesh but also the particular corruptions which were understood to prompt sexual desire. These six women then, three disguised as young men about town representing Recklessness, Idleness, and Surfeit/Greediness, and three posing as married women representing Adultery, Mistress, and Fornication, all wearing matching costumes ('in sut') and masks, dance before Mind, Will, and Understanding to the music of their hornpipe. Presumably the dancers were expected to perform in ways which in some manner suited their role as personifications of sensuality and sexual licence, while the hornpipe, it has been suggested, was chosen because of its visual and eponymous association with cuckoldry.[7]

What did the playwright mean by the expression 'Here entreth six women'? Is this a reference to the gender of the performers or of their roles? Did the playwright actually mean that women dancers should play the role, and were they actually used in

---

[5] *The N-Town Play*, ed. S. Spector, 2 vols. EETS SS 11 and 12 (1991), p. 142, l. 87.
[6] *The Digby Plays*, 40.   [7] See Eccles' note in *The Macro Plays*, 212.

performance of this play (since marginalia in the Macro manuscript show that it was actually performed)? It has been suggested in the past that the play was designed to be performed by a small professional troupe of six male actors and six boys, the latter taking the parts not only of the boys who enter at another point as devils but also of the five wits who are cast as virgins and of these three sets of dancers.[8] Doubling the parts of the three sets of dancers seems in fact beyond possibility, or at least not what the writer had in mind: no exits are marked or allowed for for the dancers until a general exit after the last trio has performed, and there is far too little text between each dance to cover the elaborate costume changes that would be called for if they were to exit and reappear as another set of dancers. The stage-directions for the previous two dances are not strictly parallel, either not specifying the players ('Her entur six dysgysyde in the sute of Mynde'), or referring to the roles they play ('Here entrethe six jorours in a sute'). When, earlier, the stage-direction reads 'Here enteryd fyve vyrgynes in white kertyllys and mantelys... and synge', the reference is presumably to their role rather than the identity of the performers; given that what they sing is a Latin hymn, and that boys are used elsewhere in the play, they could easily be choirboys. But a later stage-direction clearly refers to the performers as distinct from their roles: 'Here rennyt owt from undyr the horrybyll mantyll of the SOULL seven small boys in the lyknes of devyllys and so retorne ageyn' (912). The stage-direction about Will's dancers seems closest in form to this one, referring to 'women' as players and 'galaunts' and 'matrones' as their roles. Since three at least of Will's dancers are disguised as men, there seems no reason for the stage-direction to call them women if the performers were in fact boys.[9] It is true that Shakespeare could present boy-actors playing women who disguised themselves as men, but he did give them opportunity to

---

[8] See David Bevington, *From Mankind to Marlowe* (Cambridge, Mass., 1962), 116; *Skelton's Magnyfycence* ed. R. L. Ramsay, EETS ES 98 (1906), p. cxxxii. Chambers's view that the play was intended for school performance presumably also reflects an assumption that the dancers were played by boys.
[9] Cf. Eccles (ed.), *The Macro Plays*, p. xxxiv.

establish their female identities first; it seems inconceivable that this dramatist was counting on boy performers, in the space of a brief dance, to convey female identity beneath the disguise of gallants. The editors of both texts of the play and most commentators conclude that the dancers were in fact played by women, and this seems to fit the evidence.[10]

Yet this raises a troubling question: why did the dramatist choose to specify women here, given that three of them were playing male roles and that he did not specify the gender of the other sets of dancers?[11] Why could the roles of the gallants at least not be danced by men? There seem to be at least three possibilities here. First, one might argue that he intended the female gender of the dancers playing the gallants to be made evident to the audience, and that their femaleness was part of the dramatic point, either because of a conventional association of women, or specifically women dancers, with lechery,[12] or because women dressed as gallants were suggestive of sexual licence. Secondly, it may be that the gender of the dancers was not meant to be evident to the audience but women were specified because the kind of dancing intended required the particular skills expected of women dancers. The mixed-sex dancing of the gallants and matrons was no doubt of a different kind from the dances of the six yeomen and the six jurors (more sophisticated and less laddish perhaps), though if it was meant as a burlesque of actual social practice, that is, partnered dancing in court or hall, it cannot have been far removed from the kind of dancing commonly practised by men as well as women. Thirdly (and in many ways this is the most interesting possibility

---

[10] In a subsequent book Bevington seems to have come to accept that a larger group, including women dancers, would be needed for a full performance: see *The Macro Plays: The Castle of Perseverance, Wisdom, Mankind: A Facsimile Edition with Facing Transcription*, ed. David Bevington (New York, 1972), p. xi: 'The dancers of the retainers, which apparently could be omitted, would also require six women in silent parts.'

[11] Although the Macro manuscript shows signs of preparation for performance, the elaborate stage-directions which occur more or less identically in both copies seem to reflect the author's intentions for performance, rather than a subsequent producer's or designer's additions; they are fully integrated with the text, which could not make sense without them.

[12] Lechery is a female character in both *The Castle* and the Digby play of *Mary Magdalen*, and indeed in most medieval representations apart from *Piers Plowman*. On the associations of female dancers see further below.

for the rest of my argument), there may have been an extra-dramatic reason: the dramatist may have been moved by the moral implications of requiring performers to simulate sexual licence in a dance; to require the dancers to be all of the same sex may have safeguarded the necessary distance between the figuring of depravity and the actuality of it. But given the dramatic conventions of the time one might have expected this to prompt the use of an all-male cast, and the argument rests in turn on questions of the origin and home of this play, to which we will turn later.

The involvement of women dancers in this play, and particularly in such sensual roles, is something of a surprise and anomaly, given the well-known resistance of contemporary English drama to using women performers. Two major questions arise: what is the context for these dancers in English theatrical tradition; and how do they fit into the larger concerns of the play, which many commentators associate with monastic ideals and even monastic composition and performance?

The question of women on the medieval stage has been much discussed in recent years. It is clear that they regularly played the female roles in fifteenth-century drama on the Continent, though such roles were also played by males (since the evidence is largely records of the names of the performers, it is not usually evident whether these were boys, adolescents, or mature men). Lynette Muir shows that in Northern France it was unmarried women only who were involved, but further south it was common for respectable married women, the wives of leading citizens, to act in the lavish outdoor productions of mystery plays.[13] But in the English mystery plays evidence for women on the stage seems to be entirely lacking. As Meg Twycross has shown in what is likely to be the definitive study,[14] what records there are always give male names for those being paid for performing female roles. The Chester record noting that the 'worshipful wives' of the city were responsible for the

---

[13] 'Women on the Medieval Stage: The Evidence from France', *Medieval English Theatre*, 7/2 (1985).

[14] ' "Transvestism" in the Mystery Plays', *Medieval English Theatre* 5/2 (1983), 123–80.

play of the Assumption of the Virgin has often been cited as evidence of women on the stage,[15] but Mrs Twycross plausibly argues that they were responsible for the costs, not the performance, and that there would have been little scope for the latter; the play does not survive (it was presumably suppressed because of its Catholic associations) but the equivalent York play has only one female role against more than a dozen male roles. Even so, the evidence on the playing of female roles in the English mystery plays remains scanty and perhaps allows us to say no more than that female acting roles were normally played by males. Why this should have been so is still not entirely clear. It has been argued that there was a practical rather than prudish explanation, in that female voices did not carry sufficiently in the open-air performance conditions of the mystery plays.[16] But it would be hard to explain why this was not a problem for Continental drama, or indeed for later street pageants in the sixteenth century, which seem often to have involved women as speakers too. Yet if one falls back on the old assumption that it was a matter of social propriety, it is difficult to reconcile this with the use of women dancers.

As for female roles in the morality plays, evidence here is simply lacking, since there are no external records for the plays that survive and other records may not refer to dramatic activity. While *Mankind* has no female roles (even Mercy is male), in *The Castle of Perseverance* at least twelve of the thirty-three parts listed at the beginning of the manuscript are female. Eccles says that these 'were no doubt played by men'[17] but positive evidence is lacking; the argument depends essentially on the view that this was a touring production by a professional troupe, and that such troupes did not include women performers.[18] The playwright at least seems to have felt under no pressure to limit the female roles.

Whatever the situation with actresses, dancing girls seem to have been a familiar part of late medieval English entertainment.

---

[15] See for instance Glynne Wickham, *Early English Stages*, 3 vols. (London, 1959–81), i. 271.
[16] Glynne Wickham, *The Medieval Theatre* (3rd edn., Cambridge, 1987), 93.
[17] *The Macro Plays*, p. xxii.   [18] Bevington, *From Mankind to Marlowe*.

Chaucer himself, in the voice of the Pardoner, mentions *tombesteres* as part of the entertainment available to the young men who frequented taverns and stews, and as one of the stimulants to lechery:

> And right anon thanne comen tombesteres
> Fetys and smale, and yonge frutesteres,
> Syngeres with harpes, baudes, wafereres,
> To kyndle and blowe the fyr of lecherye,
> That is annexed unto glotonye.[19]

(This is of course Flanders not England, but I don't think Chaucer means to represent this as a specifically foreign practice.) The accounts for the town of Wells record under 1498 the receipt of money by the church for entertainments involving Robin Hood, dancing girls, and church ales.[20] Cambridge college records in the fifteenth century include regular payments to dancers, and in the case of Peterhouse often specify that they are girls (*puellae*).[21] (Nelson suggests that these were girls of the parish paid for dancing at church festivals rather than professional dancers entertaining the fellows and students, but the records do not specify.) Apart from *Wisdom*, the best evidence for the use of female dancers actually in the drama appears to be the Digby play on *The Killing of the Children*. This is another East Anglian play, copied out by the same scribe as the Digby copy of *Wisdom* around the year 1512.[22] It is clearly in the tradition of the mystery plays, but survives as a single play for separate performance on St Anne's Day, and describes itself as a sequel to a play on the shepherds and the three kings performed by the same people the previous year, with a play on the doctors in the temple to be performed the following year. This has seventeen speaking roles, including Mary, Anna the prophetess, and four mothers of the innocents, but it also has important roles for virgins who dance. The

---

[19] *The Pardoner's Tale*, ll. 476–82; *The Riverside Chaucer*, ed. Larry D. Benson (Oxford, 1988), 196.
[20] E. K. Chambers, *The Mediaeval Stage*, 2 vols. (Oxford, 1903), i. 176.
[21] *Cambridge*, ed. Alan H. Nelson, Records of Early English Drama (Toronto and London, 1989).
[22] *The Digby Plays*, 96–115. On the scribe see pp. liv–lvi.

opening proclamation, spoken by Poeta, describes the action and occasion of the play and ends by calling on the minstrels to play and the virgins to perform, presumably to dance:

> And ye menstrallis, doth youre diligens!
> And ye virgynes, shewe summe sport and plesure,
> These people to solas, and to do God reverens! (53–5)

The virgins appear again in the body of the play, in the scene of the presentation in the temple, and one of them briefly speaks. The stage-directions at this point indicate that 'virgynes, as many as a man wylle, shalle holde tapers in ther handes', and then they sing 'Nunc dimittis' while Simeon processes round the temple (ll. 465–84). At the end of the play, the stage-directions seem to indicate that Anna and the virgins dance, and the play ends with Poeta again invoking musicians to play and virgins to dance:

> Wherfor now, ye virgynes, er we go hens,
> With alle your cumpany, you goodly avaunce!
> Also, ye menstralles, doth your diligens;
> Afore oure departyng, geve us a daunce! (563–6)

The list of 'the namys of the pleyers' which follows on the next page includes only 'a virgyn' rather than a group, but that is presumably the one that speaks. The directions clearly indicate a fair though fluctuating number of virgins.

There seems to be considerable agreement that these virgins were played by females.[23] The editors of the Digby plays suggest that the main cast was provided by a professional touring troupe of players, but that they recruited village girls to play the virgins.[24] There must surely be an element of doubt, however. The virgins are required to sing the *Nunc dimittis*, apparently in Latin,[25] and it is hard to believe that this was a skill

---

[23] Lynette Muir, *The Biblical Drama of Medieval Europe* (Cambridge, 1995), 55; *Digby Plays*, pp. lxii–lxiii; John Marshall, 'Modern Productions of Medieval English Plays', in *The Cambridge Companion*, 290–311, at 308–9.
[24] *The Digby Plays*, p. lxiii.
[25] Both Simeon and the stage-direction refer to the canticle by its Latin title, and no English words are given at this point; it is conceivable that they are meant to sing the English rendering spoken a little earlier by Simeon, which has a marginal note 'Here declare *Nunc dimittis*', but this seems unlikely.

that could readily be found amongst village girls recruited for the occasion of a touring production, even with time for rehearsal. Indeed, the only women amateurs who could readily be called upon to perform liturgical song would be nuns, and this is evidently not a convent production. Women in an acting company could no doubt have learned to sing this piece, but the reference to 'virgynes, as many as a man wylle' suggests that the dramatist was not expecting to draw on the limited resources of a touring company. The obvious group to use for such a purpose, one that could be relied upon to perform such music and might be hireable in many places, is of course choirboys. The acting required of them is minimal, and the one speaking part may have been provided by the actors. In the N-town play on the Purification, a stage-direction says that the *Nunc dimittis*, which it calls a psalm, is to be 'songyn every vers' while Simeon plays with the Christ-child; when the hymn is finished, Simeon then speaks an English version of it. It does not indicate who is to sing the hymn, but the play in the same cycle on the salutation of Mary ends with angels singing the Ave Maria and it seems probable that this part of the N-town cycle was designed to use choristers or clerics. A parallel for the use of choristers dressed as virgins would be the pageants designed to celebrate the wedding of Katherine of Aragon to Prince Arthur in 1501, where a castle appeared with four turrets, in each of which 'was a litill childe apparellid like a mayden, and so all they four children syngyng full swettly and ermeniosly'.[26]

Yet the Digby play requires the virgins to dance, and whether choirboys could be relied upon to dance as well as sing is another question. The Tudor pageants seem to distinguish between the lords and ladies who danced and the choristers who sang, even if the latter were disguised as maidens or ladies. Thus the pageant-castle with the four choristers noted above also contained 'viii goodly and fresshe ladies' who subsequently came down and danced with some 'noble knyghtes'. Compare too one of the other pageants for Katherine of Aragon, which also

[26] *The Receyt of the Ladie Kateryne*, ed. G. Kipling, EETS OS 296 (1990), 56.

contains lords and ladies who dance and choristers who sing; the lords and ladies seem to be closely associated with the nobles and ladies of the court-audience who dance in their turn, and distinct from the choristers.[27] The dancing thought appropriate to temple virgins may not have been very complicated, of course, or much like dancing at court, and perhaps the boys could manage it. Yet it does appear from the text that the dancing virgins and the music of the minstrels were conceived as an important part of the entertainment that the play offered. They are used to begin the play and to end it on a note of celebration, while the virgins' dramatic role within the action is slight and easily dispensable: that is, they seem to exist in this play primarily to provide an added element of display and entertainment in the production. (One might think that the massacre of the innocents, which forms the first part of the play, would not have been thought an appropriate occasion for entertainment with music and dance, but this is a version of the massacre that allows for the comic intervention of the cowardly braggart Watkin, who will fight any man but is terrified of the women and finds himself, after gleefully slaughtering the babies, being beaten up by their mothers.) Given the role of the dance of the virgins in the theatrical production, it seems likely that they were played by skilled dancers rather than by choirboys whose main forte was song. Yet there is still the question of the *Nunc dimittis*. It seems that we have to think either of choirboys with an unexpected skill in dance, or of women dancers with an unexpected skill in Latin liturgical chant. The answer may well be that we should not be thinking of a touring troupe at all, nor of amateurs, but of professional performers in the employ of the nobility or the church, and including women who could both dance and sing.

In any case, the kind of dancing required of temple virgins in a play produced in honour of St Anne's Day and dramatizing the presentation in the temple would hardly offer a very close parallel to the dancing girls of *Wisdom*, with their implied simulation of sexual licence. A much better parallel is the

[27] Ibid. 75.

curious anecdote from the life of Henry VI provided by his chaplain John Blacman. Blacman reports the remarkably chaste and modest character (*pudicitas* is the Latin word) of the young king, noting especially his determined avoidance of the sight of naked men or women. To illustrate this impressive virtue, Blacman reports the following story:

> Tempore natalis Domini choreas, vel spectaculum quoddam generosarum juvencularum, resolutis sinibus suis nudatas mamillas proponentium, quidam adduceret magnus dominus coram eo, ut ante regis aspectum juvenes illae mulierculae sic denudatae tripudiarent, ad probandum forsan eum, vel ad alliciendum regis juvenilem animum. Sed rex iste non improvidus, nec diabolicae fraudis ignarus, his spretis praestigiis, nimium indignatus, oculos avertens, dorsum eius citius posuit, et ad cameram suam exivit dicens, 'Fy fy, for shame, forsothe ye be to blame.'[28]

> At Christmas time a dance or display of noble young ladies, with loose dress and showing their naked breasts, was brought before him by a certain great lord, so that those young women thus unclothed might dance in the sight of the king, in order to test him perhaps, or to allure the young mind of the king. But the king, by no means unseeing, nor unaware of the devilish wiles, spurning these deceptions, and very angry, averted his eyes and quickly turned his back, and went out to his chamber, saying, 'Fy fy, for shame, forsothe ye be to blame.'

Disinterring what may have actually happened, or what could plausibly have happened, behind this story is a hazardous business. The fact that Henry had the presence of mind, as he rushed out of the hall, to express his disgust and embarrassment in rhyming verse (the words are quoted by Blacman in English) suggests that literary tradition had had a hand in the story before Blacman himself got hold of it. And Blacman, as a monk, can hardly have been ignorant of, or uninfluenced by, the long tradition behind such stories, going back at least to

---

[28] *Collectarium Mansuetudinum et Bonorum Morum Regis Henrici VI*, ed. M. R. James, in *Henry the Sixth: A Reprint of John Blacman's Memoir with Translation and Notes* (Cambridge, 1919). The text is based on the sixteenth-century edition by Robert Copeland and the reprint by Thomas Hearne in 1732. I owe the reference to William Tydeman, who notes the story in 'An Introduction to Medieval English Theatre', *The Cambridge Companion*, 1–36, at 16.

the story told by Gregory the Great of St Benedict, whose success in attracting disciples so angered a local priest that he attempted to corrupt his followers by sending a troupe of girls to dance naked in their sight.[29] But it may be that the story does refer to an actual performance, or at least to something that could plausibly have been produced as royal entertainment. We should not necessarily assume that this was indecorous entertainment—burlesque. The performers are *generosae*, that is, well-born young women, or girls of high-class family. Nor should it be assumed that the great lord's intentions were really to corrupt. The second anecdote which Blacman goes on to tell to illustrate Henry's bashfulness records how he came upon a group of men bathing naked at a pool or river near Bath and instantly rode away in great indignation. The point seems to be that the bathing was a common practice, not an act of peculiar viciousness or licentiousness and not, of course, one designed to deprave or corrupt. Underlying the story of the show may be a record of a perfectly normal kind of courtly entertainment to which Henry nevertheless took exception. What the story does not reveal was whether these dancers were simply performing a dance or were in costume and acting a part, like those in *Wisdom*. Were the loose costume and uncovered breasts meant as sexual display perhaps in the manner of Chaucer's licentious (or at least lust-provoking) *tombesteres*, or were they part of a serious dramatic attempt to represent particular characters or qualities as part of a pageant or drama? Nor does the story reveal whether the women were salaried performers or ladies of the court. The costume, or rather lack of costume, seems to suggest professional performers, but the term *generosae* seems to suggest court ladies. Given the extensive part played by 'ladies' in the court shows and pageants of Tudor times, it may be that there was not always a sharp distinction.

A possible context for this kind of royal entertainment is provided by contemporary Continental entertainments. In *The Waning of the Middle Ages* Huizinga cites a number of cases,

---

[29] See Grégoire le Grand, *Dialogues*, ed. A. de Vogüé and P. Antin, Sources Chretiennes, 3 vols. (Paris, 1978–80), ii. 162.

from the fifteenth century onwards, of women performing nude as part of royal pageantry: they appeared as sirens swimming in the river Lys near the bridge over which Duke Philip passed on his entry into Ghent in 1457; there were three naked sirens playing musical instruments to greet Louis XI on his entry into Paris in 1461; and tableaux depicting the Judgement of Paris, using real and unclothed female figures, became a common and popular topos of civic pageantry.[30] The accounts seem to make it unambiguously clear that real rather than simulated nudity was involved. Huizinga remarks that 'in general an extreme licence was tolerated'. Part of the point here is that what might be indecorous in normal circumstances became acceptable at the highest level when exhibited in the name of art; nudity was all right if they were representing classical sirens or Venus and Juno.

What was acceptable in France and Burgundy may not of course have been allowable in England, always more puritanical it seems. As Nashe was proudly to remark of the Elizabethan theatre, 'Our Players are not as the players beyond sea, a sort of squirting baudie Comedians, that have whores and common Curtizens to playe womens partes, and forbeare no immodest speech of unchast action that may procure laughter.'[31] Though the English records show women playing a part in pageantry there is nothing to match the daring of the Continental examples. But the parallels do suggest that women dancers performing what might in other circumstances be thought risqué dances may have been a perfectly acceptable form (acceptable, that is, to anyone but the saintly King Henry VI) of royal and high-class entertainment in England, particularly if it involved simulating a dramatic role. But the possibility of conflicting views about erotic dance even in court circles is indicated by the story in Hall's *Chronicle* of a masque 'after the maner of Italie' in Henry VIII's court: the masquers invited the ladies of the court to dance with them, and while some

---

[30] J. Huizinga, *The Waning of the Middle Ages*, trans. F. Hopman (Harmondsworth, 1965), 300–1.
[31] 'Pierce Penilesse his Supplication to the Divell', in *The Works of Thomas Nashe*, ed. R. B. McKerrow (Oxford, 1903–10; repr. 1966), 215.

accepted others refused 'because it was not a thyng commonly seen'.³² What seems to be involved here is the fusing of two very different kinds of dance: dance as performance by entertainers before an audience (entertainers who might themselves be amateurs or professionals, and would generally be in costume or even masked), and dance as a social activity by the members of a court or other community in their ordinary dress.³³ As Wickham suggests, there is some evidence that these were normally kept separate in later medieval England, and the Italian practice being introduced here in Henry VIII's court involves a new and disturbing crossing of boundaries. The dance before Henry VI described by Blacman was evidently a 'show' of the first kind, and so are the first two dances in *Wisdom*. But the third dance, invoked by Will, may have been particularly daring because it merges the two kinds. It is of course a show like the others, performed by skilled dancers, and probably professionals, to entertain the audience of the play; but it simulates the dance of gallants with ladies, dance as a courting and mating ritual. It thus becomes a comment on the sensuality of 'social dancing', not just the performances of *tombesteres*. The audience is placed spatially and morally outside the world of dance. Alexandra Johnston has argued that Will's dancers are 'surely ... court ladies and gentlemen', and that despite the references to the stews they 'start out as court dancers'.³⁴ It is hard to reconcile this idea in the literal sense with what Will and the stage-directions say of the dancers, but there may well be an intimation in the scene that the dancing that had become accepted in court society was, from a moral point of view similar to Henry VI's, no more than the lewd seductions of gallants from the stews and their adulterous mistresses.

Turning back, then, to the question of why the author of *Wisdom* specified women to play the parts of Will's dancers, we can I think see some of the factors involved. Women dancers

---

[32] Cited in Wickham, *Early English Stages*, i. 218.

[33] The distinction is drawn and illustrated by Elsa Streitman in her helpful entry on dance in *A Companion to the Medieval Theatre*, ed. Ronald W. Vince (New York 1989), 85–98, at 86.

[34] Johnston, '*Wisdom* and the Records', 96.

played a prominent part in entertainment at various levels, probably including East Anglian drama as well as town and court displays. Their status ranged from the *tombesteres* of the tavern to the well-born if topless ladies of royal entertainment, and from the local girls of the parish in Cambridge and Wells to the ladies of the court in royal pageants. Some were evidently professionals, others perhaps paid amateurs, and the dramatist was able to count on their established skills as dancers. But at various levels there remained an association, for some, with lechery and indecency—whether for Chaucer's *tombesteres* or Henry VI's ladies—and the author of Wisdom evidently draws on these associations in using women dancers to represent lechery and sensuality. At the same time, in using them not, like the other sets of dancers, to represent six matching performers but to represent mixed dancing, three gallants and three matrons, he draws into the picture the social dancing of court and hall, suggesting (as in the Mary Magdalen play of the Digby MS) the underlying sexuality and processes of seduction involved in such dancing.

I assume they were professionals, part of a troupe of at least eighteen in the employ of a magnate or even a religious house, though it is possible that they were freelance, a travelling troupe available for use in various kinds of entertainment.

The dance of the masked and costumed women invoked by Will is only one of the more striking aspects of a play designed for the most lavish and colourful spectacle. The total cast is very large—six speaking parts, eighteen dancers, seven small boys, five virgins, three musicians—with very little scope for doubling. Costume is specified in lavish detail, and as well as the dancing and the accompanying music there is the singing of the five virgins. Though it is clear that costume, dance, and music play crucial symbolic roles in the working out of the play's themes, they must inevitably have been the main contributors to the play's appeal as spectacle and entertainment. How does all this, but most of all the lewd, or at least erotic, dancing of the women, fit with all the signs of monastic ambience that have so often been noted in connection with this play, and have become clearer with time?

These signs are partly a matter of externals. The Macro manuscript has the name Hyngham written in several places, and Richard Beadle has now firmly identified this signature with the fuller one written in another manuscript, as Thomas Hyngham, monk of Bury St Edmunds.[35] What is more, Beadle shows that Hyngham was not only the possessor of the manuscript but actually wrote out the text of *Wisdom* and most of *Mankind*. Bury abbey is now known to have staged theatrical events,[36] and a powerful case has been made for the abbey as the place where *Wisdom* itself was performed and possibly composed.[37] It was one of the wealthiest abbeys in the country, had a major role in entertaining visiting dignitaries, including the king and his parliament at times, and boasted a positively palatial set of abbot's lodgings with a vast courtyard before it. The abbot's palace was in fact rebuilt and refurbished for the visit of Henry VI, who spent Christmas and Easter there in 1433–4, and later held parliaments there. The argument remains uncertain. Alexandra Johnston has argued instead for locating the play in the house of some member of the lay nobility, and Coldewey in his study of East Anglian drama has argued that since *Mankind* is evidently a play designed for a small professional touring troupe and is associated with Cambridge and Norfolk rather than Bury, we should see Hyngham as a collector of plays from different contexts rather than a provider of drama for Bury abbey.[38] Even so, the role of Hyngham makes it clear that there was a monastic interest in *Wisdom*, and his copy of the play was evidently used for performance soon after he copied it.

Moreover, the link with monks and monasticism is not simply external: the central values and ideas of the play itself seem to be very close to those of the monks. It is in the first place a very learned play, drawing on a wide range of sources, many

---

[35] 'Monk Thomas Hyngham's Hand in the Macro Manuscript', in Richard Beadle and A. J. Piper (eds.), *New Science out of Old Books: Studies in Manuscripts and Early Printed Books in Honour of A. I. Doyle* (Aldershot, 1995). I am very grateful to Dr Beadle for letting me see his important article in advance of publication.
[36] Ibid. 337 n. 56.
[37] See especially Gibson, 'The Play of *Wisdom*', and *The Theatre of Devotion*.
[38] Johnston, '*Wisdom* and the Records'; Coldewey, 'The Non-Cycle Plays'.

of them with contemplative or monastic links: an English translation by a Carthusian monk of the *Orologium Sapientiae* by the mystic Henry Suso; Walter Hilton's *Scale of Perfection* and his *Epistle on the Mixed Life*; two treatises associated with St Bernard; and St Bonaventure's *Soliloquium*.[39] More significantly, the central theme of the play is strongly contemplative in its leanings. Its central concern is the Augustinian view of the human psyche.[40] It presents the soul and its faculties, Mind, Will, and Understanding, as taking their form from God, resembling him and being directed towards him. Lucifer's role is to draw them into the concerns of the world and thus initiate their fall. In a tradition that goes back, in English, to *Piers Plowman* (B. ix) and *Sawles Warde*, Anima is presented as a passive female figure, not acting herself but dependent on the active male representatives of the mental faculties for purity or fall, salvation or damnation. The dramatic movement of the play requires those faculties to be drawn into the action of the world, which is inevitably also the action of the play. To live and to act in this context is to fall. But the arguments which Lucifer uses are ones which might in themselves seem innocuous except in a strongly contemplative or monastic context. He accuses the faculties of idleness, and argues that they have a duty to work as well as pray and fast. When they claim that they are committed to the contemplative life, he uses against them Hilton's theory of the mixed life as a higher calling, and claims Christ himself as giving a precedent for such a life, working and living in the world as well as praying. Both arguments are thoroughly orthodox, if offensive to the monastic and fraternal orders. Similarly, what he proposes to Will in opposition to chastity is not promiscuity but marriage, preferring fair fruit to foul pollution in an adaptation of St Paul's words. Once the faculties have been moved by these arguments, they fall rapidly into the corruptions of the contemporary English scene—the maintenance of private armies

---

[39] See Eccles (ed.), *The Digby Plays*, pp. xxxiii–xxxiv.
[40] See Eugene Hill, 'The Trinitarian Allegory of the Moral Play of *Wisdom*', *Modern Philology*, 73 (1975), 121–35. Milton McC. Gatch, 'Mysticism and Satire in the Morality of *Wisdom*', *PQ* 53 (1974), 342–62, suggests a particular connection with the psychological views of the mystics.

to dominate others, the corruption of law, the sensuality of the stews. But there is no denying that they have passed to this by way of arguments that in themselves are merely arguments for a mixed spiritual life and would seem unexceptional in most contexts, though they had acquired a bit of a Lollard colouring for a while.[41] What both the arguments and the visual drama strongly suggest is a severely ascetic view that to enter the world or allow for the body at all is to sink into the very depths of corruption, mirrored by the reappearance of Anima horribly deformed. Once having accepted the idea of marriage Will passes immediately into the sexual corruptions represented by the women dancers and to the seduction of another man's wife. The faculties when they fall pass, as it were, out of the monastery and into the town.

The general structure which the dramatist is using here is a characteristic feature of the surviving English morality plays. Their story is of man's fall from a state of innocence into the corruption of the world, from which he is abruptly rescued by an act of grace. Man is an anti-hero, represented as naturally innocent but weak and vulnerable to the powerful forces of vice; to fall into vice is represented as the normal mode of experience, and escape comes not from within the individual but from divine grace. In *The Castle* Mankind is born into the world as a weak and naked baby, lost and alone in the arena where he is surrounded by the vibrant and powerful forces of the World, the Flesh, and the Devil and forced to choose a way. Even for clothing he is dependent on Lust (that is, Pleasure), and the business of living seems to involve an inevitable fall. To escape the world of corruption and return to virtue his only hope of safety is to withdraw from the arena of life into an enclosed place represented by the castle and live out his life there in the moral security of stasis and enclosure, emblematic of monastic ideals. When he is again tempted out of the castle

---

[41] Gatch, 'Mysticism', suggests that Lucifer's arguments are actually directed against the mixed life; but Lucifer does seem to be explicitly arguing *for* the mixed life, at least on the surface, and using Hilton's ideas in doing so. Bevington ('Political Satire', 51) claims that 'the playwright ultimately argues for a "vita mixta" in which the cleric's life is indeed like Christ's, both contemplative and active', but it is in fact Lucifer who argues for the *vita mixta*.

by Covetousness, there is a strong suggestion that any possession is in the domain of Avarice and hence of the World, man's enemy. Living virtuously means holding out in the Castle, untempted and unfallen, until the end comes. Action is identified with the World and the Devil. His eventual salvation is the work not of Mankind himself, who is justly carried off to Hell at the end, but of God and his four daughters, who debate his fate and decide to override the claims of Truth and Righteousness in favour of Mercy. The identification of living and action with fall is strongly imaged in the visual effects: Mankind in the arena is dwarfed by the scaffolds of World, Flesh, Devil, and Avarice, and it is they who produce all the colour, activity, and vibrant language which turn the play-text into theatre.

Mankind, the only surviving copy of which was written by Thomas Hyngham, the monk of Bury, shows a similar structure though perhaps a less extreme position. Here Mankind is not a helpless newborn innocent but a grown man already conscious of the war between body and soul. He has already entered on the active life of the world (represented by digging) and that is not here a state of sin or danger. The temptation in this play is not into the world itself but into its 'vicious new gyse' as Mercy puts it, a kind of contemporary hooliganism or gang-cult which has its own clipped way of talking as well as an engagement in crime and a fondness for earthy humour. The contrast is between the almost pastoral image of Mankind digging and the corrupted urbanized world of Newgyse and the others as vagabonds and parasites. The theme fits rather well into the rural setting implied by the East Anglian village place-names, setting the virtues of the country against the parasites of the town. In basic structure, however, the play is similar to *The Castle*: Mankind is corrupted by the vices and eventually rescued by God's representative Mercy.

Wisdom clearly reflects these patterns, taking the protagonists from an initial state of innocence to fall and corruption. As in the other two plays, redemption comes not through the efforts of man himself but through the intervention of a representative of divine grace, here Wisdom who is primarily Christ rather than a human faculty. But more than *Mankind* and even

The Castle, *Wisdom* seems to present the corruption of the soul and its faculties as an unavoidable effect of any involvement in the world of work and society. Anything but the contemplative and ascetic ideals of the mystics and monks is a temptation of Lucifer: to labour in the world for others, or to marry, is to fall. One might contrast *Mankind*, where the vices prompt the protagonist's fall by tempting him to *abandon* work. And, as in *The Castle*, this identification of activity with fall is strongly imaged in the dramatic action, as corruption is expressed through the colour and energy of the dancers.

One reason, perhaps *the* reason, for the use of this kind of structure in the morality plays is that though they seem to be telling the story of the representative individual, and in *Mankind* and *Wisdom* at least have strongly topical accounts of corruption and fall, they are also alluding to the story of mankind, and that is a narrative which involves an inevitable fall followed by redemption through an external act of grace. In *Wisdom*, the underlying pattern of redemption history is perhaps specifically suggested by the identification of the tempting devil as Lucifer and the redeemer figure as Christ. And that pattern is significant because it can suggest both the inevitability of fall and the identification of the fallen state with the essential nature of life in the world.

David Bevington has described the powerful use of costume and colour in *Wisdom*.[42] Wisdom himself opens the play, as a majestic regal figure clothed in purple and gold. Anima is dressed in white but covered with a black mantle, explicitly to symbolize the purity which can be corrupted. The five wits appear as virgins clothed in white, expressing their essential purity. The three faculties are dressed in white cloth of gold, 'cheveleryde and crestyde in sute'; once corrupted, they re-enter glorying in new 'jolly' clothing, and their restoration to virtue is marked by a reappearance in their original white costumes. Lucifer appears in 'devil's array', presumably black, but casts off the outer garb to appear as a 'proud gallant', presumably in colourful

---

[42] '"Blake and wyght, fowll and fayer": Stage Picture in *Wisdom*', in Riggio (ed.), *The Wisdom Symposium*, 18–38.

and fashionable costume. The dancers of Mind are marked by red beards and appropriate livery, while those of Understanding wear his livery and the costume of jurors, and those of Will, as we have seen, are dressed as gallants (though possibly gallants who can be seen to be 'really' women) and matrons. The turning point of the action comes when Anima reappears in 'a horrible mantle'. Yet the powerful symbolism is complicated by the fact that the characters can appear in different guises. As Lucifer says,

> I wyll change me into bryghtnes,
> And so hym to-begyle...
> Thus under colours all thynge perverse.

Whereas in *The Castle* Mankind moves from his natural nakedness to a costume provided by Lust, here the characters do not exist except in costume; and the concept of what they 'really' or 'naturally' are becomes interestingly problematic, perhaps reflecting a theological issue about the essential nature of the self. Anima and the three faculties can be clothed in different ways to reflect their spiritual state, but we never get to see the unaccommodated man—or woman. If Anima's black cloak over white garments seems to suggest that corruption by the world is in some sense 'put on' over an innate purity, that kind of interpretation of disguise is complicated by the realization that Lucifer wears his devil's garb over a gallant's costume. The women dancers disguised as gallants who seduce matrons may well have made their own contribution to this disruption of identity. There is too an underlying uncertainty in this colour and costume symbolism. If the bright colourful clothing of the gallants is associated with the vices of the world and the active life, how easily can it be distinguished from the equally rich colour of Wisdom himself, which seems to have associations with secular kingship? The costuming of Wisdom as a king is a reminder that the Fall is, paradoxically, into the world of kingship. It is a Fall into the life of the world and creates the world as a secular audience knows it. Hence the ambivalence of the dance, which associates simultaneously with the recreations of the court and the seductions of the taverns and brothels.

And some of the symbolism may well have set up further problems with the audience's own costume. A contemporary illustration of Henry VI and his parliament at Bury St Edmunds abbey shows the king, the chief secular figure and representative of the world, wearing white and gold like the wits and the faculties in their unfallen state, while the surrounding monks, representatives of the contemplative life, wear their traditional Benedictine black, a colour which in the play is emblematic of sin.[43]

Even more striking is the uncertainty of production values. As Bevington suggests, Lucifer seems to come close to identifying himself as a player, an actor, when he describes and enacts his change of costume. But this is part of a more general truth about the play. The theatrical strengths of colour, costume, acting, disguise, music, dance, vigorous language, spectacle, are focused sharply on the world and its corruption. The vices of the faculties are articulated not through their own actions on stage, or even particularly off it, but primarily by the dances. The play as text invites the audience to identify as corruption and vice all that is most attractive and entertaining in the play as theatre—not least the dancing girls.

Perhaps all this takes us back to the question of the staging of the play. The external associations of the play, its centralizing of the contemplative life as the only possible way, and its learning, all point to a monastic ambience. Yet the resources on which the play draws, particularly dancing girls, and the pleasures which it invites, in dance and colourful costume, point away from the monastery to the wider world of court and town. It may well be that the palatial lodgings of the abbot of Bury, belonging both to the monastery and to the world, could provide an appropriate locus for such a play. The choice made by the three faculties to participate in the world was a choice probably made on a daily basis by the monks of this very worldly abbey with its great estates. It is in a way a very appropriate play for such an abbey, with its wealth, its role in entertaining kings and nobles, and the town stretching immediately before its gates. Even so, that does not explain away the

---

[43] ' "Blake and wyght, fowll and fayer": Stage Picture in *Wisdom*', in Riggio (ed.), *The Wisdom Symposium*, 34–5.

curious imagination of the artist who could summon up such colour from the world in the service of such an unworldly theme. One can only hope that if the play was indeed performed at Bury, it was not during the visit of Henry VI in the 1430s: the dancing girls would have embarrassed him, evidently much more than they embarrassed the monks.

Swabian Master, *Les Amants trépassés* (late 15th century).
Musée de la Ville de Strasbourg

11 'Abject odious': Feminine and Masculine in Henryson's Testament of Cresseid

FELICITY RIDDY

In the cathedral museum in Strasbourg there is a late fifteenth-century painting attributed to an unknown Swabian Master called 'Les Amants trépassés'. It depicts the dead lovers naked, standing side by side on what looks like a stone floor which dissolves into an impenetrably black background. Their bodies are already decomposing; through their emaciated flesh the bones are visible; the skin on their faces is pulled back so that they are almost grinning skulls. They wear their winding sheets, and the woman is holding hers back to expose her withering breasts and her genitals, to which a toad clings. Snakes coil into, out of, and around the bodies of them both, and flies are feeding on their flesh. Nevertheless they are not cadavers: they stand upright. The man's face has an expression of tormented regret, as if he is weeping tearlessly. He covers his genitals with his shroud and is turned slightly away from the woman. She has placed a scrawny hand on his shoulder in a gesture of dependence or restraint; her stare is bolder than his, less comprehending, more lost. They are still in some sense a couple, and their suffering, it is implied, is related to their coupling. The painting is of death as a continuing process of pain, degradation, and decay; the two are caught forever between living and being dead. They are revenants, walkers on the boundary; excluded, abominable, defiled. The horror of the painting lies in the way it blurs the borders between life and death as well as those between repulsion and fascination.

The painting obviously draws on the iconography of Adam and Eve, expelled from the garden, hiding their nakedness in pristine shame. The posture of the man—one hand over his genitals and the other on his breast—is identical to that of Adam in Jan van Eyck's Ghent altarpiece of 1432. Van Eyck's Adam, though, is not in torment; he and Eve are on the outermost edge, but they are integral to and not excluded from the redemptive scheme which is the altarpiece's subject. So the Adam and Eve iconography does not necessarily produce the desolation of 'Les Amants trépassés', and Law does not have to be understood as only punishing. In 'Les Amants trépassés' something seems to have happened to the representation of exclusion —to the Adam and Eve model—to give it its peculiar horror. Perhaps this 'something' can be approached in another way, by trying to understand what the couple are excluded from. Van Eyck presents a different pairing in his double portrait of Giovanni and Giovanna Arnolfini, which he painted in 1434.[1] In this painting, which in some ways could not be further from 'Les Amants trépassés', the merchant and his wife, dressed from head to foot in rich but unshowy clothing, stand holding hands in their bedchamber, prayer beads hanging on the wall. Their sanctioned and unlascivious sexuality is represented in their solid bed with its carving of St Margaret with her dragon, patroness of childbirth. They are incorporated into the patriarchal institutions of marriage and the household. Looking at the pair, we can see that the dead lovers are excluded from all this: from lawfulness, marriage, domesticity, philoprogenitive love. He knows and repents, but she remains even now half outside the law, displaying her ruined nakedness without shame. And yet these couples are not disconnected: the guilty lovers' abjection enables the sanctioned lovers to hold their gaze steady. The couple in 'Les Amants trépassés' stand between the viewer and the abyss of total dissolution. They have traversed into the forbidden; the sanctioned lovers remain within the borders of

---

[1] The van Eyck double portrait is in the National Gallery, London. Much has been written on its assumed occasion and the significance of its details. See Erwin Panofsky, 'Jan van Eyck's *Arnolfini Portrait*', *Burlington Magazine*, 64 (1934), 117–27, and, for a recent bibliography, Craig Harbison, 'Sexuality and Social Standing in Jan van Eyck's Arnolfini Double Portrait', *Renaissance Quarterly*, 43 (1990), 249–91. I am grateful to my colleagues Amanda Lillie and, especially, Richard Marks for their helpful advice on art-historical matters.

the ordered and permissible. The fantasy of social, domestic, and sexual order which van Eyck has painted—because it is a fantasy despite the realism of his style—needs those borders to maintain itself in being. There are indications within the painting of what lies outside and bounds it: carved on one of the posts of the bench behind the couple's clasped hands is a grotesque crouching monster. Moreover the figure of St Margaret reminds us that the bed in which marital intercourse takes place and in which the children are born is also where the wife may die in childbirth. The marital bed is, moreover, the site of the 'tame death' of the *artes moriendi*;[2] Giovanni Arnolfini must have hoped to die in a bed like this, turning his face to the wall in the presence of his confessor and his sorrowing household. Meanwhile order and system hold sin and death at bay.

'Les Amants trépassés', then, are what the Arnolfini double portrait has excluded. Nevertheless there is more to be said about the iconography of their abjection, and the painting's focus on their suffering. The woman has antecedents in representations of *luxuria*, the deadly sin of lust who, as Marina Warner points out, appears in bas-relief at Moissac and elsewhere, naked, with snakes gnawing at her genitals and breasts and with toads issuing from her mouth.[3] The law the guilty lovers have transgressed is similarly implied through the precisely located retribution it exacts. A different parallel is provided by a late fifteenth-century limewood carving, attributed to Gregor Erhart, of *Vanitas*, the preacher's theme that all is vanity.[4] This carving is of three interlinked figures, standing back to back: two of them are a beautiful, naked young man

[2] For the 'tame death', see Philippe Ariès, *The Hour of Our Death*, trans. Helen Weaver (Harmondsworth, 1983).
[3] See Marina Warner, *Monuments and Maidens: The Allegory of the Female Form* (London, 1985), 295–6 and fig. 89, and Michael Camille, 'The Image and the Self', in Sarah Kay and Miri Rubin (eds.), *Framing Medieval Bodies* (Manchester, 1994), 79–80. I am grateful to Cordelia Beattie for these references and for the Warner reference in n. 4. See also Meyer Schapiro, *The Sculpture of Moissac* (London, 1985), 115 and fig. 131.
[4] This carving is in the Kunsthistorisches Museum in Vienna. It is reproduced in Warner, *Monuments and Maidens*, fig. 90. See also *Katalog der Sammlung für Plastik und Kunstgewerbe: Mittelalter*, 2 vols. (Vienna, 1964), 63, figs. 60 and 61, and Michael Baxandall, *The Limewood Sculptors of Renaissance Germany* (New Haven and London, 1980), 292. Baxandall thinks the sculpture is probably not by the Augsburg sculptor Erhart, but by an artist working in Passau.

and woman, while the third is a naked, scrawny old woman with flaps for breasts, missing teeth, and the same bold and desperate glare as the woman in 'Les Amants trépassés'. The young man does not need a decrepit male counterpart because the old woman can apparently make the point for both sexes. It is on the female body that the grim law of nature that beauty passes is most clearly drawn: 'all flesh is as grass... and the flower thereof falleth away'. 'Les Amants trépassés' seems to bring these elements together in an ambivalent over-determination of guilt: the figures incorporate not only the primal transgression of Adam and Eve, but both *luxuria* and *vanitas* as well, punitively intertwined. The couple are being punished for their lust by their bodily decay: they represent the sin and death which lurk in the Arnolfini double portrait.

The relevance of 'Les Amants trépassés' to *The Testament of Cresseid* is surely clear enough. Cresseid the leper is another figure of degradation and horror who is similarly positioned at the ambivalent coming-together of *luxuria* and *vanitas*, which are constantly intertwined and mistaken for one another in the poem. What Denton Fox and others have seen as the moral confusion of the narrator in lines 78–84[5]—a stanza which combines *vanitas*'s 'flour' (78) and *luxuria*'s 'giglot' (83)—is the product of this ambivalence. When Cresseid finally disposes of her disgusting leprous body in her testament, consigning it as waste, 'With wormis and with taidis to be rent' (577–8), Henryson uses an iconography of decay that locates her with 'Les Amants trépassés'. Nevertheless, poem and painting also share a wider preoccupation with defilement and exclusion, and with states of being—leper and standing corpse—that are neither living nor dead. Throughout the poem Cresseid is an outcast, an 'unworthie outwaill' (129), and the action concerns the processes whereby she is progressively excluded or excludes herself: socially, morally, spatially, temporally. She enters the poem as an exile from Troy, and her promised 'retour' (51) or

---

[5] In his separate edition of the poem, Denton Fox describes the narrator as 'stupid and passionately involved'; see *The Testament of Cresseid*, ed. Denton Fox (London, 1968), 23. All quotations in this essay from *The Testament of Cresseid* are from *The Poems of Robert Henryson*, ed. Denton Fox (Oxford, 1981).

'ganecome' (55) can never take place. She is formally repudiated by Diomeid and, 'desolait' (76) and 'maculait' (81), passes 'far out of the toun' (95) to her father's house, but once she has become a leper she cannot stay there either. In the gods' sentence on Cresseid the sufferings of leprosy are represented as another version of exclusion, not only because her repulsive disease means that 'Quhair thou cummis, ilk man sall fle the place' (341), but because she is cut off from her own former beauty and desire:

> 'Thy greit fairnes and all thy bewtie gay,
> Thy wantoun blude, and eik thy goldin hair,
> Heir I exclude fra the for euermair.' (313–15)

This exclusion is reiterated in, and structures, the complaint Cresseid speaks in the 'hospitall at the tounis end' (382) to which, as a leper, she must be consigned. The complaint first takes the form of an elaborate and moving elegy to an unrecoverable past—the past of the 'greit fairnes' the gods have cut her off from—and then develops an increasingly intense focus on the contrasting degradations of her present. The present is not a stable state; it is not 'the end' (456) although Cresseid calls it that. Rather, it is a process of 'faiding' (461) and 'rotting' (464), like the decomposing bodies of 'Les Amants trépassés'. That is, the vantage-point of retrospection is unfixed; there is further to go; there is a beyond even leprosy; in the end the narrative itself will exclude her. Her pessimistic reminder of the processes of time is directed by Cresseid at the 'ladyis fair of Troy and Grece' (452), and is one from which Troilus is apparently exempt.[6] Like the young man in the carving of *Vanitas*, the woman does his decomposing for him. She transmogrifies into unrecognizability; she is 'untrew' (602), heterogeneous and changeable, while he is 'trew' (the word is used of him repeatedly at the end of the poem) and self-consistent.

The *Testament of Cresseid* engages, in a way that is quite

---

[6] Lesley Johnson points out that Cresseid's leprosy 'literally produces the conditions of old age'; see 'Whatever Happened to Criseyde? Henryson's *Testament of Cresseid*', in Keith Busby and Erik Kooper (eds.) *Courtly Literature: Culture and Context* (Amsterdam and Philadelphia, 1990), 313–21, at 314.

beyond the reach of Chaucer's *Troilus and Criseyde*, with filth and pollution, with what Julia Kristeva, in *Powers of Horror*, calls the abject.[7] Cresseid uses the word of herself in the complaint against the gods that has such terrible consequences:

> 'Quha sall me gyde? Quha sall me now convoy,
> Sen I fra Diomeid and nobill Troylus
> Am clene excludit, as abject odious?' (131–3)[8]

In this cry 'Quha sall me gyde? Quha sall me now convoy?' can be heard the voice of the ungoverned woman whom the authorities in late-medieval society continually attempted to control; husbandless, protectorless, cast adrift from the structures of male authority which the poem does not question, she is Kristeva's 'stray'.[9] 'Lost' is a word I used of the woman in 'Les Amants trépassés' who clutches the man's shoulder even as he turns from her. Henryson's extraordinary feat is to have given her a voice, to imagine what it is to be 'abhominabill' (308).

Kristeva argues that the process of abjection—of loathing and repulsion—is the means whereby the subject, or 'I', is brought into being. What is rejected as filth and waste is not so in itself: there is nothing intrinsic to excrement, menstrual blood, corpses, or lepers to account for the abhorrence attached to them in many cultures.[10] Kristeva suggests that these things take on the meanings they do because 'Refuse and corpses *show me* what I permanently thrust aside in order to live. These bodily fluids, this defilement, this shit are what life withstands, hardly and with difficulty, on the part of death.'[11] The abject, loathed and repellent, lurks ambiguously on the borders of identity, making identity possible, yet constantly threatening

---

[7] Julia Kristeva, *Powers of Horror: An Essay on Abjection*, trans. Leon S. Roudiez (New York, 1982).

[8] Fox (ed.), *Poems of Robert Henryson*, n. to l. 133, points out that 'abject' is not recorded elsewhere in Middle Scots, nor in English until 1534.

[9] 'The one by whom the abject exists is thus a *deject* who places (himself), *separates* (himself), situates (himself), and therefore *strays* instead of getting his bearings, desiring, belonging, or refusing' (Kristeva, *Powers of Horror*, 8).

[10] 'Excrement and its equivalents (decay, infection, disease, corpse, etc.) stand for the danger to identity that comes from without: the ego threatened by the non-ego, society threatened by its outside; life by death' (ibid. 71).

[11] Ibid. 3.

its collapse. The abject is thus 'the in-between, the ambiguous, the composite'; it is heterogeneous, neither one thing nor another. Kristeva argues that abjection is the process whereby the infant begins to found an identity separate from the mother, before the intervention of the father into the mother–child dyad, before it takes up a position in language and the symbolic order. What is rejected must be—since there is as yet no separate identity—the maternal, the feminine. Moreover, Kristeva argues that it is maternal authority which maps the infant's body, delineating it as 'clean and proper':

> Through frustrations and prohibitions, this authority shapes the body as a *territory* having areas, orifices, points and lines, surfaces and hollows, where the archaic power of mastery and neglect, of the differentiation of proper-clean and improper-dirty, possible and impossible, is impressed and exerted.[12]

This mapping defines the distinction between inside and outside, self and other, subject and object; the 'clean and proper body' founds identity, order, and stability. Her reworking of Freud's *From Totem to Taboo* makes it possible for her to move from the constitution of the subject to the constitution of society, ranging over a variety of historical periods including the medieval, and to theorize the ways in which law, morality, and religion also require for their very being expulsion, repression, and purification. At the end of *Powers of Horror* she speaks of laying bare 'under the cunning, orderly surface of civilisations, the nurturing horror that they attend to pushing aside by purifying, systematizing, and thinking; the horror that they seize on in order to build themselves up and function'.[13] The horror of 'Les Amants trépassés' is what, I have been arguing, lies under the 'cunning, orderly surface' of the Arnolfini double portrait; by 'pushing aside' Cresseid, Troilus's identity is constituted within the poem.

Kristeva's conception of the abject is a good starting-point

---

[12] Ibid. 72. For 'the self's clean and proper body', see p. 71. In his 'Translator's Note', p. viii, Leon Roudiez explains that he uses the 'rather cumbersome "one's own clean and proper body" to render the French *corps propre*'.
[13] Ibid. 210.

for a reading of *The Testament of Cresseid* that focuses on Cresseid's degradation and which aims to understand why the poem treats Cresseid as cruelly as it does.[14] Of all the outcomes that might have been designed for Chaucer's Criseyde, this is surely one of the most horrible. Why was it not possible to imagine an altogether different kind of story, in which Cresseid marries a Greek, establishes a household, even has children— the story in terms of which the demure Giovanna Arnolfini is constructed? To say that Henryson is more misogynistic than Chaucer, as some readers have done, does not answer the question but simply restates it. One answer must lie in the meanings given to women's sexuality in fifteenth-century Scotland and thus to the kinds of narrative it can generate, and I shall return to this subject later. But the poem's need to represent Cresseid as defiling and abominable also seems to emanate from some more private place, from what Kristeva calls the 'uncertain spaces of unstable identity'[15] where masculinity struggles to maintain its equilibrium. And so Cresseid is made to bear the symbolic weight of the expulsion of the feminine: Troilus's famous truth, his self-consistency, is a version of the 'clean and proper body' from which hers, first defiled by promiscuity and then disfigured by leprosy, is abjected. Tracing this in the story means attending to the poem's discontinuities and incoherences; it means reading against the grain of the dominant interpretation of *The Testament of Cresseid* as a 'getting-of-wisdom poem'.[16]

The vocabulary I have adopted is modern, yet it can also be related to medieval thinking about sex and gender. Joan Cadden has shown us in great detail how medieval scientific and medical ideas about sexual difference—a two-thousand-year conversation

---

[14] Critics have long emphasized the poem's cruelty: see Douglas Duncan, 'Henryson's *Testament of Cresseid*', *Essays in Criticism*, 11 (1961), 128–35; A. C. Spearing, 'Conciseness and *The Testament of Cresseid*', in *Criticism and Medieval Poetry*, 2nd edn. (London, 1972), 157–94. For a more recent reading which, like mine, emphasizes 'debasement and expulsion', see David J. Parkinson, 'Henryson's Scottish Tragedy', *Chaucer Review*, 25 (1991), 355–62 (p. 355).

[15] Kristeva, *Powers of Horror*, 58.

[16] Quoted by Edwin D. Craun, 'Blaspheming Her "Awin God": Cresseid's "Lamentation" in Henryson's *Testament*', *SP* 82 (1985), 25–41, at 25, from Jennifer Strauss, 'To Speak Once More of Cresseid: Henryson's *Testament* Reconsidered', *Scottish Literary Journal*, 4 (1977), 5.

conducted almost exclusively by men—not only assumed but enforced a polarity (which is also a hierarchy) between male and female.[17] In scientific discourses gender as a cultural construction was not coterminous with biological sex, but was nevertheless polarized in the same way as sexual difference. Femininity mostly, although not without exception, connoted various kinds of 'moral and physical weakness' while masculinity mostly connoted 'moral and physical strength'.[18] These meanings were not arbitrarily assigned; they were believed to be grounded in nature. It was held that women's physical make-up made them frailer than men, morally and physically, so 'feminine' could be used in a transferred sense to characterize, among other things, men who showed the forms of frailty observable in women, contrary to their own nature, and vice versa. Cadden sees scientific thought as implicated in a process which she presents as oppressive:

Natural philosophy and medicine, among the authoritative arbiters of what was natural, were therefore participants in the construction of the concepts of the feminine and the masculine, in the enforcement of the duality which they applied, and in the disapprobation of what was therefore seen as deviant.[19]

The question that this raises is why it should have been so crucial to medieval scientific thinking that the categories male and female, and masculine and feminine, be kept rigorously apart. What would be at risk if sex and gender differences were to collapse, dissolving male into female and thus making it impossible to distinguish masculine from feminine? The threat of such a collapse surely takes us into 'the uncertain spaces of unstable identity', to use Kristeva's phrase. From a modern vantage point, it is possible to see that reinforcing the sex and gender binaries by appeals to nature is a way of buttressing the 'moral and physical strength' of the male, creating and confirming the masculine identity which seems to be at issue in *The Testament of Cresseid*.

Douglas Gray, in his sympathetic account of the poem in

---

[17] Joan Cadden, *Meanings of Sex Difference in the Middle Ages: Medicine, Science and Culture* (Cambridge, 1993), 170.
[18] Ibid. 208.   [19] Ibid. 226.

Robert Henryson, has provided us with the most thorough and attentive version of the getting-of-wisdom reading. He points to, though does not develop, the importance of pollution in *The Testament of Cresseid*, which he presents as medieval tragedy in the Senecan mode, citing Dante's definition of tragedy as in its end 'fetid and horrible'. Nevertheless his reading, I think it is fair to say, is more concerned with the pity he has made his special subject than with horror. Gray takes as his point of entry into the poem the analysis of character, and the liberal-humanist position from which he writes allows him to regard Cresseid as an agent, with a psychology, and to suggest that she is capable of moral understanding, choice, and development, even of undergoing 'a spiritual change of some kind'.[20] This is, as I have already said, now the dominant reading of the poem: there seems to be general agreement that it shows the awakening of conscience through suffering. Gray argues, with great sympathy, that Cresseid's final speech 'sets up an ideal of noble love, embodied in Troilus, which she has totally betrayed'.[21] This humanist move, in which Troilus's love is implicitly endorsed as a standard against which Cresseid has failed, ensures that this ideal remains unexamined. It is not only to modern feminism that his 'noble love' may not appear self-evidently universal: after all, Chaucer did not represent Troilus's love as simply noble in *Troilus and Criseyde*, though that is one of the temporary valuations the poem puts on it. At the end it is seen as reprehensible, as 'blynde lust, the which that may nat laste' (V. 1824).[22] The 'ideal of noble love' in *Troilus and Criseyde* is finally not located in humans at all. The failure of the affair and Troilus's cruel death are held to show the futility of his kind of loving ('Swich fyn hath, lo, this Troilus for love!', V. 1328) and the ineffectuality of his gods ('Lo here, what alle hire goddes may availle!', V. 1849). The *Testament of Cresseid*, by contrast, demonstrates the gods' terrible power and does not condemn his love for Cresseid. Her degradation does not contaminate him, nor is he coupled with her as a

---

[20] Douglas Gray, *Robert Henryson* (Leiden, 1979), 205.   [21] Ibid. 203.
[22] Quotations are from *The Riverside Chaucer*, ed. Larry D. Benson (Oxford, 1988).

guilty lover. The fact that the poem refuses to follow Chaucer's precedent, though, shows that the meaning it finds in Troilus is contingent, not universal, an achievement not a given, and the painfulness of Cresseid's treatment shows what it costs to achieve. The 'ideal of noble love' can be said to stand in relation to Cresseid as the Arnolfini couple do to the 'amants trépassés'. Cresseid's abjection borders and maintains Troilus's truth.

Troilus, in addition to being 'trew', is twice described as 'worthie', a word that links him with the 'worthie wemen' (610) of the final stanza to whom the whole poem turns out to be addressed.[23] Cresseid represents the 'fals deceptioun' (613) which they are exhorted to eschew. The 'ideal of noble love' which Troilus upholds is apparently one of which male readers do not need to be reminded. Douglas Gray, using his tragic model, defends this stanza as cathartic: 'its wordiness comes as something of an emotional release' as the narrator in his choric role selects 'as in the *moralitates* of the fables, a single important moral strand from his story for emphasis', and brings the poem to 'an abrupt and enigmatic conclusion'.[24] This account of the stanza, by so generous and fair-minded a commentator, simply shows up the problem, since it has to leave out the uncomfortable fact that the poem ends with the old lie that it is women who are fickle. This old lie is, of course, one which has been particularly useful for 'the cunning, orderly surface of civilisations', and Gray is right when he calls it 'an important moral strand in the poem'. It is, after all, one of the views of women that is encoded in the plot, a plot which, as I have already said, is generated by the meanings given to female sexuality in fifteenth-century Scotland. The story of Cresseid's decline into promiscuity, disease, and death is in essence the same as the one which Hogarth depicted in the eighteenth century in a series of paintings known as *The Harlot's Progress*.[25]

---

[23] Fox points out that Henryson follows Chaucer, 'in whose poem Troilus is repeatedly called *worthie* and *worthiest*.... Henryson, like Chaucer, opposes the beauty of Cresseid to the moral worth of Troilus' (*The Poems of Robert Henryson*, 343).
[24] Gray, *Robert Henryson*, 207.
[25] See Ronald Paulson, *Hogarth*, 3 vols. i: *The 'Modern Moral Subject' 1697–1732* (Cambridge, 1991). I am indebted to Mark Hallett for the Hogarth parallel and this reference.

In this sequence the young woman, Moll Hackabout, is depicted as initially arriving in London, then deceiving her elderly lover, then being arrested for prostitution, then committed to Bridewell, then dying of the pox, and finally in her coffin. There is more than one way of reading this sequence, as the contemporary responses to it show, but Ronald Paulson suggests that the 'ordinary reader of the *Harlot*, brought up on Bunyan, would have read a grim moral narrative in which the Harlot is justly punished.'[26]

The plot of the *Testament* is strikingly similar to this, and can be read in much the same way. The final stanza in fact offers this kind of reading:

> Now, worthie wemen, in this ballet schort,
> Maid for your worschip and instructioun,
> Of cheritie, I monische and exhort,
> Ming not your lufe with fals deceptioun:
> Beir in your mynd this sore conclusioun
> Of fair Cresseid... (610–15)

Such a reading makes the moralist's assumption—which innumerable women's life-histories of course disprove—that once a woman has been unfaithful, then she will inevitably become promiscuous, contract a venereal disease, and die. Because the sequence is presented as inevitable it forecloses the alternative ending I referred to earlier, in which Cresseid might have ended up married to a Greek. In fact, once the poem is read as exemplary, it is possible to see that the gods are there to enforce the inevitability of the sequence and to ensure that no other outcome to the plot is possible. Moreover they provide an explicit moral causation for events that in the Hogarth series are left more open. Leprosy is elaborately troped as a judgement on Cresseid, and not a contagion. Medieval medical science believed that leprosy was transmitted by sexual intercourse, by contact and by breath[27]—that is, that it was a social disease

---

[26] Paulson, *Hogarth*, i. 256.
[27] For the medieval belief in the contagiousness of leprosy, see Luke Demaître, 'The Description and Diagnosis of Leprosy by Fourteenth-Century Physicians', *Bulletin of the History of Medicine*, 59 (1985), 327–44, and Danielle Jacquart and Claude Thomasset, *Sexuality and Medicine in the Middle Ages*, trans. Matthew Adamson (Oxford, 1988),

—but it is crucial to the moral structure of this story that Cresseid, isolated, should infect herself. The harlot's progress, in which progression is inevitably downwards, must have been one among several narratives about female sexuality available in the fifteenth century; its obverse is the story of the harlot's success which underlies Dunbar's *Tretis of the Tua Mariit Wemen and the Wedo*. The narrative of ruin lurks in the mid-fifteenth-century advice poem, 'Thewis of Gud Women', in which young girls are warned that painting the face and keeping bad company are 'giglotrye',[28] the first step on the path to the loss of all social identity.

The harlot's progress is the kind of narrative that was depicted in the painted glass roundels which survive from late-medieval urban buildings in the Low Countries, and which were produced in narrative series aimed at conveying 'edifying allegory, ethical instruction or cautionary tale'.[29] There is evidence of a similar taste in English glazing of the period.[30] There is no surviving domestic glass from late-medieval Scotland although it is in the houses of merchants, including those members of the Dunfermline guild who traded with Flanders,[31] that we might expect to find its use. Various lurid cautionary tales

---

185–7. It was also, of course, believed to be a punishment for sin: see Saul Brody, *The Disease of the Soul: Leprosy in Medieval Literature* (Ithaca, NY, 1974). See also Peter Richards, *The Medieval Leper and his Northern Heirs* (Cambridge, 1977), and Françoise Bériac, *Histoire des lepreux aux Moyen Age: une société d'exclus* (Paris, 1988).

[28] See 'Thewis of Gud Women', in *Ratis Raving and Other Early Scots Poems on Morals*, ed. R. Girvan, STS, 3rd ser. 11 (Edinburgh and London, 1939), ll. 92 and 121. Henryson uses 'giglotlike' of Cresseid at l. 83.

[29] See Timothy B. Husband, *The Luminous Image: Painted Glass Roundels in the Lowlands, 1480–1560* (New York, 1995), 13. Subjects of surviving roundels include Susanna and the Elders, and Sorgheloos, 'a starchy allegory inveighing against spendthriftness' (p. 13). Sorgheloos (Carefree), like the Prodigal Son, leaves home and squanders all his money but, unlike the Prodigal Son, is not welcomed back by his father and ends up a destitute outcast. Sorgheloos's successful counterpart is Dick Whittington. A version of the Sorgheloos story survives in Hogarth's *The Rake's Progress*. See Husband, *The Luminous Image*, 88–97; for English examples see pp. 96 and 97. I am grateful to Richard Marks for this reference.

[30] See Richard Marks, *Stained Glass in England During the Middle Ages* (London, 1993), 97–8. Marks comments that 'the taste for these roundels appears to have derived from Flanders' (p. 97).

[31] See Elizabeth P. D. Torrie, 'The Guild in Fifteenth-Century Dunfermline', in Michael Lynch, Michael Spearman, and Geoffrey Stell (eds.), *The Scottish Medieval Town* (Edinburgh, 1988), 252.

of female sexual ruin—including that of Cresseid—are used in *The Spectacle of Lufe*, which the Edinburgh notary John Asloan copied into his manuscript in the early decades of the sixteenth century.[32] The narrative of the harlot's progress—in the late Middle Ages as in the eighteenth century—defines urban morality through the figure whose transgressiveness consigns her to the margins of civil society. Henryson's version of the harlot's ruin is not simply antifeminist but is used to shore up one kind of femininity against another: the 'worthie women' of the final stanza against the 'giglot' (83). We know these worthy women from 'Thewis of Gud Women', in which young girls are advised to conform themselves to 'the best / of women that are worthyest' (123–4), and told that 'Thai suld be chaist and cheritable, / Worthi women, wyss and abile' (225–6). Kristeva writes that 'Abjection, when all is said and done is the other facet of religious, moral and ideological codes on which rest the sleep of individuals and the breathing spells of societies'.[33] The moral and ideological codes of the late-medieval Scottish towns were maintained by men like those 'introspective, conservative' burgesses of Dunfermline whom Elizabeth Torrie has neatly characterized, with their well-designed houses and their subservient wives.[34] They certainly did not have the wealth and sophistication of Giovanni Arnolfini; their portraits were not painted by court artists, but they did, presumably, send their sons to school with Robert Henryson. The system and order of their communities required the exclusion of those whom the authorities deemed threatening and antisocial, including prostitutes and lepers: 'scho was nocht worthy to remayn in the town' was the judgement passed by one court on a woman offender,[35] and

---

[32] 'Or how quyte cresseid hir trew luffar troyelus his lang service In luf quhen scho forsuk him for dyomeid And thare efter went common amang the grekis And syn deid in gret myssere & pane': 'The Spectacle of Luf', in *The Asloan Manuscript: A Miscellany in Prose and Verse*, ed. W. A. Craigie, 2 vols., STS, 2nd ser. 14 (London and Edinburgh, 1923), 16.

[33] Kristeva, *Powers of Horror*, 209.

[34] Torrie, 'The Guild in Fifteenth-Century Dunfermline', 245–60.

[35] Quoted by Elizabeth Ewan, *Townlife in Fourteenth-Century Scotland* (Edinburgh, 1990), 57 and n., from *Early Records of the Burgh of Aberdeen, 1317, 1398–1407*, ed. W. C. Dickinson, Scottish Historical Society (Edinburgh, 1957), p. cxxvii. See also *The Acts of the Parliament of Scotland*, ed. T. Thomson and C. Innes (Edinburgh, 1844–75), ii. 12: 'Item at commoun women be put to the utmast endis of the toune quhare lest

lepers, likewise, were shunned.³⁶ In Cresseid, of course, promiscuity and disease are conflated, making her doubly abject.

If humanist readings of *The Testament of Cresseid* fail to acknowledge its antifeminism, they also overestimate its coherence. For critics to turn the exemplary narrative of the harlot's progress into an exemplary narrative of the birth of conscience requires bringing into play a notion of character that seems to me anachronistic, as I shall argue later. It also requires the reader to ignore the fact that there are discontinuities in the narrative itself which blur the whole issue of Cresseid's transgression. It might be thought crucial, if Cresseid has to learn penitence, that the reader should be allowed to know what crime she has committed. Is it her infidelity, that she did not return to Troy as she had promised to do, but instead became the mistress of Diomeid? Is it that after being repudiated by Diomeid she became promiscuous? Is it that she blamed the gods for what happened to her? Is it that she set too much store by beauty and luxury? Is it that she imagined she could be desirable for ever? All these, at some point or other in the poem, are brought to the fore as things for which she deserves to be punished. Furthermore, there is a telling hiatus between Cresseid's reception by Diomeid in lines 43–4 (apparently alluding to the scene in *Troilus and Criseyde*, V. 15–189) and his repudiation of her at 71–5, a hiatus that is filled by the stanzas in which the 'narrator' takes up the 'uther quair' (61). The old narrative stopped with Troilus despairing of her return; when the new narrative begins she is already, like some Jean Rhys heroine, being discarded by a sexually bored Diomeid. The 'betrayal' (the word is Douglas Gray's) falls into the space between the two versions. If the poem aims to show Cresseid coming to an awareness of the wrong she has done to Troilus,

---

perel of fyre is.' (Act of 1425; one of a series relating to fire regulations. Common women are the only group, apart from those who work with straw and other combustible materials, to be singled out.) I am grateful to Cordelia Beattie for this reference.

³⁶ 'Item at na lipirouss folk sit to thig nothir in kirk nor in kirk yarde na in nane uthir place within the borowis bot at thare awin hospitale ande at the porte of the toune and uthir placis outewith the borowis' (Act of 1427). See *The Acts of the Parliament of Scotland*, ed. Thomson and Innes, ii. 16. I owe this reference to Ewan, *Townlife in Fourteenth-Century Scotland*, 38.

then it must surely be a weakness that the reader is not allowed to know how that wrong came about.

Cresseid herself can be read, not as an individualized moral agent with the capacity to 'develop' in the course of the action,[37] but as a voice. Her three main speeches—her diatribe against the gods, her complaint, and her testament—are different genres that provide discontinuous subject positions: the 'I' of the moralizing mirror, as it occurs in *The Three Dead Kings* or *The Buke of the Howlat*; the *ubi sunt* 'I' from the Body and Soul tradition;[38] the testamentary 'I' of contemporary wills;[39] the 'I' of the forsaken woman, as in Chaucer's *Anelida and Arcite*;[40] the 'I' of the outcast. Trying to read these discontinuities as stages in a moral progression may prevent us from seeing that what humanist criticism takes as given in the discussion of character—its moral coherence and stability or, in medieval terms, its 'truth'—is in fact what the poem is struggling to bring into being. Moreover this 'truth' is gendered: what the *Testament of Cresseid* shows is the struggle to constitute a stable masculine identity; its constant risk of dissolution; its relation to repression, law, and punishment; and above all, its need to exclude the feminine. Cresseid, who is central to redemptive and exemplary readings of the poem, is precisely *not* where the achievement of this is located; rather, she is what has to be jettisoned both by the narrative and by the poem's symbolic codes to achieve it. Of course the poem tells a story, and a very powerful and moving one. My argument is that the power of the story comes not so much from the events, but from the way what happens is imagined and engaged with. What is obscurely at stake in the story of the much-loved woman who is cast out is the very making of masculinity.

---

[37] See 'When is a Character Not a Character? Desdemona, Olivia, Lady Macbeth and Subjectivity', in Alan Sinfield, *Faultlines: Cultural Materialism and the Politics of Dissident Reading* (Oxford, 1992), 52–79.
[38] See Fox (ed.), *Poems of Robert Henryson*, 371, n. to ll. 416–33.
[39] See Julia Boffey, 'Lydgate, Henryson, and the Literary Testament', *MLQ* 53 (1992), 41–56.
[40] See Lee W. Patterson, 'Christian and Pagan in *The Testament of Cresseid*', *PQ* 52 (1973), 696–714, esp. 705–9.

The problem of character is initiated with the 'I' of the opening stanza, an 'I' that is explicitly brought into being by the act of writing ('Richt sa it wes quhen I began to wryte / This tragedie', 3–4). This 'I' cannot be confidently identified with a really existing Henryson outside the poem or with anyone whom we can call 'the narrator'. It is not much more than a strategy for beginning a poem, a strategy that is well established by the late fifteenth century and for which Henryson had plenty of models in Chaucer, Gower, and Lydgate. This 'I' merges with the 'I' of age's retrospection on youth (as at the end of Gower's *Confessio Amantis* and in Hoccleve's *Regement of Princes*), and the 'I' of February warming himself by the fire (from innumerable 'labours of the months' illustrations), in order to focus on male sexuality. The oppositions between heat and cold, inside and outside, and youth and age construct an identity which is corporeal: the body is the place where masculinity is founded and which it struggles to transcend. The male body is to be an issue—perhaps the issue—throughout the poem. It is returned to at the moment of Troilus's last encounter with Cresseid, when a 'spark of lufe' (512) 'kendlit all his bodie in ane fyre', coding it in terms of medieval humour theory as youthful, sexual, and male, and refocusing on the opposition between inside and outside. As Troilus imposes on to the face of the leprous Cresseid the 'idole' (507) in his mind of the 'sweit visage and amorous blenking / Of fair Cresseid, sumtyme his awin darling' (503–4), loathing of and desire for the feminine can be seen to collapse into one another.

If we accept that what looks like a character here and in the opening stanzas is a means of focusing the reader's attention, there is no difficulty when the 'narrator' later swithers between moral condemnation of Cresseid and pity for her misfortune:

> O fair Creisseid, the flour and A per se
> Of Troy and Grece, how was thow fortunait
> To change in filth all thy feminitie,
> And be with fleschelie lust sa maculait,
> And go amang the Greikis air and lait,
> Sa giglotlike takand thy foull plesance!
> I have pietie thow suld fall sic mischance! (77–84)

We do not have to ask ourselves how these positions, especially the contradiction of the last two lines, can be integrated by appealing to some conception of a stable, founding character, nor do we have to explain that the narrator is a particular kind of person in order to account for this. Rather we can pay attention to the contradiction and ambivalence in the ways this language constructs Cresseid: I have already said that she is located at the intersection of discourses of *luxuria* and *vanitas*. The comment 'how was thow fortunait / To change in filth all thy feminitie' (79) is particularly revealing. We might expect cleanness to change into filth, or femininity into masculinity; there is a surprising disturbance of the binaries here. The implication is that femininity is purity, and so an unclean femininity is a contradiction whose unthinkableness produces the outrage of this line, and eventually requires the dissolution of Cresseid into the body that is consigned to rot and the soul that joins Diana in 'waist woddis and wellis' (588). What is left unspoken in line 79, of course, is the fourth term: masculinity. If the feminine is clean, then the masculine is filthy. The problem that the poem is wrestling with is not the problem of femininity but a problem within masculinity: its own uncleanness, which is coded as feminine and rejected as polluting. The feminine-unclean is expelled, repudiated first by a 'lybell of repudie' (74) or formal bill of divorce, and then by the excessive rigour of the gods' parliament. Kristeva says that an 'unshakeable adherence to Prohibition and Law' is necessary in order to thrust aside the abject: 'Religion. Morality. Law. Obviously always arbitrary, more or less; unfailingly oppressive, rather more than less; laboriously prevailing, more and more so.'[41] This seems to make sense—if that is the right word—of the judging and punitive forces ranged against Cresseid.

The 'unstabilnes' of which Cresseid accuses herself, and which she contrasts with Troilus's constancy, is the deceptive heterogeneity of the feminine which lies outside masculine singleness and into which the latter constantly threatens to slide. When she goes 'into the court, commoun' (77) Cresseid is borderless,

---

[41] Kristeva, *Powers of Horror*, 16.

dissolved. The Venus of the opening stanza is also multiple: she is not the same as the Venus of the parliament; Venus in that section is described as 'Richt unstabill and full of variance' (235), while Cynthia has no colour of her own. Against the fascination of the abject, masculinity is fragile. The male gods represent the symbolic order of prohibition and law, and yet even in them the boundaries of masculinity are under threat. Saturn, like the narrator at the beginning of the poem, is an androgynous figure of cold, androgynous because according to the theory of humours women are colder than men;[42] in winter, according to Gilbert Hay, 'all the vertues of mannis corps and bestis worthis waykare and feblare, as ane ald wyf, bludelas but naturale hete in hir, is cald and dry, nakit and trembland, gray and gretand, and all for elde drawand to the poynt of dede.'[43] Jupiter, garlanded and flower-bedecked, is 'nureis to all thingis generabill' (171), and the 'fair Phebus' is, similarly, 'Tender nureis and banischer of nicht' (201). In her final lament Cresseid herself is made to shore up the rigid dualities of sex and gender—'Fy, fals Cresseid; O trew knicht Troylus' (560)—on which masculine identity rests.

That duality has already been confirmed in the episode to which I have referred in which Troilus, riding triumphantly back from the battlefield, gives Cresseid a purse of gold without knowing who she is. She asks one of the other lepers who 'Hes done to us so greit humanitie?' (534), and is told that it is he. 'Humanitie' means 'human nature', but it also means 'kindness' and 'generosity' or, as *A Dictionary of the Older Scottish Tongue*[44] glosses it, 'conduct appropriate to human beings', which brings together both meanings. 'Don humanitie' means 'to treat kindly'; it is a performative, like 'don frendshipe' or 'don merci'. In giving Cresseid the purse Troilus has done what human beings do: he has enacted his humanity. His gesture seems to obliterate difference as it crosses the boundaries between

---

[42] See Cadden, *Meanings of Sex Difference*, 208.
[43] *The Buke of the Governaunce of Princes*, in *The Prose Works of Sir Gilbert Hay*, ed. Jonathan A. Glenn, STS, 4th ser. 21 (Edinburgh, 1993), 101.
[44] See *A Dictionary of the Older Scottish Tongue from the Twelfth Century to the End of the Seventeenth*, ed. Sir William Craigie and A. J. Aitken (Chicago and London, 1931–).

leprous and whole, between past and present, between man and woman, between prince and beggar. And yet at the same time it constitutes difference, since in order for him to do what he does, Cresseid has to be where and what she is. She has to have been exiled, repudiated, and stricken with disease so that Troilus can lay claim to the 'humanitie' which she attributes to him.

Cresseid's epitaph is her last exclusion and it leads into the moralizing detachment of the final stanza. It is famously elliptical:

> 'Lo, fair ladyis, Cresseid of Troy the toun,
> Sumtyme countit the flour of womanheid,
> Under this stane, lait lipper, lyis deid.' (607–9)

Like the couple in 'Les Amants trépassés' with whom I began, she is in the grave; the monument which Troilus is said to have erected is against his own dissolution as much as it is a memorial to hers. It is etched in 'goldin letteris' (606) with her doubleness, with the ambivalence of *vanitas* and *luxuria*: 'flour of womanheid' and 'lipper'. The marble of the tomb contrasts with the paper of her testament, as if solidifying that doubleness in stone can somehow fix its slipperiness, and halt death as a process of 'faiding' and 'rotting'. 'Refuse and corpses show me what I permanently thrust aside in order to live', says Kristeva: the monument marks the border between the 'grave quhair that scho lay' (605) and the living zone where the masculine is marked as human, stable and 'trew'.

12 'Spekyng for one's sustenance': The Rhetoric of Counsel in Mum and the Sothsegger, Skelton's Bowge of Court, and Elyot's Pasquil the Playne

HELEN BARR AND KATE WARD-PERKINS

In keeping with the ambiguous meanings of the poem as a whole, the title of Skelton's *Bowge of Court* can be understood in at least two senses. 'Bowge' is both 'an allowance of food at court' and an anglicized form of the French word for mouth: 'bouche':[1] the mouth of the court, that is, court language, is inseparable from court sustenance. This wordplay encapsulates the problem addressed in all three texts discussed here: namely, can one speak with integrity if one is, or hopes to be, retained at court? What kinds of language available to a courtier secure wise and ethical government?

> Est quid rex, nisi consilium fuerit sibi sanum
> Sunt quid consilia, rex nisi credeat ea.
>
> for ther is nothing
> Which mai be betre about a king

---

[1] In Skelton's catalogue of his works in *The Garland of Laurel*, he lists 'Item Bowche of Courte, where Drede was begyled' (1183), *John Skelton: The Complete English Poems*, ed. J. Scattergood (London, 1983). The non-anglicized form 'bowche' (the form used in *Mum*) makes more explicit the pun on 'bowche' as 'mouth; cf. *Speke Parott*: 'Maledite soyte bouche malheurewse!' (375); 'Cursed be a wicked mouth'. Arthur F. Kinney argues that 'bouge' also means to stove in the sides of a ship: *John Skelton: Priest as Poet* (Chapel Hill, NC, 1987), 11.

Than conseil, which is the substance
Of all a kinges governance.[2]

With characteristic pith Gower sums up one of the central premisses of traditional advice to princes literature: that good government depends on truthful counsel.[3] Throughout this tradition, the type of speaking that constitutes good counsel is expressed in formulations that are insistently oppositional: plain speaking versus duplicity; costly intervention versus self-interested silence; declarative criticism versus obsequious flattery. Gower's *Confessio Amantis* provides typical examples of the characteristic discourse of flatterers:

> Of feigned wordes make him wene
> That blak is whyt and blew is grene... (VII. 2187–8)

> And thus of fals thei maken soth... (VII. 2197)

> And trouthe is torned to lesinge,
> It is, as who seith, ayein kinde. (VII. 2214–15)

---

[2] Gower, *Vox Clamantis*, VI. 531–2, *The Latin Works of John Gower*, ed. G. C. Macaulay (Oxford, 1902); *Confessio Amantis*, VII. 3887–90, *The English Works of John Gower*, ed. G. C. Macaulay, 2 vols. EETS ES 81, 82 (1901).

[3] The range and different configurations of this premiss are too huge to document in full, but the following examples may serve to illustrate the persistence of the topos and its various emphases: Hoccleve, *The Regement of Princes*, ed. F. J. Furnivall, EETS ES 72 (1897), 4859–963; *The Governance of Lordschipes*, in *Three Version of the Secreta Secretorum*, ed. R. Steele, EETS ES 74 (1898), which devotes fifteen chapters to counsellors and their properties, pp. 98–103; *De Quadripartita Regis Specie*, in J.-P. Genet (ed.), *Four English Political Tracts of the Later Middle Ages*, Camden Society, 4th ser. 18 (1977), where wisdom is defined as the king sitting amongst his counsellors and nobles receiving the benefit of good advice, p. 96; *Richard the Redeless* and *The Crowned King*: both poems which offer the political advice needed by contemporary rulers; Ashby, *The Active Policy of a Prince*, in *The Poems of George Ashby*, ed. M. Bateson, EETS ES 76 (1899), 281–7, where the 'wiseman' enjoins Prince Edward to do 'all thinge with counseil', p. 281; J. Fortescue, *The Governance of England*, ed. C. Plummer (Oxford, 1885), chs. xv–xvi, where a pragmatic description of the composition of the king's council is followed by a comparison between Rome and England to illustrate that civil wars and poverty are caused by the absence of sensible and well-chosen counsellors to counsel the king, pp. 145–50, and the separate treatise, *Example What Good Counseill Helpith and Avantageth, and of the Contrare what Folowith*, pp. 346–7; Sir Thomas Elyot, *The Boke Named The Governour*, ed. H. H. S. Croft (London, 1880), which, in a humanist discussion of counsel, concludes that 'the ende of all doctrine and studie is good counsayle' (III. xxix), ii. 433. The tradition of counsel is examined at length by A. B. Ferguson, *The Articulate Citizen and the English Renaissance* (Durham, NC, 1965).

Such 'unnatural' duplicity is contrasted with the truthteller's plain-speaking 'trouthe':

> Bot wher the pleine trouthe is noted
> Ther may a Prince wel conceive
> That he schal noght himself deceive
> Of that he hiereth wordes pleine... (VII. 2340–3)

Our argument in this chapter, however, is that these uncompromising pronouncements on language and counsel are deceptive. As the texts we discuss show, the process of truthtelling is rhetorically much more complex than the traditional theory allows for. Despite the claimed oppositions between plain speaking and duplicity, intervention and silence, advice and flattery, speaking has to be strategic in order to be heard: there is no single, unmediated 'Truth' available to a speaker either sustained at court or seeking court preferment.

Skelton's *The Bowge of Court* (1480–98?)[4] shows a highly self-reflexive awareness of these issues. The pun on 'bowge' captures the rhetorical problem overlooked by oppositional formulations of the language considered appropriate for princely advice, and opens up the question of the speaker's position. If the language which circulates at court is that which is rewarded by court sustenance, how can a speaker lay claim to the transparent, honest counsel so earnestly enjoined as a 'sine qua non' of good government in conventional treatises on counsel for the king?

While a number of texts written between the fourteenth and sixteenth centuries assert the need for a wise man at court, and while, as in the debate between Peter Giles, Hythlodaeus, and Morus in Book I of *Utopia*,[5] the compatibility of public office and honest counsel is questioned, the rhetorical implications of this issue are generally taken for granted. The sceptical treatment of the problem of honest counsel in *Bowge* is highlighted when the poem is compared to other texts which are also

---

[4] *Bowge* was printed by Wynkyn de Worde in 1499 and its writing has been assigned variously to the early-to-mid 1480s, 1494–5, and 1498: see M. J. Tucker, 'Setting in Skelton's *Bowge of Court*: A Speculation', *ELN* 7 (1970), 168–75, and G. Walker, *John Skelton and the Politics of the 1520s* (Cambridge, 1988), 8–27.

[5] *The Complete Works of St Thomas More*, ed. E. Surtz and J. H. Hexter (New Haven and London, 1965), iv. 54–9.

self-conscious about the relationship between counsel, court position, and language. To illustrate the variety of this discussion we have chosen to place *Bowge* alongside an early fifteenth-century alliterative political poem, the anonymous *Mum and the Sothsegger*, and from the Tudor humanist literature of counsel, Elyot's prose treatise, *Pasquil the Playne* (1533). All three texts reveal interesting configurations of the problem of language and counsel, most especially in their treatment of the conventional polarities of plain speech and flattery. In *Mum*, *Pasquil*, and *Bowge*, though with different emphases and consequences, the equation between 'plain speaking' and ethical transparency is problematized: plain speaking emerges as a strategic discursive position. In comparing *Bowge* with earlier and later texts we also aim to suggest that Skelton's handling of the conventional elements of this issue is more explicitly radical than his status as a so-called 'transitional' poet can accommodate.[6]

In the opening section of *Mum and the Sothsegger*[7] the narrator declares that the most necessary officer in a king's court is a truthteller who will offer corrective advice to the king (31–53). Throughout the poem the type of language such a court counsellor should use is categorized unequivocally. A truthteller is 'a sicour servant' who 'pleynely telleth' (1174–5); one who does not shun this duty: 'for no salaire ne soulde that he fangeth / Ne [for no] likerous lyvelode ne loising of his office' (1176–7). Plain-speaking, proverbial transparency which is unswerving even in the face of losing remuneration or office is asserted as the guarantee of truth.

However, these confident statements, spoken by the narrator and a beekeeper, are challenged and tested in the poem. Mum, the personification not just of self-interested silence but of all the vices of speech opposed to wise counsel, advises the narrator that no truthteller was ever rewarded at court, but if you can 'parle for your profit' (257) you will be welcome everywhere.

---

[6] The debate over Skelton's designation as a transitional poet between the Middle Ages and the Renaissance is reviewed and its significance theorized in R. Halpern, 'Skelton and the Poetics of Primitive Accumulation', in P. Parker and D. Quint (eds.), *Literary Theory/Renaissance Texts* (Baltimore, 1986), 225–256; pp. 225–7.

[7] *Mum and the Sothsegger*, in H. Barr (ed.), *The Piers Plowman Tradition* (London, 1993).

'Spekyng for one's sustenance'   253

The narrator's reply affirms the interdependence of court sustenance (bouche of court, 272), flattery, and self-interested silence:

> Thou wol not putte the in prees but profit be the more
> To thy propre persone, thou passes not the bondes
> Forto gete any grucche for glaunsyng of boltes.
> Thus me semeth that thou serves thy-self and no man elles,
> And has housholde and hire to holde up thy oyles,
> And eke bouche of court for colte and for [cnave];
> And [yit] thou suffris thy souvrayn to shame hym-self
> There thou mightes amende hym many tyme and ofte.
>
> (267–74)

But despite the narrator's insistence on the fraudulence of this self-interested discourse, Mum succeeds in convincing him that the only kind of language tolerated at court is duplicitous, for truthtelling invites trouble:

> And ever he concludid with colorable wordes
> That who-so mellid muche more than hit nedeth
> Shuld rather wynne weping watre thenne robes.
> And cleerly Caton construeth the same,
> And seyth soethly, I saw hit in youthe,
> Nam nulli tacuisse nocet, nocet esse locutum
> For of 'bable' cometh blame and of 'be stille' never.
>
> (281–92)

What is interesting here is that the ostensibly separate discursive positions of Mum and the 'sothsegger' begin to merge. The would-be-truthteller narrator is sufficiently impressionable to pervert a quotation from Cato's *Distichs* to support Mum's position. Though the narrator continues to align himself with the discourse of truthtelling ('seying soethly', 289) the Latin aphorism at 291a is more usually cited to warn against speaking when it is either imprudent or unethical to do so[8] than to

---

[8] e.g. in Albertanus of Brescia's *De Arte Loquendi et Tacendi*, in *Brunetto Latinos Levnet og Skrifter*, ed. J. Thor Sundby (Copenhagen, 1869), pp. xcvii–xvciii, where the tag is used to advise that ethical caution in speech is to be preferred against rash pronouncement. This is a text which Skelton may have translated: see *Garland of Laurel*: 'Item the Boke to Speke Well or be Styll' (1175). A version of the distich is cited in *Piers Plowman*, C. XIII. 223b (*Piers Plowman by William Langland: An Edition of the 'C' Text*, ed. D. Pearsall (London, 1978)) as a rebuke to the Dreamer for having interrupted Reason; and at the end of *The Manciple's Tale* to warn of the dangers of speaking ill-advisedly (*The Riverside Chaucer*, ed. L. D. Benson (Oxford, 1988), ll. 325–8 and 359).

endorse a speaking position which is at odds with the ethical uses of speech the narrator had earlier promulgated so clearly.

The ease with which 'soeth seying' elides with the manipulative language use associated with 'mumming' illustrates both the fragility of the discourse of truthtelling, and the provisionality of the oppositional terms that are used to describe it. A further demonstration of this occurs in a later exchange when Mum apparently turns 'sothsigger' himself, declaring that if one refuses to speak out against abuses, one is implicated in them: 'qui tacet consentire videtur' (745). A more hard-hitting speech could scarcely have come from the narrator himself, as he acknowledges:

> 'Now treuly,' cothe I, 'thy talking me pleasith,
> For thou has saide as sothe, so me God helpe,
> As ever sage saide sith Crist was in erthe,
> For thou has rubbid on the rote of the rede galle
> And eeke y-serchid the sore and sought alle the woundz.
> And yf thou woldes do wel wende to thaym alle
> And telle the same tale that thou has tolde here'. (767–73)

However, Mum declines to repeat his words in the very context where they are sorely needed—

> 'Nay, there I leve the, lucas, go loke [for] an othir;
> For I wil wende no waie but wit go bifore' (775–6)

—and the scene changes to a banquet where the narrator watches Mum corrupt the assembled company through lies, ellipses, 'plaisant wordes', and speech which is 'ful couchant and coy and curtoys' (808–12). Mum is rewarded for his verbal display with gifts and pride of place at the feast. The narrator asks if any 'sothe-sigger were sette in the halle' (828) but learns that he

> Dyneth this day with Dreede in a chambre,
> And hath y-drunke dum-seede, and dar not be seye. (838–9)

Truthtelling is associated with Dread, and, significantly, with silence, which is a discursive position more usually associated with dishonest language use. The location of the truthteller in an anonymous 'chambre' without power or position signals his impotence.

At the very moment, however, in which both the narrator's words and the narrative strategy which frames them recognize that the only place from which a truthteller can speak with integrity is a place in which they won't be heard, the narrator also falls back on the assertion that a 'soth-sigger' would be a 'better barne to abide stille / And to lyve with a lord to his life-is ende' (851–2) than Mum is.[9] Ultimately the poem, for all its awareness of the rhetorical complexities of truthtelling, recuperates plain-speaking as an effective discursive strategy. In the dream-vision section of *Mum* the narrator meets a beekeeper who speaks the truthtelling discourse for which he has been searching: plain-speaking, altruistic, and corrective. The beekeeper renews the narrator's faith in truthtelling, and, further, commissions the narrator to turn truthteller himself. And so, with a new discursive strategy, the narrator makes a fresh start. He opens a bag of books which Mum had confiscated and provides a plain-speaking guide to their truthtelling contents: 'forto conseille the king' (1343). In this new narrative context the narrator quotes the first half of the Cato distich which he had distorted earlier in the poem, but here the aphorism 'Shun gossip lest you be thought an originator of it' (1403a) is quoted to assert the importance of offering corrective advice rather than resorting to seditious rumour-mongering. After a long struggle the last section of the poem proclaims a truthtelling discourse from a dominant, uninterrupted position.

It is important, however, that while the poem chronicles its own empowerment to speak the truth, the positions from which it does so are marginal. The beekeeper is a member of the third estate; and though he bids the narrator give a copy of his book to the king, its writer is *not* sustained by court: 'for with the king-is cunseil I come but silde' (151). Further, the vernacular, uplandish style of the poem positions it outside the discourses of dominant institutions,[10] even while its hard-hitting mode of

---

[9] The permeability of the truthtelling discourse is seen even here in that 'stille' also means silence. *Mum* also uses this pun in ll. 755 and 823: see H. Barr, *Signes and Sothe: Language in the Piers Plowman Tradition* (Cambridge, 1994), 81.

[10] The alliterative register of *Mum* supplements rather than endorses dominant, institutionalized discourses. This is discussed in more detail in Barr, *Signes and Sothe*, 39–50.

complaint claims a kind of vatic authority. Although *Mum* offers honest counsel to the king for the good of the common weal, and dramatizes the eventual victory of honest criticism over fraudulent language use, it does so from a position where integrity of speech depends on its divorce from centres of power.

At first sight, this stance looks similar to that of Elyot's *Pasquil the Playne* (1533), 'a mery treatise wherin plainnes and flateri do come in trial'.[11] The treatise is cast in the form of a Lucianic dialogue between plain-speaking Pasquil and two 'cousins germane', Gnatho, a loquacious flatterer, and Harpocrates, a practitioner of self-interested silence. Elyot informs his readers in the preface that Pasquil 'is an image of stone, sitting in the citie of Rome openly: on whome ones in the yere, it is leful to every man, to set in verse or prose any taunte that he wil, agayne whom he list, howe great an astate so ever he be' (p. 42). This is a reference to the popular Roman custom of attaching anonymous lampoons of the Pope and other Roman prelates to an ancient statue which had been unearthed in 1501 and erected at the corner of the Piazza Navona.[12] Elyot's account suggests that he was familiar with this custom, and the satirical genre of 'pasquillades' which derived from it, in which the responsibility for writing scurrilous verses and lampoons was evaded by claiming that they were attached to the statue of Pasquil, or were reports of exchanges between Pasquil and another statue called Marforius. A collection of these pasquillades was published in Rome in 1512, and another in 1544.[13] The verses published in the later collection were known in England in the early 1530s: Edmund Bonner, later bishop of London, who had been sent to Rome by Henry VIII to protest against the Pope's attitude towards divorce proceedings, sent

---

[11] *Pasquil the Playne* (London, 1553), quoted from the facsimile ed. Lillian Gottesman, in Sir Thomas Elyot, *Four Political Treatises* (Gainesville, Fla, 1967), 42. All subsequent references to this edition are cited in the text.

[12] S. E. Lehmberg, *Sir Thomas Elyot: Tudor Humanist* (Austin, Tex., 1960), 117 n. 8.

[13] An edition of the 1512 collection, *Carmina Apposita Pasquillo*, is preserved in MS Bodley Mortara adds. I. 72 and the 1544 *Pasquillorum Tomi Duo* in MS Bodley Douce P. 562. Two of the most extreme anti-papal invectives are a verse in which Christ and the pope are described in a series of antitheses, and the 'Third Gospel according to Pasquil', which, in a parody of St Matthew's enumeration of the genealogy of Christ, narrates a genealogy of the pope which starts with the devil, moves through bulls and indulgences, and concludes with Antichrist, pp. 26–7 and 115–24.

one of these works to Elyot's friend Thomas Cromwell on 24 December 1542, writing: 'Your Maystership dothe, I knowe, well remember that great statua lyeng benethe the Capitole which is called Marforius; and as for Mr Pasquillus ye knowe, I know well.'[14]

Elyot's treatise is also clearly dependent on the advice to princes tradition. The traditional topoi of discussions of counsel —the need for honest speaking and the dangers of flattery—are played out in the confrontation between the different speakers of the dialogue. The initial topic of dispute between Gnatho and Pasquil is the significance of a sentence from one of Aeschylus's tragedies: 'holdyng thy tonge wher it behoveth the. And spekyng in tyme that whiche is convenient' (p. 49). Rather as the narrator in *Mum* wrenches Cato's distich, Gnatho interprets the sentence to endorse a time-serving, self-interested mode of speech. Pasquil, however, interprets Aeschylus's doctrine with pragmatic highmindedness. Its thrust, he argues, is to judge the occasion and the moment at which counsel can be most effective: 'For oportunite and tyme for a counsayllour to speke do not depend of the affection and appetite of hym that is counsayled: mary than counsaylle were but a vayne worde, and every man wolde do as hym lyste' (pp. 55–6). Having led Gnatho on to parade his own obsequious pursuit of preferment, Pasquil turns his attention to Harpocrates' claim that 'in silence is suretie' (p. 65), and similarly exposes the self-seeking and politically damaging nature of this kind of verbal behaviour. The dialogue thus reproduces the familiar contours of traditional discussions of counsel: duplicitous speech and time-serving silence are oppositionally contrasted with honest truthtelling.

Read in this light, *Pasquil the Playne* appears to be a conventional treatise on the topic of counsel. As such, it continues Elyot's humanist concern with this topic, exemplified in his translation of the earliest known example of the 'advice to princes' genre, Isocrates' *Ad Nicolem*,[15] and in the emphasis

---

[14] Quoted in *The Boke Named The Governour*, ed. Croft, p. xcviii, from *State Papers*, vii. 397. The responses of Marforius are found in verses printed only in the later 1544 collection.
[15] This is edited in *Four Political Treatises* under the title 'The Doctrinal of Princes' by Lillian Gottesman.

placed on counsel in *The Governour* (1530). The latter is strongly informed by the central humanist belief in the importance of humane education as a foundation for the provision of the best political advice.[16] The supreme significance of such humanist counsel is asserted in the closing address to the reader:

> Therefore these thinges I have rehersed concernyng consultation ought to be of all men in authoritie substancially pondered and moost vigilauntly observed, if they intende to be to their publike weale profitable, for the whiche purpose onely they be called to be governours. And this conclude I to write any more of consultation, whiche is the last part of morall Sapience and the begynnyng of Sapience politike.[17]

A closer reading of *Pasquil the Playne*, however, suggests that its relation to the optimistic humanist view of the political and ethical integrity of the rhetorically educated counsellor is more ambivalent than this contextualization might suggest. Elyot's preface asserts that 'plainnes in speking is of wise men commended' and 'diverse do abhorre longe prohemes of Rhetorike' (p. 42). This anti-rhetorical stance is reinforced by his description of Gnatho as 'a Greke borne and therfore he savorith some what of rethorike' (p. 43). Pasquil, by contrast, is 'an olde Romane, but by longe sittinge in the strete, and heringe market men chat, he is become rude and homely' (p. 43). It is tempting to read the transformation of the classical statue into a demotic speaker as a figure for Elyot's own shift of discursive position since writing *The Governour*.

This wariness about rhetoric is paralleled elsewhere in the treatise by a surprisingly ambivalent attitude towards classical learning. It is Gnatho who cites 'Aeschylus counsaylle' (p. 49) as an authority for 'how I mought sonest come to promotion', and Pasquil's jaundiced reaction is significant:

---

[16] Q. Skinner, *The Foundations of Modern Political Thought* (Cambridge, 1978), i. 122 refers to 'the familiar humanist assumption that, since the right kind of education is of crucial importance in shaping the character of the "vir virtutis", there must be a close connection between the provision of the best education and the best political advice'. A crucial element in this is the recovery of Plato's *Republic* because of the prominence given to education and the programme of studies to be followed by the Guardians of the State.

[17] *The Governour*, ii. 446-7.

Mary Gnatho . . . thou arte moche wysar than I supposed. I had wende al this whyle that by nature onely thou haddest ben instructed to flatter, but by saint Jone I se now, that thou joynest also therto a shrewde wyt, and preparest to the helping therof as it were a crafte gathered of lernynge and scripture. (p. 49)

In contrast to *The Governour*'s uncomplicated use of humanist discourse, and its insistence on the ethical and political value of learning, here knowledge of the ancients is shown to be a dangerous 'crafte' in the mouth of a rhetorically trained speaker.

Another suggestive point of contrast with *The Governour* can be detected in Pasquil's critique of Harpocrates' use of a Latin neologism. Elyot is famous for his willingness in *The Governour* 'to usurpe a latine worde . . . for the necessary augmentation of our langage'.[18] Yet in *Pasquil* neologism is represented as an instrument of obscurity rather than illumination. In his dispute with Harpocrates over the ethics of silence, Pasquil backs his opponent into a corner with the question of whether one should speak if one sees a master or friend about to be murdered. Harpocrates replies that he would bide his time to see if the danger might pass: 'but whan hit were imminent thanne wolde I give warninge' (pp. 76–7). Pasquil seizes on his choice of diction as a wilful strategy to obfuscate a clear moral argument: 'Imminent, what calle ye that? . . . but teache me I pray you, what ye calle imminent, for hit is a worde taken out of latine and not commenly used' (pp. 77–8).[19] Harpocrates replies that 'imminent' is 'whan it appereth to be in the instante to be done or to happen: and after some mens exposition as it thretned to come' (p. 78). With heavy irony Pasquil commends Harpocrates' exposition as 'clerkly' and adds that if he is to divide time into instants then he is a good 'Duns man'.[20] Harpocrates' use of the Latin loan-word exploits the humanist

---

[18] Ibid. i. 243–5.

[19] In *The Governour*, Elyot uses 'imminent' in the sentence: 'Surely whan there was any difficulte warre immynent, then were thay constrained to electe one soveraine chiefe of all other . . .' (i. 19). No attention is drawn to its Latinity and the inclusion of the word is part of Elyot's explictly stated aim in the first chapter to explicate the senses of English words borrowed from Latin in order to enlighten political opinions (i. 1–3).

[20] See *OED* dunce 1. Tindale, *Par Wikked Mammon* Wks (1573) 88: 'A Duns man would make xx distinctions'.

strategy of *The Governour* to completely antithetical ends; in affecting the Classics he sounds like a medieval schoolman. Pasquil's alternative definition of 'imminent' exposes the expedience of Harpocrates' explanation[21] and Harpocrates is forced to agree that 'sylence were out of season'. Defeat of the silent flatterer hence turns on an argument centred around the true and false exposition of Latin. Pasquil is constructed as a plain speaker who can see through the disingenuous use of learning.

It is possible to interpret these satirical portrayals of the opportunistic use of humanist learning as reflecting a growing scepticism in Elyot over whether an ethically based humanism can ever be politically effective. Elsewhere in the treatise it is suggested that a humanist education is out of fashion at court. Pasquil laments that: 'In olde tyme men used to occupie the mornynge in deepe and subtile studies and in counsailes concernynge the comune weale, and other matters of great importaunce' (p. 64).[22] Gnatho sees such concerns as a political liability. He cynically advises Pasquil that 'if thou woldist... laye apart the lesson of gentiles, called humanite' and 'pike out here and there sentences out of holy scripture to fournisshe thy reason with authoritie. I make god avowe... whan thy conversion and good opinion is knowen, than shalt thou be called fore' (p. 61). The implication that politically opportunistic piety is the present key to preferment connects suggestively with Elyot's own political fortunes. Elyot wrote *Pasquil* after 'the Kinges opinyon mynisshid towarde me' and he had been recalled as Ambassador to Spain in 1532 and replaced by Cranmer:[23] *Pasquil* appears to have grown out of Elyot's personal failure to secure influence at court.[24] Thus it is possible

---

[21] If one sees a man on the point of being murdered, the peril is not 'nowe imminent, that is to say, to be done, or to happen: but it is in the instant of happening'. It is, he says, in the very point of: 'executing. Wherefore ther is repugnancie in your owne resoninge, if this worde, Imminent be truely expouned' (pp. 78-9).

[22] Pasquil's subsequent description of the lifestyle of counsellors 'in olde tyme' echoes the education of the humanist 'vir virtutis' in *The Governour*, but he concludes: 'now all this is tourned into an other fascion, god helpe us, the worlde is almost at an ende' (p. 65).

[23] Elyot wrote this to Thomas Cromwell in November 1532, and added that he was held in 'lasse estimation than I was in whan I servid the King first in his Counsayle' ('The Letters of Sir Thomas Elyot', ed. K. J. Wilson, *SP* 73 (1976), pp. i-xxx, 1-78; p. 9).

[24] This is argued by Alistair Fox, 'Sir Thomas Elyot and the Humanist Dilemma', in A. Fox and J. Guy (eds.), *Reassessing the Henrician Age* (Oxford, 1986), 52-73.

to read the treatise both as a response to specific political circumstances and as a more general exploration of the problem of 'spekyng for one's sustenance'. Cranmer's preferment at Elyot's expense provides the topical context for the persistently hostile references to scriptural learning.[25] Moreover, Elyot's adoption of the persona and rhetorical licence of Pasquil can be read as an attempt to find a new, more sceptical discourse in which to express not only his sense of injustice at seeing 'other men avauncid openly to the place of Counsaylours which neither in the importaunce of service neither in chargis have servyd the king as I have doone',[26] but also his awareness of the double bind of the humanist counsellor: that political expediency is incompatible with moral integrity, but speaking the truth inevitably forfeits political favour.[27]

As in *Mum*, Pasquil's plain style of speaking is constructed as a discursive position which is grounded in integrity precisely because it is removed from centres of power. Gnatho and Harpocrates vilify Pasquil's plainness as 'babillyng', 'raylyng', and 'praytyng'.[28] Pasquil's assertion that 'I have professed from my chyldehode never to speke in ernest to my mayster or frende, contrarye to that, that I thinke' draws an unequivocal reaction from Gnatho: 'Ergo thou haste professed to stande styl in the rayne and ones perchance to be throwen in to Tyber, or broken in pieces' (p. 69). When Harpocrates counsels Pasquil that 'thou shuldest do more good, if thou spakest privily', Pasquil replies: 'Tusshe man, my playnnes is so well knowen that I shall never come unto privie chambre or galeri' (p. 98). Such an unswerving insistence on political self-exile suggests that Elyot had arrived at a discursive position remarkably similar to the narrator of *Mum*: the construction of the plain style as politically

---

[25] See pp. 46–7, 49, 51, 61, 67, 88.
[26] 'Letters', ed. Wilson, p. 9.
[27] This dilemma is remarkably similar to that analysed by More in Book I of *Utopia*. Elyot's preoccupation with the problem at this date is suggested by the fact that in *Of the Knowledge that Maketh a Wise Man* (1533), Elyot tells a fable drawn from Diogenes Laertius of Plato's experience when he tried to warn Dionysus that the latter was becoming a tyrant. In fury Dionysus gave Plato to Polidis, who sold him into slavery, from which he barely escaped alive. Fox discusses the relevance of this story to Elyot's situation at some length (pp. 70–3).
[28] Cf. *Mum*, 50 where the 'sothsigger' is described as one who 'bablith fourth bustusely as barn un-y-lerid'.

marginal is simultaneously a claim for plenitude of speech and superior authority. But while *Mum* clings to the authority of the 'outsider' with its uplandish vernacular, Elyot invests plain speech with the authority of classical learning. For all its anti-rhetorical positioning, the treatise is underwritten by recourse to the very traditions which it purports to eschew. The Lucianic form and style of the piece; the choice of classical protagonists, including Pasquil himself, who, even if he stands in the marketplace, is a classical statue in Rome;[29] the sustained use of Latinate diction in the treatise as a whole;[30] all these features illustrate the extent to which, for all its claims to transparency, plain speech is itself a rhetorical construction.

Furthermore it is possible to read the treatise as a piece of rhetorical self-fashioning in which Elyot constructs himself as the archetypal honest counsellor in an attempt to jog the conscience of the King.[31] That *Pasquil* is indirectly a plea for preferment is suggested not only by Elyot's 1533 letter to Cromwell, expressing the hope that 'it shall please you to recommend one of theise bookes unto the kinges highness',[32] but also by the bid for the reader's support at the end of the Preface:

And if it seme to you that Pasquill sayth true in declaringe howe moche ye do favoure truthe defende hym ageynste venemous tunges

---

[29] Gnatho is the servant/parasite in Terence's comedy *Eunuchus* and Harpocrates is the Greek equivalent of the Egyptian Horus, who, in his character of the youthful sun, was represented as a boy with his finger on his mouth. From this posture he came to be regarded by the Greeks and Romans as a god of Silence. The Romans placed statues of him at the entrance to their temples, and the phrase 'Harpocratum reddere' became proverbial to imply silence and secrecy.

[30] See e.g. citation in n. 21 where, in the same breath as criticizing Harpocrates' uses of neologism, Pasquil uses 'executing', 'repugnancie', and 'expounded' (pp. 77–8).

[31] Another possible instance may be found in his letter to the English ambassador to the Low Countries in which he expresses the hope 'that truthe may be freely and thankfully herd. For my part I am finally determyned to lyve and dye therin. Neither myn importable expences unrecompencid shall so moche feare me, nor the advauncement of my Successor the busshop of Caunterbury so moche alure me that I shall ever deklyne from trouthe or abuse my soveraigne lorde unto whome I am sworn' ('Letters', ed. Wilson, p. 17. Fox discusses this letter in rather different terms (pp. 63–4).

[32] 'Letters', ed. Wilson, pp. 22–3. At the start of this letter Elyot states that he has sent Cromwell a brief treatise, which Wilson takes to be *Of the Knowledge that Maketh a Wise Man*, which was dedicated to Cromwell. But the later mention of 'one of theise bokes', together with the comment about Elyot's own writing, 'it is sometyme goode to here the poure gardyner' (a reference to Zenobius's dictum, 'Do not despise the rustic speaker'), suggests that he also sent a copy of *Pasquil* with this letter.

and overthwart wittis, whiche doeth more myschieffe, than Pasquillus babillinge. (p. 44)

Unlike *Mum*, the plain style in *Pasquil* embraces marginality as a mode of self-recommendation: there is an internal faultline between the actual complexity of the speech-act which the treatise performs and the apparently monosemic self-image of the honest counsellor. The literary tradition of the 'pasquillade' renders this internal contradiction all the more complex. It seems improbable that Elyot was unaware of its anti-papal associations.[33] At one point Pasquil reminds Gnatho that Pope Leo had threatened to throw him into the Tiber on account of his 'babblynge' (p. 57). Elyot's political difficulties appear to have stemmed from his ineffectiveness in negotiating the king's divorce, and his apparent ambivalence about the wisdom of Henry's intentions is reflected in the overall religious conservatism of the treatise.[34] Yet in the choice of an anti-papal discourse Elyot appears to align himself with the king's party. Plain speaking in this text can thus be seen as a Janus-faced rhetorical strategy which both guarantees Elyot's political integrity and simultaneously flatters Henry with its anti-papal subtext. The unmediated linguistic 'truth' that the treatise claims to construct is, according to our reading, not transparent but rhetorically strategic. Elyot's own writing career illustrates this: the very different discourses he adopts in *The Governour* and *Pasquil the Playne* make clear that 'speaking in tyme which is convenient' is not only a question of judging the moment or occasion, but also of finding an appropriate position from which to speak.

This close correlation between literary output and political aspiration is seen also in the career of John Skelton. Like Elyot's,

---

[33] See p. 256 above and n. 13.

[34] Despite writing a letter to Henry in June 1532 which remonstrated with the king over his divorce from Katherine of Aragon, Elyot's name appears in the list of knights and gentlemen to be servitors at the coronation of Anne Boleyn (Fox and Guy (eds.), *Reassessing The Henrician Age*, 61). That *Pasquil* is conservative in its religous views can be seen from Pasquil's condemnation of German Protestantism and his defence of miracles and saints (p. 58) and of confessors (p. 91). The hostile references to the use of scriptural learning (see above, p. 260) are localized attacks on Cranmer rather than expressions of religious radicalism.

Skelton's court fortunes fluctuated. Until the death of Henry VII's heir, Arthur, in 1502, he was tutor to the young Prince Henry, and however great or small the importance of that position[35] he appears to have imbibed the ideals of the court's literary establishment. His brief *Speculum principis*, apparently written in 1501, stresses the importance of learning and virtue, and the need for princes to cultivate poets, orators, and university men:[36]

Nephas esset hoc Scipionis tacere memorabile eulogium. Illud certe, inquit, regnum cuius principes probitate vacant neque sunt nobilitate litterarum bene prediti, nunquam posse prosperari.

It would be wrong not to mention the famous eulogy of Scipio which asserts that the kingdom, whose princes lack virtue and are not well endowed with the nobility of letters, can never prosper.[37]

The connection between learning and counsel is made clear in the closing exhortation:

Adulatores prosequere odio. Acquiesce sano consilio. . . . Famulos respice et illos refice. Honora medicos, consule philosophos, venerare theologos. Amplectere poetas et cole camerarias tanquam Micenas; quia multi mulliones sed pauci Polliones.

Pursue flatterers with hatred. Assent to wise counsel. . . . Be considerate to your servants and re-appoint them. Honour doctors, consult philosophers, venerate theologians. Embrace poets and cultivate chamber knights such as Maecenas because there are many mulekeepers but few Pollios. (pp. 35–6)

Although Skelton repeats here the conventional injunction that the king should seek honest counsel and shun flatterers, his own treatise in fact collapses the distinction between these two discourses. The references to Maecenas (Virgil's patron) and

[35] W. Nelson, *John Skelton: Poet Laureate* (New York, 1964), 7–39; Walker, *John Skelton and the Politics of the 1520s*, 36–51.

[36] Gordon Kipling, in *The Triumph of Honour: Burgundian Origins of the Elizabethan Renaissance* (Leiden, 1977), 1–40, has argued that Henry's court was deeply indebted for both ideology and for scholars to the rhetoriqueur tradition of the court of Burgundy, whose dukes had promoted an ideal of 'learned chivalry' throughout the fifteenth century. He argues that Skelton was in essential agreement with the moral structure of Burgundian literature (pp. 23–30).

[37] 'Skelton's *Speculum Principis*, ed. F. M. Salter, *Speculum*, 9 (1934), 25–37; p. 33.

Pollio (Roman consul, patron, orator, poet, and dedicatee of Virgil's Fourth Eclogue) confer oblique prestige on Skelton himself as a poet and orator: the prince's tutor/orator/poet urges the prince to employ men such as himself. Further, the prince is urged not just to be considerate to his servants, but, significantly, to reappoint ('refice') them. The treatise is simultaneously a collection of wise aphorisms and a speech for Skelton's sustenance.

When in 1511 Skelton re-presents the treatise to Henry, now king, moral/political sapience and request for sustenance are even more closely entangled. The fresh presentation was a birthday gift and Skelton wrote a new epilogue and soliloquy. The epilogue describes the author as given over totally to oblivion ('vir totus obliuioni datus') and one upon whom neither the king's munificence nor the blessing of Fortune has so far thought worthy to breathe on with favour more richly ('cui nec regalis munificentia, nec fortuna benignitas adhuc opulentius dignature aspirare', p. 37). At this time, Skelton was living at Diss, and that he sought the medium of an advice-to-princes manual to make a carefully engineered plea for recall to court favour demonstrates how readily the conventions of wise counsel could be used to make a bid for court sustenance. This inseparability of wise counsel from strategic speech is unsurprising given that Skelton had already written *The Bowge of Court*, where the very title of the poem makes reward at court dependent upon the mouth,[38] and where, since the Bowge of Court is the name of the ship of state, speaking, courtliness, government, and court sustenance are indistinguishable. The title anticipates the way that the poem calls into question the power of learning and language to produce moral action.

The poem takes the form of a nightmare vision in which the scholar/dreamer, Drede, dreams that he boards a ship called the Bowge of Courte, steered by Fortune and laden with 'favor'.

---

[38] A. Wawn argues that in the Prologue Drede wishes to become an articulate citizen but fears that articulate citizenship and the bouche of court are incompatible. 'Bowge' names both the reward and the means by which that reward was lost: the mouth ('Truth-Telling and the Tradition of *Mum and the Sothsegger*, YES 13 (1983), 270–87; p. 272).

On board, Drede is assailed by seven courtiers who so bewilder him with their mixture of advice, flattery, and intimidation that he is about to jump off the ship, and so wakes from the dream. Heiserman's analysis of the poem convincingly shows how it dramatizes long-standing topics of anti-court satire in medieval treatises.[39] This dramatization, however, also stages these topics as conventions, and in so doing collapses many of their binary oppositions. For instance, the dreamer figure Drede, as both consciousness and object of the vices of courtiers, represents a conflation of the two personae of earlier epistolary court satire, the author as literary man employed in, but alienated from, the court, and his correspondent whom he seeks to persuade to eschew it. In Bowge, Drede is both writer and addressee.[40]

Further, Drede is repeatedly characterized as a solemn scholar and a poet. Although Favell compliments him on his learning to his face, he describes him to Suspecte as a 'soleyne freke' (187); Ryote advises him to be less 'sadde' and quit his studying for 'ete, drynke and slepe' (384); Dyssymulation laments that Drede's 'vertu' and 'lytterature' are being maligned (449–51). For all his scholarliness, Drede is also the personification of anxiety. One might view him as representing the anxiety of the lack of influence of the man of learning whose constructive importance in government Skelton was so keen to stress in his *Speculum principis*. Drede personifies the inevitability of the scholar-counsellor's falling victim to non-truthtelling political careerism.

This situation is dramatized in the prologue. The port where Drede (though unnamed as yet) falls asleep and into which the 'Bowge of Court' sails is called 'Powers Keye' (35). Real wharf or not, the topology is apt to highlight the narrator's interest in the key to power, namely the royal merchandise of favour carried on board the 'Bowge of Court':[41]

---

[39] A. R. Heiserman, *Skelton and Satire* (Chicago, 1961), 14–65.
[40] Ibid. 27.
[41] It has been proposed, though not universally accepted, that 'Powers Key' indicates a connection between Skelton and the Howard family: see A. Fox, *Politics and Literature in the Reigns of Henry VII and Henry VIII* (Oxford, 1988), 28; M. J. Tucker, 'Setting in Skelton's *Bowge of Court*'; and Walker, *John Skelton and The Politics of The 1520s*, 9–10.

> Marchauntes her borded to see what she had lode.
> Therein they founde royall marchaundyse,
> Fraghted with plesure to what ye coude devyse.
> But than I thoughte I wolde not dwell behynde;
> Amonge all other I put myselfe in prece. (40–4)

Drede thus occupies exactly the position of Mum in *Mum and the Sothsegger*: 'Thou wol not putte the in prees but profit be the more' (267). Unlike the narrator of *Mum*, who struggles to remain outside the discourse of self-interested language use, and Pasquil, ostensibly content to stand out in the rain, the narrator of *Bowge* strives to join the discourse of 'Who spareth to speke . . . he spareth to spede' (91), which Desire describes as the means to gain the material goods loaded on board the 'Bowge of Court'. Whereas in *Mum* the personification Drede dines with the truthteller in a private chamber and dares not be seen, in *Bowge* Drede is one of a throng of merchants who sue Fortune for a place at court in complete disregard of the function of a courtier to offer wise, constructive advice to the king:

> Of Bowge of Court she asketh what we wold have,
> And we asked favoure, and favour she us gave. (125–6)

Drede is both caught up in this slippery climb to power, and yet as narrator of the poem chronicles it as observer. The discursive speaking positions that *Mum* and *Pasquil* purport to separate are, in *Bowge*, overtly one and the same.

The same conclusion may be drawn from the dialogue on board ship.[42] Drede's first conversation is with Favell, who, as his name suggests, flatters Drede and promises to support him while intending to plot against him:

> But this one thynge ye maye be sure of me,
> For by that Lorde that boughte dere all mankynde,
> I can not flater, I must be playne to the.

---

[42] The menacing nature of the exchanges on board is discussed by S. E. Fish, *John Skelton's Poetry* (New Haven, 1965), 69–70; Heiserman, *Skelton and Satire*, 22–6; A. C. Spearing, *Medieval to Renaissance in English Poetry* (Cambridge, 1985), 263–5; and B. Sharratt, 'John Skelton: Finding a Voice—Notes after Bakhtin', in D. Aers (ed.), *Medieval Literature: Criticism, Ideology and History* (Brighton, 1986), 192–222.

> And ye nede ought, man, shewe to me your mynde,
> For ye have me whome faythfull ye shall fynde. (162–6)

Favell asserts that he uses the 'playne' speech of the truthtelling tradition[43]—which is clearly a fiction given that his speech to Drede is a tissue of unsubstantiated accolades and references to conversations that may never have taken place. Yet, simultaneously, the speech of the flatterer is propositionally valid. One of his axiomatic statements, 'Loo, what it is a man to have connynge! / All erthely tresoure it is surmountynge' (153–4), expresses exactly the sentiments that a good scholar-counsellor might wish to promulgate, but is simultaneously an attempt to flatter Drede. Drede's response follows a similar double movement:

> Than thanked I hym for his grete gentylnes.
> But, as me thoughte, he ware on hym a cloke
> That lyned was with doubtfull doublenes. (176–8)

Drede's flattering phrase 'grete gentylnes' goes alongside exposing Favell's duplicity. Truth and collusion are inseparable.

All the language on board ship is double. The owner of the ship, Dame Saunce-Pere, sits on a throne which bears the inscription: 'Garder le fortune que est mavelz et bone' (67). This has two meanings: either 'preserve fortune which is both good and bad' or 'defend yourself against Fortune which is both good and bad'. The surface structure suggests axiomatic wisdom but there is no stability of sense. What purports to be wisdom is actually just a dubious 'sentence' but, nevertheless, characteristic of the type of proverbial truisms so frequently found in advice to princes literature.[44]

Proverbs are especially associated with plain-speaking. In *Mum* a truthteller always 'hitteth on the heed of the nayle-is ende, / That the pure poynt pricketh on the sothe' (51–2). In his later *Collyn Clout* Skelton uses the same image to illustrate how

---

[43] Fish notes the appropriation of the norms of the plain-speaking tradition (*John Skelton's Poetry*, 69).
[44] See Wawn, 'Truth-Telling', and the series of maxims collected by, for example, Albertanus of Brescia in *De Arte Loquendi et Tacendi* and by Erasmus, *The Adages of Erasmus: A Study with Translations*, ed. Margaret Mann Phillips (Cambridge, 1964).

those who castigate vice are not heard: 'And yf that he hytte / The nayle on the hede / It standeth in no stede' (33–5).[45] In *Bowge*, however, this proverbial transparency is problematized. The surface structure of lines such as 'The soveraynst thynge that ony man maye have / Is lytyll to saye and moche to here and see' (211–12) and 'Woo is hym that is blynde and maye not see!' (518) suggests axiomatic wisdom because what characterizes proverbs is their absence of modality. The speaker believes and asserts that the predicate attributes an essential and immutable quality.[46] These proverbs, however, are spoken by Suspycyon and Disceyte, whose language is otherwise so slippery and divorced from referentiality that the proverbs' universal claims appear merely performative. The poem's placing of plain speech in the mouths of flatterers and time-serving connivers once again deconstructs the polarity of two apparently antithetical discursive positions.

It is very hard in *Bowge* to find any stability of position. For all the linguistic energy on board ship there is a crucial absence at the centre of the poem. There is a court, but no king. Fortune guides the ship but she never appears on board. The figure on the throne in the Prologue is Dame Saunce-Pere, whose name suggests absence or lack. Instead of a court presided over by regal male authority, its guides and authorities are presented in fickle—and female—terms.[47] This suggests an emasculated court, consonant with the image in the prologue of the muse Ignorance advising Drede to withdraw his pen from the page. It also hints that the linguistic practices and questing for favour at court are close to prostitution. Those in pursuit of favour 'her borded to see what she had lode' (40); they find her 'fraghted

---

[45] A similar image is used in *Speke Parott* when, having won his almond for his string of obsequious platitudes about Henry and Katherine, Parott turns to attack. The ladies warn him to shut up: 'Tecez-vous, Parrot, tenez vous coye', because he has 'res acu tangitur' (55–6).

[46] R. Fowler discusses the linguistic forms of universal generics in *Literature and Social Discourse* (London, 1981), 113–14.

[47] The grammatical slippages of the first stanza are noted by S. Dickey, 'Seven Come Eleven: Gambling for the Laurel in *The Bowge of Court*, YES 22 (1992), 238–54; p. 253, and the instability of the Prologue by Fish (*John Skelton's Poetry*, 60–2). Spearing notes the resemblances of the women to personifications in the *Roman de la Rose* but comments that the allegory of love becomes an allegory of trade. He links the acquisitory greed of merchants to the passion of blind lovers (*Medieval to Renaissance*, 262–3).

with plesure' but must 'paye therfore dere' (53)—terminology akin to Ryote's praise of his prostitute Malkyn, who has 'gote me more money with her tayle / Than hath some shyppe that into Bordews sayle' (405–6). Speaking in this court is presented as a series of dubious transactions which connote unbridled desire and prostitution, at odds with the moral value of eloquence which Skelton argues for in the *Speculum principis*, and which he certainly read about—and amplified—in Diodorus Siculus.[48]

The *Mum*-narrator, if he is to tell the truth, must learn to leap out of trouble;[49] Pasquil stands resolutely in the marketplace; but we are never told whether Drede actually leaps from the ship, or indeed whether he wakes up outside court:

> And as they came, the shypborde faste I hente,
> And thoughte to lepe; and even with that woke,
> Caughte penne and ynke, and wroth this lytell boke. (530–2)

Nor does he make any attempt to claim a particular moral speaking position by supplying an ethical interpretation of the events he has narrated. Instead the poem is open-ended:[50]

> I wolde therwith no man were myscontente;
> Besechynge you that shall it see or rede,
> In every poynte to be indyfferente,
> Syth all in substaunce of slumbrynge doth procede.
> I wyll not saye it is mater in dede,

---

[48] Skelton's translation of Poggio's version of *Diodorus Siculus* 'is yet another example of the revival of interest in antiquity inspired by fifteenth century humanism' (*OBLMVP*, p. 382), and one of Skelton's expansions praises the wise and fecund eloquence of King Celum which converted his people from wild conversation and bestial living to quiet, honest, and productive living (*The Bibliotheca Historica of Diodorus Siculus, translated by John Skelton*, ed. F. M. Salter and H. L. R. Edwards, 2 vols., EETS OS 233, 239 (1956, 1957), i. 295–7). Albertanus of Brescia concludes the second section of his treatise with a list of linguistic vices that his son should avoid if his speech is to be efficacious and honest. This includes malicious, obscure, crooked, slanderous, and sophistical speech (p. cv); a list which well characterizes the speech acts on board the 'Bowge of Court'.

[49] See his leaps away from the fraudulent language of the friars (533) and Mum's warning that he must leap from the clutches of the clergy (698).

[50] Fish observes that the interpretation and value of Drede's dream remain problematical because it offers neither the reader nor Drede anything authoritative (*John Skelton's Poetry*, 74); *Bowge* is a poem ultimately about the absence of advice and ultimately of faith (ibid. 79).

But yet oftyme suche dremes be founde trewe.
Now constrewe ye what is the resydewe. (533–9)

The responsibility for interpretation is transferred to the reader, but Drede is unwilling even to guarantee that there is anything to be interpreted.[51] There may be 'resydewe' for the reader to tease out but also to be teased by; for these lines are reminiscent of a moment earlier in the poem which stages the possibility of allegorical interpretation seemingly only to cancel it when Dame Saunce-Pere is described as sitting

behynde a traves of sylke fyne,
Of golde of tessew the fynest that myghte be. (57–8)

There is a long literary tradition which uses the image of the veil as a symbol of allegory:[52] the veil must be lifted in order to discern the matter of the writing. Here, however, the focus on the costly veil itself perhaps suggests that there is nothing behind it; but this very possibility is simultaneously figurative, suggesting the absence of stable moral instruction and sound language practices at court. This is why Spearing's observation that the allegory in *Bowge* conceals meaning is only half right.[53] To be sure, in the absence of referentiality and resolution, the poem deconstructs the encyclopaedic instruction of popular allegorical pieces such as the *Court of Sapience* or Hawes's later *Pastime of Pleasure*.[54] But *Bowge*'s irresolutions and indeterminacies are themselves allegorically significant. In the

[51] Fish argues that the horror of court intrigue is reflected in the narrator's inability to satirize that horror (ibid. 61).
[52] The literary history of the image of the veil is discussed in A. J. Minnis and A. B. Scott (eds.), *Medieval Literary Theory and Criticism c.1100–c.1375: The Commentary Tradition* (Oxford, 1988), 118–19. Boccaccio's celebrated discussion of the veiled truth to be found in the fiction of poetry is excerpted pp. 426–7.
[53] Spearing queries whether there is real meaning to be concealed or whether the peerless lady allegedly hidden behind the Boccaccian veil whom no one ever actually sees exists only as a projection of each of the merchants' desires (*Medieval to Renaissance*, 264–5).
[54] Fish notes how the dreamer's uneasiness in *The Court of Sapience* is immediately dispelled on meeting the personification Sapience (*John Skelton's Poetry*, 62). Sapience's court, with its fostering of 'connyng, knowlege, wyt, and al wysedome' (1492–3) is the antithesis of the 'bowge of court' and its seven deadly courtiers (*The Court of Sapience* ed. E. Ruth Harvey (Toronto, 1984)). The second book of *Sapience* is an encyclopaedia of moral instruction which Stephen Hawes imitated in his *Pastime of Pleasure*, ed. W. E. Mead, EETS OS 173 (1928).

poem's refusal to endorse discrete discursive positions we can see a deconstruction of the linguistic premisses on which other texts on counsel depend. Although truthtelling in *Mum* and *Pasquil* is revealed to be necessarily rhetorical, truthtelling discourse is nevertheless invested with claims of efficacy. *Bowge*, however, articulates its awareness of the rhetorical status of truthtelling from a much more pessimistic perspective. Its staging of the topoi associated with language and counsel demonstrates how speaking at court is always already strategic, and resistant to ethical classification.

Bowge's refusal of discursive stability resembles no text so much as Puttenham's 1589 *The Arte of English Poesie*, in which, to provide an example of metaphor where one speaks 'in sence transative and wrested from the owne signification', Puttenham significantly turns to the image of the ship of state. The courtly figure of 'allegoria' is described, in terms suggestively reminiscent of *Bowge*, as a 'figure of duplicitie, false semblant or dissimulation'. To speak one thing and think another—'when words and meanings meet not'—is claimed by Puttenham to be the mode of discourse 'not onely of every common Courtier, but also the gravest Counsellour'.[55]

[55] G. Puttenham, *The Arte of English Poesie*, ed. G. D. Willcock and A. Walker (Cambridge, 1936), 158.

13 Justification by Faith: Skelton's Replycacion

VINCENT GILLESPIE

Shortly after the deaths in 1509 of his patrons Margaret Beaufort and Henry VII, two Latin eulogies to them by John Skelton were erected in the Lady Chapel of Westminster Abbey. They were displayed in tabular format, either painted on wood, carved into stone, or engraved in brass, near to the tombs of their subjects, as was the fashion with this kind of funerary poetry. In the early 1520s, two further laments by Skelton were also displayed in the royal chapel. With the Latin verses added to the fabric of Henry's tomb, these poems represented a concrete manifestation of Skelton's much-vaunted but often unstable status as an *Orator Regius* to his former pupil, now King Henry VIII.[1]

On his way back from admiring his poetic handiwork in the Lady Chapel, Skelton's eye might have been caught by another text-table, 'hongyng on a pylere' near the entrance to St Benedict's Chapel. Like Skelton's poems, this table also contained an 'epitaphye maad by a poete laureat'. But the recipient was neither royal nor noble, though he may have been as important to Skelton's poetic self-perception as the patrons whose tombs he had left behind in the royal chapel. For the epitaph was Chaucer's, and its author the Italian humanist poet laureate, teacher of eloquence, and priest Stephen Surigo.

Surigo comes to praise Chaucer—'hic vates'—as well as bury him:

---

[1] David R. Carlson, *The Latin Writings of John Skelton*, SP, Texts and Studies, 88/4 (1991), items XVI (datable 1512); XX (datable 1516); XXIII (datable *c.*1522); XXIV (dateable *c.*1522); Appendix 4, pp. 115–21.

> Heu quantum fuerat prisca britanna rudis
> Reddidit insignem maternis versibus . vt iam
> Aurea splendescat . ferrea facta prius.[2]

Unlike most epitaphs, Surigo's allows its object to have the last word, putting into Chaucer's mouth, 'as spoken on his own behalf', the description of him as a 'vates: et fama poesis / Materne' ('poet-seer, and glory of my native poetry').

The epitaph was probably already familiar to Skelton: Caxton had printed it as long ago as 1478 in the prologue to his edition of Chaucer's *Boece*, while in the c.1484 edition of *The Canterbury Tales*, Caxton had eulogized Chaucer in neo-humanist terms, 'the whiche for his ornate writyng in our tongue may wel have the name of a laureate poete'.[3]

Skelton was perhaps keener on burying Chaucer than on praising him. But the status and fame accorded to his predecessor played its part in Skelton's estimation of his own status and the fame he deserved. After all, as he reminds us in *The Garland*, strictly speaking, Chaucer 'wantid... the laurell' (397), which Skelton had achieved. In 1490, perhaps near the peak of his reputation for learning, Skelton's own humanist eloquence and literary skill had in turn been praised by Caxton in the preface to his 1490 *Eneydos*, where he is described as 'late created poete laureate in the Unyversite of Oxenforde'.[4] And there is some evidence that Skelton saw himself in Chaucerian terms as a founder of English eloquence. Indeed, Skelton attempts an effect similar to Surigo's Chaucer epitaph when, in

---

[2] Throughout this article, Latin verse will be quoted in the original in the body of the text, with translations in the notes. Latin prose will normally be cited in translation, with reference in the notes to the Latin edition. The epitaph is printed and translated in full in Derek Brewer (ed.), *Chaucer: The Critical Heritage*, 2 vols. (London, 1978), i. 77–80: 'By the verses [that he composed] in his mother tongue he made it [as] illustrious as, alas, it had once been uncouth so that now it takes on a golden splendour where formerly it was iron' (pp. 78–9). Surigo was active in England for most of the third quarter of the fifteenth century, including spells teaching in Oxford. Derek Pearsall, 'Chaucer's Tomb: The Politics of Reburial', *MÆ*, 64 (1995), 51–73, esp. 51–9; Seth Lerer, *Chaucer and his Readers: Imagining the Author in Late Medieval England* (Princeton, 1993), 147–75.

[3] N. F. Blake, *Caxton's Own Prose*, The Language Library (London, 1973), 58–60 (Boethius), 61 (Canterbury Tales).

[4] Ibid. 80–1; Lerer, *Chaucer*, 172–4.

The Garland, he comments in Latin on his own poetic prowess as the 'British Catullus... Adonis... Homer':

> Barbara cum Latio pariter jam currite versu;
> Et licet est verbo pars maxima texta Britanno,
> Non magis incompta nostra Thalya patet,
> Est magis inculta nec mea Caliope.   (1525-8)[5]

But however superior to (or challenged by) his predecessor Skelton may have felt, Surigo's description of Chaucer as a *vates*, the noblest of poetic titles, would undoubtedly have struck a chord with his own sense of the dignity of his calling. As laureate poets, priests, and teachers of eloquence, Surigo and Skelton shared a common humanist view of the name and nature of poetry. As *vates* and glory of his country's letters, Chaucer's epitaph traced out a poetic trajectory that Skelton passionately wished to emulate.

The last decade of Skelton's life saw him address and articulate with increasing explicitness his complex and idiosyncratic conception of the role of the poet in society. *The Garland of Laurel*, though based on much earlier writings, was substantially revised and expanded prior to its publication in 1523, and explores his poetic identity in relation to the secular writers of pagan antiquity and of the recent humanist past.[6] This facet of his poetic self-knowledge is founded on and much influenced by the new humanist school curricula that had begun to emerge in England and throughout Europe in the last

---

[5] 'Though barbarous, you now compete in an equal race with Latin verse. And though for the most part it is made up of British words our Thalia is not too rude, nor is my Calliope too uncultured' (*John Skelton: The Complete English Poems*, ed. John Scattergood (Harmondsworth, 1983), 355; Scattergood's translation, p. 512). All citations of Skelton's poetry will be from this edition unless otherwise indicated. On Skelton's poetic relationship to Chaucer, see Lerer, *Chaucer*, 170-5, 193-208; Andrew Hadfield, *Literature, Politics and National Identity: Reformation to Renaissance* (Cambridge, 1994), 23-50; David Lawton, *Chaucer's Narrators*, Chaucer Studies, 13 (Cambridge, 1985), 136, 142; Lois Ebin, *Illuminator, Makar, Vates: Visions of Poetry in the Fifteenth Century* (Lincoln, Nebr., 1988), 163-91.

[6] On the date of *The Garland*, see *John Skelton: The Book of the Laurel*, ed. F. W. Brownlow (London, 1990), 30-6; Greg Walker, *John Skelton and the Politics of the 1520s*, Cambridge Studies in Early Modern British History (Cambridge, 1988), 5-34; Vincent Gillespie, 'Justification by Good Works: Skelton's *The Garland of Laurel*', *Reading Medieval Studies*, 7 (1981), 19-31.

years of the fifteenth century. These were the years of Skelton's own academic and intellectual formation, when he had enjoyed a modest but real reputation as 'the light and glory of British letters' and had served as part of an intellectually distinguished and artistically gifted team of tutors to the royal princes.[7]

His reassertion in the 1523 *Garland* of this by now perhaps rather dated tradition of scholarship and poetic idealism may have had something to do with the eclipse of his academic and poetic reputation over the preceding years. His somewhat equivocal status as a traditionalist concerning the teaching of Latin grammar, for example, emerges not only in his own poetic attacks on inadequate grammatical preparation in academic training but also in his association with the traditional preceptive school of thought in the Grammarians' War in 1520. His apparent support for that approach as opposed to the increasingly fashionable emphasis on imitation as a way of learning Latin led to the notorious gibe from one of his opponents that Skelton's claims for his academic and poetic status were ill-founded: 'Doctrinam nec habes, nec es poeta.'[8]

The Garland of Laurel and the other poems of the early 1520s thus defiantly restate a pedagogic and poetic position that perhaps owes more to the 1490s than to their own time. They are Skelton's self-justification by good work, relating his own claim to laureate fame to the Latin tradition of poetry in the service of the state. But the most passionate and emphatic defence of his poetic calling and of his academic and intellectual philosophy comes surprisingly and unexpectedly in perhaps his last English poem, the *Replication*. This poem, probably published in 1528, was ostensibly written to correct and rebuke

---

[7] David R. Carlson, 'Royal Tutors in the Reign of Henry VII', *Sixteenth Century Journal*, 22 (1991), 253–79, esp. 264–70. Erasmus refers to Skelton as a *vates* in this famous letter, praising him to Henry as 'a bard of your own...who can not only inspire but perfect your studies' (ibid. 265). For a text of Erasmus's comments, and for his *Carmen extemporale* in praise of Skelton, where he calls him 'aeterna vates', see A. S. G. Edwards (ed.), *Skelton: The Critical Heritage* (London, 1981), 44.

[8] For Lily's epigram, see Edwards (ed.), *Critical Heritage*, 48. David R. Carlson, 'The "Grammarians' War" 1519–21, Humanist Careerism in Early Tudor England, and Printing', *Medievalia et Humanistica*, NS 18 (1992), 157–81, and id., *English Humanist Books: Writers and Patrons, Manuscript and Print, 1475–1525* (Toronto, 1993), 103–22.

Justification by Faith 277

the errors of two young Cambridge scholars, who had recently abjured their heretical preaching. It may have been the verse arm of a co-ordinated campaign on the part of the ecclesiastical establishment to address the rise of heterodox thought in the two universities, which also involved a more extensive and measured prose confutation by Thomas More and a purge of suspect colleges.[9]

Although much concerned initially with the theological errors attributed to the young preachers, and anxious to defend and apologize to the University of Cambridge as his and their common *alma mater*, Skelton's onslaught against them has two peculiar features that make the poem more than a commissioned smear. In the first place, the poem goes out of its way to pour scorn on the inadequacy of their learning and the deficiencies of their command of scholastic method. Secondly, and in response to real or imagined criticism of his own role and status as a judge of their behaviour, the poem concludes with the most explicit and heartfelt of all Skelton's justifications for his own poetic vocation. The two are inextricably linked in Skelton's mind because of his strong identification with the intellectual, moral, and poetic characteristics of early Humanism.

Thomas Arthur and Thomas Bilney were tried in 1527. They were accused of a range of offences, most of which were more Lollard than Lutheran in flavour. In particular, they were accused of preaching against image worship and pilgrimage, of arguing in favour of the translation of Scripture into the vernacular (Tyndale's English New Testament had appeared in 1526), and of criticizing the use of pardons. At the root of the

---

[9] J. F. Davis, 'The Trials of Thomas Bilney and the English Reformation', *Historical Journal*, 24 (1981), 775–90; John Scattergood, 'Skelton and Heresy', in D. Williams (ed.), *Early Tudor England: Proceedings of the 1987 Harlaxton Conference* (Woodbridge, 1989), 157–70; Greg Walker, 'Saint or Schemer: The 1527 Heresy Trial of Thomas Bilney Reconsidered', *Journal of Ecclesiastical History*, 40 (1989), 219–38, and 'John Skelton, Thomas More, and the "Lost" History of the Early Reformation in England', *Parergon*, 9 (1991), 75–85; Peter Gwyn, *The King's Cardinal: The Rise and Fall of Thomas Wolsey* (London, 1990), 493–500. The proceedings of the trial and many documents relating to Bilney's later recusancy and execution are collected in *The Acts and Monuments of John Foxe*, ed. J. Pratt, 4th edn. (London, 1877).

trial, however, was their abuse of the pulpit to raise matters more properly confined to the privileged arena of the university and to the properly trained audience of a clerical academic élite. As the depositions made by laymen to the tribunal exemplify, there was ample opportunity for a lay audience to over-simplify or misrepresent the academic sophistications and scriptural ambiguities deployed by the men in their preaching.[10]

Although he criticizes their doctrinal errors, particularly concerning the veneration due to Mary and the saints, there is little sign that Skelton had first-hand evidence of the charges against Bilney and Arthur, and no sign that he had access to the documentation of the trial. His scepticism about the integrity of their recantation proved, of course, to be well founded, but doubt concerning the genuineness of their penitence was a matter of common gossip at the time. The poem invokes their failings with the broadest of brushes, only engaging in any detail with the Marian controversy (which itself is of little significance in the surviving accounts of the trial proper). Instead Skelton chooses to generalize and broaden the attack on them. It is the *effect* of their preaching as well as its content that exercises Skelton in his condemnation of their activities: they are 'rechelesse', hasty and careless (prologue):

> For all that they preche and teche
> Is farther than their wytte wyll reche. (12–13)

Puffed up by academic vanity, they have allowed themselves to be misled by the apparent logic of their reasoning on these matters, and by the subjective and cavalier exegetical play of their scriptural expositions:

> Of the gospell and the pystels
> Ye pyke out many thystels,
> And bremely with your bristels
> Ye cobble and clout
> Holy scripture so about,
> That people are in great dout

---

[10] *Acts and Monuments*, iv. 619–56 and the documents in the Appendix to vol. iv. Davis, 'The Trials of Thomas Bilney', 777; Walker, 'John Skelton, Thomas More', 76–7.

> And feare leest they be out
> Of all good Christen order.
> Thus all thyng ye disorder
> Thorowe out every border. (219–28)

Thus an important part of Skelton's case against them, and one which is only implicit in the official process, is the disordering effect of their teaching on the body politic and on the body of Christ, which is the Church. This is consistent with the attitude he articulates in many of his earlier polemics against the corruption of the Church, such as *Collyn Clout*.[11] The priest has the responsibility of the *cura animarum*, and deserves to pay heavily for it if he neglects or abuses his role as teacher and leader. The bishop has an overriding responsibility to correct error by public preaching:

> Ye bysshoppes of estates
> Shulde open the brode gates
> For your spirytuall charge,
> And com forthe at large,
> Lyke lanternes of lyght,
> In the peoples syght,
> In pulpyttes autentyke,
> For the wele publyke
> Of preesthode in this case. (*Collyn Clout*, 690–8)

It is precisely this episcopal responsibility that had been found wanting in many of Skelton's attacks on Wolsey (who, perhaps significantly, was ordained in the same year as Skelton himself took orders), and that he at last saw, perhaps at first hand, beginning to be exercised by the bishops in their action against heresy in 1527 and in the anti-Lollard *magna abjurata* of 1528.[12]

---

[11] The major studies are William Nelson, *John Skelton, Laureate* (New York, 1939); I. A. Gordon, *John Skelton: Poet Laureate* (Melbourne, 1943); H. L. R. Edwards, *Skelton: The Life and Times of a Tudor Laureate* (London, 1949); Maurice Pollet, *John Skelton, Poet of Tudor England*, trans. John Warrington (London, 1971); Stanley E. Fish, *John Skelton's Poetry*, Yale Studies in English, 157 (New Haven, 1965); A. F. Kinney, *John Skelton: Priest as Poet* (Chapel Hill, NC, 1987), 134–87; Alistair Fox, *Politics and Literature in the Reigns of Henry VII and Henry VIII* (Oxford, 1989).

[12] Scattergood, 'Skelton and Heresy', 157, suggests that Skelton was a witness at the 1528 heresy trial of Thomas Bowgas, who, like Bilney and Arthur, was tried before Cuthbert Tunstall, Bishop of London.

Thus, although the *Replication* pays lip service to the charge-sheet faced by Bilney and Arthur, the poem also, and perhaps more emphatically, arraigns the errant priest-academics on a new set of charges generated from an agenda of concerns that Skelton had been addressing for much of his writing career. At the root of these offences, Skelton argues, is a system of academic training that inadequately prepares its students for the difficulties and rigours of scriptural exegesis and fails to imbue in them the necessary modesty and humility in the face of tradition and authority. The initial characterization of the young scholars in the *Replication* stresses the partial formation they have received in scholastic method and in the liberal arts:

> A lytell ragge of rethorike,
> A lesse lumpe of logyke,
> A pece or patche of philosophy,
> Than forthwith by and by
> They tumble so in theology,
> Drowned in dregges of divinite,
> That they juge them selfe able to be
> Doctours of the chayre in the Vyntre
> At the Thre Cranes. (1–9)

This reprises a passage in *Collyn Clout* (composed 1521–2) where drunkenness leads to poor scholarship, imperfect interpretation of Scripture, and error in preaching:

> He can nothynge smatter
> Of logyke nor scole matter,
> Neyther *sylogysare*,
> Nor of *enthymemare*;
> Nor knoweth not his *elenkes*,
> Nor his predicamentes;
> And yet he wyll melle
> To amende the gospell,
> And wyll preche and tell
> What they do in hell. (814–23)[13]

Indeed, the 'smear scholastic' is a frequently deployed weapon in Skelton's battle against clerical corruption. As early as *Ware*

---

[13] Line 818 is echoed by *Replication*, 126 (ed. Scattergood, p. 377).

the Hauke (? before 1505), the errant hunting priest (a popular type in medieval anti-clerical satire) is berated for his academic pretensions:

> Maister *sophista*,
> Ye *simplex silogista*,
> Ye develysh dogmatista... (253-5)

while in *Why Come Ye Nat to Courte?* (c.1522), Wolsey himself is lampooned for his modest academic achievements:

> For he was, parde,
> No doctor of devinyte,
> Nor doctor of the law,
> Nor of none other saw;
> But a poore maister of arte!
> God wot, had lytell parte
> Of the quatrivials,
> Or yet of trivials;
> Nor of philosophy,
> Nor of philology,
> Nor of good pollycy,
> Nor of astronomy...
> . . . . .
> His Latyne tonge dothe hobbyll,
> He doth but cloute and cobbill
> In Tullis faculte
> Called humanyte. (508-19; 526-9)[14]

Nor is this simple hostility to the new learning. Skelton is no intellectual Luddite. His ambivalent attitude to the old and new learning is encapsulated in *The Garland*:

> Mens tibi sit consulta, petis? Sic consule menti;
> Emula sit Jani, retro speculetur et ante. (1519-20)[15]

Like many of his English contemporaries, he would have been closer to Reuchlin (whose *Vocabularius* he knew and used) than to the Cologne Dominicans in the great humanist battle

---
[14] Line 527 is echoed by *Replication*, 222 (ed. Scattergood, p. 380).
[15] 'Do you wish your mind to be skilful? In that case, pay attention to your mind; let it be like that of Janus which looks back and forward' (trans. Scattergood, p. 512).

of the books.[16] Indeed, Reuchlin's English supporters included More and Tunstall, active with him in the campaign against heresy. The simplistic distinction in the *Epistolae obscurorum virorum* (published 1516) between the 'modern' Poets and the archaic and barbarous Theologians would never have held good in England. Skelton has the humanist interests of the Poets and the scholastic discipline of the Dominicans in equal measure: he takes pleasure in the syllogism and the cento alike.

In the *Replication*, the 'friscajoly yonkerkyns' are upbraided for their ignorance of the theology of worship as developed by patristic authorities such as Gregory, Ambrose, Jerome, and *moderni* such as Thomas Aquinas, and are criticized in scholastic Latin for their errors in logic and in scholastic method: 'Ye are but lydder *logici* / But moche worse *isagogici*' (234–5). In *Speke Parott* (1519), in a passage that appears to allude to the Grammarians' War, Parott praises 'aurea lyngua Greca' as worthy to be magnified, while criticizing the slapdash and inadequate training offered in the language, suggesting that curricular reforms have led to insufficient rigour in grammar and in scholarly philosophical method. Once again, the result is detrimental to the common good, causing erroneous interpretations of Scripture and confusion:

> For ye scrape out good scrypture, and set in a gall:
> Ye go about to amende, and ye mare all.   (*Speke Parott*, 153–4)

These passages offer glimpses of Skelton's multi-faceted academic and clerical identity: Skelton the Trojan, Skelton the preceptive grammarian, Skelton the Latin humanist, and Skelton the upholder of an ideal of clerical learning and behaviour. But they are also an important part of the process by which Skelton is able to define and articulate his own poetic identity. The elect, whether academics, priests, or poets, have special responsibilities which they ignore at the peril of their soul. Skelton, as academic, priest, and poet, has no intention of making that mistake. That he had aspirations to be regarded as a learned poet—a kind of *poeta theologus*, to borrow the early humanist

---

[16] On which, see Gordon, *John Skelton*, pp. 82–91; *Epistolae Obscurorum Virorum*, ed. and trans. Francis Griffin Stokes (London, 1909); and p. 295 below.

Justification by Faith 283

term—is implicit in Robert Whittinton's epigram on him, where he is described as a 'culte poeta', and equally implicit in William Lily's riposte that he had failed to achieve those aspirations:

> Doctrinae tibi dum parare famam
> Et doctus fieri studes poeta,
> Doctrinam nec habes, nec es poeta.[17]

Skelton's self-proclaimed role as a *vox clamantis* in the wilderness of Wolsey's England is sustained by a powerful and highly idiosyncratic synthesis of intellectual, scriptural, spiritual, and literary influences, held together by an equally eclectic but powerful belief in himself as a member of an elect and learned poetic fraternity moved by the inspiration of the Holy Spirit and illuminated by a long tradition of classical and Christian poetry. As we shall see later, Skelton's repeated description of himself as *vates* explicitly invokes the early humanist discussions of the name and nature of poetry and the poet, and his much-advertised status as a laureate of both Universities (and perhaps of Louvain) similarly harks back self-consciously to the world of Mussato and Petrarch.[18] For, while his laureation may have been a poor imitation of that awarded to Petrarch and his classical predecessors, for Skelton it served as an outward and visible sign of the inward invisible grace that he felt impelled him to take on the role of Juvenalian scourge of hypocrisy, shoddy scholarship, and failed idealism:

> Quia difficile est satiram non scribere.[19]

---

[17] Edwards (ed.), *Critical Heritage*, 49 (Whittinton) and 48 (Lily), translated in Fuller's *Worthies* (1662) as 'While thou to get the more esteem / A learned poet fain would seem, / Skelton, thou art, let all men know it, / Neither learned, nor a poet.' They were opponents in the Grammarians' War and Whittinton had claimed the support of Skelton. He was the author of a Latin poem on the laurel that may be related to *The Garland of Laurel*; David R. Carlson, 'Skelton's *Garland of Laurel* and Robert Whittinton's "Lauri apud Palladem Expostulatio"', *RES*, 42 (1991), 417–24.

[18] On Skelton's laureation, see Edwards, *Skelton*, 287–8; Carlson, 'Royal Tutors', 269. On laureation in early humanist circles, see J. B. Trapp, 'The Owl's Ivy and the Poet's Bays: An Enquiry into Poetic Garlands', *Journal of the Warburg and Courtauld Institutes*, 21 (1958), 227–55; id., 'The Poet Laureate: Rome, Renovatio and Translatio Imperii', in P. A. Ramsey (ed.), *Rome in the Renaissance: The City and the Myth*, Medieval and Renaissance Texts and Studies, 18 (New York, 1982), 93–130.

[19] *Why Come Ye Nat to Courte?*, 1216–17 ('Because it is difficult not to write satire'), citing Juvenal, *Satire*, 1. 30. Skelton also quotes this line in his *Speculum Principis*, ed. Carlson, *Latin Writings*, VIII. 95 (p. 36).

The ritual denigration of his opponents' academic credentials is more than a routine flyting manœuvre (though it is found in his flytings as well). In his clerical satires, and in particular in the *Replication*, Skelton's criticisms of the academic and intellectual failings of his fellow members of the clerical élite are often figured as part of a contrast between his own inspired and authorized role as a kenotic mouthpiece of 'elect utterance' and the solipsistic and self-regarding vainglory of those he is criticizing. The contrast might be articulated in Pauline terms: *Scientia inflat; caritas autem edificat* (1 Cor. 8: 1).

Failure through heresy or academic error disqualifies from membership of the elect and, implicitly, from the right to judge the utterances of the elect. Thus, at the end of *Collyn Clout* the Latin Epilogue allows Colin to define the elect as those who agree with him, already using the language of poetic inspiration:

> Colinus Cloutus, 'Quanquam mea carmina multis
> Sordescunt stulte, sed pneumata sunt rara cultis,
> Pneumatis altisoni divino flamine flatis.'[20]

In the first part of the *Replication*, the young scholars are repeatedly described as 'puffed up' with the wind of secular learning, in an explicit parody of Pentecostal enlightenment:

enbolned with the flyblowen blast of the moche vayne glorious pipplyng wynde, whan they have delectably lycked a lytell of the lycorous electuary of lusty lernyng, in the moche studious scolehous of scrupulous philology, countyng them selfe clerkes exellently enformed and transcendingly sped in moche high connyng.[21]

The rash and hasty utterances of these 'demy divines' are 'enbrased and enterlased with a moche fantasticall frenesy of their insensate sensualyte' with the result that they are 'puffed so full of vaynglorious pompe and surcudant elacyon, that popholy and pevysshe presumpcion provoked them to publysshe

---

[20] 'Although to the multitude my songs are foolishly contemptible, yet they are rare inspirations to the cultivated who are inspired by the divine breath of the sublime spirit' (trans. Scattergood, p. 481).

[21] Ed. Scattergood, pp. 373–4. On the 'flyblown' image, see V. I. Scherb, 'Conception, Flies and Heresy in Skelton's "Replycacion"', *MÆ*, 62 (1993), 51–60.

Justification by Faith 285

and to preche to people imprudent perilously'. This view is succinctly summed up later in the poem:

> Your madde ipocrisy,
> And your idiosy,
> And your vayne glorie
> Have made you eate the flye,
> Pufte full of heresy.   (249-53)

It would have been better, the poem argues, for the scholars to have followed the example of Harpocrates, the god of silence, whose admonishing statue stood at the entrance to the temple of Isis:[22]

> Whan ye logyke chopped,
> And in the pulpete hopped,
> And folysshly there fopped,
> And porisshly forthe popped
> Your sysmaticate sawes
> Agaynst Goddes lawes,
> And shewed your selfe dawes.   (118-24)

Instead of the wind and flame of Pentecostal enlightenment, and openness to the loss of self that is implied in the apostolic calling, they have fanned the flames of their own egotism to light a fire of heresy, 'and baththed in their wylde burblyng and boyling blode, fervently reboyled with the infatuate flames of their rechelesse youthe and wytlesse wontonnese'. Not only have they revealed themselves to be foolish instead of wise, but they have also misjudged the material appropriate for a lay audience. In other words, they are guilty of a double betrayal of the élite. And, in that betrayal, they have cast themselves into the outer darkness where they can no longer exercise the 'opus evangelii' which is food for the elect:

> Opus evangelii est cibus perfectorum;
> Sed quia non estis de genere bonorum,
> Qui catechisatis categorias cacedemoniarum,
>   Ergo

---

[22] On this passage, see Walker, 'John Skelton, Thomas More', 80-1.

> Et reliqua vestra problemata, schemata,
> Dilemata, sinto anathemata![23]   (p. 382)

It is, as Skelton claims, an 'ineluctabile argumentum'. But it functions not only as a criticism of heresy, but as a pre-emptive disabling manœuvre against any disagreement with Skelton's own argument, or his right to articulate it.

The utterance of the young scholars, 'puffed full of heresy', contrasts strikingly with Skelton's claims for his own discourse outlined in the second part of the poem:

> Hinc omne est rarum carum: reor ergo poetas
> Ante alios omnes divine flamine flatos.[24]   (p. 386)

Poets are inhabited by God:

> By whose inflammacion
> Of spyrituall instygacion
> And divyne inspyracion
> We are kyndled in suche facyon
> With hete of the Holy Gost.   (379–83)

The divine *afflatus* descends on the chosen poets with flame and wind: poets are true apostles. Therefore Skelton's defence of poetry's right to discuss such high matters as theology and heresy is already what he calls 'a confutacion responsyve, or an inevytably prepensed answere'. It is inevitable and premeditated because it proceeds from and is a function of his long-nurtured belief in his elect status. *Hec vates ille de quo loquntur mille (Why Come Ye Nat to Courte?, 29–30).*

But whereas the arabesques of self-advertisement in his earlier poems invoke secular traditions of poetic selection and inspiration, the *Replication* develops into a full-blown exercise in Theological Poetics which is as manically eclectic as it is culturally wide-ranging. The second half of the poem finds

---

[23] 'The gospels are food for the elect; but, because you are not of the race of the good, you who give instruction in the categories of evil spirits, therefore also the rest of your problems, schemes and dilemmas shall be anathema' (trans. Scattergood, p. 519).

[24] 'Thus, everything that is rare is precious. Therefore, I think that poets, before all others, are filled with divine inspiration' (trans. Scattergood, p. 520).

Justification by Faith 287

Skelton busily shoring fragments of poetic mythology against his own poetic ruin.

Skelton is defending himself against two main charges. The first invokes the ultimately Aristotelian assertion that Poetics, as the last and lowest book of the *Organon,* is least suitable for the treatment of high matters:

> Ye saye that poetry
> Maye nat flye so hye
> In theology,
> Nor analogy,
> Nor philology,
> Nor philosophy,
> To answere or reply
> Agaynst suche heresy. (306–13)

The second is the older, ultimately Platonic charge that poets are liars:

> Why have ye than disdayne
> At poetes, and complayne
> How poetes do but fayne? (351–3)

Skelton's first line of defence is the argument from authority. He invokes St Jerome, 'that doctour glorious', whose Epistle 53 (ad Paulinum presbyterum divinum) praises the poetry of David as comparable to that of the great classical lyric poets. Invoking the Epistle by name, he invites his opponent to 'rede what Jerome there dothe say', first citing it in its original and authoritative form: 'David, inquit, Simonides noster, Pindarus, et Alceus, Flaccus quoque, Catullus, atque Serenus, Christum lyra personat, et in decachordo psalterio ab inferis excitat resurgentem.'[25]

Skelton's brief citation of Jerome needs to be put into context if its role in the poem and in Skelton's poetics is to be fully understood. In 394 Jerome wrote to the newly ordained

---

[25] 'David, our Simonides, Pindarus and Alceus, Horace also, Catullus and Serenus, sang of Christ with his lyre and with the ten-stringed psaltery celebrated his awakening and his resurrection from the lower regions' (my translation). For the Latin text, see *Saint Jérôme: Lettres,* vol. iii, ed. J. Labourt (Paris, 1953), 8–25. References in the text are to page and line of this edition.

Paulinus, praising his zeal for biblical studies, but warning him of the dangers of false guides and partial understanding of the many mysteries in Scripture. In particular, Jerome admonishes his admirer against the assumption that a good classical education provides an adequate key to the rhetorical strategies of revealed Scripture. Jerome's strictures had received wide circulation in the medieval Latin West because this letter was often prefixed to the Vulgate Bible and to the Glossa Ordinaria, both in its manuscript circulation and in its early appearances in print. This was probably because the letter contained a succinct survey of all the books of the Old and New Testaments, with thumbnail judgements by Jerome of the special interpretative difficulties posed by each. His brief sketch of David, cited by Skelton, comes from his exposition of the prophetic books of the Old Testament.

Jerome's comments are both an exercise in cultural assimilation (David has the same status as a lyrical poet as the great figures of classical secular poetry) and an exercise in cultural difference (David is OUR Simonides, Pindar, and Catullus), stressing the common rhetorical heritage of the Latin Scriptures and Latin literature and, simultaneously, the very different objectives that the common rhetorical strategies are seeking to serve. Jerome is both a syncretist and an élitist, arguing for the superiority and absolute worth of revealed Scripture while recognizing that classical literary tropes provide a hermeneutic matrix through which the revealed truths may be approached. This sophisticated Hieronimic blend of literary continuity and absolute moral superiority parallels in many respects Skelton's own attitude to classical antiquity. He clearly knew the letter well: in *The Garland of Laurel* (162–8), he cites its account of Aeschinus's praise of the style of Demosthenes' attack on him. While he labours energetically in *The Garland* to create and invoke a tradition of poetry in the service of the state (along the way likening himself to Catullus, Adonis, and Homer, 1519–32), ultimately the invocation of such a tradition serves mainly to allow the insertion of his own poetic persona at the head of that tradition, as 'prothonotary' of Fame's court, rather as David is inserted at the head of the pantheon of Christian Latin poets.

But there is more to Jerome's Epistle than shows itself above the surface in Skelton's brief citation in the *Replication*. It is the letter's pedagogic ideas that make it such a pertinent authority to invoke at this point in the poem. Jerome praises Paulinus' eagerness for learning and his humility (attributes Skelton has found wanting in the two heretics): 'ingenium docibile et sine doctore laudabile est' (10. 25). Learning is important in a priest, because it is a priestly responsibility to respond with sound answers when asked about the law ('in tantum sacerdotis officium est interrogatum respondere de lege': 11. 23–5); David had characterized the just man as meditating on the law day and night (Ps. 1: 2). In the Acts of the Apostles 9: 15, Jerome continues, a distinction is drawn between the splendour of the 'docti' and the eternal glory of those who teach justice to the multitudes (12. 1–12).

Skelton had reproved the heretics for misleading the laity, had shown them to be misplaced 'docti', and, by implication, had often throughout his career characterized himself as teaching justice to the multitudes ('Si veritatem dico, quare non creditis michi?': *Agaynst the Scottes*, 39[26]). Jerome argues that the apostles Peter and John were not learned men, but were inspired by the Word of God to utter truths beyond the understanding of Plato and Demosthenes. True wisdom destroys false wisdom. Paul speaks of wisdom 'inter perfectos', but this is not the wisdom of this world but a wisdom 'in mysterio absconditus', a wisdom who is Christ, a wisdom predestined and prefigured in the law and Prophets (12. 32–13. 27).

Thus, Jerome argues, the interpretation of Scripture is perilous without a guide. But, he asserts, he does not mean the guidance provided by grammar, rhetoric, philosophy, and the other liberal arts. In a sarcastic tone remarkably similar to that adopted by Skelton in his attack on the heretics, Jerome flays the pride and arrogance of those who presume to expound Scripture without proper discipline and humility. The art of Scripture, he argues, is different from all others, but everyone

---

[26] 'If I speak the truth, why do you not believe me?' (trans. Scattergood, p. 424). On this theme, see Fish, *John Skelton's Poetry*, 13–26.

thinks they have something to say on the matter—learned and lewd, garrulous old women, rambling old men, the verbose, all seek to teach what they have failed to understand. Proud men play philosophy with Holy Scripture to admiring groups of young women. Others learn from women what they should teach to men. Gifted with a certain verbal facility, they explain to others what they have failed to understand themselves. If they come to study Sacred Scripture after secular literature, and can please the populace with their rhetorical skills, then they begin to develop highly idiosyncratic interpretations of Scripture without deigning to acquaint themselves with the teachings of the prophets and the apostles. They alter the meaning of the Scriptures and ignore the intention or will of the text (15. 11–16. 13). Rather than seek to play exegetical games with the text of Scripture, Paulinus is recommended to avoid these pitfalls and to live within the texts and meditate on them in humility (23. 13–19).

Much of this letter is pertinent to, and perhaps informs Skelton's criticisms of the young heretics, particularly as so many of Jerome's criticisms relate to interpretative and social practices that were routinely attributed to Lollards as well as Lutherans. A common feature of the depositions against Bilney and Arthur and Skelton's criticisms of them is their ability to pervert Scripture to support their arguments. Bilney had preached in favour of translating the Scriptures into English, and had admitted in a letter written to Tunstall during the trial that he had originally bought Erasmus's new Latin version of the New Testament out of admiration for the Ciceronian beauty of its language and had only then been inspired by the teachings therein.[27] Skelton's use of the epistle that traditionally prefaced Jerome's Vulgate can thus be seen as an implicit restatement of the authority of 'orthodox' Scripture. In tone and in detail, therefore, Jerome's attack on subjective interpretation of Scripture finds its echo in the case Skelton mounts against the heretics.

Jerome recommends to Paulinus a more modest and humble approach to the mysteries of Scripture, deploying the Socratic

---

[27] *Acts and Monuments*, iv. 624, item XVIII; 635.

dictum, 'hoc tantum scio quod nescio' ('This much I know: that I do not know', 22. 14). But he goes some way to characterizing his ideal scriptural commentator in his description of the evangelists, whom he describes as true *cherubim*, glossing the word as 'scientiae multitudo', an abundance of knowledge. Respecting the intractable mysteries revealed to them, they obeyed the directions of the Holy Spirit: 'pergunt, quocumque eos flatus sancti spiritus duxerit' ('they went on wherever the breath of the Holy Spirit led', 22. 22–3). Here again, Jerome's characterization of the ideal interpreter as one full of learning but humble and obedient to the stirrings of the divine *afflatus* in a true spirit of apostolic charity chimes effectively with Skelton's attempt to characterize his own poetic vocation in apostolic and ultimately prophetic terms:

> We are kyndled in suche facyon
> With hete of the Holy Gost
> . . . . .
> That he our penne doth lede,
> And maketh in us suche spede
> That forthwith we must nede
> With penne and ynke procede.   (382–3, 385–8)

Jerome's characterization of David, then, functions metonymically in the *Replication* as an invocation of the role of the Christian poet as the equal of and successor to the poets of classical antiquity. But the broader context of Jerome's letter provided Skelton with both an argumentative precedent in his attack on heresy and a catalyst to his thinking about the role and status of the poet. This becomes clear when his additions to and elaborations of Jerome's characterization of David are explored in more detail.

Skelton's translation and gloss of Jerome's words makes his Christian supremacist views explicit and goes much further than Jerome in claiming the superiority of Christian rhetoric:

> Flaccus nor Catullus with hym [David] may nat compare,
> Nor solempne Serenus, for all his armony
> In metricall muses, his harpyng we may spare.   (336–8)

His singing has the power to translate from one mystical plane to another: he harped so melodiously about Christ:

> That at his resurrection he harped out of hell
> Old patriarkes and prophetes in heven with him to dwell.
>
> (341–2)

This Christian Orpheus, therefore, is linked in Skelton's mind with the prophets of the Old Testament who, according to Jerome, were 'seers' and saw what others could not see.[28] This may account for Skelton's major elaboration of Jerome: his repeated description of David as 'poete of poetes all, / And prophete princypall', which on each occurrence he attributes explicitly to Jerome himself:

> Kyng David the prophete, of prophetes principall,
> Of poetes chefe poete, saint Jerome dothe wright,
> Resembled to Symonides, that poete lyricall
> Among the Grekes most relucent of lyght. (329–32)

David addressed 'suche theologicall thynges':

> With his harpe of prophecy
> And spyrituall poetry. (345–6)

Therefore, Skelton argues, the charges against him have no force. For this argument to work, of course, the link between David's poetry and his prophetic status has to be clearly established, and the further link between David's prophetic status and Skelton's must also be accepted.

In fact Jerome nowhere in this epistle explicitly describes David as principal prophet, although his discussion does occur in the context of his account of the prophetic force of the Old Testament. There is clearly more at work here than a close and motivated reading of Jerome's Epistle to Paulinus. For, even in his paraphrase of Jerome's words, Skelton broadens his own defence from the narrow patristic terms of Jerome's discussion (useful though that had proved to be in his invective) to the much broader debate on the nature of poetry that follows:

---

[28] 'Vnde et prophetae appelabantur uidentes, quia uidebant eum qui ceteri non uidebant' (13. 19–21).

> Ye do moche great outrage,
> For to disparage,
> And to discorage,
> The fame matryculate
> Of poetes laureate. (354–8)

Here, perhaps for the first time explicitly in all his writings, Skelton is able to conflate his laureate status with his perception of his role as the priest-prophet-poet. Skelton had highlighted in his rime-royal paraphrase of the Epistle that Jerome's likening of David to Simonides implied a link between the Greek tradition of inspiration and the Christian. Now he invokes a lost work of his own, *The Boke of Good Advertysement*, to develop (albeit vaguely) that Greek conception of poetry:

> Howe there is a spyrituall,
> And a mysteriall,
> And a mysticall
> Effecte energiall,
> As Grekes do it call,
> Of suche an industry
> And suche a pregnacy,
> Of hevenly inspyracion
> In laureate creacyon,
> Of poetes commendacion. (365–74)

It is likely that Skelton had in mind throughout this part of the poem some of the themes and vocabulary of the early humanist defences of poetry. Indeed, when those texts are compared with Skelton's *Replication* they offer both a plausible source for his highly condensed and allusive theory of Theological Poetics and, in many cases, a surprising structural analogue to the form, tone, and content of Skelton's poem.

What has come to be seen as the tradition of humanist defences of poetry is scarcely as organized and as systematic as it appears.[29] From the turn of the fourteenth century onwards,

[29] In this section I am greatly indebted to C. C. Greenfield, *Humanist and Scholastic Poetics, 1250–1500* (Lewisburg, 1981), which offers an indispensable overview of the field. See also Ernst Robert Curtius, *European Literature and the Latin Middle Ages*, trans. Willard R. Trask (London, 1953), esp. ch. 12 and Excursus VIII and XI; A. J.

Italian writers sought to define for themselves the nature and distinctive attributes of poetry as opposed to rhetoric and the other liberal and mechanic arts. Key topics that recurred in such discussions were the meaning of the name of poet; the rarity of poets; the nature of poetic discourse; the sustainability of the claim (based ultimately on a misunderstanding of Aristotle) that all poets, including the writers of classical antiquity, could be regarded as theologians; the defence of poetry against the ancient charge that all poets were liars; and the discussion of the utility of reading pagan authors. The need for a firm grounding in grammar (as the science which taught the core skills needed to expound poetry) is also frequently discussed.[30] Early commentary on Dante acted as a spur and catalyst to such discussions, and helped to refine and explore the possibility that a contemporary Christian poet could be considered as contributing to the work of revelation and could therefore be regarded as a *poeta theologus*.[31] But the writings of many poetic theorists were also sharpened on the whetstone of strong opposition to the claims that were made for poetry to be regarded as a supreme art, and as a divine rather than a human science.

A key text in the debate was Aristotle's *Metaphysics*, as commented on by Aquinas and other scholastic commentators, and as understood (or misunderstood) by early humanist readers.[32] Because of their role in the mythography of ancient gods, Aristotle had stated that poets were the first people to do theology, because they had been the first to memorialize and interpret the deeds of the gods. The syncretist argument that this established both a continuity between ancient and modern theology and a special role for poets in interpreting theological issues was widely deployed by the humanists, but was

Minnis and A. B. Scott (eds.), *Medieval Literary Theory and Criticism c.1100–c.1375: The Commentary Tradition* (Oxford, 1988).

[30] See Greenfield's 'Conclusion', *Humanist and Scholastic Poetics*, 308–16; D. Robey, 'Humanist Views on the Study of Poetry in the Early Italian Renaissance', *History of Education*, 13 (1984), 7–25.

[31] Cf. Minnis and Scott (eds.), *Medieval Literary Criticism*, 439–519.

[32] *Metaphysics*, bk. 1. Curtius, *European Literature*, 217–18; Greenfield, *Humanist and Scholastic Poetics*, 41–53, esp. 45–53; Minnis and Scott (eds.), *Medieval Literary Criticism*, 210–11; Ronald G. Witt, 'Coluccio Salutati and the Conception of the *Poeta Theologus* in the Fourteenth Century', *Renaissance Quarterly*, 30 (1977), 538–63.

Justification by Faith 295

unacceptable to many theologians, and especially to Thomists. Thus it emerged that the most vehement opponents of the humanist claim that poetry was a divine science and that poets were inspired by God tended to be scholastically trained Dominicans: Mussato was opposed by the Dominican Giovannino of Mantua; Salutati responded to attacks on poetry by the Dominican Domenici, and rebuffed a young Camuldensian monk who had attacked the Muses; Leonardi Bruni criticized the ignorant Aristotelianism of the theologians; Guarino opposed Giovanni da Prato. A lively debate between theologians and humanists took place in the mid-fifteenth century at the Veronese court of bishop Ermolao Barbaro, involving Antonio Becaria. Late in the fifteenth century, Fontius defends poetry and poets against the charges of 'certain ignorant theologians', arguing that 'the fact that certain semi-barbarians detest and damn them as though they were contrary to the Christian religion [should not] deter you from our common studies'.[33]

Such debates between the Poets and the Theologians became the stuff of parody in the early sixteenth century, when the Dominican faculty of theology at the University of Cologne attempted to have the writings of the humanist Reuchlin suppressed. The humanist response was the highly successful and influential *Epistolae obscurorum virorum* (1515 × 16), which ruthlessly lampooned the syllogistic and barbarously archaic attitudes of the Dominicans in a series of scathingly executed parodies of their views on poetry in particular and secular literature in general.[34]

Other defences of poetry emerged out of similar sites of contention (real or imagined). Petrarch's letters to his brother

---

[33] On Mussato (d. 1329), see Curtius, *European Literature*, 215–21; Witt, 'Coluccio Salutati', 540–2; Greenfield, *Humanist and Scholastic Poetics*, 87–90. On Salutati (d. 1406), see Witt; J. Reginald O'Donnell, 'Coluccio Salutati on the Poet-Teacher', *Medieval Studies*, 22 (1960), 240–56; Greenfield, 129–45 and (on Domenici) 146–63. On Bruni (d. 1444), see Greenfield, 178–94; p. 182. On Guarino (d. 1460), see Greenfield, 187–91. On Becaria (fl. c.1450) and the court of Barbaro, see Greenfield, 195–213. On Fontius (d. 1513), see Greenfield, 283–307; Charles Trinkaus, 'A Humanist's Image of Humanism: The Inaugural Orations of Bartollomeo della Fonte', *Studies in the Renaissance*, 7 (1960), 90–132 (the quotation is on p. 98), and 'The Unknown Quattrocento Poetics of Bartollomeo della Fonte', *Studies in the Renaissance*, 13 (1966), 40–122.

[34] See, for example, *Epistolae*, ed. Stokes, 1. 5, 1. 7, 1. 17, 1. 18, 1. 27, 1. 28, which mimic the rhetorical tropes and gestures of the humanist defences.

Gherardo, in demonstrating the versatility of poetic exegesis and claiming high status for the inspired poet, were not just an exercise in fraternal persuasion. For Gherardo was a Carthusian monk whom Petrarch expects 'will shudder at the poem enclosed with this letter as inharmonious with your profession and contrary to your goals'.[35] His most extended defence of his poetic calling comes, likewise, in the course of a spirited exchange with a medical doctor who has argued for the supremacy of his calling and the degeneracy of Petrarch's.[36] Boccaccio's manifesto for poetry in his *De genealogia deorum gentilium* similarly addresses the detractors of poetry, and in particular the jurists who have sought to denigrate its status and the Thomist theologians who have abandoned wisdom for 'trifling matters' of a largely technical kind.[37] Cristoforo Landino's poetic theory is articulated through a series of disputations conducted in 1468 at the invitation of the Abbot of the strict hermitage at Camoldoli.[38]

Many of these defences adopt a highly polemical and often abusive tone towards their opponents. Petrarch's *Invectivae*, as their name suggests, often address the doctor in robust tones:

Lege, miser, et relege locum illum aristotelicum ... unde male tornatum sillogismum elicis; neque hoc aut illud verbum excerpas nichil intelligens, ut videaris Aristotilem legisse, sed totum locum excute. Invenies —si tamen intelliges—hominem illum ardentis ingenii et complecti omnia cupientem ...

Petrarch at one point calls him a hoopoe bird ('upopa'), and his tone is often derisive and sarcastic.[39] Boccaccio describes

---

[35] Greenfield, *Humanist and Scholastic Poetics*, 95–109. Minnis and Scott (eds.), *Medieval Literary Criticism*, 413–15 (*Letters on Familiar Matters*, 10. 4); Francesco Petrarca, *Letters on Familiar Matters: Rerum familiarum libri, IX–XVI*, trans. Aldo S. Bernardo (Baltimore, 1982), 10. 3–5; pp. 57–82, esp. 69–70.

[36] Charles Trinkaus, '*Theologia Poetica* and *Theologia Rhetorica* in Petrarch's *Invectives*', in *The Poet as Philosopher: Petrarch and the Formation of Renaissance Consciousness* (New Haven, 1979), 90–113.

[37] Greenfield, *Humanist and Scholastic Poetics*, 110–28; for the *De genealogia*, see *Boccaccio on Poetry*, trans. C. G. Osgood (Princeton, 1930), 19; Minnis and Scott (eds.), *Medieval Literary Criticism*, 420–38 and their discussion on pp. 387–92.

[38] Mario A. Di Cesare, 'Cristoforo Landino on the Name and Nature of Poetry: The Critic as Hero', *Chaucer Review*, 21 (1986), 155–81; Greenfield, *Humanist and Scholastic Poetics*, 214–29.

[39] *Invective contra medicum*, liber tertius; Francesco Petrarca, *Prose*, ed. G. Martellotti et al. (Milan and Naples, n.d.), 648–93.

his opponents as 'madmen' in his Dante Commentary, and as 'ignorant triflers' in his *Genealogia*, calling on 'the babblers' to 'stop their nonsense and silence their pride if they can'.[40] Similarly, Salutati calls the Camuldensian monk an 'adulescens, puer, lacteolus' who reduces him to laughter because he does not know what he is talking about. His own educational formation is to blame if he is unable to understand the poets. Boccaccio similarly recommends that his opponents should go back to the grammar school if they find poetry obscure.[41]

When seen in the general context of these humanist defences, therefore, Skelton's *Replication*, with its attack on failed scholastic method linked to passionate defence of the sacral nature of poetry, looks less odd than it otherwise might. Skelton goes out of his way in his highly personal invective against them to characterize the heretics as clumsy scholastics who, through youthful haste and superficiality, stumble over the rudiments of their Aristotelian methodology:

> Ye argued argumentes,
> As it were upon the elenkes,
> *De rebus apparentibus*
> *Et non existentibus.*
> And ye wolde appere wyse
> But ye were folysshe nyse. (125–30)

Like the Dominicans of the *Epistolae obscurorum virorum* and the earlier humanist epistles, therefore, their argument that 'poetry / Maye nat flye so hye / In theology' (306–8) is disqualified by scholarly myopia and academic incompetence. Perhaps something of Skelton's own career as a grammar master and teacher of Prince Henry emerges here, reflecting the common humanist argument that learning, a grasp of the basic hermeneutical skills, and application to study and reading were necessary for a proper appreciation of poetry. (Skelton reflects

---

[40] *Tratatello in laude di Dante*, trans. David Wallace, in Minnis and Scott (eds.), *Medieval Literary Criticism*, 492–519; p. 498; *De genealogia*, 14. 10, Minnis and Scott, p. 428.
[41] O'Donnell, 'Coluccio Salutati', 243; *De genealogia*, 14. 3, trans. Osgood, p. 21. On the role of poetry in humanist theories of education, see Eugenio Garin, *Il Pensiero Pedagogico dell' Umanesimo* (Florence, 1958); Helen Wieruszowski, 'Rhetoric and Classics in Italian Education of the Thirteenth Century', *Studia Gratiana*, 11 (1967), 171–207.

these views in his description of the training he gave the young Henry.)[42] Wittingly or not, Skelton is repeating a humanist manœuvre and ventriloquizing a humanist tone of scorn in his own apology for his art. The *Replication* is a minor key reprise of a major humanist genre.

There are, however, important differences as well as similarities. Skelton does not seek to denigrate scholastic method and traditional learning in the manner of the anti-Cologne satires or the earlier epistles. Indeed, he seems to be an advocate of Thomistic authority. And, like Petrarch in the *Invectivae*, he enjoys beating the scholars at their own game. Similarly, he is not presenting himself as a Poet seeking to challenge the assumptions of the Theologians. Quite the opposite: he seeks to justify his own poetic activity within the framework of the sacerdotal theology that defines his identity. But however eccentric (and perhaps pragmatic) his claims may appear to be in the light of his own poetic practice, it is clear that the *Replication* alludes to many of the key debates of humanist poetic theory. So it is important to calibrate with some care the ways in which Skelton's defence parallels and echoes those of the earlier writers if his idiosyncratic stand in this poem is to be fully understood.

The key terms in Skelton's vocabulary of poetic self-classification are *Orator Regius*, 'laureate poet', and *vates*. The three are mixed and permutated throughout his career. The most recurrent title, and the one which most emphatically invokes the authority he claims in his public poetry, is that of poet laureate. As here in the *Replication*, he deploys this title repeatedly against real or imagined antagonists as an apotropaic totem which puts him above criticism and gives his writings extra

---

[42] Carlson, 'Royal Tutors', discusses the humanist context of the Royal Tutors and, on p. 256, prints Bernard André's humanist list of authors studied by Prince Arthur. Skelton calls himself 'creaunser' to Henry (*Agaynst Garnesche* (1514), 102), alluding to how he taught him to read classical poetry, and Erasmus describes him as showing Henry the 'sacred fonts' (Carlson, ibid. 265). On English Humanism generally, see Roberto Weiss, *Humanism in England during the Fifteenth Century*, Medium Aevum Monographs, 4 (3rd edn., Oxford, 1967); Gordon, *John Skelton*, 82–101; Carlson, *English Humanist Books*; Douglas Gray, 'Humanism and Humanisms in the Literature of Late Medieval England', in S. Rossi and D. Savoia (eds.), *Italy and the English Renaissance*, (Milan, 1989), 27–44.

Justification by Faith 299

status and power. Linked with this, his use of *Orator Regius* and his claim on occasion to write 'By the kynges most noble commandement' invokes his formal and public office, even in the unlikely context of his flyting against Garnesche. We know how seriously Skelton took this role and how flamboyantly he advertised his status in his dress as well as in his verse.[43] But beneath the sartorial and verbal display of poetic plumage, it may be that the consistent juxtaposition of 'laureate' and 'orator' consciously harks back to an important strand in humanist poetic theory. It became commonplace in late quattrocento humanist discussions of poetry to assert the rediscovered common ground between the poet and the orator, a recognition that reached its apogee in Salutati's appropriation of the Ciceronian definition of the orator as 'vir bonus dicendi peritus' for his definition of the *poeta* as 'vir optimus laudandi vituperandique peritus' ('the best of men, skilled in the art of praise and blame').[44] This is a cliché spun from clichés: the Ciceronian is grafted on to the Averroistic definition of poetry as an art of praise and blame to create a highly moral definition that does not sit uncomfortably with Skelton's own very high opinion of his calling and praxis. Similarly it is not unusual for the humanist theorists to discuss the high moral seriousness of Latin satire at some length, often praising and invoking the spirit of Juvenal (the titular deity of Skelton's own satirical universe). Indeed, Petrarch quotes extensively from Juvenal in the oration he delivered at his own laureation ceremony in 1341.[45] Thus Skelton's satirical upbraiding of the young heretics by means of robust invective fits squarely into what Skelton could have thought of as a typically humanist sense of poetic responsibility.

But the term that comes closest to Skelton's interest in the *Replication* in the interface between priesthood, prophecy, and

---

[43] See his *Calliope* (ed. Scattergood, pp. 112–13); Gillespie, 'Justification', 19–22.

[44] *Colucii Salutati: De Laboribus Herculis*, ed. B. L. Ullmann (Turin, 1951), 1. 63, 68; Greenfield, *Humanist and Scholastic Poetics*, 110–28; O'Donnell, 'Coluccio Salutati'; Witt, 'Coluccio Salutati'.

[45] Carlo Godi, 'La "Collatio Laureationis" del Petrarca', *Italia Medioevale e Umanistica*, 13 (1970), 1–27; for a translation, see E. H. Wilkins, *Studies in the Life and Works of Petrarch*, Medieval Academy of America Publication No. 63 (Cambridge, Mass., 1955), Appendix, pp. 300–13. Fontius devotes an entire Oration to the satirists: see Trinkaus, 'A Humanist's Image'.

poetry is *vates*. The encyclopaedic tradition, for which Skelton seems to have had some taste, had invariably linked discussion of *vates* with discussion of *poeta*. Isidore's *Etymologies* forged an explicit link between poetry, prophecy, and divine inspiration in its brief attempt at etymology:

Vates a vi mentis appelatos Varro auctor est; vel a viendis carminibus, id est flectendis, hoc est modulandis: et proindae poetae Latine vates olim, scripta eorum vaticinia dicebantur, quod vi quadam et quasi vesania in scribendo commoverentur... Etiam per furorem divini eodem erant nomine, quia et ipsi quoque pleraque versibus efferebant.

Varro is the authority for *vates* being so called from force of mind; or else from their 'plaiting' songs, that is, bending them into shape in modulating them; and hence poets were once called 'vates', prophets, in Latin, and their writings called prophecies, because in writing they were moved with a certain force and something like madness... Priests went by the same name likewise on account of their crazed inspiration, because they too used also to make many of their utterances in verses.

Other encyclopaedists and lexicographers followed suit. Papias repeats Isidore. John Balbus of Genoa's *Catholicon* glosses *vates* with the terms *sacerdos, propheta*, and *poeta divinus* (in that order). The humanist Reuchlin's *Vocabularius* links *vates* with *poeta* and *propheta*. Salutati's *De laboribus Herculis* synthesizes Isidore and Papias, chaining the standard definitions together and stating that the words *vates* and prophet are now considered synonymous.[46]

Discussion of the poet as *vates* was a commonplace of the early humanist defences of poetry and their discussions of divine inspiration. Albertino Mussato, the Paduan pre-Humanist who received the laurel in 1315 in recognition of his poetic achievements, claimed that the *vates* was a poet who spoke of theological truths under the inspiration of the deity. Significantly, his opponent in an epistolary debate about the nature of poetry, the Dominican Friar Giovannino of Mantua, argued

---

[46] *Isidori Etymologiarum sive Originum*, 2 vols., ed. W. M. Lindsay (Oxford, 1911), 8. 7 (De poetis); Joannes Balbus, *Catholicon* (Mainz, 1460; repr. Farnborough, 1971), s.v. *vates*; Johannes Reuchlin, *Vocabularius Breviloquus* (Basle, 1478) s.v. *vates; De Laboribus Herculis*, ed. Ullmann, 1. 16.

Justification by Faith 301

on the authority of Church Fathers that the term could not be used of poets alone, because it was used also to describe philosophers, priests, and prophets.[47] Petrarch's letter to his Carthusian brother links the name *poet* with the high-style 'sacred flattery' offered to the gods by primitive men, arguing on the authority of Jerome that it is proper to call David 'the poet of the Christians' because the psalms were written in Hebrew verse. Boccaccio repeats this argument in his commentary on Dante, and in the *Genealogia* uses Jerome's letters to develop the argument that poetry was sacralized by the poetic books of the Old Testament.[48] Jerome's Epistle 53 to Paulinus, which seems to have informed so much of Skelton's thinking in the *Replication*, describes St Paul as the 'vas electionis' (10. 5). Leonardi Bruni argues for the divinity of poetry by showing that *vates* is used to describe both poets and prophets. Cristoforo Landino in his *Disputationes camuldulenses* argues that poetry is the truest form of contemplation and that poets have a god-like character as divine *vates* and 'sacri Musarum sacerdotes' ('priests consecrated to the Muses')—a rather Skeltonic conception. Politian calls on the authority of Jerome to assert that poets and prophets are both *vates*. Ficino argues that poetry and prophecy both rely on inspiration and an elevated state of the soul.[49]

In his Coronation Oration, Petrarch links the prophetic power of the poet with the notion of divine inspiration:

The inherent difficulty of the poet's task lies in this, that whereas in the other arts one may attain his goal through sheer toil and study, it is far otherwise with the art of poetry, in which nothing can be

---

[47] Greenfield, *Humanist and Scholastic Poetics*, 81–90, esp. 89; Witt, 'Coluccio Salutati', 540–2; for the text of the letters see Albertino Mussato, *Opera* (Venice, 1630), reprinted in J. G. Graevius, *Thesaurus Antiquitarum et Historiarum Italiae* (Leyden, 1722), 6. 2, cols. 34–62. Giovannino's epistle is in cols. 54D–57E; the discussion of *vates* is col. 56B.

[48] *Fam.* 10. 4, *Letters*, ed. Bernardo, pp. 69–70, also citing Isidore on poets; substantially repeated in Boccaccio's *Tratatello*, Minnis and Scott (eds.), *Medieval Literary Criticism*, 492–3. For the *De genealogia*, see 14. 3 and 14. 4, where Boccaccio uses Jerome's Epistles 53 and 70, and the Prefatory Letter from book 2 of Jerome's translation of Eusebius's *Chronicon*; trans. Osgood, pp. 19–25, 147–9.

[49] On Bruni, see Greenfield, *Humanist and Scholastic Poetics*, 178–85, esp. 180; Robey, 'Humanist Views', 17–19. On Landino, see Di Cesare, 'Cristoforo Landino', esp. 166–76. On Politian, see Greenfield, 257–7, esp. 263. On Ficino, see Greenfield, 230–6, esp. 235.

accomplished unless a certain inner and divinely given energy is infused in the poet's spirit [*in animum vatis infusa vi*].

Petrarch supports this with a citation from Cicero's *Pro Archia*, widely used in discussions of inspiration, but he is in fact going further than Cicero and is defining his own Christian poetics and his own sense of the *poeta theologus* in terms that are slightly different from the classical view. Cicero argues that the poet achieves insight from his own talents: 'the poet attains through his very nature, is moved by the energy that is within his mind and is as it were inspired by a divine inbreathing [*et quasi divino quodam spiritu afflari*]', and he quotes Ennius as calling poets sacred in their own right because they possess a divine gift.[50] This passage, and in particular Cicero's use of one word—*quasi*—is at the nub of the debate about the human or divine nature of poetry, and about whether pagan poets could be regarded as theologians and as 'Christians without Christ'.

Isidore had baldly stated without authority that ancient poets were called theologians because they made songs about the gods. Later encyclopaedists, such as Vincent of Beauvais, repeated this bald assertion.[51] But Mussato had been the first humanist apologist to deploy what was in fact Aristotle's argument in the *Metaphysics* that poets were the first theologians as part of his argument for the inspired nature of classical poetry, going so far as to argue that 'Nostra fides sancto tota est praedicta Maroni'. But his Dominican opponent, a better Aristotelian, or at least a better Thomist, had pointed out that the pagan poets had been describing false gods, and could not therefore be likened to the theology that undertook to expound the mysteries of Christian revelation. Indeed, on the authority of the same Jerome Epistle used by Skelton in the *Replication*, he dismisses Mussato's claim that Christian truths can be discerned in pagan texts, arguing that this effect can only be achieved by taking passages out of context and coupling them together for false effect in a manner that Jerome ridicules as

---

[50] Godi, 'Collatio Laureationis', 14; Wilkins, *Studies in Petrarch*, 301–2.
[51] 'Quidam autem poetae theologi dicti sunt, quoniam de diis carmina faciebant', ed. Lindsay, 8. 7; Vincent of Beauvais, *Speculum doctrinale*, col. 288 in *Speculum maius* (Douai, 1624; repr. Graz, 1964–5).

'puerilia... et circulatorum ludo similia' (16. 11). Likewise, he responds to Mussato's claim that the presence of verse in Scripture justifies poetic composition with the scornful response that metre is not the essence of poetry, merely a mode of expression.[52]

Petrarch and Boccaccio repeated Mussato's arguments in their discussion of Aristotle's anthropological analysis of early poets. But, unlike Mussato, they begin to open up clear water between the pagan notion of the divine frenzy and the Christian notion of divine inspiration. Petrarch tries to persuade his eremitical brother that 'poetry is not at all inimical to theology', indeed that 'I would almost say that theology is poetry written about God.' Passing quickly over the pagan origins of poetic theology, he focuses instead on the use of poetic techniques in Scripture and by later Christian authors. In his *Invectivae* he cites Aristotle's description of poets as the first theologians, and praises the endeavours of these 'investigators of truth' but recognizes that their studies were fuelled by human genius rather than superhuman insight. He rapidly moves on to assert that perfect knowledge of the true God is a gift from heaven and not the result of human study, putting an implicit wedge between pagan poets and Christian poets, just as he does in the Coronation Oration, where Cicero's use of *quasi* allows the pagan imagery of inspiration to stand as merely analogous to but different in kind from the divine inspiration he finds at work in his own writings and those of other Christians.[53]

Boccaccio is heavily dependent on Petrarch in his handling of the issue of inspiration. Poetry, he argues, 'proceeds from the bosom of God', and pagan poets of mythology are theologians in the Aristotelian sense of being early collectors and interpreters of myth. But the Christian writers were the first to receive 'the sublime effects of this great art', he argues, not the pagans: 'Rather it was instilled into the most sacred prophets dedicated

---

[52] Graevius, *Thesaurus*, col. 55D–F. See Greenfield, *Humanist and Scholastic Poetics*, 87–90; Witt, 'Coluccio Salutati', 540–2.
[53] *Fam.* 10. 4, Minnis and Scott (eds.), *Medieval Literary Criticism*, 413; alternative translation, *Letters*, ed. Bernardo, p. 69; *Invective contra medicum, Prose*, ed. Martellotti et al. 658, 674; Godi, 'Collatio Laureationis', 14; Wilkins, *Studies in Petrarch*, 301–2.

to God. For we read that Moses, impelled by what I take to be this poetic longing, at dictation of the Holy Ghost, wrote the larger part of the Pentateuch not in prose but heroic verse.' The influence of Jerome's Epistles, including the letter to Paulinus, hangs heavy over this part of Boccaccio's argument. Whereas holy men were filled with the Holy Ghost and wrote under its impulse, the others were prompted by mere energy of mind. In his Dante commentary, Boccaccio argues that poetry and Scripture 'which we call theology' share a common manner of literary treatment, and that critics of poetry may, through their censure of the poets, fall into the error of criticizing the Holy Spirit. Indeed, echoing Petrarch, he argues that: 'theology and poetry can be spoken of almost as one and the same thing, when they share the same subject . . . theology is nothing more than a poetry of God'.[54] Both Boccaccio and Petrarch mount their defence of Theological Poetics in contexts which also include extensive discussion of laureation and its meaning for poets, but both of them are envisaging a new Christian poetics and a new Christian concept of laureation exisiting in a deferential but distinct relationship to their classical antecedents. For both, true poetic vocation is a rare and wonderful phenomenon:

This poetry, which ignorant triflers cast aside, is a sort of fervid and exquisite invention, with fervid expression, in speech or writing, of that which the mind has invented. It proceeds from the bosom of God, and few, I find, are the souls in which this gift is born; indeed so wonderful a gift is it that true poets have always been the rarest of men.[55]

The rarity of poets is implicit in Cristoforo Landino's view of the poet as a a superhuman figure: 'And indeed whichever *vates* were worthy of the name, they have been seen to be capable of something beyond human strength.' But Landino is less clear than Petrarch and Boccaccio about the differences

---

[54] Robey, 'Humanist Views', 7–12; Greenfield, *Humanist and Scholastic Poetics*, 110–25; *De genealogia*, trans. Osgood, p. 46; *Tratatello*, paras. 141 and 154, Minnis and Scott (eds.), *Medieval Literary Criticism*, 495, 498.

[55] *De genealogia*, 14. 7, Minnis and Scott (eds.), *Medieval Literary Criticism*, 420; trans. Osgood, p. 39. On the Ciceronian basis of this trope, see Greenfield, *Humanist and Scholastic Poetics*, 114–18.

between pagan and Hebrew/Christian inspiration.[56] Similarly, in his Ciceronian and Averroistic poetics, Salutati tends in *De laboribus Herculis* to blur the distinction between pagan and Christian theories of inspiration (though his later correspondence suggests that he may have changed his position to one closer to Petrarch and Boccaccio). In a manner which is perhaps characteristic of fifteenth-century humanist poetics, he moves the definition of poet closer to the traditional definition of orator. He cites Cicero's *Pro Archia,* offers a long mythographic exposition of the significance of the Muses and Apollo in the context of his discussion of inspiration, and expounds in some detail the *officium* of poets using the Averroistic *Poetics* as his starting point. 'Poetry is an art in which *studia, praecepta* and *doctrina* play a part, but in the final analysis, it is *natura* which distinguishes a great poet.' The role of poetry is to praise and blame by means of a range of imaginative devices.[57] And, for Salutati, it is the allegorical nature of poetry that is its final justification and, because of its similarity to the *modus agendi* of scripture, its ultimate defence against those *apud religiosus* who denigrate it. But there is less of the *poeta theologus* in his writing and more of the *poeta orator et historiographus* who comes to the fore in later humanist writing.

Many of these discussions of the nature of poetry and the character of the poet were available in print by the time Skelton's intellectual formation was under way; others appeared in good new editions in the course of his lifetime.[58] Even if his awareness of the terms of the debate was gleaned largely from dictionaries,

---

[56] Di Cesare, 'Cristoforo Landino', 172; Greenfield, *Humanist and Scholastic Poetics,* 213–20.

[57] Robey, 'Humanist Views', 11–14; O'Donnell, 'Coluccio Salutati', 246–52, quoting from p. 248; Witt, 'Coluccio Salutati', 546–63; *De Laboribus Herculis,* ed. Ullmann, liber primus, *passim,* esp. cap. 12, pp. 61–8.

[58] e.g. the editions of Petrarch's Latin works (Venice, 1501) and *Opera* (Venice, 1515); the many editions of Boccaccio's *De genealogia* from the Venice edition of 1472 onwards; Landino's *Disputationes* (Florence, c.1480; Paris, 1511); Fontius's *Orationes* (1486–7); and the many editions of Jerome's letters (Rome, 1468/9 onwards) and *Opera* (Basle, 1516). Given that Skelton chooses Lydgate (rather than Chaucer) to admit him into the court of Fame in *The Garland of Laurel,* it is interesting that the prologues of books 4 and 8 of his *Fall of Princes* praise Petrarch and Boccaccio, *Lydgate's Fall of Princes,* ed. Henry Bergen, 4 vols. EETS ES 121–4 (London, 1924–7); Ebin, *Illuminator, Makar, Vates,* 19–48.

encyclopaedias, and those collections of aphoristic *dicta* for which he had a particular liking, it is remarkable how closely his mediation of those terms ventriloquizes the tone and trajectory of earlier defences.[59]

Moreover the earlier humanist view of the *poeta theologus* was still being expressed even in Skelton's own lifetime. The Inaugural Orations of Bartollomeo della Fonte (Fontius), professor of poetry and oratory in Florence in the 1480s, represent a highly traditional, even clichéd view of the role and nature of the poet:

> But he who comes to the doorposts of the poets without the inspiration of the muses, thinking he can make himself a bard by technique and learning, is vain and puerile in his poetising. For noble *vates*, who are very few, create poetry not by art or by science, but rather by the divine spirit... For God alone excites the madness of the poet and uses him as though a minister and messenger of his oracles.[60]

For Fontius, all whom the divine madness inspires are called prophets, and he gives a historical survey of poetry from the times of the Egyptians, Assyrians, and Greeks down to the biblical poets and their Christian successors, including Dante (who equalled all earlier prophetic poets) and Petrarch. Many of these ideas are repeated at greater length in his *Poetics* written for Lorenzo de Medici: poets are 'prophetae summi atque theologi'; the Old Testament Prophets and later Christian writers like Jerome were inspired to write songs 'divino spiritu afflati'. Poets are the friends of God; many have been lifted up into the contemplation of sublime mysteries, like the apostle Paul 'in vas electionis electus et et in tertium caelum amore contemplationis attractus', he argues, echoing Jerome's characterization of Paul in the Paulinus Epistle. Poetry serves a range of functions: 'For whoever now soothes, now torments, partly

---

[59] For evidence of Skelton's reading, see *The Bibliotheca Historica of Diodorus Siculus*, translated by John Skelton, EETS OS 239 (1957), Appendices B and C; Gillespie, 'Justification by Good Works'; David R. Carlson, 'John Skelton and Ancient Authors', *Humanistica Lovaniensia*, 38 (1989), 100–9, suggests that Skelton's learning may have been derivative.

[60] Trinkaus, 'A Humanist's Image', 105–6. The oration *On the Good Arts* was delivered in 1484, *In Praise of the Poetic Art* was delivered in 1485/6. The orations were printed in Florence in 1487/8.

relaxes, partly coerces, sometimes terrifies, occasionally diverts, occasionally instructs the mind of the reader fully carries out the poetic function.'[61] This may be compared with Petrarch's list in the *Invectivae* of the 'work' of the orator/rhetor (and by implication of the poet): 'To accuse, to excuse, to console, to irritate, to calm the soul, to move to tears and to restrain them, to provoke anger and extinguish it, to make things colourful, to avert infamy, to transfer blame, to stir up suspicion.'[62]

Such lists of the varied functions performed by poetry link it firmly to the multiple literary modes which medieval exegetes had argued to be operative in Scripture, and, most notably, to the range of functions performed by the poetry of the Psalms, and by extension to the hymns and poems of early Christian writers:

The sange of psalmes chaces fendes, excites aungels tille oure help, it dose oway synne, it qwemes God, it enfourmes parfitnes, it dose oway and destroys noy and angere of saule and makes pees bytwix body and saule, it bringes desire of heven and despite of erthly thinge. Sothely this shinand boke es a chosen sange bifor God, als laumpe lyghtenand oure lyf, hele of a seke hert, huny til a bitter saule, dignite of gastly persones, tunge of prive vertus; the whilke heldes the proude tille meknes and kynges til pouer menne makis underloute, fosterand barnes with hamelynes.[63]

The humanists are, in general theoretical terms and in the details of their literary modes, closing a hermeneutical circle and establishing the continuity of their literary practice with that of the inspired authors of Scripture. This is, of course, precisely what

---

[61] The treatise was composed between 1490 and 1492; the unique manuscript has been edited by Trinkaus, 'The Unknown Quattrocento Poetics', these quotations on pp. 98, 99, 105 (leading to a citation of Jerome's Epistle 70), and 78–9.

[62] *Prose*, ed. Martellotti *et al.* 688.

[63] *English Writings of Richard Rolle, Hermit of Hampole*, ed. Hope Emily Allen (Oxford, 1931), 4–5; Vincent Gillespie, 'Mystic's Foot: Rolle and Affectivity', in Marion Glasscoe (ed.), *The Medieval Mystical Tradition in England*, vol. ii (Exeter, 1982), 199–230; A. J. Minnis, *Medieval Theory of Authorship: Scholastic Literary Attitudes in the Later Middle Ages*, 2nd edn. (Aldershot, 1988), s.v. *David*; *Psalter*, esp. pp. 42–56, 85–93, 103–12. In a sense this is where I came in, as my first encounters with Douglas Gray were as an undergraduate and graduate student interested in the poetics of religious lyrics and my first explorations of poetic and affective theory were undertaken under his benign, tolerant, and immensely wise and well-read guidance. Thank you, Douglas: you have only yourself to blame.

Skelton is also trying to do in the *Replication* when he argues that inspired poets write:

> Somtyme for affection,
> Sometyme for sadde dyrection,
> Somtyme for correction,
> Somtyme under protection
> Of pacient sufferance,
> With sobre cyrcumstance,
> Our myndes to avaunce
> To no mannes anoyance. (389–96)

The link is made explicit when, in a Latin sidenote at this point in the poem, Skelton quotes from the opening of Vulgate Psalm 44: 'My tongue is the pen of a scrivener that writeth swiftly.'[64]

Because of his sense of its sacred nature, Fontius was prepared to defend poetry against the charges of its enemies and to defy their criticisms: 'If divine poetics is near to them, if lovable poets are inspired by divine power, what do I care if they are less pleasing to certain ignorant theologians?'[65] His tone is similar to that adopted by Skelton in reply to 'certain ignorant theologians' of his own time, and Skelton in his turn can be shown to echo and allude to many of the gestures of his predecessors in defending poetry's status and the divinely inspired role of the poet. His choice of Jerome's Epistle 53 to Paulinus as his main proof text allows him to invoke a distinct branch of humanist thought on the issue of poetic theology. He sidesteps the contentious issue of the theological validity of pagan poetry —the 'Christians without Christ' argument—because it had been emphatically dealt with by Jerome in that same epistle. Instead he positions himself in the humanist mainstream which had consistently argued that poetry was indeed capable of examining at a profound level just those issues of theology, analogy, philology, and philosophy that Skelton's opponents seek to deny to him. Similarly his response to the argument 'Howe

---

[64] The Latin sidenotes are printed in *The Poetical Works of Skelton*, ed. Alexander Dyce, 2 vols. (London, 1843), i. 206–24, this quote p. 222. Only some of these are translated by Scattergood in his notes on the poem.

[65] Trinkaus, 'The Unknown Quattrocento Poetics', 68.

poetes do but fayne' is to invoke the 'fame matryculate / Of poetes laureate' (358), because the humanist defence to that charge is always mounted on the grounds of the allegorical force of true poetry and usually in the context of celebrating the laureate status of its greatest exponents, notably Virgil.

His discussion of the mechanics of inspiration emphasizes the Greek concept of 'effecte energiall' (this is glossed philologically in one of the authorial sidenotes that stress the learned and serious tenor of Skelton's argument: 'Energia grece, latine efficax operatio. Internoque quodam spiritus impulsu inopinabiliter originata'[66]); and in the peroration he cites Socrates and Plato as authorities. The Platonic strand of poetic theory had long been assimilated into humanist aesthetics, though Bruni, Ficino, and Fontius had given it more prominence than some of the earlier writers. But Skelton's emphasis that inspiration is an act of divine grace, and is only given to poets who have strenuously prepared themselves to receive the gift, reflects the teaching of the early writers:[67]

> That of divyne myseracion
> God maketh his habytacion
> In poetes whiche excelles,
> And sojourns with them and dwelles. (375–8)

Here the marginal note cites Ovid's *Fasti*, VI. 5–6, a standard proof text in humanist discussions of inspiration. But, following Jerome, Skelton's inspiration is emphatically Christian: as with the prophets of the Old Testament, it is 'hete of the Holy Gost' that leads him to take up his pen and urgently write (here the sidenotes cite Jerome and Baptist Mantuan as well as the Psalms). He claims for himself Davidic authority for the divine frenzy that urges him to argue against the misplaced motivation of the 'frenetykes ... lunatykes ... sysmatykes ... heretykes' who have opposed him, citing in Latin Vulgate Psalm 74: 5: 'I said to the wicked: Do not act wickedly: and to the sinners: Lift not up the horn.' By preaching openly throughout East

---

[66] Dyce (ed.), *Poetical Works of Skelton*, 222.
[67] Robey, 'Humanist Views'; Witt, 'Coluccio Salutati'; Greenfield, *Humanist and Scholastic Poetics*, 315–16 and *passim*.

Anglia, Hertfordshire, and London, Bilney and Arthur had lifted up the horn of heresy. Skelton felt impelled to reply, but in so doing found himself defending not only clerical orthodoxy and sound learning, but also his own calling as a poet. His Latin peroration triumphantly proclaims a sense of literary self-worth and poetic rarity that places him firmly in the tradition of the humanist defences:

> De raritate poetarum, deque gimnosophistarum, philosophorum, theologorum, ceterumque eruditorum infinita numerositate, Skeltonidis Laureati epitoma.[68]

The laureate poet is pitted against the others as possessing a wisdom that is different in kind, not just in degee, from the knowledge of other 'docti': *scientia inflat; caritas autem edificat.*

> Sunt infiniti, sunt innumerique sophiste,
> Sunt infiniti, sunt innumerique logiste,
> Innumeri sunt philosophi, sunt theologique,
> Sunt infiniti doctores, suntque magistri
> Innumeri; sed sunt pauci rarique poete.
> Hinc omne est rarum carum: reor ergo poetas
> Ante alios omnes divine flamine flatos...
> Sic magnus Macedo, sic Caesar, maximus heros
> Romanus, celebres semper coluere poetas.[69]

It is not an impressive syllogism, but it is clearly heartfelt, and distils into a few lines that idiosyncratic synthesis of spleen, idealism, self-advertisement, eclectic learning, and attention-seeking behaviour that characterizes his life and work. A Latin sidenote refers the reader (and perhaps the monarch by whose privilege the poem was printed) to Valerius Maximus's account of the proper veneration due to notable poets. Even at the end

---

[68] 'The epitome of Skelton, the laureate poet, is about the rarity of poets and about the infinite abundance of gymnosophists, philosophers, theologians and the rest of the learned sort' (trans. Scattergood, p. 520).

[69] 'Infinite and innumerable are the sophists, infinite and innumerable are the logicians, innumerable are the philosophers and theologians, infinite the doctors and innumerable the masters, but poets are few and rare. Thus, everything that is rare is precious. Therefore, I think that poets, before all others, are filled with divine inspiration... thus the great Macedonian, thus Caesar, the greatest of Roman heroes, always honoured famous poets' (trans. Scattergood, p. 520).

of his writing career, and in his most high-minded account of his own poetic and prophetic vocation, Skelton is still striving to create the taste by which he was to be appreciated, and doing so by ventriloquizing tropes and gestures found in his humanist antecedents.

If in the public poetry celebrated in *The Garland of Laurel* Skelton can most usefully be seen as presenting himself as a *poeta orator et historiographus* (and this is in keeping with the character and output of those classical and humanist writers he invokes there), the *Replication* invites us to see Skelton from a different perspective: as a committed and skilled synthesizer of the three roles of poet, priest, and prophet. At the end of his writing career he exchanges the singing robes of *Calliope* for the borrowed robes of a *poeta theologus*.

Hec vates ille de quo loquntur mille.

After his death in 1529, according to Bale, Skelton was buried before the high altar of St Margaret's, Westminster. Engraved on his tombstone was the legend:

Ioannes Skeltonvs Vates Pierius Hic Situs Est
Here lies John Skelton, *vates* of the Muses/of Poetry.

The tombstone and its legend has since disappeared. In 1556, Chaucer was moved to a grander tomb in the Abbey.[70]

[70] Pollet, *John Skelton*, 160; Pearsall, 'Chaucer's Tomb', 59–67.

14 Visio Baleii: An Early Literary Historian

ANNE HUDSON

The idea of a chair in English Literature and Language would have struck John Bale as a surprising, indeed probably a bizarre, notion. Yet the work of this irascible, prejudiced antiquarian has a claim to recognition as one of the first foundations to the edifice of vernacular literary scholarship, even if its author's objectives were theological, ecclesiological, or historical rather than literary. Bale's life was eventful: first a Carmelite friar, zealous for the reputation and history of his order, in the early 1530s the views of the reformers persuaded him to abandon his fraternal profession in 1536, but not his intellectual pursuits. His extreme Protestant views led, after a brief period of favour under the patronage of Thomas Cromwell, to a first exile between 1540 and the death of Henry VIII in 1547; he returned probably in 1548, was nominated as bishop of Ossory in October 1552, but had to flee less than a year later after Mary's accession. His second Continental exile ended in 1559, when he was given a canonry at Canterbury; he lived there until his death in November 1563. The complexity of this career, the number of his publications, and the profuse signs of revision, amplification, and repetition revealed by his surviving notebooks (only a fraction though they obviously are of his output), have meant that no full or adequate account of his importance has yet been written.[1] This chapter is intended as a brief indication of one further area that will need consideration

---

[1] Probably the best so far available, though the title reveals the author's primary interest, is L. P. Fairfield, *John Bale: Mythmaker for the English Reformation* (West Lafayette, 1976), with its bibliography listing most important previous work; for the majority of Bale's work published before 1640 see *STC*.

when that account comes to be put together. Bale is perhaps the earliest historian of English literary works still regularly consulted by modern scholars; that consultation has been primarily for bibliographical information, but it is worth considering whether his comments do not offer an interesting sidelight on the construction of the literary canon and on the consequent view of literary history. My discussion will largely be limited to Bale's comments on fifteenth-century writers in English, with particular concern for those included in *The Oxford Book of Late Medieval Verse and Prose*.[2] I shall, however, extend the limits slightly by including a few somewhat earlier writers, and by adding the Latin and French works composed by those who are now remembered primarily as 'English' writers.

Bale's preoccupation throughout his career was the preservation, and as a means to that end the cataloguing, of England's historical heritage; though influenced by his older contemporary John Leland, Bale's concern found more publicity by virtue of his own prolific writing.[3] The basis for the study here is primarily Bale's *Scriptorum illustrium maioris Brytanniae... Catalogus*, published first in two volumes in Basel, 1557 and 1559. This was an expansion of the briefer *Illustrium maioris Britanniae scriptorum summarium* that had appeared in 1548 with an Ipswich imprint.[4] Both of these are arranged after prefatory material as a series of biographies of individual writers, divided in the *Catalogus* into groups of a hundred, and laid out roughly chronologically (the 'centuries' are not of time but of number). The format is regular: a brief outline of the writer's life is given, followed by a list of works by title, number of books, and incipit, though the last piece of information is in perhaps more than half the cases missing; a brief comment follows, with sometimes an appendix of information usually

---

[2] Identification of authors or works excerpted in this anthology is shown by bold-face numbers here.

[3] See Fairfield, *John Bale*, and *The Vocacyon of Johan Bale*, ed. P. Happé and J. N. King, Medieval and Renaissance Texts and Studies, 70 (1990).

[4] The longer work, because of its declared place of publication, does not appear in *STC*; the second is there no. 1295 and the actual place of printing is likely to have been Wesel. Bale's *Summarium* was largely put together during his first exile from 1541 to 1548.

declaredly deriving from some other authority. The language is throughout Latin, for titles and incipits, as well as for commentary; since the work appears usually as the object of a sentence the main words of the titles are normally in the accusative case. The information in the *Catalogus* can usefully be supplemented from the work that has come to be known as his *Index Britanniae scriptorum*; this was not published in Bale's lifetime nor intended to be so. In its modern edition it is an alphabetization of the material provided in one of Bale's notebooks, now Oxford Bodleian MS Selden supra 64, a notebook mostly compiled between 1548 and 1552 when Bale was back in Britain following his first exile.[5] The information in this notebook is again a catalogue of British writers, here without most of the biographical detail; the valuable material is the account of the manuscripts in which Bale saw the works of those he lists (again with title, book number, and sometimes incipit). Although inevitably the owners, institutional let alone individual, of the manuscripts mentioned are rarely the same now as they were when Bale saw them, and difficulties of identification exist, this listing has many interests. It is a reasonable guide to what Bale actually saw, rather than what he took over from earlier secondary sources; further it offers important information about materials that were available in England between c.1520 and 1557, materials that may be much depleted now.[6]

Bale's *Summarium* and the larger *Catalogus* were designed, as their titles imply, to list British writers and thereby to celebrate the British nation; as becomes quickly evident, a second purpose was undeclared in those titles, namely to indicate the long desire expressed in English writers for the reform of the Roman church, a reform only later brought to fruition partially by Henry VIII but fully by his son Edward.[7] But the format and

---

[5] Edited by R. L. Poole and M. Bateson (London, 1902), and reissued with a supplementary introduction by C. Brett and J. P. Carley (Cambridge, 1990); see the latter, p. xiv.

[6] For instance, Bale's *Index*, pp. 264–74 reveals a number of works by Wyclif in English collections that now survive only in Bohemian copies in central European libraries; it also makes clear that Balliol and The Queen's Colleges, Oxford, and Pembroke College, Cambridge, possessed manuscripts of Wyclif's works that are no longer there.

[7] See *Index*, new introduction, pp. xii–xiii.

method of both had been laid down long before this second purpose had come to dominate Bale's mind. In the surviving notebooks from Bale's early life as a Carmelite friar appear prolific notes largely on Carmelite writers, covering again their lives and the titles, books, and incipits of their writings; here the outlook is, from a medieval viewpoint, entirely orthodox and his own order is the object of Bale's praise. Thus, for instance, in the notebook now Oxford MS Bodley 73, a notebook that seems to date from 1522–7, appear, alongside more diverse materials, biographies of this kind, evidently written as information came to hand: Thomas Netter of Walden, John Kyningham, both noted opponents of John Wyclif, recur.[8] Other comparable notebooks are now Bodleian MSS Selden supra 41 and 72, British Library MS Harley 1819, and Cambridge University Library MS Ff. 6. 28, all of them from before Bale's disenchantment with the Carmelite order around 1532; the same information reappears in many places, sometimes apparently at random, sometimes from Bale's reading of another source.[9]

The regular format for the listing of a writer's works is probably to be derived from Johan Trithemius's *Liber de scriptoribus ecclesiasticis*, itself first printed in Basel in 1494 and several times later; though Trithemius was a Benedictine, his work attracted rapid attention and is quoted with some frequency in Bale's own *Catalogus*.[10] An alternative source of earlier date is the medieval listing in the author Bale knew as 'Boston of Bury', where again the fullest form provides the same information in the same order.[11] The model was a well-

[8] For the dating see Fairfield, *John Bale*, 158–9; details about Netter appear fos. 1^{r-v}, 11^v–12^v, 40, 56^v, 57^v–8, 62^{r-v}, 72, 78, 81^{r-v}, 94^v–103^v, 108^v, 113^v, 133^v, 183, 186, 196^v, 199^v, 204–5, 208, 217^v, on Kyningham fos. 40^v, 42^v, 56–57^v, 81, 119, 133^v, 196^v, 205.

[9] For the dating see Fairfield, *John Bale*, 157–61; British Library MS Harley 3838 consists of three parts, the third of which, fos. 156–249, probably also dates from before 1533 (ibid. 161–3).

[10] Trithemius's *De laudibus ordinis Carmelitarum* was only much later printed in 1575, and cannot have been known to Bale. For a brief biography see the introduction by K. Arnold to R. Behrendt's translation of *Johannes Trithemius In Praise of Scribes* (*De laude scriptorum*), (Lawrence, Kan., 1974), 1–12. For Bale's use see, for instance, *Catalogus*, i. 473, 476, ii. 208, etc.

[11] See, most recently, *Registrum Anglie de libris doctorum et auctorum veterum*, ed. R. H. Rouse and M. A. Rouse (London, 1991), where 'Boston' is identified with Henry of Kirkestede; 'Boston' is extensively cited by Bale (e.g. *Catalogus* i. 409, 410, 128, etc.).

Visio Baleii: An Early Literary Historian

established one in late medieval times: there exists, for instance, an early fifteenth-century Hussite listing of the works of John Wyclif with the same format of book title, number of chapters (or sermons), and incipit.[12] The aim of these catalogues was identification of works that might in manuscript be unascribed (and, in the case of the *Registrum*, location); that function is still evident not only in Bale's *Catalogus* but also in modern critics' utilization of his materials (as will be seen below).

Bale's syllabus for his endeavours is thus strictly historically based, and author based. There is no theory of literature, no basis for inclusion or exclusion beyond the availability of information concerning an author and his work. But this last requirement imposes a major restriction on Bale's view of earlier English literature: all the works included are there by virtue of their authors, and thus almost all anonymous texts are missing.[13] This inevitably means that perhaps a half or more of the works normally studied by modern readers do not appear: the wealth of fifteenth-century lyric poetry (*OBLMVP* 11), the bulk of ballads (12) and romances (14), letters (2), practical and comic materials (9 and 23), and almost all the plays are absent (16, 21).[14] This cannot in many cases be the result of Bale's ignorance of their existence: his investigation of medieval manuscripts was wide, almost unbelievably wide, and it is inconceivable that he had not encountered many examples of all kinds. Their absence is the result of Bale's self-restriction to a biographical mode. The same cannot be said in explanation of

---

[12] These are printed by R. Buddensieg, *John Wyclif: Polemical Works*, 2 vols., Wyclif Society (London, 1883), i, pp. lix–lxxxiv, and see my paper, 'The Hussite Catalogues of Wyclif's Works', in J. Pánek, M. Polívka, N. Rejchrtová (eds.), *Husitství Reformace Renesance*, i (Prague, 1994), 401–17. The ordering of the items in the Hussite catalogue is in some respects more sophisticated than either Trithemius or Bale: the incipit is the ordering item, arranged in alphabetical order (first letter only), followed by explicit and book number, with the title placed above the incipit and rubricated. In Bale the title is given first, in random order, then book number, but with no explicit and often no incipit.

[13] A few anonymous works appear in the *Index*, collected in the edition under appendices I–III; there can be found works such as *Mum and the Sothsegger* (p. 479) or *Speculum Christiani* (p. 480)—for the first see H. Barr, *The Piers Plowman Tradition* (London, 1993) especially p. 15, for the second *Speculum Christiani*, ed. G. Holmstedt, EETS OS 182 (1933), pp. ci–cii.

[14] The entry for Ranulph Higden (*Catalogus*, i. 462) does not include the legend about his responsibility for the Chester Plays; when a play's author is known, as with Skelton's *Magnyficence*, the work is included (i. 652).

318 *Anne Hudson*

certain other omissions. Whilst he might not have regarded Alain Chartier (8C) as properly a British author, John Walton (17A) and Osbern Bokenham (17D), the second from Bale's own East Anglian area, seem strange omissions.[15] Some appear under slightly incorrect forms: John Fortescue (8B) is entered as *Foskevve Cancellarius* (i. 613), and appears with some variations under *F* in the *Index* (p. 72). Bale's knowledge of Scots vernacular writers seems to have been limited, drawing apparently exclusively on printed sources. Gavin Douglas is included, but his biography is largely attributed to Polydore Vergil, and the only works for which an incipit are given are *The Palace of Honour* and the *Aeneid* translation.[16] From John Major and Polydore Vergil he derives the information about James I (5); the title of the first of three works listed (and the only one certainly identifiable, as *The Kingis Quair*), *Super uxore futura*, makes it plain that Bale had never read the work, though since it survives now only in a single manuscript, this is not very surprising.[17] Neither Robert Henryson (18) nor William Dunbar (19) is included, though both appear, in one case in garbled form, in a list of Scottish writers in the *Index*.[18]

Less surprising is the fact that neither Julian of Norwich nor Margery Kempe (7D) figures in Bale's *Catalogus*: disapproval of women writers cannot be the reason since Dame Juliana Barnes (9T, W) is included,[19] but the paucity of surviving manuscripts of both Julian and Margery (even granted that more might have been available in his time) can excuse Bale. But the combination of the exclusion of anonymous works and the

---

[15] As the editor of Walton's *Boethius*, M. Science (EETS OS 170 (1927)) comments, pp. xlix–l, Walton first appears in Thomas Tanner's *Bibliotheca Britannico-Hibernica* (London, 1748), 753, and then with details that confuse two men with the same name.

[16] See *Catalogus*, ii. 218, *Index*, p. 83; Bale may have known the *Palace* from the Edinburgh edition of *c.*1535 (*STC* 7072.8), and the *Aeneid* from Copland's 1553 edition (*STC* 24797).

[17] *Catalogus*, ii. 217; see J. Norton-Smith (ed.), *The Kingis Quair* (Leiden, 1981), p. xix; see further here Sally Mapstone's comments, pp. 52 n. 4, 68.

[18] For prints of some poems before 1557 by Henryson see *STC* 13166 and by Dunbar *STC* 7347–9, 7350; *Index*, p. 496 includes 'Dunbar . . . Rolandus Harryson'.

[19] *Catalogus*, i. 611; three treatises, on hawking, hunting, and the laws of arms (i.e. heraldry) are specified, suggesting Bale knew the St Albans edition of 1486 (*STC* 3308); he adds 'Dicitur et de piscatione edidisse opusculum', indicating that he had not seen Wynkyn de Worde's 1496 edition (*STC* 3309) or later versions which included such a section.

probable invisibility of writers such as Julian and Margery to Bale means that those we know as 'the Middle English mystics' are very poorly represented in the *Catalogus*: Richard Rolle from the early fourteenth century and Walter Hilton are the only writers whom we should recognize from this field. To Hilton is ascribed *De ecclesiastica musica*, the name by which Thomas a Kempis's *De imitatione Christi* (7G) was characteristically known in England.[20] The vernacular nature of works from writers who predominantly used Latin often passes unremarked: in the long list of John Fisher's texts (7L), none is acknowledged to be in English, though at least two are identifiable with such texts;[21] a long biography of John Colet is provided, but only in the *Index* is his use of English (and the suspicion that this brought him under) mentioned;[22] John Alcock (7I) is said to have written 'Homelias uulgares' (no incipit), but the use of English in *Montem perfectionis* is unremarked.[23]

Bale's work is perhaps most often consulted now by those interested in the manuscript circulation of medieval works. But it is worth noting that, despite his concern for the preservation of manuscripts after the dispersal of libraries formerly in religious hands, Bale also extensively utilized printed editions. His knowledge, for instance, of the works of Stephen Hawes (22A) seems to derive entirely from the various printed editions available at his time—though, given the lack of an incipit to any of them, it is perhaps legitimate to wonder how carefully Bale had scrutinized them. The six titles given are *Delectamentum spiritus* (*Pastime of Pleasure*), *Amantium consolamen* (*Comfourt of Lovers*), *Virtutis exemplar* (*Example of virtue*), *De coniugio principis* (*Joyfull Meditacioun*), *Alphabetarium auicularum* (lost),

---

[20] See R. Lovatt, 'The *Imitation of Christ* in Late Medieval England', *Transactions of the Royal Historical Society*, 5th ser. 18 (1968), 97–121; it seems likely that Bale was referring to the Latin version and not to its English translation (which was later than Walter Hilton), since the incipit is precisely that of the Latin.

[21] *Catalogus*, i. 654; *In septem Psalmos* and *Sermones contra Lutherum* appear in *The English Works of John Fisher*, ed. J. E. B. Mayor, EETS ES 27 (1876), 1–267 and 311–48 respectively.

[22] *Catalogus*, i. 648–9, *Index*, p. 195.

[23] *Catalogus*, i. 631–2, see STC 278–81; to Alcock is also ascribed (with neither incipit nor language) *Abbatiam Spiritus sancti*, doubtless from one of the three prints, STC 13608.7, 13609–10.

and *Templum crystallinum* (*Temple of Glass*).²⁴ The last is, of course, no longer attributed to Hawes.²⁵

If Bale's list of Hawes's works indicates a lack of close knowledge, the same cannot be said of his account of John Skelton's writings (24). Here a much longer list is found, with only two exceptions, without incipit. Forty of these items derive from a close reading of *The Garland of Laurel* lines 1172–502, as is obvious not only from the titles but more clearly from the order in which they are cited; that reading must have been earlier than Bale's inclusion of Skelton in his *Index*, and indeed that earlier listing corrects one mistake in the order in the *Catalogus*.²⁶ Added to this are twelve items not from this source: the *Garland* itself is a logical entry, plus *Philippum passerculum* and *Cur ad curiam non uenis*, both probably from independent printed editions; seven more entries include the translation of Diodorus Siculus (24A) without incipit and two texts with incipits.²⁷ But did Bale obtain so much from printed sources?— the *Index* does not list the *Garland* at all, and gives the source of the list as 'Ex collectis Edwardi Braynewode', a London acquaintance of Bale's.²⁸

The longest entry concerning a medieval writer in the vernacular is inevitably that for Chaucer. Since this entry has been much examined by critics previously, only the most important points need mention. The first twenty-four items, all but one with incipits, seem to be drawn from and ordered by the 1542 reissue of Thynne's edition of 1532; that it was the reissue is shown by the inclusion of the *Plowman's Tale*, first found along with Chaucer's works in 1542.²⁹ This explains the inclusion of items such as the *Testament of Criseyde*, *The Flour of Curtesy*,

---

[24] Respectively STC 12948, 12942.5, 12945, 12953, and 17033.3; see *Stephen Hawes: The Minor Poems*, ed. F. W. Gluck and A. B. Morgan, EETS OS 271 (1974), pp. xi–xii.
[25] See the edition of the poem by J. Schick, EETS ES 60 (1891), pp. lxxv–lxxxv.
[26] *Catalogus*, i. 651–2, *Index*, p. 254; both listings omit 'The Balade also of the Mustarde Tarte' (*Garland* 1245); see *John Skelton: The Complete English Poems*, ed. J. Scattergood (Harmondsworth, 1983), no. xxi.
[27] The three identified works are STC 22610, 22594, and 22615–17 respectively.
[28] See *Index*, new introduction, p. xx, and *Catalogus*, i. 718.
[29] *Catalogus*, i. 525–7, cf. *Index*, pp. 74–8. The 1532 edition is STC 5068, the 1542 edition appeared in two, very slightly differing, prints, STC 5069, 5070. See J. E. Blodgett, 'William Thynne', in P. G. Ruggiers (ed.), *Editing Chaucer: The Great Tradition* (Norman, Okla., 1984), 35–52.

The Testament of Love, La Belle Dame sans Mercy (6B, here *Super impia domina*) under Chaucer's name. The remainder of the list goes back to pick up some items from the edition that had been omitted in their due sequence, but in part derives from further research. The Retractions to the *Canterbury Tales* presumably furnished the title, without incipit, of *De leone et eius dignitate*, and possibly *Hymnos amatorios*; the Prologue to the *Legend of Good Women* the *Vitam D. Ceciliae*, *Origenis tractatum*, and probably *Amores Palaemonis et Arcyti* (since the incipit given to the first item, *The Canterbury Tales*, is that of the Knight's Tale). One item, *De curia Veneris* with its incipit *In Maio cum uirescerent*, seems identifiable with a poem now known to survive in only one manuscript, now Cambridge University Library Gg. 4. 27 (part 1, fo. 8b), but there is no evidence that it was known to Bale.[30]

In some ways Bale's information about Gower is more interesting than that about Chaucer: Chaucer was already accepted as the most important native poet, and most of his works had appeared, often more than once, in print. Gower's English *Confessio Amantis* had, by 1557, been printed three times, by Caxton in 1493, and by Berthelette in 1532 and 1554.[31] But, though this duly appears as the second item on Bale's list, Bale also reveals an extensive knowledge of Gower's Latin and, more surprisingly, also French writings. The *Index* reveals that Bale had seen a manuscript at All Souls' College, Oxford (now numbered 98), which provided him with eight of his Latin works and their incipits, including the *Vox clamantis* and the *Chronica Tripertita* and also the French *De coniugii dignitate* (noted as *Gallice* in the *Index*).[32] It is probably from a Latin

---

[30] *IMEV* 1506; see facsimile of the manuscript with introductory material by M. B. Parkes and R. Beadle (3 vols., Norman, Okla., 1979), and E. P. Hammond, 'A Parliament of Birds', *Journal of English and Germanic Philology*, 7 (1907–8), 105–9.

[31] *STC* 12142–4.

[32] *Catalogus*, i. 524–5, *Index*, pp. 208–10. See the account of the manuscript in G. C. Macaulay, *The Complete Works of John Gower*, 4 vols. (Oxford, 1899–1902), iv, pp. lx–lxii; I am indebted also to the generosity of Professor Andrew Watson for allowing me to see his forthcoming new description. The incipit Bale gives for the French text, 'Qualiter creator omnium rerum Deus', shows that All Souls 98, when Bale saw it, had not lost a folio after fo. 131 with the start of the French text (known as *Traitié*, Macaulay, i. 379–92).

statement found in that same manuscript (fo. 135ᵛ) that Bale learned of his first entry, *Speculum meditantis, Gallicè*, which he knew to be in ten books but for which he produces no incipit. The work seems to have gained little circulation: in the single surviving manuscript, now Cambridge University Library MS Additional 3035, it is indeed divided into ten parts, but there is no indication that this copy could have been known to Bale. The source of the *Ad eundem [sc. Henricum quartum] de laude pacis*, beginning *Nobilis ac digne rex Henrice*, is Thynne's edition of Chaucer (fo. 375ᵛ) where it is correctly assigned to Gower.[33]

Manuscripts again supplemented and perhaps replaced the meagre printed materials in the information concerning Walter Hilton. The *Scalam spiritualem* could have been known from the Wynkyn de Worde edition, produced first in 1494 but reissued several times up to 1533.[34] But the *Index* shows Bale to have seen the text in Magdalen College, Oxford, where MS Lat. 141 contains a copy.[35] The only other Hilton text that was printed was that known now as *Mixed Life*, issued separately in [1530?] *STC* 14041 and along with the *Scale* subsequently; this appears as *De communi uita, ad laicum* (in the *Index* as *De vita communi*). Manuscripts are the source of the remainder. The *De utilitate religionis* is identifiable from its incipit as the text now known as *Epistola de utilitate et prerogativis religionis*; the *De consolatione in tentationibus* as *Epistola ad quemdam seculo renunciare volentem*.[36] But Bale seems to have become confused by the similarity of opening of a number of Hilton's personal Latin writings: these last two wisely omit the address; but the greeting seems to have produced two titles for the work now known as *De imagine peccati—De idolo cordis* and, more puzzlingly, *De tolerandis imaginibus*.[37] The interest

---

[33] The *Chronicon Ricardi secundi*, with incipit 'Opus humanum sit inquirere', is a double of the *Cronica Tripertita* with the gloss (iv. 314 margin) giving the incipit; the *Epigrammata quaedam*, with incipit 'Alta petens aquila uolat alitque', resembles Macaulay, iv. 344 *Prophecia*, but is not identical with it.
[34] *Catalogus*, i. 569; *STC* 14042–5. [35] *Index*, p. 106.
[36] See *Walter Hilton's Latin Writings*, ed. J. P. H. Clark and C. Taylor, Analecta Cartusiana, 124 (1987), i. 103–73, ii. 245–98.
[37] Ibid. i. 69–102.

Visio Baleii: *An Early Literary Historian* 323

of the second lies in the fact that Hilton did indeed write on this subject, and that Bale includes the tract, there called *De adorandis imaginibus*, with its correct incipit *Nunquid Domini nostri crucifixi*, under the name of the Dominican Thomas Palmer; the source of Bale's misattribution to Palmer seems to be a manuscript then as now in Merton College Oxford (now 68), where Hilton's work is so ascribed.[38] But the source of his confusion under Hilton appears to have been a copy belonging to Aylot Holte, a pensioned Benedictine from Bury St Edmunds, which may well have come from Bury.[39]

Hilton's *Mixed Life* had also appeared in print as the second item of a Pynson volume in 1516, along with an abbreviated version of Capgrave's *Nova legenda Anglie*; the full edition of this work came from de Worde's press the same year.[40] Capgrave's text duly appears in Bale's *Catalogus* with its correct incipit, but after a long list of other works, almost all of them biblical commentaries.[41] Two other secular works are included. The first is *De nobilibus Henricis*, now known as *Liber de illustribus Henricis*; Bale, according to the *Index* (p. 188), saw this at Magdalen College, Oxford, but it is now no longer there.[42] The second is *Vitam Hunfridi ducis*, that is of Humfrey, duke of Gloucester (with no incipit); the text is mentioned in *Liber de illustribus Henricis*, from which Bale took his information. Two of the commentaries, that on Acts and that on the

---

[38] *Catalogus*, i. 540, and for Bale's knowledge of the Merton manuscript see *Index*, p. 449; see same edition i. 175–214—the confusion over the attribution was first sorted out by J. Russell-Smith, 'Walter Hilton and a Tract in Defence of the Veneration of Images', *Dominican Studies*, 7 (1954), 180–214.

[39] See *Index*, pp. 105–6 and added note, p. xxv; the other text in the manuscript was the *Epistola ad quemdam seculo renunciare volentem*, but neither of the surviving copies of that text seems to derive from Bury—nor does either contain the *De imagine peccati*. Two other works, both with incipits, complete Bale's listing.

[40] *STC* 4602 and 4601 respectively; the attribution to Capgrave seems to be a confusion on Bale's part (see P. J. Lucas, 'John Capgrave and the *Nova Legenda Anglie*: A Survey', *The Library*, 5th ser. 25 (1970), 1–10).

[41] *Catalogus*, i. 582–3, *Index*, pp. 188–9. For a detailed examination of Capgrave's works, extensively using Bale, see A.de Meijer, 'John Capgrave, OESA (1393–1464)', *Augustiniana*, 5 (1955), 400–40, 7 (1957), 118–48, 531–75, and P. J. Lucas 'John Capgrave, OSA (1393–1464), Scribe and "Publisher"', *Transactions of the Cambridge Bibliographical Society*, 5 (1969), 1–35.

[42] *Index*, p. 188; the text was edited by F. C. Hingeston, *Memorials of Henry the Fifth*, Rolls Series (1858), 63–75; the manuscripts now known are Corpus Christi College Cambridge 408 (Capgrave's autograph) and BL Cotton Tiberius A. viii.

creeds, are still to be found where Bale saw them, in Balliol College library.⁴³ But the *Index* does not include the remaining commentaries, and it is uncertain where Bale saw them—for see them he certainly did, judging by the nine incipits provided in the *Catalogus*. Only two of them have yet been identified in surviving manuscripts, but they may give the clue to the source of Bale's knowledge: the commentary on Genesis is to be found in Oriel College MS 32, that on Exodus in Oxford Bodleian MS Duke Humfrey b. 1.⁴⁴ Both these copies are presentation volumes for Duke Humfrey, written by the same scribe almost certainly at Capgrave's own Augustinian friary at King's Lynn under the author's guidance.⁴⁵ It seems likely, rather than these copies, it was their ancestors or congeners that Bale had seen.⁴⁶ Bale shows no awareness of Capgrave's many English writings.⁴⁷

Of John Lydgate's works (4), as might be expected, Bale provides an ample list, though it is one largely without incipits. Much had appeared in print, and for some those editions may be the source.⁴⁸ This probably explains *De bello Thebano* (*Sege* (or *Destruction*) *of Thebes*), issued about 1497 by Wynkyn de Worde, *Vitam S. Mariae ad Henricum 5* (*Life of our Lady*), first produced by Caxton in 1484, *De casibus uirorum illustrium* (*Fall of Princes*), and from the last *The Dance Machabre* (whose title has been mangled in both *Catalogus* and *Index* to *De saltu Machabaei*!) and some others.⁴⁹ But Bale's investigations had certainly not stopped with printed texts: he has a title and

---

⁴³ As located by *Index*, p. 188, now respectively Balliol 189 and 190; Lucas, 'John Capgrave', 3–4 identifies these as the presentation copies made for bishop William Grey of Ely, and given by him to Balliol.

⁴⁴ See F. Stegmüller, *Repertorium*, 11 vols. (Madrid, 1950–80), nos. 4283–7, 4291, 4302, 4301, 4303.1, 4303.2).

⁴⁵ See exhibition catalogue *Duke Humfrey's Library and the Divinity School 1488–1988* (Oxford, 1988), items nos. 30–1 with reproductions from each.

⁴⁶ Bale cites materials from what he describes as the University Library at Oxford (see *Index*, index, p. 578). Bale owned three Capgrave manuscripts, but none of them included biblical commentary: see H. McCusker, 'Books and Manuscripts formerly in the Possession of John Bale', *The Library*, 4th ser. 16 (1935), 144–65 at p. 151 nos. 41–3.

⁴⁷ For instance, the lives of St Augustine or St Gilbert of Sempringham, or the *Tretis of the Orderes* (all ed. J. J. Munro, EETS OS 140 (1910)), the *Chronicle of England* (ed. F. C. Hingeston, Rolls Series (1858)), the *Life of St Katharine of Alexandria* (ed. C. Horstmann, EETS OS 100 (1893)), the *Solace of Pilgrimes* (ed. C. A. Mills (London, 1911)), or the *Life of St Norbert* (ed. C. L. Smetana (Toronto, 1977)).

⁴⁸ See the early items listed in *STC* 17005–38.

⁴⁹ Catalogus, i. 586–7, *Index*, pp. 228–31; *STC* 17031, 17023, 3175, 3177.

Visio Baleii: *An Early Literary Historian* 325

incipit for *Lives of St Edmund and St Fremund*, the *Kalendar*, and others. Hoccleve (3), like Lydgate, was known as a disciple of Chaucer. His *Regement of Princes* is mentioned without incipit, and six short works, the first five of which have an incipit. These six appear in the same order in the *Index*, where Bale's knowledge is said to derive from a manuscript 'Ex museo domini de Russell'.[50]

In the case of Reginald Pecock (8A) Bale acknowledges the source of his information as the account given by the fifteenth-century Thomas Gascoigne, and it is from the same source that he gives a fairly full history of Pecock's career. Only one of the twenty-four works listed has an incipit: this is *De fide (The Book of Faith)*. Though, like the rest of Pecock's works, this text survived the destruction of its author's books at his recantation or soon after in only one copy, it seems that Bale had indeed seen it.[51] A religious writer with whom Bale had much more sympathy was William Thorpe (1G). Here the source of his information was the English print put out in [1530?], of which Bale himself had made a Latin translation.[52]

The importance of translation in the late medieval period is made clear in the biographies of Alexander Barclay (22B–D) and of Lord Berners (25). 'Multa tamen in Anglicum sermonem eleganter ille transtulit ac scripsit', Bale says of Barclay, and lists *Nauim stultiferam* (22B), the five eclogues attributed to Mantuan (22C), the *De bello Iugurthino* of Sallust (22D), the last, together with the *De pronunciatione Gallica*, with incipit.[53] Bale claims that Lord Berners, John Bourchier, likewise enriched English with translations from French, Spanish, and Italian: his renderings of Froissart (25A), *Huon of Burdeux* (25B),

---

[50] *Catalogus*, i. 537, *Index*, p. 448; the list of Russell's books at a later date, M. St Clare Byrne and G. S. Thomson, '"My Lord's Books": The Library of Francis, Second Earl of Bedford, in 1584', *RES* 7 (1931), 385–405 does not reveal this.

[51] *Catalogus*, i. 594, *Index*, pp. 337–9 where a list of titles in English is also given; for Gascoigne see the extracts printed by J. E. Thorold Rogers, *Loci e libro veritatum* (Oxford, 1881), 26–49, 99, 104, 208–18, and the biography in A. B. Emden, *A Biographical Register of the University of Oxford to AD 1500*, 3 vols. (Oxford, 1957–9), ii. 745–8. Whether Bale had seen Trinity College, Cambridge MS B. 14. 45 is uncertain.

[52] *Catalogus*, i, 538; the translation, now surviving only partially, was entered by Bale into the manuscript of *Fasciculus Zizaniorum*, now Bodleian e Mus. 86, for which see my edition, EETS OS 301 (1993), pp. xxx–xxxvii.

[53] *Catalogus*, i. 723, *Index*, pp. 19–20; nine other works are listed, all without incipit.

Arthur of Lytell Brytayne (25C) all derive from French, *The Golden Boke of Marcus Aurelius* (25D) and *Castellum amoris* ultimately from Spanish though directly from French, but it is not clear what Bale had in mind for Italian.⁵⁴ Not surprisingly, Bale's account of Sir Thomas More (26) is intemperate in its opprobrium, and his listing of More's literary achievement is partial. There is a concentration on More's polemic, on his letters, and translations. The text that we know as *The History of King Richard III* (26B) appears under the title of *Vitam Eduardi quinti*, with an incipit that makes it clear that, despite the Latin language in which it is clothed, Bale knew it from the English version incorporated into the chronicles of Hall and Hardyng.⁵⁵

Bale's chief interest for the modern critic may well be for his information about manuscripts, and the circulation of medieval texts—the first at least was certainly one of Bale's own concerns. Bale's preference for manuscripts is very evident from his brief entry for William Caxton (15), a figure that he damns with faint praise as 'uir non omnino stupidus, aut ignauia torpens, sed propagandae suae gentis memoriae studiosus admodum'.⁵⁶ The first six works listed are evidently regarded as historical, even though they include as the final item a *Historiam Arthuri regis* recognizable from its opening words as Thomas Malory's *Morte Darthur* (though Malory's name (13), perhaps surprisingly, seems to appear nowhere in Bale's works). The remaining seven titles show again a strong historical bent, though they are recognized as translations. Bale also mentions Caxton's printing of Chaucer.⁵⁷ Caxton is acknowledged as the source for most of Bale's information on John Tiptoft (17E): only *Tullius*

---

⁵⁴ *Catalogus*, i. 706, *Index*, pp. 183-4; for the first three see *OBLMVP* nn. pp. 488-91, for the last *STC* 21739.5; the *Index* states enigmatically 'Ex lingua Italica, li. plu.'. See N. F. Blake, 'Lord Berners: A Survey', *Medievalia et Humanistica*, NS 2 (1971), 119-32.

⁵⁵ *Catalogus*, i. 655, incipit 'Aeternus Deus ad suam miser.', for which see the opening paragraph (omitted in the 1557 edition) printed by R. S. Sylvester (New Haven, 1963), p. xxv; this text does not appear in the long list in *Index*, pp. 445-7.

⁵⁶ *Catalogus*, i. 618, *Index*, pp. 119-21.

⁵⁷ The second half appear to be *STC* 7269, 4920, 15375, 3259, 13175, perhaps 4602 (but erroneously, since the print is Pynson's), and 14077 e.6 or 8 respectively.

de Amicitia is provided with an incipit, though six other texts are mentioned.[58]

Has Bale anything more than a catalogue to offer? His literary judgement is certainly often subordinated to his sectarian bias: Walter Hilton comes in for grave disapproval as a member of a 'private religion', though Bale erroneously placed him in the Carthusian order, and unwarranted slurs are cast upon his idleness and morals (i. 569). Capgrave, though also a member of a despised religious order, fares rather better, the superstitions of his biblical commentaries being attributed to the unhappiness of the times (i. 582–3); judging by Bale's comments, this is explicable from Capgrave's greater interest in England's history and from his admiration for Humfrey, duke of Gloucester, one whom Bale in the very next entry praised in the most fulsome terms (i. 583–4). Lydgate similarly escapes condemnation for his monastic status: here the acclaim comes both for his enrichment of the English language from imitation of Chaucer and of foreign models, and for his translations especially of classical (pseudo-)historical texts, and of Dante and Petrarch (i. 586–7). Skelton, despite the deplorable concubine, gains credit for his invectives against Wolsey. Langland, however, though given the wrong christian name of Robert, is recognized as a disciple of John Wyclif, and hence as one rightly battling 'contra apertas Papistarum blasphemias', prophesying from afar the happy state achieved in Bale's own time (i. 474) —achieved, however, despite the persecutions of men such as More, 'impudens Christi aduersarius' (i. 656).

Despite his obvious prejudices, however, Bale was an astute critic. He was entirely willing to admit the limitations on his knowledge: he had been unable to discover whether Langland wrote anything before *Visionem Petri Aratoris*, nor whether he had obtained his undoubted erudition at Oxford or Cambridge. The enrichment of the English language he regarded as a worthy objective: John Tiptoft (i. 621), 'Musarum dulcedine captus', drew material from Italian into English. James I 'in uernaculo sermone, ornatissima carmina faciebat' (ii. 217—though, as

---

[58] *Catalogus*, i. 620, *Index*, p. 259; the surname in both is given as 'Tipitotus'.

noted above, p. 318, the opinion must be second-hand), whilst Hoccleve, 'exquisita quadam Anglici sermonis eloquentia, post Chaucerum, cuius fuerat discipulus, patriam ornauit linguam' (i. 537). The vernacular is not, however, in itself a concept to which Bale devotes much attention: the writers who had provided the record of England's history had written in several languages, and a reader who came to the *Catalogus* without antecedent preoccupations might be forgiven for overlooking the comments that have been selected here. Most of the fourteen hundred authors included in the two volumes wrote entirely in Latin; the works even of authors such as Langland, whose output was only in English, appear in Latin dress. The entry for Chaucer is certainly a comparatively lengthy one (i. 525–7); but even then it must be admitted that Wyclif (i. 450–6), or even the earlier and less controversial Robert Grosseteste (i. 304–7) gain more space. It is, however, important that a start had been made: Bale had acknowledged the contribution of the common tongue.

Much remains to be done before Bale's standing as a bibliographer, let alone as an incipient literary critic, can be properly assessed. Bale himself often acknowledged that his information came indirectly, through earlier biographies, through chronicles, or through surveys; in particular, the extent of Bale's debt to his forerunner in England, John Leland, a debt often warmly noted, remains to be gauged, even if, because of the loss of materials, it can never be accurately quantified. Equally uncharted is Bale's influence on others, outside the evident debt of men such as Thomas Tanner who later engaged in updating Bale's bio-bibliographical information.[59] It would perhaps be fanciful to suggest that Bale's work had more wide-ranging effects: that it focused literary study on the historical development of named writers, to the diminution of interest either in form or in works regardless of authorship, and that consequently only in very recent times have major areas of fifteenth-century writing (areas such as lyrics, plays, and much religious prose) been reclaimed as legitimate areas of study. Acceptance

---

[59] See his *Bibliotheca Britannico-Hibernica* (London, 1748).

Visio Baleii: *An Early Literary Historian* 329

of anonymity remains highly reluctant, and neglect tends to follow its establishment. But Bale's method, even if not a direct cause of later critical concentration, at least coincided with it in some areas: the preoccupation of much study of fifteenth-century English writing with the 'Chaucer tradition' could trace its lineage through John Bale's *Catalogus*.[60] Even though Bale himself had more theological and social sympathy with 'Robert' Langland than with John Lydgate, the disciples of Chaucer tended to have discoverable names, whereas the imitators of *Piers Plowman* did not. The importance of *The Oxford Book of Late Medieval Verse and Prose* lies not least in its liberal boundaries: unlike Bale's view of the fifteenth-century literary scene, Douglas Gray's makes generous admission of the interests of anonymous texts. As such it fills out some part of the gap which Bale lamented even whilst he celebrated his native inheritance: 'ingens ille librorum thesaurus, quem collegi, et hoc in opere coaceruaui, in Bibliothecis ac coenobijs nostris aliquando delituit: quos nunc partim obliuio deleuit et obliterauit, partim iniuria ac iniquitas exulceratissimorum temporum obscurauit et extinxit.'[61]

---

[60] For a recent example see S. Lerer, *Chaucer and his Readers: Imagining the Author in Late Medieval England* (Princeton, 1993), which gives references to earlier comparable studies.
[61] *Catalogus*, i. *Epistola Nuncupatoria*, sig.α.3.

A Bibliography of the Published Writings of Douglas Gray

COMPILED BY JOERG O. FICHTE

1960
'In what estate so euer I be', *N&Q* 7 (1960), 403–4.

1961
'A Middle English Epitaph', *N&Q* 8 (1961), 132–5.
'Sir Orfeo, l. 565', *Archiv*, 198 (1961), 167–9.

1962
'An Inscription at Hexham', *Archaeologia Aeliana*, 40 (1962), 185–8.

1963
'Two Songs of Death', *Neuphilologische Mitteilungen*, 64 (1963), 52–74.
'The Five Wounds of Our Lord', *N&Q* 10 (1963), 50–1, 82–9, 127–34, 163–8.

1967
'A Middle English Verse at Warkworth', *N&Q* 14 (1967), 131–2.

1968
'Two Middle English Quatrains and Robert Holcot', *N&Q* 15 (1968), 125.
'A Copy of Lydgate's *Dietary* at Lille', *N&Q* 15 (1968), 245–6.

1969
Spenser, *The Faerie Queene*, Book I, ed. (London, 1969).
(With J. C. Maxwell) 'An Echo of Chaucer', *N&Q* 16 (1969), 170.

1970
'Later Poetry: The Courtly Tradition', in W. F. Bolton (ed.), *The New History of Literature*, Vol. 1: *The Middle Ages*. Sphere History of Literature, 1 (London, 1970), 313–67; repr. as The Penguin History of Literature, Vol. 1 (1993).

1972
Themes and Images in the Medieval English Religious Lyric (London and Boston, 1972).

1974
'A Scottish "Flower of Chivalry" and his Book', *Words: Wai-te-ata Studies in Literature*, 4 (1974), 22–34.

'Notes on some Middle English Charms', in B. Rowland (ed.), *Chaucer and Middle English Studies in Honour of Rossell Hope Robbins* (1974), 56–71.

1975
A Selection of Religious Lyrics, ed., Clarendon and Medieval and Tudor Series (Oxford, 1975; repr. Exeter, 1992).

Guillaume Caoursin: The Siege of Rhodes (1482), Translated by John Kaye; and Aesopus: The Book of Subtyl Histories and Fables of Esope (1484); Facsim. Reproduction, introd. (Delmar, NY, 1975).

1979
'Chaucer and "Pite"', in Mary Salu and Robert T. Farrell (eds.), *J. R. R. Tolkien, Scholar and Storyteller: Essays in Memoriam* (Ithaca, NY and London, 1979), 173–203.

Robert Henryson, Medieval and Renaissance Authors Series (Leiden, 1979).

Norman Davis, Douglas Gray, Patricia Ingham, and Anne Wallace-Hadrill (eds.), *A Chaucer Glossary* (Oxford, 1979).

1981
'A Middle English Illustrated Poem', in P. L. Heyworth (ed.), *Medieval Studies for J. A. W. Bennett Aetatis suae LXX* (Oxford, 1981), 185–205.

'A Tribute to J. A. W. Bennett (1911–1981)', *MÆ* 50 (1981), 205–14.

'"Th'ende is every tales strengthe": Henryson's *Fables*', in Roderick J. Lyall and Felicity Riddy (eds.) *Proceedings of the Third International Conference on Scottish Language and Literature (Medieval and Renaissance)* (Stirling and Glasgow, 1981), 225–50.

1982
'Death in Late Medieval Literature', *Australasian Language and Literature Association XXI: Proceedings and Papers* (Palmerston North, 1982), 40–63.

A Marriage of Mercury and Philology. An Inaugural Lecture delivered before the University of Oxford, 21 May 1981 (Oxford, 1982).

1983

'Songs and Lyrics', in Piero Boitani and Anna Torti (eds.), *Literature in Fourteenth-Century England*, Tübinger Beiträge zur Anglistik, 5 (Tübingen and Cambridge, 1983), 83–98.

'Captain Cook and the English Vocabulary', in E. G. Stanley and Douglas Gray (eds.), *Five Hundred Years of Words and Sounds: A Festschrift for Eric Dobson* (Cambridge, 1983), 49–62.

Douglas Gray and E. G. Stanley (eds.), *Middle English Studies Presented to Norman Davis in Honour of His Seventieth Birthday* (Oxford, 1983).

E. G. Stanley and Douglas Gray (eds.), *Five Hundred Years of Words and Sounds: A Festschrift for Eric Dobson* (Cambridge, 1983).

1984

'Rough Music: Some Early Invectives and Flytings', *YES* 14 (1984), 21–43; repr. in Claude Rawson (ed. and introd.), Alvin Kernan (introd.), *English Satire and the Satiric Tradition* (Oxford, 1984).

'The Robin Hood Poems', *Poetica*, 18 (1984), 1–39.

'Chaucer and Allusion', in Sergio Rossi (ed.), *Saggi sul Rinascimento* (Milan, 1984), 7–26.

1985

'Eric John Dobson 1913–1984', *Proceedings of the British Academy*, 71 (1985), 533–8.

The Oxford Book of Late Medieval Verse and Prose, ed. (Oxford, 1985).

1986

J. A. W. Bennett, edited and completed by Douglas Gray, *Middle English Literature*, Oxford History of English Literature, Vol. 1, Part 2 (Oxford, 1986).

'La poesia religiosa inglese e la tradizione latina', in Claudio Leonardi and Giovanni Orlandi (eds.) *Aspetti della Letteratura Latina nel Secolo XIII*, Quaderni del Centro per il collegamento degli studi medievali e umanistici nell'Università di Perugia, 15 (Perugia, Florence, 1986), 169–92.

'Books of Comfort', in Gregory Kratzmann and James Simpson (eds.), *Medieval English Religious and Ethical Literature: Essays in Honour of G. H. Russell* (Cambridge, 1986), 209–21.

1987

'A Middle English Secular Illustrated Poem', *Journal of the Department of English, University of Calcutta*, 22 (1986–7), 1–4.

'Chaucer and "Gentilesse"', in G. H. V. Bunt, E. S. Kooper, J. L. Mackenzie, and D. R. M. Wilkinson (eds.), *One Hundred Years of English Studies in Dutch Universities* (Amsterdam, 1987), 1–27.

Explanatory notes to *The Miller's Prologue and Tale*, *The Reeve's Prologue and Tale*, and *The Cook's Prologue and Tale* in *The Riverside Chaucer*, ed. L. D. Benson (Cambridge, Mass., 1987).

1988

'Medieval English Studies at Oxford', *Medieval English Studies Newsletter*, 19 (1988), 1–3.

'A Note on Sixteenth-Century Purism', in E. G. Stanley and T. F. Hoad (eds.), *Words for Robert Burchfield's Sixty-Fifth Birthday* (Woodbridge, 1988), 103–19.

'St Augustine and Medieval Literature', in Edward B. King and Jacqueline T. Shaefer (eds.), *St Augustine and his Influence in the Middle Ages*, Sewanee Medieval Studies, 3 (Sewanee, 1988), 19–58.

'A Seventeenth-Century Collector of Medieval Devotional Verse', in D. M. Reeks (ed.), *Sentences: Essays presented to Alan Ward* (Southampton, 1988), 119–29.

The collected papers of Nevill Coghill: Shakespearean and Medievalist, introd. (Brighton, 1988).

1989

'Sailing in Another Direction: Some Early New Zealand Writing', in Luigi Sampietro (ed.), *Declarations of Cultural Independence in the English-Speaking World: A Symposium* (Milan, 1989), 69–97.

'Humanism and Humanisms in Late Medieval English Literature', in Sergio Rossi and Dianella Savoia (eds.), *Italy and the English Renaissance* (Milan, 1989), 25–44.

'Medieval English Ballads', in Patricia Shaw *et al.* (eds.), *Actas del Primer Congreso Internacional de la Sociedad Española de Lengua y Literatura Inglesa Medieval* (Oviedo, 1989), 129–54.

1990

'Some Chaucerian Themes in Scottish Writers', in Ruth Morse and Barry Windeatt (eds.), *Chaucer Traditions: Studies in Honour of Derek Brewer* (Cambridge, 1990), 81–90.

'Some Pre-Elizabethan Examples of an Elizabethan Art', in Edward Chaney and Peter Mack (eds.) *England and the Continental Renaissance: Essays in Honour of J. B. Trapp* (Woodbridge, 1990), 23–36.

'Notes on Some Medieval Mystical, Magical and Moral Cats', in H. Phillips (ed.), *Langland, the Mystics and the Medieval English Religious Tradition: Essays in Honour of S. S. Hussey* (Woodbridge, 1990), 185–202.
'Popular Religion and Late Medieval Literature', in Piero Boitani and Anna Torti (eds.) *Religion in the Poetry and Drama of the Late Middle Ages in England* (Cambridge, 1990), 1–28.
'Medieval Literature and the Medieval World', in M. Coyle *et al*. (eds.) *Encyclopedia of Literature and Criticism* (London, 1990), 69–81.

1991

'"Of sunne ne mone had thay no nede": Notes on the Imagery of Light in a Middle English Text', in Robert G. Benson and Eric W. Naylor (eds.) *Essays in Honor of Edward B. King* (Sewanee, 1991), 87–108.

1992

'Typology and Some Middle English Religious Lyrics', in Hugh Keenan (ed.), *Typology and English Medieval Literature*, Georgia State Literary Studies (New York, 1992), 275–88.
'*Hadlowe*: An Unrecorded Middle English Hare Word?', *N&Q* 39 (1992), 1, 26.

1993

'Norman Davis 1913–1989', *Proceedings of the British Academy*, 80 (1993), 261–73.
'Josiah Relph: Dialect Poet', in L. Bauer and C. Franzen (eds.), *Of Pavlovas, Poetry and Paradigms: Essays in Honour of Harry Orsman* (Wellington, 1993), 175–9.
'Nicholas Bozon' and 'Sir Richard Roos', in C. S. Nicholls (ed.), *The Dictionary of National Biography: Missing Persons* (Oxford, 1993).

1994

Malcolm Godden, Douglas Gray, and T. F. Hoad (eds.), *From Anglo-Saxon to Early Middle English: Studies Presented to E. G. Stanley* (Oxford, 1994).
'An Early English *Entführung*: A Note on *Floris and Blauncheflur*', in Malcolm Godden, Douglas Gray, and T. F. Hoad (eds.) *From Anglo-Saxon to Early Middle English: Studies Presented to E. G. Stanley* (Oxford, 1994), 206–13.
'Bocase in Kent', in Renzo S. Crivelli and Luigi Sampietro (eds.), *Il passaggiere italiano: Saggi sulle letterature di lingua inglese in onore di Sergio Rossi*, Biblioteca di anglistica, 4 (Rome, 1994), 59–71.

'Virgil in Late Medieval Scotland: *Aeneid* and *Eneydos*', in G. Bystydzieńska and L. Kolek (eds.) *Papers for the 2nd Conference of the Polish Association for the Study of English, Kazimierz '93* (Lublin, 1994), 11–22.

1995

'"Pite for to here—Pite for to se": Some Scenes of Pathos in Late Medieval English Literature', Sir Israel Gollancz Memorial Lecture, *Proceedings of the British Academy*, 87 (1995), 67–99.

1996

Robert Henryson and William Dunbar, Authors of the Middle Ages 9 and 10 (Aldershot, 1996).

'Chaucer and the Art of Digression', *Studies in Medieval Language and Literature*, 11, The Japan Society for Medieval English Studies (1996), 21–47.

'Ends and Beginnings in the Earlier Sixteenth-Century Drama', in Ana M. Manzanas Calvo (ed.), *SEDERI VI* (Sociedad Española de Estudios Renacentistas Ingleses) (Spain, 1996), 75–91.

1997

'Medieval English Mystical Lyrics', in William F. Pollard and Robert Boenig (eds.), *Mysticism and Spirituality in Medieval England* (Cambridge, 1997).

'The Royal Entry in Sixteenth-Century Scotland', in S. Mapstone and J. Wood (eds.), *The Thistle and the Rose* (East Lothian, 1997).

Select Bibliography

(Place of publication is London, unless otherwise stated.)

PRIMARY SOURCES

ARBER, EDWARD (ed.), *The Revelation to the Monk of Evesham* (Westminster, 1869; repr. 1901).

AUDELAY, JOHN, 'Fifteenth Century Carols by John Audelay', ed. E. K. Chambers and F. Sidgwick, *Modern Language Review*, 5 (1910), 473–91; 6 (1911), 68–84.

—— *The Poems of John Audelay*, ed. James Orchard Halliwell, Percy Society, 14 (1844).

—— *The Poems of John Audelay*, ed. Ella Keats Whiting, EETS OS 184 (1931).

BALE, JOHN, *Index Britanniae Scriptorum*, ed. Reginald L. Poole and M. Bateson (1902); with supplementary introduction ed. Caroline Brett and James P. Carley (Cambridge, 1990).

—— *The Vocacyon of Johan Bale*, ed. Peter Happé and John N. King, Medieval and Renaissance Texts and Studies, 70 (1990).

BARR, HELEN (ed.), *The Piers Plowman Tradition* (1993).

BOCCACCIO, GIOVANNI, *Boccaccio on Poetry*, trans. C. G. Osgood (Princeton, 1930).

The Book of Vices and Virtues, ed. W. Nelson Francis, EETS OS 217 (1942).

BOWER, WALTER, *Scotichronicon*, vol. viii, ed. D. E. R. Watt (Aberdeen, 1987).

BRADSHAW, HENRY, *Life of Saint Werburge*, ed. Carl Horstmann, EETS OS 88 (1887).

BRAMPTON, THOMAS, *A Paraphrase on the Seven Penitential Psalms*, ed. William Henry Black, Percy Society, 7 (1843).

BRIDGET, ST, OF SWEDEN, *The Liber Celestis of St Bridget of Sweden*, ed. Roger Ellis, EETS OS 291 (1987).

—— *The Revelations of Saint Birgitta*, ed. William Patterson Cumming, EETS OS 178 (1929).

BRONSON, BERTRAND H. (ed.), *The Traditional Tunes of the Child Ballads*, 4 vols. (Princeton, 1959–72).

BROWN, CARLETON (ed.), *Religious Lyrics of the XVth Century* (Oxford, 1952).
CAVENDISH, GEORGE, *Metrical Visions by George Cavendish*, ed. A. S. G. Edwards (Columbia, SC, 1980).
CHAMPAGNE, THIBAUT DE, *Lyrics of Thibaut de Champagne*, ed. and trans. Kathleen J. Brahney, Garland Library of Medieval Literature, series A, 41 (New York, 1989).
CHARTIER, ALAIN, *The Poetical Works of Alain Chartier*, ed. J. C. Laidlaw (Cambridge, 1974).
CHAUCER, GEOFFREY, *The Riverside Chaucer*, ed. Larry D. Benson, 3rd edn. (Oxford, 1988).
Le Chevalier des Dames du Dolant Fortuné, ed. Jean Miquet (Ottawa, 1990).
CHILD, FRANCIS JAMES (ed.), *The English and Scottish Popular Ballads*, 5 vols. (Boston, 1882–98; repr. New York, 1965).
CHRISTINE DE PIZAN, *Poems of Cupid, God of Love: Christine de Pizan's 'Epistre au dieu d'Amours' and 'Dit de la Rose', Thomas Hoccleve's 'The Letter of Cupid'*, ed. Thelma. S. Fenster and Mary Carpenter Erler (Leiden, 1990).
CICERO, *De officiis*, ed. Walter Miller (Cambridge, Mass. and London, 1913)
—— *De inventione*, ed. and trans. H. M. Hubbell (London and Cambridge, Mass., 1949).
—— *On Duties [De officiis]*, ed. M. T. Griffin and E. M. Atkins (Cambridge, 1991).
DAVIS, NORMAN (ed.), *Non-Cycle Plays and Fragments*, EETS SS 1 (1970).
DESCHAMPS, EUSTACE, *Œuvres complètes*, ed. Le Marquis de Queux de Saint-Hilaire and Gaston Raynaud, 11 vols., SATF (Paris, 1878–1903).
The Digby Plays, ed. Donald C. Baker, John Murphy, and Louis B. Hall, EETS OS 283 (1982).
DOUGLAS, GAVIN, *The Shorter Poems of Gavin Douglas*, ed. Priscilla J. Bawcutt, STS, 4th ser. 3 (Edinburgh and London, 1967).
—— *Virgil's Aeneid, Translated into Scottish Verse by Gavin Douglas*, ed. David F. C. Coldwell, 4 vols., STS, 3rd ser. 25, 27, 28, 30 (Edinburgh and London, 1957–64).
DYBOSKI, ROMAN (ed.), *Songs, Carols, and other Miscellaneous Poems, from the Balliol MS 354, Richard Hill's Commonplace-Book*, EETS ES 101 (1908).
ELYOT, SIR THOMAS, *The Book Named The Governour*, ed. Henry Herbert Stephen Croft (1880).

—— *Four Political Treatises*, ed. Lillian Gottesman (Gainesville, Fla., 1967).

—— 'The Letters of Sir Thomas Elyot', ed. K. J. Wilson, *SP* 73 (1976), pp. i–xxx, 1–78.

Epistolae Obscurorum Virorum, ed. and trans. Francis Griffin Stokes (1909).

Evangelia Apocrypha, ed. Constantin Tischendorf (1876; Hildesheim, 1966).

FISHER, JOHN, *The English Works of John Fisher*, ed. John E. B. Mayor, EETS ES 27 (1876).

The Floure and the Leafe, The Assembly of Ladies, The Isle of Ladies, ed. Derek Pearsall, TEAMS (Kalamazoo, 1990).

Four Sons of Aymon: The Right Pleasant and Goodly History of the Four Sons of Aymon, ed. Octavia Richardson, 2 vols., EETS ES 44, 45 (1884–5).

FOXE, JOHN, *The Acts and Monuments of John Foxe*, 4th edn., ed. J. Pratt, 8 vols. (1877).

GOWER, JOHN, *The English Works of John Gower*, ed. G. C. Macaulay, 2 vols., EETS ES 81–2 (1900–1).

—— *The Latin Works of John Gower*, ed. G. C. Macaulay (Oxford, 1902).

GRANSON, OTON DE, *Oton de Granson: Sa vie et ses poésies*, ed. Arthur Piaget, Mémoires et documents publiés par la société de l'histoire de la Suisse romane (Lausanne and Geneva, 1941).

GREENE, RICHARD LEIGHTON (ed.), *The Early English Carols*, 2nd edn. (Oxford, 1977).

HARDYNG, JOHN, *The Chronicle of Iohn Hardyng*, ed. Henry Ellis (1812).

HAWES, STEPHEN, *Stephen Hawes: The Minor Poems*, ed. Florence W. Gluck and Alice B. Morgan, EETS OS 271 (1974).

[HAY, GILBERT], *The Buik of King Alexander the Conquerour*, ed. John Cartwright, 2 vols., STS, 4th ser. 16, 18 (Edinburgh, 1986; Aberdeen 1990).

HAY, GILBERT, *The Prose Works of Sir Gilbert Hay*, vol. iii, ed. Jonathan A. Glenn, STS, 4th ser. 21 (Edinburgh, 1993).

HENRYSON, ROBERT, *The Poems of Robert Henryson*, ed. Denton Fox (Oxford, 1981).

HILTON, WALTER, *Walter Hilton's Latin Writings*, ed. John P. H. Clark and Cheryl Taylor, Analecta Cartusiana, 124 (1987).

HOCCLEVE, THOMAS, 'The Formulary of Thomas Hoccleve', ed. E.-J. Y. Bentley, Ph.D. thesis (Emory, 1965).

HOCCLEVE, THOMAS, *Hoccleve's Works: The Minor Poems*, ed. Frederick J. Furnivall and I. Gollancz, 2 vols., EETS ES 61, 73 (1892, 1925), rev. Jerome Mitchell and A. I. Doyle (1970).
—— *The Letter of Cupid*, see Christine de Pizan.
—— *The Regement of Princes*, ed. Frederick J. Furnivall, EETS ES 72 (1897).
HORSTMANN, C. (ed.), *Yorkshire Writers, Richard Rolle of Hampole, an English Father of the Church and his Followers*, 2 vols. (1895–6).
HULL, ELEANOR, *The Seven Psalms: A Commentary on the Penitential Psalms translated from French into English by Dame Eleanor Hull*, ed. Alexandra Barratt, EETS OS 307 (1995).
JAMES I, *The Kingis Quair*, ed. John Norton-Smith (Leiden, 1981).
JEROME, ST, *Saint Jérôme: Lettres*, vol. iii, ed. J. Labourt (Paris, 1953).
JULIAN OF NORWICH, *A Book of Showings to the Anchoress Julian of Norwich*, ed. Edmund Colledge and James Walsh (Toronto, 1978).
KEMPE, MARGERY, *The Book of Margery Kempe*, ed. Sanford Brown Meech and Hope Emily Allen, EETS OS 212 (1940).
KENNEDY, PETER (ed.), *Folksongs of Britain and Ireland* (1975).
Lamprechts Alexander, ed. Karl Kinzel (Halle␣␣Salle, 1884).
Lancelot of the Laik, ed. W. W. Skeat, EETS OS 6 (1895; repr. 1965).
LEVERSEDGE, EDMUND, *The Vision of Edmund Leversedge*, ed. Wiesje Fimke Nijenhuis (Nijmegen, 1991).
Lollard Sermons, ed. Gloria Cigman, EETS OS 294 (1989).
LYDGATE, JOHN, *Lydgate's Fall of Princes*, ed. Henry Bergen, 4 vols., EETS ES 121–4 (1924–7).
—— *Minor Poems of John Lydgate*, ed. Henry Noble MacCracken, EETS OS 192 (1934).
—— *The Serpent of Division*, ed. Henry Noble MacCracken (London and New Haven, 1911).
—— *Lydgate's 'Siege of Thebes'*, ed. Axel Erdmann and Eilert Ekwall, 2 vols., EETS ES 108, 125 (1911, 1930).
—— *Lydgate's Temple of Glas*, ed. J. Schick, EETS ES 60 (1891).
The Macro Plays: The Castle of Perseverance, Wisdom, Mankind: A Facsimile Edition with Facing Transcription, ed. David Bevington (New York, 1972).
The Macro Plays, ed. Mark Eccles, EETS OS 262 (1969).
MAJOR, JOHN, *A History of Greater Britain*, ed. and trans. Archibald Constable, Scottish History Society, 10 (Edinburgh, 1892).
MALORY, THOMAS, *The Works of Sir Thomas Malory*, ed. Eugene Vinaver, 3 vols., 3rd edn. rev. P. J. C. Field (Oxford, 1990).

Melusine, ed. A. K. Donald, EETS ES 68 (1895).
Merlin, ed. Henry B. Wheatley, EETS OS 21 (rev. edn. 1877).
METHAM, JOHN, *The Works of John Metham*, ed. Hardin Craig, EETS OS 132 (1916).
MINNIS, A. J., and SCOTT, A. B. (eds.), *Medieval Literary Theory and Criticism c.1100–c.1375: The Commentary Tradition* (Oxford, 1988).
MONTAIGLON, ANATOLE, and ROTHSCHILD, J. DE (eds.), *Recueil des poésies françoises des xve et xvie siècles*, 13 vols. (Paris, 1855–78).
MORE, THOMAS, *The Complete Works of Sir Thomas More*, 15 vols., various editors (New Haven and London, 1963–).
—— *The English Works of Sir Thomas More*, ed. W. E. Campbell (1931).
MORRIS, RICHARD (ed.), *An Old English Miscellany*, EETS OS 49 (1872).
Morte Darthur (Alliterative and *Stanzaic)*, ed. Larry D. Benson, *King Arthur's Death* (Exeter, 1986).
The N-Town Play, ed. Stephen Spector, 2 vols., EETS SS 11 and 12 (Oxford, 1991).
NEVILL, WILLIAM, *The Castell of Pleasure*, ed. Roberta D. Cornelius, EETS OS 179 (1930).
Partenay: The Romans of Partenay, ed. Walter W. Skeat, EETS ES 22 (rev. edn. 1899).
PERCY, BISHOP THOMAS, *Bishop Percy's Folio Manuscript: Ballads and Romances*, ed. John W. Hales and Frederick J. Furnivall, 3 vols. (1868).
—— *Reliques of Ancient English Poetry... by Thomas Percy*, ed. Henry B. Wheatley, 3 vols. (1885).
PETRARCH, FRANCESCO, *Letters on Familiar Matters: Rerum familiarum libri, IX–XVI*, trans. Aldo S. Bernardo (Baltimore, 1982).
—— *Prose*, ed. G. Martellotti *et al.* (Milan and Naples, n.d.).
The Pilgrimage of the Soul, A Critical Edition of the Middle English Dream Vision, ed. Rosemary Potts McGerr, vol. i (New York, 1990).
PORETE, MARGUERITE, 'Margaret Porete: "The Mirror of Simple Souls", A Middle English Translation', ed. M. Doiron, *Archivo italiana per la storia della pietà*, 5 (1968), 247–382.
The Prose Life of Alexander, ed. J. S. Westlake, EETS OS 143 (1913).
The Quare of Jelusy, ed. J. Norton-Smith and I. Pravda, Middle English Texts, 3 (Heidelberg, 1976).
Ratis Raving, ed. R. Girvan, *Ratis Raving and Other Early Scots Poems on Morals*, STS, 3rd ser. 11 (Edinburgh and London, 1939).

The Receyt of the Ladie Kateryne, ed. Gordon Kipling, EETS OS 296 (Oxford, 1990).
A Revelation of Purgatory by an Unknown, Fifteenth-Century Woman Visionary, ed. Marta Powell Harley (Lewiston, 1985).
ROBBINS, ROSSELL HOPE (ed.), *Secular Lyrics of the XIVth and XVth Centuries* (2nd edn., Oxford, 1955).
The St Albans Chronicle, 1406–1420, ed. V. H. Galbraith, (Oxford, 1937).
St Patrick's Purgatory, ed. Robert Easting, EETS OS 298 (1991).
SKEAT, W. W. (ed.), *Chaucerian and Other Pieces*, supplement to *The Works of Geoffrey Chaucer*, 7 vols. (Oxford, 1897).
SKELTON, JOHN, *The Bibliotheca Historica of Diodorus Siculus, translated by John Skelton*, ed. F. M. Salter and H. L. R. Edwards, 2 vols., EETS OS 233, 239 (1956, 1957).
—— *The Book of the Laurel*, ed. F. W. Brownlow (1990).
—— *The Complete English Poems*, ed. John Scattergood (Harmondsworth, 1983).
—— *The Latin Writings of John Skelton*, ed. David R. Carlson, *SP*, Texts and Studies, 88 (1991).
—— *The Poetical Works of Skelton*, ed. Alexander Dyce, 2 vols. (1843).
—— *Skelton's Magnyfycence*, ed. Robert Lee Ramsay, EETS ES 98 (1906).
—— 'Skelton's *Speculum Principis*', ed. F. M. Salter, *Speculum*, 9 (1934), 25–37.
Speculum Christiani, ed. Gustaf Holmstedt, EETS OS 182 (1933).
STEFFENS, KARL (ed.), *Die Historia de preliis Alexandri Magni: Rezension J³* (Meisenheim am Glan, 1975).
STEVENS, JOHN (ed.), *Mediaeval Carols*, Musica Britannica, IV (1st edn. 1958, 2nd edn. 1970).
[*Suite du Merlin*]: *Merlin: roman en prose du xiiie siècle*, ed. Gaston Paris and Jacob Ulrich, 2 vols., SATF (Paris, 1886).
Thomas of Ercledoune, ed. Ingeborg Nixon, University of Copenhagen, Publications of the Department of English, 9 (Copenhagen, 1980–3).
THORPE, WILLIAM, *Testimony of William Thorpe 1407*, in *Two Wycliffite Texts*, ed. Anne Hudson, EETS OS 301 (1993).
TUBACH, FREDERIC C., *Index Exemplorum: A Handbook of Medieval Religious Tales*, FF Communications, 204 (Helsinki, 1969).
TURVILLE-PETRE, THORLAC (ed.), *Alliterative Poetry of the Later Middle Ages: An Anthology* (1989).

Valentine and Orson, ed. Arthur Dickson, EETS OS 204 (1937).
WALTON, JOHN, *Boethius: De Consolatione Philosophiae*, ed. Mark Science, EETS OS 170 (1927).
The Wars of Alexander, ed. Hoyt N. Duggan and Thorlac Turville-Petre, EETS SS 10 (1989).

SECONDARY SOURCES

ANDERSEN, FLEMMING G., and PETTITT, THOMAS, 'Mrs Brown of Falkland: A Singer of Tales', *Journal of American Folklore*, 92 (1979), 1–24.
AYERS, ROBERT W., 'Medieval History, Moral Purpose, and the Structure of Lydgate's *Siege of Thebes*', *PMLA* 73 (1958), 463–74.
BARR, HELEN, *Signes and Sothe: Language in the Piers Plowman Tradition* (Cambridge, 1994).
BEADLE, RICHARD, 'Monk Thomas Hyngham's Hand in the Macro Manuscript', in Richard Beadle and A. J. Piper (eds.), *New Science out of Old Books: Studies in Manuscripts and Early Printed Books in Honour of A. I. Doyle* (Aldershot, 1995).
—— (ed.), *The Cambridge Companion to Medieval English Theatre* (Cambridge, 1994).
BEVINGTON, DAVID, *From Mankind to Marlowe* (Cambridge, Mass., 1962).
BLAKE, N. F., *Caxton's Own Prose* (1973).
—— 'Lord Berners: A Survey', *Medievalia et Humanistica* NS 2 (1971), 119–32.
BLYTH, CHARLES R., 'Thomas Hoccleve's Other Master', *Mediaevalia*, 16 (1993), 349–59.
BOFFEY, JULIA, 'English Dream Poems of the Fifteenth Century and their French Connections', in Donald Maddox and Sara Sturm-Maddox (eds.), *Literary Aspects of Courtly Culture*, International Courtly Literature Society (Cambridge, 1994), 113–21.
—— 'Lydgate, Henryson, and the Literary Testament', *MLQ* 53 (1992), 41–56.
—— *Manuscripts of English Courtly Love Lyrics in the Later Middle Ages* (Woodbridge, 1985).
—— 'Richard Pynson's *Book of Fame* and the *Letter of Dydo*', *Viator*, 19 (1988), 339–53.
—— 'Women Authors and Women's Literacy in Fourteenth- and Fifteenth-Century England', in Carol M. Meale (ed.), *Women and*

Literature in Britain 1150–1500, Cambridge Studies in Medieval Literature, 17 (Cambridge, 1993), 159–82.

BOFFEY, JULIA and COWEN, JANET (eds.), *Chaucer and Fifteenth-Century Poetry*, King's College, London, Medieval Studies, 5 (1991).

BOKLUND-LAGOPOULOU, Karin, '*Judas*: The First English Ballad?', *MÆ* 62 (1993), 20–34.

BOWERS, JOHN M., 'Hoccleve's Huntington Holographs: The First "Collected Poems" in English', *Fifteenth-Century Studies*, 15 (1989), 27–51.

BREWER, DEREK (ed.), *Chaucer: The Critical Heritage*, 2 vols. (1978).

BRIE, FRIEDRICH, 'Zwei mittelenglische Prosaromane: *The Sege of Thebes* und *The Sege of Troy*', *Anglia*, 130 (1913), 40–52, 269–85.

BROWN, ANDREW D., *Popular Piety in Late Medieval England* (Oxford, 1995).

BROWN, MICHAEL, *James I* (Edinburgh, 1994).

BUNT, G. H. V., *Alexander the Great in the Literature of Medieval Britain*, Medievalia Groningana, 14 (Groningen, 1994).

BURNLEY, J. D., *Chaucer's Language and the Philosophers' Tradition*, Chaucer Studies, 2 (Cambridge, 1979).

BURROW, J. A., *Thomas Hoccleve*, Authors of the Middle Ages, 4 (Aldershot, 1994).

CADDEN, JOAN, *Meanings of Sex Difference in the Middle Ages: Medicine, Science and Culture* (Cambridge, 1993).

CARLSON, DAVID R., *English Humanist Books: Writers and Patrons, Manuscript and Print, 1475–1525* (Toronto, 1993).

—— 'The "Grammarians' War" 1519–21, Humanist Careerism in Early Tudor England, and Printing', *Medievalia et Humanistica* NS 18 (1992), 157–81.

—— 'Royal Tutors in the Reign of Henry VII', *Sixteenth Century Journal*, 22 (1991), 253–79.

CERQUIGLINI, JACQUELINE, 'Le Clerc et l'écriture: le *voir dit* de Guillaume de Machaut et la définition du dit', in Hans Ulrich Gumbrecht (ed.), *Literatur in der Gesellschaft des Spätmittelalters* (Heidelberg, 1980), 151–68.

CERQUIGLINI-TOULET, JACQUELINE, *La Couleur de la mélancolie* (Paris, 1993).

CHAMBERS, E. K., *English Literature at the Close of the Middle Ages* (Oxford, 1945).

—— *The Mediaeval Stage*, 2 vols. (Oxford, 1903).

CONNOLLY, MARGARET, 'The Dethe of the Kynge of Scotis: A New Edition', *Scottish Historical Review*, 71 (1992), 46–69.

COOPER, HELEN, 'Romance after 1400', in *The Cambridge History of Medieval English Literature: Writing in Britain, 1066–1547*, ed. David Wallace (Cambridge, forthcoming).
COURCELLE, PIERRE, *La Consolation de Philosophie dans la tradition littéraire, antécédents et posterité de Boece* (Paris, 1967).
CRAUN, EDWIN D., 'Blaspheming Her "Awin God": Cresseid's "Lamentation" in Henryson's *Testament*', *SP* 82 (1985), 25–41.
CURTIUS, ERNST ROBERT, *European Literature and the Latin Middle Ages*, trans. Willard R. Trask (1953).
DAVENPORT, W. A., *Fifteenth Century Drama* (Cambridge, 1982).
DAVIDOFF, JUDITH M., *Beginning Well: Framing Fictions in Late Middle English Poetry* (London and Toronto, 1988).
DAVIS, J. F., 'The Trials of Thomas Bilney and the English Reformation', *Historical Journal*, 24 (1981) 775–90.
DE MEIJER, A., 'John Capgrave, OESA (1393–1464)', *Augustiniana*, 5 (1955), 400–40, 7 (1957), 119–48, 531–75.
DI CESARE, MARIO A., 'Cristoforo Landino on the Name and Nature of Poetry: The Critic as Hero', *Chaucer Review*, 21 (1986), 155–81.
DINZELBACHER, PETER, *Vision und Visionsliteratur im Mittelalter* (Stuttgart, 1981).
DUFFY, EAMON, *The Stripping of the Altars: Traditional Religion in England c.1400–c.1580* (New Haven, 1992).
EASTING, ROBERT, 'Purgatory and the Earthly Paradise in the *Tractatus de Purgatorio Sancti Patricii*', *Cîteaux*, 37 (1986), 23–48.
EBIN, LOIS A., 'Boethius, Chaucer, and *The Kingis Quair*', *PQ* 53 (1974), 321–41.
—— *Illuminator, Makar, Vates: Visions of Poetry in the Fifteenth Century* (Lincoln, Nebr. and London, 1988).
EDWARDS, A. S. G. (ed.), *Skelton: The Critical Heritage* (1981).
—— (ed.), 'Tradition and Innovation in Fifteenth-Century Poetry', *MLQ* 53 (1992).
EDWARDS, H. L. R., *Skelton: The Life and Times of a Tudor Laureate* (1949).
EWAN, ELIZABETH, *Townlife in Fourteenth-Century Scotland* (Edinburgh, 1990).
FAIRFIELD, LESLIE P., *John Bale: Mythmaker for the English Reformation* (West Lafayette, 1976).
FISH, STANLEY E., *John Skelton's Poetry*, Yale Studies in English, 157 (New Haven, 1965).
FOWLER, DAVID C., *A Literary History of the Popular Ballad* (Durham, NC, 1968).

Fox, Alistair, *Politics and Literature in the Reigns of Henry VII and Henry VIII* (Oxford, 1989).
—— 'Sir Thomas Elyot and the Humanist Dilemma', in Alistair Fox and John Guy (eds.), *Reassessing the Henrician Age* (Oxford, 1986), 52–73.
Gatch, Milton McC., 'Mysticism and Satire in the Morality of *Wisdom*', *PQ* 53 (1974), 342–62.
Gibson, Gail McMurray, *The Theatre of Devotion: East Anglian Drama and Society in the Late Middle Ages* (Chicago and London, 1989).
Gillespie, Vincent, 'Justification by Good Works: Skelton's *The Garland of Laurel*', *Reading Medieval Studies*, 7 (1981), 19–31.
Gordon, I. A., *John Skelton: Poet Laureate* (Melbourne, 1943).
Gray, Douglas, 'Chaucer and "Pite"', in Mary Salu and Robert T. Farrell (eds.), *J. R. R. Tolkien, Scholar and Storyteller: Essays in Memoriam* (Ithaca, NY and London, 1979).
—— 'Medieval English Ballads', in Patricia Shaw *et al.* (eds.), *Actas del Primer Congreso Internacional de la Sociedad Española de Lengua y Literatura Inglesa Medieval* (Oviedo, 1989).
—— *Robert Henryson* (Leiden, 1979).
—— 'The Robin Hood Poems', *Poetica*, 18 (1984), 1–39.
—— *Themes and Images in the Medieval English Religious Lyric* (1972).
Green, Richard Firth, *Poets and Princepleasers: Literature in the English Court in the Late Middle Ages* (Toronto, 1980).
Greenfield, C. C., *Humanist and Scholastic Poetics, 1250–1500* (Lewisburg, 1981).
Griffiths, Jeremy, and Pearsall, Derek (eds.), *Book Production and Publishing in Britain 1375–1475* (Cambridge, 1989).
Halpern, Richard, 'Skelton and the Poetics of Primitive Accumulation', in Patricia Parker and David Quint (eds.), *Literary Theory/Renaissance Texts* (Baltimore, 1986), 225–56.
Harbison, Craig, 'Sexuality and Social Standing in Jan van Eyck's Arnolfini Double Portrait', *Renaissance Quarterly*, 43 (1990), 249–91.
Heiserman, A. R., *Skelton and Satire* (Chicago, 1961).
Hicks, M. A., 'The Piety of Margaret, Lady Hungerford (d. 1478)', *Journal of Ecclesiastical History*, 38 (1987), 19–38.
Hill, Eugene D., 'The Trinitarian Allegory of the Moral Play of *Wisdom*', *Modern Philology*, 73 (1975), 121–35.
Horstmann, K., 'Orologium Sapientiae or The Seven Poyntes of Trewe Wisdom aus MS Douce 114', *Anglia*, 10 (1887), 323–89.

HUIZINGA, JOHAN, *The Waning of the Middle Ages*, trans. F. Hopman (1965).
HUOT, SYLVIA, *From Song to Book: The Poetics of Writing in Old French Lyric and Lyrical Narrative Poetry* (Ithaca, NY, 1987).
JEFFERSON, JUDITH A., 'The Hoccleve Holographs and Hoccleve's Metrical Practice', in Derek Pearsall (ed.), *Manuscripts and Texts: Editorial Problems in Later Middle English Literature* (Cambridge, 1987), 95–109.
KEEN, M. H., *England in the Later Middle Ages: A Political History* (London and New York, 1973).
KERN, J. H., 'Zum Texte einiger Dichtungen Thomas Hoccleve's', *Anglia*, 39 (1916), 389–494.
KERRIGAN, JOHN, *Motives of Woe: Shakespeare and the 'Female Complaint'* (Oxford, 1991).
KINNEY, A. F., *John Skelton: Priest as Poet* (Chapel Hill, NC, 1987).
KRISTEVA, JULIA, *Powers of Horror: An Essay on Abjection*, trans. Leon S. Roudiez (New York, 1982).
LANGLOIS, ERNEST, *Recueil d'arts de seconde rhétorique* (Paris, 1902; repr. Geneva, 1974).
LAWTON, DAVID, 'Dullness and the Fifteenth Century', *ELH* 54 (1987), 761–99.
LERER, SETH, *Chaucer and his Readers: Imagining the Author in Late Medieval England* (Princeton, 1993).
LEWIS, C. S., *English Literature in the Sixteenth Century, excluding Drama* (Oxford, 1954).
LOOMIS, ROGER SHERMAN (ed.), *Arthurian Literature in the Middle Ages* (Oxford, 1979).
LOTE, GEORGES, *Histoire du vers français*, première partie, *Le Moyen Âge*, 3 vols. (Paris, 1949–55).
LOVATT, R., 'The *Imitation of Christ* in Late Medieval England', *Transactions of the Royal Historical Society*, 5th ser. 18 (1968), 97–121.
LUCAS, PETER J., 'John Capgrave, OSA (1393–1464), Scribe and "Publisher"', *Transactions of the Cambridge Bibliographical Society*, 5 (1969), 1–35.
LYLE, E. B., 'The Relationship between *Thomas the Rymer* and *Thomas of Erceldoune*', *Leeds Studies in English*, NS 4 (1970), 23–30.
MCINTOSH, ANGUS, 'Some Notes on the Text of the Middle English Poem *De Tribus Regibus Mortuis*', *RES* NS 28 (1977), 385–92.
MCNAMER, SARAH, 'Female Authors, Provincial Setting: The Re-Versing of Courtly Love in the Findern Manuscript', *Viator*, 22 (1991), 279–310.

MAPSTONE, SALLY, 'Was there a Court Literature in Fifteenth-Century Scotland?', *SSL* 26 (1991), 410–22.
MASON, ROGER, 'Kingship, Tyranny and the Right to Resist in Fifteenth Century Scotland', *Scottish Historical Review*, 66 (1987), 125–51.
MEALE, CAROL M., '"... alle the bokes that I haue of latyn, englisch and frensch: Laywomen and their Books in Late Medieval England', in Carol M. Meale (ed.), *Women and Literature in Britain 1150–1500*, Cambridge Studies in Medieval Literature, 17 (Cambridge, 1993), 128–58.
MORGAN, ALISON, *Dante and the Medieval Other World* (Cambridge, 1990).
MUIR, LYNETTE R., 'Women on the Medieval Stage: The Evidence from France', *Medieval English Theatre*, 7 (1985), 107–19.
NELSON, WILLIAM, *John Skelton, Laureate* (New York, 1939).
NIJENHUIS, WIESJE F., 'Truncated Topoi in *The Vision of Edmund Leversedge*', *MÆ* 63 (1994), 84–97.
NOLAN, BARBARA, *Chaucer and the Tradition of the 'Roman Antique'*, Cambridge Studies in Medieval Literature, 15 (Cambridge, 1992).
O'DONNELL, J. REGINALD, 'Coluccio Salutati on the Poet-Teacher', *Medieval Studies*, 22 (1960), 240–56.
PANOFSKY, ERWIN, 'Jan van Eyck's *Arnolfini Portrait*', *Burlington Magazine*, 64 (1934), 117–27.
PARKINSON, DAVID J., 'Henryson's Scottish Tragedy', *Chaucer Review*, 25 (1991), 355–62.
PARR, JOHNSTONE, 'Astronomical Dating for Some of Lydgate's Poems', *PMLA* 67 (1952), 251–8.
PATTERSON, LEE, *Chaucer and the Subject of History* (1991).
—— 'Christian and Pagan in *The Testament of Cresseid*', *PQ* 52 (1973), 696–714.
—— 'Making Identities in Fifteenth-Century England: Henry II and John Lydgate', in Jeffrey N. Cox and Larry J. Reynolds (eds.), *New Historical Literary Study: Essays in Reading Texts, Representing History* (Princeton, 1993), 69–107.
PEARSALL, DEREK, 'Chaucer's Tomb: The Politics of Reburial', *MÆ* 64 (1995), 51–73.
—— 'The English Romance in the Fifteenth Century', *Essays and Studies*, 29 (1976), 56–83.
—— *John Lydgate* (1970).
—— 'Lydgate as Innovator', *MLQ* 53 (1992), 5–22.

PERKINS, GEORGE, 'A Medieval Carol Survival: "The Fox and the Goose"', *Journal of American Folklore*, 74 (1961), 235–44.
PIAGET, A., '*La Belle Dame sans merci* et ses imitations', *Romania*, 30 (1901), 22–48, 317–51; 31 (102), 315–49; 33 (1904), 179–208; 34 (1905), 375–428, 559–97.
POLLET, MAURICE, *John Skelton, Poet of Tudor England*, trans. John Warrington (1971).
RASMUSSEN, J. K., *Die Sprache John Audelay's, Laut- und Flexionslehre* (diss., Bonn, 1914).
RENOIR, Alain, 'The Immediate Source of Lydgate's *Siege of Thebes*', *Studia Neophilologica*, 33 (1961), 86–95.
RIDDY, FELICITY, *Sir Thomas Malory* (Leiden, 1987).
RIGGIO, MILLA COZART (ed.), *The Wisdom Symposium: Papers from the Trinity College Medieval Festival* (New York, 1986).
ROBEY, D., 'Humanist Views on the Study of Poetry in the Early Italian Renaissance', *History of Education*, 13 (1984), 7–25.
ROSS, D. JAMES, *Musick Fyne: Robert Carver and the Art of Music in Sixteenth-Century Scotland* (Edinburgh, 1993).
ROSS, D. J. A., *Alexander Historiatus*, Warburg Institute Surveys, 1 (1963).
SALTER, H. E., 'Vision of the Monk of Eynsham', *Cartulary of the Abbey of Eynsham*, II, Oxford Historical Society, 51 (1908), 257–371.
SANDISON, H. E., 'En mon deduit a moys de may', in C. F. Fiske (ed.), *Vassar Mediaeval Studies* (New Haven, 1923), 235–45.
SCANLON, LARRY, *Narrative, Authority, and Power: The Medieval Exemplum and the Chaucerian Tradition* (Cambridge, 1994).
SCATTERGOOD, JOHN, 'Skelton and Heresy', in D. Williams (ed.), *Eearly Tudor England: Proceedings of the 1987 Harlaxton Conference* (Woodbridge, 1989), 157–70.
SCATTERGOOD, V. J., *Politics and Poetry in the Fifteenth Century* (1971).
—— and SHERBORNE, J. W. (eds.), *English Court Culture in the Later Middle Ages* (1983).
SCHEPS, WALTER, and LOONEY, J. ANNA, *Middle Scots Poets: A Reference Guide to James I of Scotland, Robert Henryson, William Dunbar, and Gavin Douglas* (Boston, 1986).
SCHIRMER, WALTER F., *John Lydgate: A Study in the Culture of the Fifteenth Century*, trans. Ann E. Kemp (1952).
SCHMITZ, GÖTZ, *The Fall of Women in Early English Narrative Verse* (Cambridge, 1990).

SCHULZ, H. C., 'Thomas Hoccleve, Scribe', *Speculum*, 12 (1937), 71-6.
SHULDHAM-SHAW, PATRICK, 'The Ballad of "King Orfeo"', *Scottish Studies*, 20 (1976), 124-6.
SIMPSON, JAMES, *Sciences and the Self in Medieval Poetry: Alan of Lille's 'Anticlaudianus' and John Gower's 'Confessio Amantis'*, Cambridge Studies in Medieval Literature, 25 (Cambridge, 1995).
SPEARING, A. C., *The Medieval Poet as Voyeur: Looking and Listening in Medieval Love-Narrative* (Cambridge, 1993).
—— *Medieval to Renaissance in English Poetry* (Cambridge, 1985).
STEWART, MARION, '"King Orphius"', *Scottish Studies*, 17 (1973), 1-16.
—— 'A Recently-Discovered Manuscript: "ane taill of Sir colling ye kny"', *Scottish Studies*, 16 (1972), 23-39.
STOKES, CHARITY SCOTT, 'Thomas Hoccleve's *Mother of God* and *Balade to the Virgin and Christ*: Latin and Anglo-Norman Sources', *MÆ* 64 (1995), 74-84.
STROHM, PAUL, 'Hoccleve, Lydgate and the Lancastrian Court', in *The Cambridge History of Medieval English Literature: Writing in Britain, 1066-1547*, ed. David Wallace (Cambridge, forthcoming).
STROHM, REINHARD, *The Rise of European Music 1380-1500* (Cambridge, 1993).
SWANSON, R. N., *Catholic England: Faith, Religion and Observance before the Reformation* (Manchester, 1993).
TORRIE, ELIZABETH P. D., 'The Guild in Fifteenth-Century Dunfermline', in Michael Lynch, Michael Spearman, and Geoffrey Stell (eds.), *The Scottish Medieval Town* (Edinburgh, 1988), 245-60.
TORTI, ANNA, *The Glass of Form: Mirroring Structures from Chaucer to Skelton* (Cambridge, 1991).
TRINKAUS, CHARLES, '*Theologia Poetica* and *Theologia Rhetorica* in Petrarch's *Invectives*', in *The Poet as Philospher: Petrarch and the Formation of Renaissance Consciousness* (New Haven, 1979).
TUCKER, MELVIN J., 'Setting in Skelton's *Bowge of Courte*: A Speculation', *ELN* 7 (1970), 168-75.
TURVILLE-PETRE, THORLAC, '"Summer Sunday", "De Tribus Regibus Mortuis", and "The Awntyrs off Arthure": Three Poems in the Thirteen-Line Stanza', *RES* NS 25 (1974), 1-14.
TWYCROSS, MEG, '"Transvestism" in the Mystery Plays', *Medieval English Theatre*, 5 (1983), 123-80.
VINCE, RONALD W. (ed.), *A Companion to The Medieval Theatre* (New York, 1989).

WALKER, GREG, *John Skelton and the Politics of the 1520s* (Cambridge, 1988).
—— 'John Skelton, Thomas More, and the "Lost" History of the Early Reformation in England', *Parergon*, 9 (1991) 75–85.
WARNER, MARINA, *Monuments and Maidens: The Allegory of the Female Form* (1985).
WAWN, A., 'Truth-Telling and the Tradition of *Mum and the Sothsegger*', *YES* 13 (1983), 270–87.
WEISS, ROBERTO, *Humanism in England during the Fifteenth Century*, Medium Aevum Monographs, 4 (3rd edn., Oxford, 1967).
WICKHAM, GLYNNE, *Early English Stages*, 3 vols. (1959–81).
WILKINS, E. H., *Studies in the Life and Works of Petrarch* (Cambridge, Mass., 1955).
WIMSATT, JAMES I., *Chaucer and his French Contemporaries: Natural Music in the Fourteenth Century* (Toronto, 1991).
WITT, RONALD G., 'Coluccio Salutati and the Conception of the *Poeta Theologus* in the Fourteenth Century', *Renaissance Quarterly*, 30 (1977), 538–63.
WOOLF, ROSEMARY, *The English Religious Lyric in the Middle Ages* (Oxford, 1968).
WÜLFING, J. E., 'Der Dichter John Audelay und sein Werk', *Anglia*, 18 (1896), 175–217.
YEAGER, ROBERT F. (ed.), *Fifteenth-Century Studies: Recent Essays* (Hamden, Conn., 1984).

Index

advice to princes literature 6, 57, 59, 250–1, 257, 264, 268
  English 60, 64
  Scottish 52, 59, 60–6
Alcock, John 319
Alexander, Prose 141, 146–7, 157
Alexander the Great, in Middle English and Middle Scots literature 12–13, 123, 138, 145, 146, 185
  in *The Prose Life of Alexander* 123, 141, 146–7, 157
  in *The Wars of Alexander* 123–39
alliterative poetry 3, 12
'Amants trépassés', painting 229–32, 233, 234, 235, 239, 248
Aquinas, St Thomas 282, 294
Aragon, Katherine of 212–13, 263 n. 34, 269
Aristotle 7 n. 13, 287, 294, 302, 303
Arnolfini portrait, *see* van Eyck, Jan
Arthur 61–2, 142, 145, 146, 149–55
Arthur, Prince 212, 264, 298 n. 42
Arthur, Thomas 277–80, 284–90, 297, 299, 310
Asloan, John 241
Assembly of Ladies 82, 84, 88–9, 94, 96
Audelay, John 12, 99–121
  carols of 107, 108, 117–21
  and scribes of Bodleian MS Douce 302 99–105, 111, 115
  verse forms of 99–121
  'An Exhortation I' 104 n. 13, 107
  'An Exhortation, II' 100, 104 n. 11, 110 n. 35

'De effusione sanguinis Christi' 107, 117–18
'De passione Domini ... et de horis canonicis' 104 n. 13, 113, 114
'De rege Henrico sexto' 101, 102 n. 7, 104, 107
'De sancta Maria I' 111, 119–20
'De tribus regibus mortuis', see *Three Dead Kings*
'Ihesus Christus apparuit sancto Gregorio' 103–4, 113
'In die circumcicionis domini' 102, 119, 120
In die natalis Domini' 102 n. 7, 118
'Pater noster' 108, 110, 112–13
'Prayer to St Winifred' 104, 107, 108, 117
'Salutacio in honore sancte Anne' 106–7, 113, 115
'Salutacio sancte Brigitte' 107, 114–15
Three Dead Kings ('De tribus regibus mortuis') 12, 99–100, 101, 108–14, 121, 243
Averroes 7 n. 13, 299, 305

Bale, John 2, 13–14, 311, 313–29
  Illustrium maioris Britanniae scriptorum summarium 314, 315
  Index Britanniae scriptorum 315–29
  Scriptorum illustrium maioris Brytanniae ... Catalogus 314–29
ballad, history of 3, 4, 7, 12, 163–84, 317
Barbour, John, *Bruce* 58
Barclay, Alexander 325

Index

Barnes, Dame Juliana 318
Beadle, Richard 221
Beaufort, Joan 55, 56, 68
Beaufort, Margaret 273
Bedford, Duke of, *see* John, Duke of Bedford
Belle Dame sans Mercy 74, 80, 83, 321
  see also Chartier, Alain; Roos, Sir Richard; Pynson, Richard
Berners, Lord 325
  Arthour of Lytell Brytane 326
  Castellum amoris 326
  Golden Boke of Marcus Aurelius 326
  Huon of Burdeux 325
Bevington, David 208–9, 225, 227
Bilney, Thomas 277–80, 284–90, 297, 299, 310
Blacman, John 216–17, 219
'Blancheflour and Jellyflorice', ballad 169
Boccaccio, Giovanni 17, 91, 297, 301, 303–4, 305
  De genealogia deorum gentilium 31 n. 26, 296, 297, 301, 303–4
Boece, Hector 151 n. 16
Boethius, *Consolation of Philosophy* 13 n. 20, 53–4, 55, 59
Boffey, Julia 89
Bokenham, Osbern 318
Bold, Henry, *Latine Songs* 176
Bonner, Edmund 256–7
Book of Cupid 87
Book of Vices and Virtues 189
'Boston of Bury' 316–17
Bower, Walter, *Scotichronicon* 65–6, 67, 68
Bradshaw, Henry, *Lyfe of Saint Werburge* 76
Bramham, Peter of 187, 198
Brampton, Thomas, *Penitential Psalms* 76
Bridget of Sweden, St 9, 189–90, 191, 192, 198
Brown, Mrs Anna, of Falkirk 165–6, 168–9, 177, 179
Bruni, Leonardi 295, 301, 309
Brut, prose 142, 144, 151

Buik of Alexander 52, 123 n. 2
Buik of King Alexander the Conquerour 13 n. 19, 52 n. 3, 61 n. 17, 62, 63–4, 123 n. 2
Buke of the Howlat 244
Bury St Edmunds, abbey 8, 221, 227

Cadden, Joan 236–7
Campbell, Thomas 102–3
Capgrave, John 323–4, 327
  Biblical commentaries 323–4
  Liber de illustribus Henricis 323
  Nova legenda Anglie 323
  Vita Hunfridi ducis 323
'Carnal and the Crane', ballad 179–81
carols 107, 108, 117, 171
Castle of Perseverance 205, 209 n. 12, 211, 223–5, 226
Cato, *Distichs* 253–4, 255, 257
Cavendish George, *Metrical Visions* 76, 79
Caxton, William 2, 144–5, 321, 324, 326
  Boece 274
  Canterbury Tales 274
  Charles the Great 146, 148
  Dicts and Sayings of the Philosophers 145 n. 9
  Eneydos 274
  Four Sons of Aymon 146, 148, 160
  Godfrey of Bouillon 146
  Morte Darthur 326
Cerquiglini-Toulet, Jacqueline 43–5, 49, 73 n. 3
Chambers, E. K. 105, 106, 205
Champagne, Thibaut de 78–9
Chanson de Roland 7, 146
Charlemagne romances 145, 146, 148
Charles d'Orléans 41, 42, 76, 80
Chartier, Alain 35, 39, 318
  Belle Dame sans Merci 74–5, 80, 83, 91–4
Chaucer, Geoffrey 1, 3, 7, 11, 12, 13, 21, 29, 35, 38, 39, 40, 49, 53, 71–99, 245, 273–5, 305 n. 58, 311, 320–1, 326, 327, 328, 329

Anelida and Arcite 28, 29 n. 23, 88, 244
Book of the Duchess 54–5, 83, 84, 88, 96
Canterbury Tales 21, 22–3, 25, 33, 43, 44, 101, 274, 321; Franklin's Tale 88; Knight's Tale 6, 16, 20, 21–33, 53, 321; Manciple's Tale 253 n. 8; Monk's Tale 21–2; Nun's Priest's Tale 172; Pardoner's Tale 212, 217, 220; Prioress's Tale 199; Reeve's Tale 110, 175; Retractions 321; Wife of Bath's Tale 183–4
Complaint of Mars 96
Complaint of Venus 88
Complaint to his Purse 46
Envoy to Scogan 46, 49
Fortune 46
House of Fame 39, 74, 86, 89, 163
Legend of Good Women 29 n. 23, 36 n. 7, 74, 75, 88, 89–90, 93, 321
Troilus and Criseyde 19 n. 10, 24, 25, 27–8, 40, 53, 74, 77, 81, 82, 89, 145, 234, 236, 238–9, 243
Chaucerian poetry 2, 3, 9, 11, 12, 13, 53, 71–99, 329
Chester mystery play cycle 317 Assumption of the Virgin 210–11
Chevalier des Dames du Dolant Fortuné 83
Child, F. J. 164–5, 177–8, 180
'Choristers' Lament' 110
Christine de Pizan 9, 35, 40, 41, 42, 75, 88
L'Epistre au dieu d'amours 36, 37, 95
Cicero 17, 290, 299, 303, 304, 305
 De inventione 20
 De officiis 18–20
 Pro Archia 302, 305
Colet, John 319
Columbus, Christopher 185
'Complaint Against Blacksmiths' 110

Condé, Jean de, Messe des oiseaux 74
Court of Sapience 271
Court of Venus 76
Cranmer, Thomas 260–1, 263 n. 34
Cromwell, Thomas 260, 262, 313

dance, in court entertainments 215, 217–19, 220
dancing girls 211–17, 219, 220
 see also Wisdom
Dante 184, 199, 201, 202, 238, 294, 297, 301, 304, 306, 327
Deguileville, Guillaume de
 Pèlerinage de l'âme 36–7, 186, 187
 see also Pylgremage of the Sowle
Deschamps, Eustache 5, 38, 40 n. 15, 41, 45–9, 73
De spiritu Guidonis 187, 194
Dethe of the Kynge of Scotis 51–2
De Worde, Wynkyn 251 n. 4, 318 n. 19, 322, 323, 324
Digby plays 212
 Mary Magdalen 207, 209 n. 12, 220
 The Killing of the Children 212–13
Douglas, Gavin 1, 2, 67, 318
 Eneados prologues 81, 86, 91
 Palice of Honour 86, 88 n. 42, 91, 318
Dryden, John 31 n. 24
Dunbar, William 1, 2, 3, 75, 318
 Golden Targe 62, 78, 80
 Tretis of the Tua Mariit Wemen and the Wedo 3, 241
Dunfermline 241, 242
Dunstable, John 1

earthly paradise 185, 188, 191, 192, 194, 200–1
Ebin, Lois 2, 3 n. 6, 17–18
Edward V 5
Elyot, Sir Thomas: The Boke Named the Governour 250 n. 3, 258–60, 263
 Of the Knowledge that maketh a Wise Man 261 n. 27, 262 n. 32

Elyot, Sir Thomas (*cont.*):
  Pasquil the Playne 7, 252, 256–63, 267, 270, 272; and 'pasquillade' tradition 256–7, 263; and plea for preferment 262–3
Emperour and the Childe 161–2
Epistolae obscurorum virorum 282, 295, 297
Erasmus, Desiderius 276, 290, 298
Erhart, Gregor, carving of *Vanitas* attributed to 231–2, 233
Everyman 10, 205
Exodus 182
Eynsham, Adam of 191, 200
Eynsham, Edmund of, see *Revelation to the Monk of Eynsham*

'False Fox', see Ryman, James
Ficino, Marsilio 301, 309
Field, P. J. C. 149
Fisher, John 319
Florice and Blancheflour 159
Flour of Curtesye 86, 88 n. 42, 320
Floure and the Leafe 74, 81 n. 23, 87–8
Fonte, Bartollomeo della, (Fontius) 295, 299, 306–7, 308, 309
Fordun, John of, *Chronica Gentis Scotorum* 55, 151 n. 16
Fortescue, John 250 n. 3, 318
'Fox and the Goose', ballad 170–1, 174–5
Fox, Denton 232
Fowler, David C. 164–6, 168–9, 170, 171, 177
'Frog and the Mouse', ballad 171
Froissart, Jean 35, 41, 43, 73, 76, 325
  Espinette Amoureuse 44
Furnivall, Frederick 116

gallants, see *Vision of Edmund Leversedge*; *Wisdom*
Gascoigne, Thomas 325
Gast of Gy 187
Geoffrey of Monmouth 150–1
'Gest of Robyn Hode', ballad 173
Gesta Romanorum 44

Geu des trois roys 180–1
Giovannino of Mantua 295, 300–1, 302–3
Gloucester, Duke of, see Humphrey, Duke of Gloucester
Gospel of Pseudo-Matthew, Greek 179
Gospel of Thomas, Latin 179, 181
Gower, John 6, 13, 35 n. 1, 41, 80, 245, 249–50, 321–2
  Confessio Amantis 250–1, 321
Grammarians' War 276, 282, 283 n. 17
Granson, Oton de 35, 41, 76
  Livre Messire Ode 44, 83
Gray, Douglas v–vi, 10, 11, 15 n., 83 n. 30, 99, 164 n. 5, 237–8, 239, 243, 307 n. 63, 330–5
  OBLMVP 1–14, 36 n. 7, 83, 164, 185, 314, 329
Greene, R. L. 102, 106, 108 n. 25, 119 n. 52, 171
'Grey Cock', ballad 175–6
Grosseteste, Robert 328
Gy, in visionary literature 187, 192, 194, 199
'Gypsy Laddie', ballad 174

'Half Hitch', ballad 167, 183
Hall, Joseph, *Chronicle* 218–19, 326
Hardying, John 149, 150, 151, 326
Harris, Mrs, of Perthshire 177–8
Hawes, Stephen 319–20
  Pastime of Pleasure 271
Hay, Gilbert 67 n. 27, 246
Henry IV 4, 7, 46
Henry V 4–5, 15–16, 36
Henry VI 5, 16, 216–17, 218, 219, 220, 221, 227, 228
Henry VII 264, 273
Henry VIII 7, 218–19, 256, 262, 263, 264–5, 269, 273, 297–8, 313, 315
Henryson, Robert 1, 3, 10, 318
  Testament of Cresseid 10, 82–3, 87, 91, 232–48, 320; abjection in 234–7, 242, 246, 248; anti-feminism in 232–4,

236–7, 239–43, 244, 245, 248;
humanist readings of 237–40,
243, 244–6; leprosy in 232–3,
240–1, 243, 248; male body
and masculinity in 236, 244–8;
reading of Cresseid in 244–8;
see also Kristeva, Julia
Higden, Ranulph 317 n. 14
Hild of Whitby, St 192
Hilton, Walter 203, 319, 322–3, 327
  Epistle on the Mixed Life 222,
    322, 323
  'Of Angels Song' 191
  Scale of Pefection 189, 222, 322
'Hind Horn', ballad 166, 167–8
Historia de preliis Alexandri Magni
  123–39
Hoccleve, Thomas 3, 6, 8, 11, 12,
  35–49, 325, 328
  Formulary compiled by 35
  holograph manuscripts of 35,
    38–49
  and metre 38–40, 116
  and Middle French poetry
    35–49
  and stanzaic forms 38–40
  Balade to the Virgin and Christ
    37–8
  balades 40
  Complaint of the Virgin 36–7
  Dialogue with a Friend 36, 39,
    40
  Learn to Die 44
  Letter of Cupid 36, 88
  Male Regle 45, 46–9
  Regiment of Princes 35, 36, 40,
    48, 49, 245, 250 n. 3, 325
  Series 39, 43–5
Hogarth:
  The Harlot's Progress 239–40, 242
  The Rake's Progress 241
Hogg, Margaret 166
Holy Boke Gratia Dei 189
Huizinga, Johan 143, 217–18
Hull, Dame Eleanor 9
Humphrey, Duke of Gloucester
  15–16, 45, 323, 324, 327
Huot, Sylvia 41–2, 43, 72, 73 n. 3,
  74
Hyngham, Thomas 221, 224

Infancy Gospel of Thomas, Greek
  79
Interlude of the Four Elements
  173
Isidore 301, 302
  Etymologies 300
Isle of Ladies 89

James I of Scotland 3, 5, 55–6, 57,
  65, 318, 327–8
  death of 51–2, 63, 65, 68–9
  other poetry by 67–8, 318
  The Kingis Quair 8, 51–69,
    84–6, 318; and advice to
    princes tradition 52, 57–66;
    authorship of 66–9; and
    Boethius 53–4, 55, 59, 85; and
    Chaucerian tradition 52–3, 83,
    84–6; dream episode in 54–5,
    59, 60, 85; manuscript of
    52 n. 4, 57, 67 n. 27;
    self-government in 53–69
James II of Scotland 5, 63, 65
James III of Scotland 5, 63, 65
James IV of Scotland 5, 69
Jefferson, Judith 38–9, 40
Jerome, St 282, 301, 305, 306,
  307, 309
  Epistle 53 to Paulinus 287–93,
    301, 302–3, 304, 306, 309
John, Duke of Bedford 15–16
John of Bridlington, St 192
Judas 153
  ballad on 170
Julian of Norwich 9, 190, 191,
  200, 318–19
Juvenal 283

Kempe, Margery 2, 9, 190–1, 202,
  318–19
'King Arthur and King Cornwall'
  169
'King Henry', ballad 183–4
'King Orfeo', ballad 166, 167
King Orphius 167, 177
'Knight and the Shepherd's
  Daughter', ballad 182
Kristeva, Julia, *Powers of Horror*
  234–6, 237, 242, 246, 248
Kyningham, John 316

358 Index

Lamprechts Alexander 135, 137
Lancelot of the Laik 61–2, 149
Landino, Cristoforo 296, 301, 304, 305
Langland, William, Piers Plowman 6, 110 n. 35, 209, 222, 253 n. 8, 327, 328, 329
Laud Troy Book 145–6
Lay of Sorrow 88
Leland, John 314, 328
Lerer, Seth 3 n. 6, 21 n. 15
Letter of Dydo 74, 77, 89–91
Leversedge, Edmund, see Vision of Edmund Leversedge
Liber Pluscardensis 64
Life of Alexander 145 n. 10
Lily, William 276, 283
Lollardy 4, 5, 8, 188, 202, 223, 277, 279, 290
Lovelich, Henry:
  History of the Holy Grail 149
  Merlin 149
Lover's Mass 74
Lydgate, John 1, 6, 12, 13, 73, 245, 305, 327, 329
  'Ballade to King Henry VI Upon his Coronation' 102 n. 7
  Complaint of the Black Knight 79–80, 94, 96
  Dance Machabre 324
  Destruction of Thebes 6, 15–33, 145, 324; dating of 15–16; relation to the Knight's Tale 16, 21–33; prudence in 18–21, 25–7, 30; source of 20–1; title of 15–16; 'truthe' in 16–21, 32
  Fall of Princes 15 n. 1, 31 n. 24, 77, 305 n. 58, 324
  Gentlewoman's Lament 88
  Kalendar 324–5
  Life of our Lady 324
  Lives of St Edmund and St Fremund 324–5
  Serpent of Division 16 n. 2
  Temple of Glass 53, 54, 56, 77, 86, 88 n. 42, 94, 95, 320
  Troy Book 145
lyric, the 11–12, 176, 317
  Harley lyrics 109–10, 117
  lyrico-narrative poetry 71–2

Machaut, Guillaume de 35, 41, 42, 43, 49, 73, 76
  Fonteinne amoureuse 79, 96
  Jugement dou Roy de Navarre 44–5
  Voir Dit 43–4
Major, John 57 n. 11, 67 n. 28, 68, 318
Malory, Sir Thomas 1, 3, 4, 7 n. 13, 62, 72, 144, 145, 148–9, 152, 326
  Morte Darthur 148–55, 326
  Tristram 150
Mandeville's Travels 185
Mankind 205, 211, 221, 224–5
manuscripts:
  All Souls College, Oxford MS 98 (Gower) 321–2
  Balliol College, Oxford MS 189 (Capgrave) 323–4
  Balliol College, Oxford MS 190 (Capgrave) 323–4
  Balliol College, Oxford MS 228 (Bramham) 187
  Bibliothèque Nationale MS fr. 840 (Deschamps) 41
  Bibliothèque Nationale MS fr. 1584 (Machaut) 41
  Bibliothèque Nationale MS fr. 25458 (Charles d'Orléans) 42
  Bodleian Library MS 73 (Bale) 316
  Bodleian Library MS 462 (St Albans Chronicle) 187
  Bodleian Library MS Arch. Selden. B. 24 (Chaucerian poetry, Kingis Quair) 52 n. 4, 57, 67 n. 27
  Bodleian Library MS Digby 133 (Wisdom) 205–6
  Bodleian Library MS Douce 302 (Audelay) 99–105, 111, 115
  Bodleian Library MS Duke Humfrey b. I (Capgrave) 324
  Bodleian Library Fairfax MS 16 (Chaucerian poetry) 72, 74 n. 4
  Bodleian Library MS Selden supra 41 (Bale) 316
  Bodleian Library MS Selden supra 64 (Bale) 315

Bodleian Library MS Selden
  supra 72 (Bale) 316
British Library MS Add. 34,193
  (*Vision of William of Stranton*,
  Vision of Edmund Leversedge)
  194
British Library MS Arundel 119
  (*Destruction of Thebes*) 15
British Library MS Arundel 292
  (alliterative poetry) 110
British Library MS Cotton
  Tiberius A. viii (Capgrave) 323
British Library MS Harley 1819
  (Bale) 316
British Library MS Harley 2253
  (Harley lyrics) 109–10
British Library MS Harley 4431
  (Christine de Pizan) 42 n. 21
Cambridge University Library MS
  Additional 3035 (Gower) 322
Cambridge University Library MS
  Ff. 6. 28 (Bale) 316
Corpus Christi College,
  Cambridge 408 (Capgrave) 323
Durham University Library MS
  Cosin V.iii. 9 (Hoccleve)
  38–49
Folger Library, Washington MS
  V. a. 354 (*Wisdom*) 205–9
Huntington Library MS HM 111
  (Hoccleve) 38–49
Huntington Library MS HM 744
  (Hoccleve) 38–49
Magdalen College, Oxford, MS
  Lat. 141 (Hilton) 322
Oriel College, Oxford MS 32
  (Capgrave) 324
Vatican Library, MS Vaticano
  Latino 3195 (Petrarch) 41
Margery Kempe, *see* Kempe,
  Margery
'Marriage of Sir Gawain', ballad
  166
Martianus Capella, *De nuptiis* 20,
  27
Matthew Paris, *Chronica maiora*
  170
Melusine 145, 146, 155–8
Merlin, English prose 144, 149,
  152

Merlin, Vulgate 151–2
Messagier d'Amours 83
Metham, John 5 n. 10, 143
  Amoryus and Cleopes 143
Middle French poetry 12, 13,
  35–49, 73
  dits amoureux 71, 73, 75, 78,
  80, 94, 95, 96–7
Mills, Farmer, of Beaminster 175–6
Mordred 149–55, 162
More, Sir Thomas 2, 188, 277,
  282, 326, 327
  History of King Richard III 326
  Utopia 251, 261
Mort le roi Artu 154
Morte Arthur, stanzaic 149, 154
Morte Arthure, alliterative 149,
  150, 151, 153
Mum and the Sothsegger 7, 252–6,
  257, 261, 262, 263, 267, 268,
  270, 272, 317 n. 13
Mussato, Albertino 283, 295, 300,
  302–3
mystery plays 210–11
  see also Chester; N-town;
  Towneley plays; York

N-Town mystery plays 205
  Mary and Joseph 214
  Purification 214
Nashe, Thomas 218
Netter, Thomas 316
Nevill, William, *Castle of Pleasure* 86
Nicholas, St 200, 201–2

Of Arthour and Merlin 149
'Old Daddy Fox', ballad 170–1,
  174–5
Orléans, Charles de, *see* Charles
  d'Orléans
Otuel and Roland 148
Ovid 31 n. 24
  Fasti 309
  Heroides 88, 90
  Metamorphoses 86
Owein, visionary at St Patrick's
  Purgatory 186, 192, 202
*Oxford Book of Late Medieval
  Verse and Prose*, *see* Gray,
  Douglas

Paston family 9, 196
Paul, St 186, 192
Pearsall, Derek 21 n. 14, 99–100
Pecock, Reginald, *The Book of Faith* 325
Percy, Bishop, Folio MS 161, 165, 167, 177, 178
  Reliques 177–8
Petrarch, [Francesco] 11, 13 n. 20, 41, 283, 295–6, 301–2, 303, 304, 305, 306, 327
  Invectivae 296, 298, 307
Petrarch, Gherardo 296, 301
Pizan, Christine de, *see* Christine de Pizan
Plowman's Tale 320
Politian, Angelo 301
Porete, Marguerite 9
Pricke of Conscience 198 n. 39, 203
Privy Seal office 35–6, 46
Prose Solomon and Saturn 182
Pseudo-Turpin Chronicle 146, 148
purgatory, in other-world visions 8, 9, 185–203
Puttenham, George, *The Arte of English Poesie* 272
Pylgremage of the Sowle 37, 187–8, 194, 197
Pynson, Richard 74, 76, 90 nn. 47–8, 91, 94, 323, 326 n. 57

Quare of Jelusy 83–4, 94–6
Queste del Saint Graal 150

Rastell, John 173
Receyt of the Ladie Kateryne (1501) 214
Reuchlin, Johannes 281–2, 295, 300
Revelation of Purgatory to an unknown woman 9, 191, 197–9
Revelation to the Monk of Eynsham 191, 194, 198, 199–203
Richard II 2, 5
Richard III 5, 326
Ritson, Joseph 165, 167, 176
Robert III of Scotland 55, 63

Robin Hood 173, 212
'Robin Hood and Allen a Dale', ballad 173
Rolland, John, *Court of Venus* 80
Rolle, Richard 307, 319
Roman de Edipus 20, 24 n. 20
Roman de la Rose 36, 80, 89, 95, 269 n. 47
Roman de Thebes 20
Romance of Horn, Anglo-Norman romance 168
Romance of Partenay 157
Romanz de Saint Fanuel 181
Roos, Sir Richard 76
  Belle Dame sans Mercy 74, 80, 81, 83, 91, 93–4
Ryman, James, 'The False Fox', ballad 171–2, 173, 174

Saint-Gelais, Octavien de, *Epistres d'Ovide* 74
St Patrick's Purgatory 186, 192, 194
Salutati, Coluccio 295, 297, 299, 300, 305
Sawles Warde 189, 222
Scotish Feilde 3
Scotland 5, 51, 71, 236, 239, 241, 242–3
Scott, Walter 165–6
  Minstrelsy of the Scottish Border 168–9
'Sermon of dead men' 188–9
Shakespeare, William 141, 208
  Macbeth 21 n. 13
  The Winter's Tale 162
Shirley, John 51
Siege of Thebes, *see* Lydgate, John, *Destruction of Thebes*
Siege of Thebes, prose 145–6, 147–8
Siege of Troy, prose 145–6, 147–8
Sinclair, William 67
'Sir Aldingar', ballad 169, 181
'Sir Cawline', ballad 177
'Sir Colin', ballad 177–8
Sir Colling 177–8
Sir Gawain and the Green Knight 78, 109, 155

Sir Launfal 155
Sir Orfeo 167
Skelton, John 1, 8, 72, 263, 283,
    320, 327
  and idea of poet laureate 273–7,
    298–311
  Latin eulogies by 273
  Agaynst Garnesche 298, 299
  Agaynst the Scottes 289
  Boke of Good Advertysement 293
  Bowge of Court 7, 82, 249,
    251–2, 265–72
  Collyn Clout 268–9, 279, 280,
    284
  Diodorus Siculus 270 n. 48, 320
  Garland of Laurel 76, 249 n. 1,
    253, 274–6, 281, 283 n. 17,
    288, 305 n. 58, 311, 320
  Magnificence 317 n. 14
  Phillip Sparrow 320
  Replication 276–80, 281, 282,
    284–93, 297–8, 299, 302,
    308–11; and David in 288–91,
    292, 309–10; and influence of
    Jerome upon 287–93; and
    term *vates* in 283, 300–11
  Speculum Principis 264–5, 266,
    270, 283
  Speke Parott 249 n. 1, 269 n. 45,
    282
  Ware the Hauke 280–1
  Why Come Ye Nat to Courte?
    281, 283, 286, 320
Song of Roland (English) 148
Spearing, A. C. 3 n. 6, 21 n. 15, 78,
    271
Spectacle of Lufe 242
Spiegel, Gabrielle 143
Statius 20
  Thebaid 31
Stewart, Marion 167, 177–8
Stranton, William of, see *Vision of
  William of Stranton*
Suite du Merlin 149, 150, 152–3
Surigo, Stephen 273–4
Suso, Henry, *Orologium Sapientiae*
    188, 222

'Thewis of Gud Women' 241, 242
Thomas à Kempis 319

Thomas of Erceldoune 168–9, 177,
    179
'Thomas Rymer', ballad 166,
    168–9, 177
Thorpe, William 325
Three Dead Kings, see Audelay, John
Tiptoft, John 326, 327
Torti, Anna 77
Towneley plays 101, 110
*Tractatus de purgatorio Sancti
  Patricii* 194
'Treatise of Ghostly Battle' 188
Trithemius, John, *Liber de
  scriptoribus Ecclesiasticis* 316,
    317
Troyes, Treaty of (1420) 5, 15, 16
Tuck, Elizabeth, 'Vallis Valle. Part
    II' 195
Tundale, visionary 186, 192, 202
  see also *Vision of Tundale*
Tunstall, Cuthbert 279, 282, 290
Turville-Petre, Thorlac 106, 108–9,
    111 n. 36
'Twa Magiciens', ballad 182
Twycross, Meg 210–11
Tyndale, William, English New
    Testament 277

Udall, Nicholas 173

Valentine and Orson 145, 146,
    158–62
van Eyck, Jan:
  Arnolfini portrait 230–1, 232,
    235, 242
  Ghent altarpiece 230
Vergil, Polydore 318
Virgil 7, 264–5
  Aeneid 86, 284, 309
Vision of Edmund Leversedge 191,
    194–7, 198, 199, 200, 201
  alias of William Wreche in
    196–7
  gallants in 195–6
  MS of 194
Vision of Tundale 194
Vision of William of Stranton 191,
    192–4, 195, 197, 198, 199,
    201
  MSS of 194

visionary literature 8, 9, 185–203
visions, of the otherworld
    185–203
Voeux du Paon 52
Vulgate Cycle 150, 154

Walton, John 318
Wars of Alexander 3, 13, 123–39
    Candace in 134–7
    Jerusalem in 132–4
Wars of the Roses 4–5, 143, 150
*Wedding of Sir Gawain and
    Dame Ragnell* 149–50,
    166–7
Westminster Abbey 273, 311
'Westron Wynde' 176
Whiting, E. K. 100, 103–4 n. 11
Whittinton, Robert 283
'Wife of Usher's Well', ballad
    183
William of Malmesbury 170

Wisdom 205–28
    costume in 217, 220, 225–7
    dance in 206–10, 212, 215–16,
        217, 219–20, 225, 226, 227
    gallants in 207, 208–9, 219,
        220, 225, 226
    music in 206–7, 220, 227
    staging of 208, 209, 220–1,
        227–8
    women in 206–10, 212, 215,
        219–20, 223, 227
Wolsey, Thomas 279, 281, 283, 327
Wreche, William, see *Vision of
    Edmund Leversedge*
Wülfing, J. E. 105
Wyclif, John 315, 316, 317, 327,
    328

York mystery play cycle,
    Assumption of the Virgin 211
'Young Hunting', ballad 181

OHIO UNIVERSITY LIBRARY

Please return this book as soon as you have finished with it. In order to avoid a fine it must be returned by the latest date stamped below. All books are subject to recall after two weeks or immediately if needed for reserve.

DEC 1 6 2004

JUN 1 5 2019

CF